COMPREHENDING ORAL AND WRITTEN LANGUAGE

EDITED BY

ROSALIND HOROWITZ

College of Social and Behavioral Sciences
Division of Education
The University of Texas
San Antonio, Texas

S. JAY SAMUELS

Department of Educational Psychology
and Center for Research in Learning, Perception, and Cognition
University of Minnesota
Minneapolis, Minnesota

ACADEMIC PRESS, INC.
Harcourt Brace Jovanovich, Publishers
San Diego   New York   Berkeley   Boston
London   Sydney   Tokyo   Toronto

ACADEMIC PRESS, INC.
1250 Sixth Avenue, San Diego, California 92101

United Kingdom Edition published by
ACADEMIC PRESS INC. (LONDON) LTD.
24–28 Oval Road, London NW1 7DX

Library of Congress Cataloging in Publication Data

Comprehending oral and written language.

Includes index.
1. Psycholinguistics.   2. Comprehension.
3. Discourse analysis.   4. Oral communication.
5. Written communication.   6. Literacy.   I. Horowitz,
Rosalind.   II. Samuels, S. Jay.
PS37.C595   1987   401'.9   87-1077
ISBN 0–12–356110–8 (alk. paper)

To the memory of my mother
Fannie Hartman Horowitz
1905–1985
who taught me to value the
possibilities of schooling
and
To the memory of my father
Cantor Louis Horowitz
1905–1972
who taught me to value the
sound and meaning of text

RH

To my wife
Nancy
and
To my colleagues and students

SJS

Contents

CHAPTER **1**

Comprehending Oral and Written Language:
Critical Contrasts for Literacy and Schooling   **1**

Rosalind Horowitz and S. Jay Samuels

PART **1**

THE LANGUAGE OF SPOKEN
AND WRITTEN DISCOURSE

CHAPTER **2**

Spoken and Written Modes of Meaning   55

M. A. K. Halliday

CHAPTER **3**

Properties of Spoken and Written Language   83

Wallace Chafe and Jane Danielewicz

PART **II**

PROCESSING STRATEGIES: RHETORICAL, SOCIAL-SITUATIONAL, AND CONTEXTUAL CONSTRAINTS

CHAPTER **6**

The Role of Context
in Written Communication   **197**
Martin Nystrand

PART **III**

PROCESSING STRATEGIES:
PERCEPTUAL AND COGNITIVE DEMANDS
IN LISTENING AND READING

CHAPTER **7**

Listening and Reading Processes
in College- and Middle School-Age Readers   **217**
David J. Townsend, Caroline Carrithers,
and Thomas G. Bever

CHAPTER **13**

A Comparison of the Two Theories about Development in Written Language: Implications for Pedagogy and Research 371

Sandra Stotsky

Contributors

Numbers in parentheses indicate the pages on which the authors' contributions begin.

THOMAS G. BEVER (217), Department of Psychology, University of Rochester, Rochester, New York 14627

CAROLINE CARRITHERS (217), Department of Psychology, Johns Hopkins University, Baltimore, Maryland 21218

WALLACE CHAFE (83), Department of Linguistics, University of California, Santa Barbara, California 93106

JANE DANIELEWICZ (83), Department of English and The Writing Center, Hobart and William Smith Colleges, Geneva, New York 14556

JOSEPH H. DANKS (271), Department of Psychology, Kent State University, Kent, Ohio 44242

LAUREL J. END (271), Department of Psychology, Salve Regina College, Newport, Rhode Island 02840

M. A. K. HALLIDAY (55), Department of Linguistics, University of Sydney, N.S.W. 2006, Australia

ROSALIND HOROWITZ (1, 117), College of Social and Behavioral Sciences, Division of Education, The University of Texas, San Antonio, Texas 78285

MARTIN NYSTRAND (197), Department of English, and Wisconsin Center for Education Research, University of Wisconsin, Madison, Madison, Wisconsin 53706

DAVID R. OLSON (329), Center for Applied Cognitive Science, Ontario Institute for Studies in Education, Toronto, Ontario, Canada M5S 1V6, and The McLuhan Program in Culture and Technology, University of Toronto, Toronto, Ontario, Canada M5S 1A1

CHARLES A. PERFETTI (355), Department of Psychology, Learning, Research, and Development Center, University of Pittsburgh, Pittsburgh, Pennsylvania 15260

S. JAY SAMUELS (1, 295), Department of Educational Psychology, and Center for Research in Learning, Perception, and Cognition, University of Minnesota, Minneapolis, Minnesota 55455

PETER A. SCHREIBER (243), Departments of English and Linguistics, and Wisconsin Center for Education Research, University of Wisconsin, Madison, Madison, Wisconsin 53706

SANDRA STOTSKY (371), Graduate School of Education, Harvard University, Cambridge, Massachusetts 02138

DAVID J. TOWNSEND (217), Department of Psychology, Montclair State College, Upper Montclair, New Jersey 07043

TEUN A. VAN DIJK (161), Department of General Literary Studies, Section of Discourse Studies, University of Amsterdam, 1012 VT Amsterdam, The Netherlands

RITA WATSON (329), Department of Educational Psychology, University of British Columbia, Vancouver, British Columbia, Canada V6T 1Z5

Preface

Comprehending Oral and Written Language is written for researchers and graduate students who have an interest in theoretical and research questions associated with the relationships among oral and written language, listening and reading, and speaking and writing. This book will be useful in courses on applied linguistics, cognitive and educational psychology, rhetoric and speech communication, reading and English education, as well as in discourse analysis and the study of literacy. The chapters are strongly oriented toward theory and scientific research. The state of the art is such that these are desperately needed. The book is not designed to bring closure to the complex relationships presented but rather to ignite further work, increase fine-grained analyses, and promote theoretical and experimental inquiry. This work, however, will also bear on more applied recommendations. From some of the material presented in this book, one may, for instance, begin to develop approaches that classroom teachers can use to improve listening and reading comprehension.

The chapters that follow should be of value to a rather diverse readership—to those who have an interest in comprehension and interpretation of language—in oral and written language as communication products and listening and reading, speaking and writing as communication processes. These essays may prove informative for the way that we think about daily discourse, communication through and with schoolbooks, through the media or press, computers, and in our understanding of the language used in spoken and written learning and instruction in the schools.

Some readers will be surprised to find that our contrasts are quite recent ones. For instance, the study of discourse comprehension, by way of oral and written language with attention to extended stretches of discourse, was not possible a mere 10 years ago. We simply did not have the proper tools or, more so, dare we say, the inclination. Moreover, this volume explicates several hypotheses regarding the nature of comprehension that we could not envision a mere decade ago. We are no longer asking only, Are oral and written language the same or different? Nor are we asking, Are listening and reading the same or different? As this book demonstrates, the questions have become multilayered, more focused, and consequently more engaging. Attention has been directed to particular communication tasks, situational contexts, and listener and reader audiences.

The book is organized into four parts designed to highlight critical contrasts: Part I, "The Language of Spoken and Written Discourse," approaches the comprehension of oral and written language by contrasting features of spoken and written discourse. This section considers lexical density, clause and sentential and intersentential features, and grammatical intricacy and metaphor (Chapter 2), and clause and sentence construction and oral and written language as expressions of involvement and detachment in communication (Chapter 3).

Part II, "Processing Strategies: Rhetorical, Social-Situational, and Contextual Constraints," explores social-psychological factors that influence oral and written discourse-processing strategies. Chapter 4 begins with attention to the rhetorical features within text and moves from the writer outward toward the intellectual structures of the reader. Chapter 5 examines mental models within the reader and moves outward to the text and writer. Chapter 6 considers the role of context in the production of written communication and gives arguments against an autonomous view of text. These arguments have striking implications for an autonomous view of literacy—a view of literacy that ignores task, text, and several layers of social and psychological context.

Part III, "Processing Strategies: Perceptual and Cognitive Demands in Listening and Reading," looks for similarities and differences between listening and reading by examining perceptual and cognitive demands of each on select listener and reader audiences. Chapter 7 contrasts theories of reading comprehension and discusses experimental research in sentence and discourse thematic processing of middle grade and college skilled and average readers. Chapter 8 summarizes experimental research that compares child and adult perception of prosody and structure in syntactic processing of spoken language. Chapter 9 pinpoints specifically how the design of an experiment may actually determine whether or not one finds similarities or differences in listening and reading comprehension. Finally, Chapter 10 discusses inside-the-head and outside-the-head factors that should be taken into account in diagnosing listening and reading problems, and, thereby, sets the stage for the remaining section on schooling.

Part IV, "The Acquisition of Literacy and Schooling," brings the book closer to issues of theory building and particular problems associated with literacy development in schools. Chapter 11 discusses the acquisition of literacy through study of the ontogenesis of definitions inside and outside schools, and Chapter 12 characterizes the shifts from oral to written language and from written language development to oral language development through graphic representations. A final chapter compares and contrasts two theories about development in written language and discusses their implications for pedagogical practices and research.

These chapters have been prepared by cognitive scientists, socio- and psycholinguists, and English, reading, and language arts educators, many of whom are highly visible in their respective research committees and recognized for their outstanding contributions to literacy research. They are truly diamonds in their respective fields. And although there is considerable research talent represented here, this should not suggest that there is unity in perspective or agreement on important matters. Quite the contrary. In this book, one should expect to find and extrapolate differences of opinion on critical issues. Once juxtaposed, many of the chapters bring to the foreground the kind of dialectic that we believe is desperately needed and that permits scholarship to advance and grow. This book should be read in the spirit of learning from the differences of opinion and by capitalizing on the variation set in the context of a single text.

Acknowledgments

We are grateful to the contributors to this volume for their study of the questions and topics that are so integral to comprehending oral and written language, and we thank them for working tenaciously and enthusiastically at producing their thoughts on the theme for the present volume. Each scholar has contributed a solid chapter that stands on its own and can be read as an insightful contribution to the literature, independently of the whole. However, each chapter is also part of a collective endeavor and is better for each of the contributions that constitute the whole. In unison, these chapters enable us to achieve greater understanding of complex and precious questions.

The participants in our International Reading Association Symposium "Comprehending Oral and Written Language," Richard C. Anderson, Joseph H. Danks, John T. Guthrie, Charles A. Perfetti, and Thomas G. Sticht, may be said to have sparked this work, though they may not have known so at the time that they accepted our invitation to deliver a paper at our symposium. After six years of work, extensive dialoguing about the theme, and redrafting of chapters, we have not forgotten, and we thank them.

Special appreciation is extended to our colleague Martin Nystrand, who supported this project from its inception, read manuscripts, and offered many suggestions not to mention inspiration which strengthened this effort.

Appreciation is extended to The National Academy of Education for a Spencer Fellowship awarded to Rosalind Horowitz for 1985–1988, through the generous assistance of The Spencer Foundation. This award helped defray a number of expenses associated with the production of this volume. It allowed us to expand our vision of the project and influenced its orchestration. In essence, the award brought this book to fruition and is acknowledged with the deepest of gratitude. The opinions expressed here, however, do not reflect those of The Academy, The Spencer Foundation, nor of the other funding offices or agencies acknowledged throughout the manuscript.

Dwight F. Henderson, Acting Vice President for Academic Affairs at The University of Texas at San Antonio, graciously granted funds for assistance on this book during his tenure in the Office of the Dean of the College of Social and Behavioral Sciences.

Graduate and undergraduate students assisted the editors far beyond the call of duty. Special appreciation is due to Lucinda Canavan, Dahlia Ryle, Anne Dunivan, Amy Harris, Steven Tanner, Marilyn Walsh, and many others at The University of Texas at San Antonio. In particular, Anna Budzinski saw the project through to completion and was at side in a variety of capacities through the final stages of this work. Melissa Beams faithfully typed and proofed a number of versions of this work.

Finally, special appreciation is warmly extended to the staff at Academic Press. We thereby thank Fiona Stevens and Joe Ingram, our superb editors, for their advice, meticulous care with the manuscript, and constant support throughout the project.

Chapter 1

Comprehending Oral and Written Language: Critical Contrasts for Literacy and Schooling

Rosalind Horowitz
S. Jay Samuels

INTRODUCTION[1]

In the next century it will be virtually impossible to pursue the study of written language and literacy without attention to oral language. If the observations of the contributors to this volume are correct, our knowledge of written language will be significantly influenced by our knowledge of oral language. More so, the study of the comprehension and uses of written language will be dramatically influenced by our understanding of the comprehension and uses of oral language. What have been seemingly separate lines of research, conducted by seemingly separate communities of inquiry, will ultimately coalesce in some surprising and important ways.

Speculations are that 100 years from now, not only will there be a mingling of research perspectives, but since features associated with oral and written language and social-psychological factors associated with language processes are constantly in a state of flux, our very object of study will also change dramatically. The lexis, grammar, and larger structures of oral and written language may become alike, with the norm being a writing that is largely indistinguishable from speech. How we view the comprehension of oral and written language will change as daily language uses and technology change and reshape what form or function oral and written language assumes. How we view the comprehension of oral and written language will also influence what possibilities exist for listening and reading and speaking and writing, both inside and outside of schools.

This book brings together essays that explore theoretical and research questions that will influence the comprehension of oral and written language in schools. Chapters examine similarities and differences between elements of oral and written language, the mutual and unique components and processes that underlie listening and reading, and theoretical models that depict oral and written language development and processes. These chapters have been commissioned with the expectation that critical contrasts would surface that would extend our understanding of language and literacy in and for schooling. There has been, to our knowledge, no systematic study and presentation of the various lines of research and contrasts that we present under the cover of a single publication.

Comprehending Oral and Written Language focuses on studies of oral and written language, with attention to reading and writing literacy. But this work is about more than literacy development. It also indirectly addresses questions that are basic to human learning. The bulk of what we understand and learn inside or outside of schools comes through oral or written exchange, by way of the ear or the eye, and through listening and reading, speaking and writing, by teacher, text, or technology. Yet we have little explanation of these processes in ways that inform our understanding of them and the learning possibilities that students should be able to avail themselves of in thoughtfully and creatively designed schools (see Scheffler, 1985).

This book is motivated by the realization that the processing of discourse in schools can best be explained through theoretical models that characterize an individual's growth and development in the uses of oral and written language in particular situational contexts. Models and scientific studies that characterize learning and cognition by way of prototypical oral and written discourse of the schools by and large do not exist. Work in discourse analysis and text processing and comprehension is recent, and psycho- and sociolinguistic analyses have not been adequately applied to educational questions and everyday psychological issues of the most pressing sort, although the potential for such application is quite good (van Dijk, 1985; Stubbs, 1986).

In this chapter, then, we set the stage for the book. In the first section we give a brief historical overview of the comparisons and contrasts that follow. We identify past assertions that are problematic. We identify issues that are raised in the past work and pose questions not raised. We note new research directions.

To do so, we briefly examine definitions of oral and written language, work on oral and written language from a historical angle, the search for laws of oral and written language, and the search for laws of listening and reading comprehension. Finally, we consider advancements in technology as they influence our definitions and bear on the development of oral and written language in schools.

In the second part we give an overview in some detail of the chapters that follow, highlight critical differences of opinion, and discuss interrelationships between ideas in this book and those elsewhere in the literature.

It should be noted that there are similarities but also differences of opinion on many important matters. Our goal in this chapter is to isolate and highlight some of these with the expectation that this will stimulate further inquiry by those who have an interest in language, literacy, and cognitive studies for schooling.

New Research Directions

Nearly a century of reading research exists. There is less writing research, perhaps 40 years at best. But reading research can be said to date back to the late 1800s. In this literature, one finds a substantial and impressive body of research that has examined the perceptual and psychomotor operations associated with learning to read. Only recently in the United States has this research been extended to incorporate comprehension and higher-order cognitive processes associated with learning from complex discourse such as is found in extended texts and lectures of the upper grades.

This change in research perspective is reflected in recent national reports in the United States (*Becoming a Nation of Readers, The Reading Report Card, The Writing Report Card, Literacy: Profiles of America's Young Adults* and its follow-up report *The Subtle Danger: Reflections on the Literacy Abilities of America's Young Adults,* and others). These reports indicate that most students acquire word-recognition skills, that is, basic reading skills, by Grade 4 but fail to acquire higher-order comprehension skills— such as the ability to summarize, synthesize, evaluate, and engage in analytical and critical thinking.

Further only since the early 1980s have scholars begun to investigate certain complex language relationships including that of reading and the other language arts. After nearly 80 years of separation, reading and writing are being studied in relationship to one another. Principles gleaned from a century of research on reading are being applied to writing research. Scholars have also begun to look at the cognitive, linguistic, and social knowledge needed to read and write. This work on reading and writing has revealed that neither reading nor writing can stand in isolation. What writers know about reading influences how they write; and conversely, what readers know about writing consciously or unconsciously influences how they read. The reading–writing comparisons (and they have largely been comparisons, although contrasts are also needed) have set the stage and provided the momentum for other kinds of comparisons, and contrasts, including some we wish to consider in this volume and hope to expand upon elsewhere.

It is apparent that work on reading and writing cannot advance without serious attention to oral language. Written language is processed not only by what we know about writing, but also by what we know about oral language and the ways in which the two combine. Oral language, however, is processed in unconscious or conscious ways depending upon whether the language is spontaneous or highly planned and depending upon whom the audience might be.

For the most part, oral language has been neglected in accounts of school literacy. However, oral and written language need to be understood in relation to one another. They often function as interdependent systems of communication in schools. We better understand what we have heard in a lecture after we have read a chapter, and conversely, the chapter reading becomes dependent on the lecture processing. As we show here and in the chapters that follow, not only is there an interdependency between oral and written language, but the interaction (or mingling) between oral and written language occurs frequently in schools (as in society). In schools, students read along as they hear a text read by a teacher. Students listen in round robin reading as they follow the oral reading by a peer in the next seat. Finally, there is a juxtaposition between oral and written language in schools (as in work places). Oral language discussions, for example, occur before students read a basal reader or after reading a textbook chapter. Such discussions usually accompany reading, but do not take place alone, and this juxtaposition influences the final meaning and the differences in interpretation that children reach about texts.

There is growing international concern, for schools and beyond, about some of the questions that we have discussed. In particular, *A Nation Prepared: Teachers for the 21st Century* (Carnegie Forum, 1986) directly calls for literacy instruction of the highest order in schools of the next century. When we began this volume, there were few theoretical papers or research studies in the United States or in other countries for that matter that considered oral and written discourse and listening and reading processes. As chapters were added to the project, we found leading scholars in the United States, Canada, Europe, and Australia posing questions relevant to this effort. As we have noted, however, this work remains a scattered and disparate literature.

Certain trends are apparent:

1. There are growing systematic and scientific comparisons of oral and written language as discourse types and as systems of communication. Oral and written language are viewed as existing along a continuum of discourse and mediating potentials for communication (see Halliday, this volume). The lexical, grammatical, rhetorical, and pragmatic aspects of oral and written language (also referred to as *speech and writing* or *spoken and written* language) are being studied in ways that will influence our concepts of language, cognition, and literacy (see Horowitz, this volume).[2] Ongoing studies look at spontaneous discourse, conversations, natural discourse processing, narratives, explanatory discourse in schoolbooks, scientific and news texts, and argumentative prose in political and legal debates. See samples in this volume.

2. There is growing study of speaking and writing as acts of performance and processes that employ specific oral or written language forms (e.g., Chafe and Danielewicz, this volume). This book only touches upon these, and another full volume would be necessary to address this comparison.[3]

3. There is growing study of the role of interlocutors in the communication process. The rule-governed behavior of the writer and reader, speaker and listener is no longer defined a priori to a discourse. These rules are discovered through reciprocity between interlocutors and with the audience functioning as a "co-author" in particular contexts of text use (Duranti & Brenneis, 1986; Nystrand, 1982, 1986, also this volume).

4. The kinds of cognitive models that language users employ during listening or reading are being given attention in work on episodic or mental models in communication (including models about ethnic minority groups) as these interact with discourse structures and arguments, such as used by a majority population (see van Dijk, this volume, and his more recent publications which have implications for multiethnic and -cultural classrooms).

5. There is growing scientific study of listening and reading comprehension as mutual and unique processes that employ specific oral and written language (see Danks & End; Townsend, Carrithers, & Bever; Samuels, all this volume).

6. Relatedly, what it means to learn and understand, given certain human biological possibilities and constraints and in select environments from classroom to computer-based or real world, is being considered with attention to the perceptual systems (e.g., J. J. Gibson, 1966).

Perceptual mechanisms used in learning by the eye and ear (in the case of writing, see Emig, 1978; Frith, 1979) and by the ear, eye, and hand by way of computer manipulations are being studied. These are gaining attention in research reports (Gottlieb & Krasnegor, 1985; Freeman & Cox, 1985).

The various contrasts and comparisons that we present in this chapter are of more than academic interest. The discussion that follows indicates that the way in which oral and written language and listening and reading are defined and treated has important ramifications for school practices.

DEFINITION OF ORAL AND WRITTEN LANGUAGE

What constitutes oral or written language? The terms *oral* and *written language* have not been adequately defined. They have been used to refer to the products of speaking and the writing system, which may or may not include the processes of listening and reading. Some use written language to refer to not only the *products* of writing but also the *acts* of reading and writing. The confusion is compounded as others use oral and written language for just the products of speaking and writing, while still others (as we have in this chapter) use oral and written language for both products *and* both processes—spoken–written language (as products), listening–speaking and reading–writing (as processes). Orality, however, implies both speaking and listening, and literacy implies both reading and writing.

Our review of the various essays or research studies that contrast oral and written language reveals that although there is growing scientific discussion about oral and written language in many English-speaking nations, there is no agreed-upon definition of what is to be included or excluded under each. Further, there is no clear definition of these for purposes of literacy instruction in the school environment. However, we do find that there has been oversimplification and many erroneous assumptions in the literature based on sheer myth or the dichotomization of oral and written language.[4]

A number of leading scholars of the English language have considered several factors critical to oral and written comparison-contrasts (see the work of Wallace Chafe, Robert de Beaugrande, Michael Halliday, Martin Nystrand, Michael Stubbs, Deborah Tannen, and others).[5] Differences of opinion exist regarding a number of matters including (1) the relationship between interlocutors in oral and written communication, (2) the role of context in oral and written communication, (3) the type of structure and cohesive devices characteristic of oral and written language, (4) the way in which language mediates meaning under each language form and from the perspective of the aural or visual modalities, (5) the way in which oral and written language interact to convey meaning.

Oral language is typically associated by linguists with conversation that is produced, processed, and then evaluated in the context of face-to-face exchange and grounded in interpersonal relationships that are often clearly established. Oral language is adapted to a specific audience and to sociocultural settings and communities that are presumably present, functioning in a context of here and now. This language is characterized as episodic and narrative-like. It is noted that speaking is the natural, while writing is the artificial, form of language, and that oral language involves use of an informal register—a style of language adapted to a social context. Cohesion is expressed through **deixis** (references to items outside of a discourse or text) but also through **prosodic cues** (the pitch, stress, and pauses expressed by the language) and **paralinguistic devices** (such as facial expressions, lifts of the eyebrow, smiles or frowns, or body language such as pointing or distancing oneself from a listener). It is argued that much can remain unsaid, that oral language need not be explicit because these nonverbal cues and the voice can convey considerable information which evokes the meanings that are normally carried by the written discourse. Relatedly, because there is a sharing of context, this primarily **phatic communication** (communication designed to express feelings or interpret relationships, such as expressed by a birthday card) can be swift, brief, linear, with constructions that are based on a single predication and simplicity. For example, imagine the talk between lovers or intimate friends. Little need be said, but much is known and understood. What seems to hold the message together lies not so much within the words, but within the subtle nonverbal cues and the interpersonal relations that go beyond the immediate space and time. (Vygotsky, 1962, citing Tolstoy, discusses the language of lovers to make a similar point.)

Finally, oral language is used for specific purposes, different from those of writing and for interpersonal communication that demands face-to-face exchange, e.g., conversations across a neighborhood yard, a proposal of marriage, a board meeting, a prayer meeting, a medical report to a patient, or a legal proceeding.

In contrast, written language is typically associated with language of books and explanatory prose such as is found in schools. Written language is formal, academic, and planned; it hinges on the past and is reconstructed in such a way that in the future it can be processed by varied readerships. Written language is often characterized as secondary to speech. Writing is often portrayed as an autonomous language, one without context or where context is not visible, although as we show in this volume, this, among other claims, is a highly controversial matter. In written language, unlike oral language, cohesion is expressed through **lexical choices** (sometimes redundancy of those choices), **nominalization** (the formation of a noun from a verb), **anaphoric relations** (reference to a previous part of a text), **cataphoric relations** (reference to a subsequent portion of a text), **signal words** or **cohesive ties** (e.g., connectives such as *however, moreover*), and is explicitly marked through symbolic devices (including punctuation marks such as ! ? — ( ) ,) that show intra- and intersentential relations. While oral language has been characterized as the personal and spontaneous language, written language is said to be depersonalized and objective, content- or idea-based, formalized and controlled. Finally, written language has been characterized as more complex than oral language, with multiple predication, subordination, and extended clauses, where elaboration is necessary should the unknown reader misunderstand. Complex hierarchical organization replaces the linear, additive, and formulaic motif of oral discourse. Table 1.1 shows the oral and written dichotomy.

Despite our picture of what is found in the literature, it must be emphasized that this dichotomy between oral and written language begs for research. Oral and written language do not constitute unitary constructs. Rather there is much variation and overlap. Oral and written language forms depend upon the purposes for which they are used and the listener and reader audience that they will serve. Oral and written language can be further broken down into still other discourse types and registers (varieties of language that are adapted to particular occasions of use). Oral and written language will change in form and complexion, in tenor and texture, depending upon the degree of formality of a topic, one's degree of familiarity with an audience, the immediacy of a situation or problem, and the content covered or genre. Oral language may be spontaneously produced for informal speech and in conversational situations (speech among friends) or may be systematically prepared for a formal address and addressee, a speech that is organized through writing for oral reading at a lecturn. Likewise, some written language is produced with minimal planning for reading (e.g., an informal letter) and some is prepared for a formal community and unknown audience (e.g., an essay); still other writing is produced for oral reading (e.g., legal documents) or for speaking (e.g., court proceedings). As Table 1.2 illustrates, there are a number of decisions to be made about oral and written language production and uses given the varieties of oral and written language in our world.

TABLE 1.1
The Oral–Written Dichotomy

Oral language *Talk*	Written language *Text*
Face-to-face conversation with reciprocity between speaker and listener	Face-to-text with limited reciprocity between author and reader
Narrativelike	Expositorylike
Action oriented	Idea oriented
Event oriented	Argument oriented
Story oriented	Explanatory prose
Here and now	Future and past
In given space and time	Not space- or time-bound
Informal	Formal
Primary discourse	Secondary discourse
Natural communication	Artificial communication
Interpersonal	Objective and distanced
Spontaneous	Planned
Sharing of context (situational)	No common context
Ellipsis	Explicitness in text
Structureless	Highly structured
Cohesion through paralinguistic cues	Cohesion through lexical cues
Single predication	Multiple predication
Repetition	Succinctness
Simple linear structures	Complex hierarchical structures
Paratactic patterns	Hypotactic patterns
Right branching with limited subordination	Left branching with multiple levels of subordination
Fleeting	Permanent
Unconscious	Conscious and restructures consciousness

Further, school oral discourse may be characterized by its own rules of operation, and unlike oral language of the home or peer group may prove to be objective, depersonalized, and decontextualized for many students. Similarly, school written discourse, found in schoolbooks or used by teachers in classroom discussion (e.g., direction-giving) may also be decontextualized or arhetorical. However, some students often learn to appeal to their teachers' expectations for certain kinds of manuscript form. Oral and written discourse of the schools may also require entry into particular communities of discourse, with the acceptance of the belief systems, values, and reward structures of those communities. For example, particular content fields taught in schools, such as science or world geography, have their own technical language systems, meaning systems, and communities of understanding and beliefs.

TABLE 1.2
Varieties of Oral and Written Language

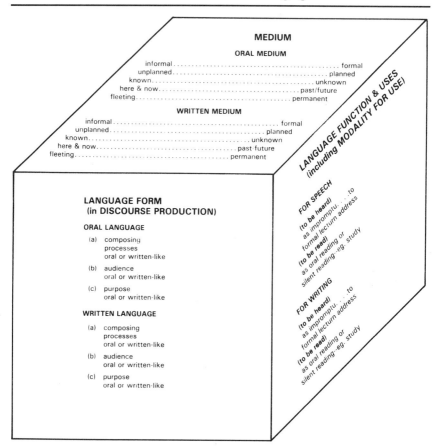

Readers who enjoy science may learn to acquire not only the vocabulary of science, but an appreciation for the ways of knowing science through school oral and written discourse. While it may appear that there is no specific audience in mind in much of the written discourse of the schoolbook, it may be that the audience is of a qualitatively different nature than we have conceived in other types of written language (e.g., personal letter writing). (See Lemke, 1985, for examples.)

Relatedly, school listening is a more intense and analytical kind of listening than listening at home. Thomas G. Sticht introduced the concept of **auding,** some 15 years ago, to refer to this specialized listening which he says is needed in school learning and is different from other kinds of listening. Auding is an active process under the direct control of an individual's attention and requires selectivity in information gathering and appropriate "tracking" of communication (Sticht, Beck, Hauke, Kleiman, & James, 1974). This kind of listening, unlike other kinds of listening often intended to maintain social relationships, is oriented toward propositions and argument processing, analysis, and synthesis. It is not like the listening one engages in during chitchat on the street or in a pub!

School reading, similarly, requires new kinds of reading skills suitable to the academic goals and type of text read and tasks required by the institution. School reading is not the same as reading at home. It is not like that done in a lounge chair with a glass of wine. Students at quite young an age (as young as first grade) know that in school reading they will be tested, judged in relation to others, and held accountable to the institution.

Additionally, in schools there are many unique shifts in language usage and many unique kinds of mingling of oral and written language that have barely been touched upon in the research literature.[6] In schools, one finds that there is written language that is converted into spoken language (when text is read aloud by teachers or students, in oral reading of writing protocols, or when round robin reading occurs). There is a written language (textbook information) that is transformed into oral language (when fiery discussions are held). And vice versa, we have oral language (discussion) that is transformed into written language (through writing assignments that teachers require) and oral language that is transcribed into written language (e.g., in language experience approaches to reading). How students manage these shifts and manipulate discourse forms in these modalities in order to meet the needs of school assignments remains a fascinating and untouched question worthy of research![7]

Table 1.3 calls attention to select discussions and studies of oral and written language in and for schooling in this volume and elsewhere. This table also gives a list of the different types of oral and written language that we have in mind and that are relevant to the goals of this book.

The types of oral and written language treated in Table 1.3 are of a qualitatively different form and nature than were observed in schools some 50 years ago. In the past, recitation-type communication dominated in the schools. Learning revolved around teacher-controlled talk and resulted in limited reciprocity between student and teacher or student and student.

TABLE 1.3
Select Discussions and Studies of Oral and Written
Language in and for Schooling

Natural speech *outside* schools (Halliday, this volume)

Conversation (Bereiter & Scardamalia, 1981; Buchmann, 1983; Chafe & Danielewicz, this volume; Edmondson, 1981; Emerson, 1983; Fox, 1986; Tannen, 1984; Wardaugh, 1985; Wertsch, 1980)

Movement from conversation and dyadic dialogues *outside* and *inside* schools (including parent–child, child–child, and teacher–child interactions, Horowitz, 1973; Horowitz & Davis, 1984; McLane, 1981) to interaction with text (Ruddell & Haggard, 1986; Staton, Shuy, Kreeft, & Reed, in press)

Dialogue journal writing as a corpus for analysis, with conversation between a student and teacher *around* journal-diary texts (Staton, Shuy, Kreeft, & Reed, in press; Steiner, 1978)

Self-talk (inner speech) *in* listening	(Stotsky, this volume; van Dijk, this volume)
in reading	(Stotsky, this volume; van Dijk, this volume)
in speaking	(Wertsch, 1980, 1985)
in writing	(Daiute, 1985a) and
vital to the concept of the history of *la parole*	(Steiner, 1978)

Letters (Chafe & Danielewicz, this volume)

Natural speech *inside* schools (Halliday, this volume)

Monologues or lectures (Chafe & Danielewicz, this volume)

Schooled writing (McCutchen, in press; Scinto, 1986)

Academic essays (Chafe & Danielewicz, this volume)

Oral reading (Danks, 1980; Danks & End, this volume; Danks, Bohn, & Fears, 1983; Glushko, 1981; Jorm & Share, 1983; Juel & Holmes, 1981)

Speech processes *in* reading (Perfetti, 1985; Perfetti & McCutchen, 1982)

Discussions *around* classroom text (Heath, 1986; Schallert & Kleiman, 1979)

Teacher-led discussions in particular domains of knowledge (e.g., science, Lemke, 1985)

Oral and written code elaboration (Poole & Field, 1976) and oral and written commentaries (Greenberg, 1983; Rabin, 1986) *around* student writing (Faigley, Cherry, Jolliffee, & Skinner, 1985), as part of text revision (Faigley, Cherry, Jolliffee, & Skinner, 1985; Sawkins, 1971), oral and written language around a film (Beaman, 1984)

Oral versus written knowledge and definitions of vocabulary in homes versus schools (Graves, 1986; Gruner, Kibler, & Gibson, 1967; Hall, Nagy, & Linn, 1984; Nagy & Anderson, 1984; Watson & Olson, this volume)

Speech recognition from infancy (Eimas, 1986) to speech recognition by children and adults (Savin, 1972; Schreiber, this volume) and by computer (Levinson & Liberman, 1986)

Voice feedback as a scaffold for writing (Lehrer, Levin, DeHart, & Comeaux, 1986) and speech synthesis for word-processor writing (Borgh & Dickson, 1986)

Speech and writing production by computer (Daiute, 1985b; Greenfield, 1984; Olson, 1985) and writing by electronic mail (Duranti, 1986; Quinn, Mehan, Levin, & Black, 1983)

Oral exchanges and social interaction have been revitalized perhaps due to the work of Lev Vygotsky (and other Russian psychologists). Work on cooperative learning is gaining unprecedented attention and becoming the subject of training programs and research in the United States and Europe. We are now interested in paired reading and learning. Perhaps based on old European models of paired study, paired learning increases oral exchange and encourages reciprocal questioning, elaboration, and interpersonal teamwork. Oral reading and talk may occur in dyads at home between parents and children or in schools between peers or older children teaching younger ones. Peer conferencing has also increased: There is oral reading, writing, and learning about writing processes through open peer exchanges and listening.

Group learning has been used more readily in schools particularly in the past few years. In group discussion, students engage in cooperative projects and group evaluation. Use of these and other nonrecitation types of oral language appear to promote mutual exchanges and reciprocity among learners that is quite different from the one-sided exchanges typical of the turn of the century and the years following. Research on each of these types of discourse is only beginning and holds great promise for comprehension studies.

A serious comparison of the preceding types of oral and written discourse has not been possible in the past for numerous reasons:

First, for most of this century, language was viewed as a phonological, lexical, or syntactic system in its own right, self-contained and separate from discourse or listener and reader audiences. Language study has been separated from other fields of research or disciplines, including the cognitive sciences, because meaning was believed to reside within language and to be a purely linguistic matter. Moreover, the various language and cognitive processes (speaking, listening, writing, and reading) have been analyzed as separate psychological phenomena within the provinces of separate fields of research.

There are signs that this situation is being altered and that we wish to redress imbalances of our notions of oral and written language. We are taking a closer look at each of the language arts and are moving toward an integrated theory of the language arts; scholars from various fields are interacting about the relationship between speaking and writing, and listening and reading (although the latter two are less highlighted), between the roles of speaker and writer, listener and reader (although the latter two are also less highlighted).

Second, scholars have not only neglected to consider oral and written language contrasts, they have only recently systematically tackled difficult comparisons of the comprehension of oral and written language. It has been implicitly assumed that the processing of oral and written language involved use of consistently similar perceptual and cognitive processes and strategies across ages and development, social groups and settings, and purposes (see Danks & End, this volume). With growing interest in literacy and the broadening of approaches, a number of scholars have begun to compare and contrast the comprehension of oral and written language in order to explain why comprehension may be achieved with certain oral language but may not be achieved with written language, what new skills are needed for comprehending written language, or what similarities exist between these two language codes and modes of processing. These comparisons have resulted in some reassessment of traditional assumptions and in new kinds of questions critical for schooling: How is listening to a lecture or participating in a classroom debate the same as or different from reading about the lecture or debate? Is reading in school just another form of listening? Is writing just another form of speaking? When is the teacher easier to understand than the text? When is the text easier to understand than the teacher? When is the classroom discussion more informative than both the teacher and the text? When do oral and written language combine in schools to form "new" meanings that neither can do alone?

Third, it is clear that literacy research, be it the study of reading or writing, cannot advance with certain precision without greater understanding of speech, speech processing, and, above all, the speakers engaged in communication acts. A more comprehensive study of language comprehension must include oral and written language—and the language users involved.

Fourth, without comparing and contrasting oral and written language, the acts of listening and reading, speaking and writing, and the readers and writers, listeners and speakers involved, it is virtually impossible to chart the development and acquisition of literacy—and furthermore to intelligently and systematically design instruction in the schools. For how can we know what literacy is until we know what orality is and how the two interrelate and interconnect?

Readers and writers are first and foremost listeners and speakers. The acquisition of literacy entails a shift (or shifts) from psychological, linguistic, and social-cultural experiences as a speaker and oral-language processor (including listener) to those of a reader and user of more formal oral and written language registers in school (and other written forms, thereafter, outside of schools). This shift from orality to literacy is clearly more than one of processing a new register, i.e., a new variation of language; this shift has been described from a social-historical perspective as a shift to markedly new kinds of consciousness and intellectual possibilities (Havelock, 1980; Heath, 1986; Olson, 1977, 1980, 1985; Ong, 1982). There are, however, many ideas expressed about the new consciousness that require further explanation.

Ong (1982) notes that of the possibly tens of thousands of languages spoken in the course of human history, only around 106 have ever been committed to writing, and most have never appeared in print. Only 78 have a literature. Many have disappeared. Many were not written at all. Consequently, he emphasizes that "The basic orality of language is permanent" (p. 7).

However, we also face a second level of orality. It is not a preliterate but a "postliterate society's orality" which has infiltrated our society and schools. With this "secondary orality" will come continued familiarity with computers and other electronic communication systems that suggest new ways of processing and interpreting messages. Ong's secondary orality depends upon writing for its very existence! What is thus orallike and writtenlike has become blurred and continues to change with time.

Fifth, there is reason to believe that the study of literacy and written language comprehension can be greatly enhanced by the study of oral language since the study of oral language permits analysis of many features of the language that may not be directly visible or accessible in written language but are essential to theories of language comprehension and cognition. What children can demonstrate through oral communication may begin to also tell us something about their potential for understanding and constructing written communication. In other instances, performance with written communication may tell us about the potential for producing and understanding oral communication.

Sixth, it is becoming increasingly evident that written language (text) does not exist in a vacuum, without oral language, be it in the real world or in school settings. The text has meaning and undergoes interpretation only in the context of teaching and in the context of oral uses of language.

We have operated from a rather simplistic point of view, expecting that it is with writing or reading alone that higher order abstract reasoning and cognitive development emerge. Rather, it may be that reading and writing coupled with oral exchange about the ideas are what in the final analysis produce advanced thinking and knowledge. In essence, the written word alone may produce a rather minimal level of literacy. The incorporation of the oral with the written, and the addition of listening with reading, may promote literacy and offers new insights about what literacy is and how it develops. It is unrealistic to address school texts without some exploration of the oral language environment in which they are produced, comprehended, and used (see Horowitz, 1987).

Figure 1.1 summarizes the range of questions that must be considered in the study of the comprehension of oral and written language. This boxology includes three variables treated in this chapter and throughout the book. The figure summarizes *potential antecedent variables* associated with oral and written language systems. In considering the comprehension of discourse, we must consider the speaker or writer (the person and personality), the object of interaction (the speech or text), the processes of speaking or writing (the acts), the community to be addressed, and the listeners and readers (Townsend et al., this volume). The *mediated discourse* can be further studied for its linguistic, rhetorical, and social-contextual features and its epistomological and domain of knowledge differences (Nystrand, this volume). Oral and written language can be examined for its *consequences on learners*, can result in certain comprehension, memory or recall, motivational, and attitudinal changes (van Dijk, this volume). Developmental differences exist across each of the three components represented in the figure—antecedent, mediating, and consequent variables—that will need to be researched (Stotsky, this volume). Each of the three variables will also be influenced by the possibilities or limitations of technological advancements discussed later in this chapter.

ORAL AND WRITTEN LANGUAGE HISTORICALLY CONTRASTED

Comparisons of oral and written language have largely taken a historical angle, with little attention to individual development in a literate culture. For example, one focus has been early semitic cultures. These cultures placed literacy with the elite, the priesthood. The mastery of the writing system required extensive leisure time. As may perhaps still be the case today, the general community did not have access to this leisure time and thus processed an oral, formulaic language. This form of communication was dependent upon rhapsodic thought, rituals, and the use of repetition and was event based to facilitate memory. The Hebrew term for *word* is *devar*— ר ב ד —which interestingly enough also means *place* and *event*. Hebrew was focused around people, places, and events that could be orally processed, memorized, and recalled in formulaic poetry and song. Aramaic was originally cast in oral form to be ad-

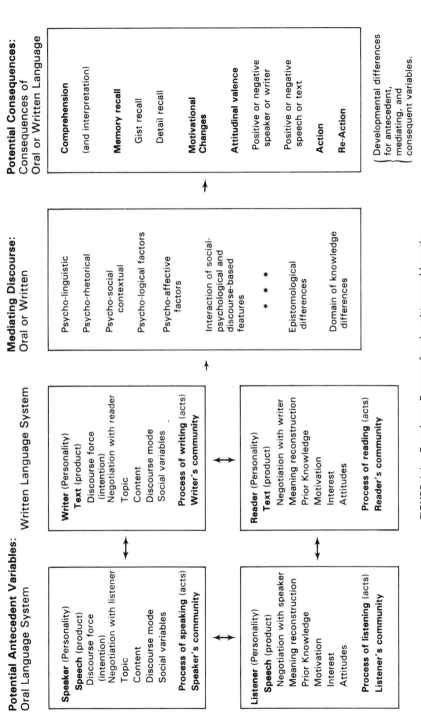

Potential Antecedent Variables:
Oral Language System   Written Language System

Mediating Discourse:
Oral or Written

Potential Consequences:
Consequences of
Oral or Written Language

Speaker (Personality)
Speech (product)
Discourse force
(intention)
Negotiation with listener
Topic
Content
Discourse mode
Social variables
Process of speaking (acts)
Speaker's community

Listener (Personality)
Speech (product)
Negotiation with speaker
Meaning reconstruction
Prior Knowledge
Motivation
Interest
Attitudes
Process of listening (acts)
Listener's community

Writer (Personality)
Text (product)
Discourse force
(intention)
Negotiation with reader
Topic
Content
Discourse mode
Social variables
Process of writing (acts)
Writer's community

Reader (Personality)
Text (product)
Negotiation with writer
Meaning reconstruction
Prior Knowledge
Motivation
Interest
Attitudes
Process of reading (acts)
Reader's community

Psycho-linguistic
Psycho-rhetorical
Psycho-social
contextual
Psycho-logical factors
Psycho-affective
factors
Interaction of social-
psychological and
discourse-based
features
    * * *
Epistomological
differences
Domain of knowledge
differences

Comprehension
(and interpretation)

Memory recall
Gist recall
Detail recall

**Motivational
Changes**

Attitudinal valence
Positive or negative
speaker or writer
Positive or negative
speech or text

Action
Re-Action

⎧ Developmental differences
⎨ for antecedent,
⎩ mediating, and
   consequent variables.

FIGURE 1.1. Boxology: Range of oral–written problematics.

dressed to audiences who did not read, but listened, memorized, and orally rehearsed what they heard.

It is impossible to fathom the shift in mind (and soul) that emerged with the use of script and later the invention of print. It is a miracle that somehow we made these shifts and that we can decode squiggles on a page and arrive at a meaning that an author or speaker, near or distant, intended. But, as many historians point out, the vast majority of the earth's population has not been literate, and most communication has historically been oral, not written.

The earliest form of script, and the miracle it brought about, has typically been said to date back some 6000 years (Ong, 1982). However, the work of Schmandt-Besserat (1986) demonstrates that "the appearance of writing in Mesopotamia represents a logical step in the evolution of a system of recordkeeping that originated some 11,000 years ago" (p. 40). The precursors of writing, the earliest code, served and fostered certain civil functions related to trade, commerce, law, and government (Nystrand, 1982). With the advent of the Greek, Hebrew, Roman, Arabic, and Chinese alphabets came substantial changes in script (Havelock, 1976). "With the rise of cities and the development of large-scale trade the system was pushed onto a new track. Images of the tokens soon supplanted the tokens themselves, and the evolution of symbolic objects into ideographs led to the rapid adoption of writing all across western Asia" (Schmandt-Besserat, 1986, p. 40). Ultimately, the printing press altered language production and form, cognition, and memory capacity (Eisenstein, 1968, 1981, 1985), "although the gulf separating the age of scribes from that of printers has not been as fully probed" (Eisenstein, 1985, p. 32) as one might expect.

The written word offered the following: (1) One could plan and produce elaborate, limitless discourse, and a language user did not have to digest it all at once. (2) Its structure need not be formulaic or time and event based, nor follow demands and limits of memory and the musical rhythm of language as did past oral language. (3) It permitted reprocessing and reflection, criticism and reevaluation. (4) It permitted new structures, e.g., hypotaxis (Halliday, this volume; Horowitz, this volume), which may have depended upon spatial representation rather than strictly temporal representation. Above all, Ong and others suggest that written language, literacy, meant a new consciousness, the development of higher psychological processes (see also Vygotsky, 1978).

Havelock (1980) characterizes the coming of literate communication (in Athens, fifth century, reinvented by the child across the globe and time) as a movement from the ear to the eye, from an acoustic kind of discourse organization and meaning to an optic kind of discourse organization, an architectural arrangement of language which permitted analysis and appreciation of the shape of an extended organization. Movement from that of an oral composer to that of a written composer meant new ways of composing, but also created and continues to create new ways of structuring and using language. When considering the effect of written language on speakers, Havelock comments, "In orality the speaker and his speech remained one, what was spoken was his creation, in a sense it was himself. . . . As language assumed a new identity, so did the personality that spoke and used it" (p. 98).

While there is a growing literature that captures and describes the advent of literacy in Western civilization (Clifford, 1984; Eisenstein, 1968, 1985; Gelb, 1963; Havelock, 1976; Ohmann, 1972; Ong, 1982; Resnick, 1983; Resnick & Resnick, 1977; Rosenberg, 1985), we lack an explanation of the oral-to-written shift(s) within the individual child, adolescent, and low-literate adult in various social groups. We lack explanation of the growth that emerges as an individual moves from oral to written language and back to orality. We furthermore lack an explanation of how the social order influences this shift as it is experienced by various populations in our society. Halliday (1978), Olson (1977), and Watson and Olson (this volume) address how the oral–written shift is naturally experienced inside and outside of schools. Greenfield (1984), Olson (1985), and Ong (1982) address computer-technological advances. Kaestle (1985) reports what was read and what the readership in the United States consisted of from 1880 to 1980. He reports that, at least from 1600 to 1850, "the bias in literacy was toward the upper classes, toward males, and toward urban settings. Higher literacy was also associated with northern areas of Europe, Protestant areas, and industrializing areas" (p. 22). We await his full report on changes in literacy in the past 100 years. The expansion of literacy beyond the elite to the masses and traditionally neglected populations in our society is also gaining attention. For a start, see Stedman & Kaestle (1987).

Havelock is a scholar who expresses the oral-to-written shift within the child, and promotes the unique role of the oral.

> For millenia we have been biologically conditioned to use and understand language only as it is spoken and heard, and in the interest of preserving some of that language for recall, we have schooled ourselves as a species to develop a poetic language. . . . If it is desirable that a large majority of the population be literate can this be accomplished without prior linkage to the poetic and musical inheritance—in short should children be rushed into reading before they have learned to speak fluently, to recite, to memorize, and to sing suitable verse available in their own tongue? (Havelock, 1980, p. 97)

THE SEARCH FOR LAWS OF ORAL
AND WRITTEN LANGUAGE

A brief review of the literature on oral and written language follows. We find that there has been limited scientific study of extended oral and written language and a neglect of oral and written contrasts. We touch upon these omissions in this section. More is included in the chapters that follow.

Ferdinand de Saussure (1916/1959), Edward Sapir (1921), Leonard Bloomfield (1933), Charles Hockett (1958), and other linguists focused on the sound system and excluded written language from their domain of language study. Bloomfield notes that "writing is not language but merely a way of recoding language by means of visible marks" (p. 21). While Saussure considered *la langue* and *la parole*, he insisted on the supremacy of *la langue* (language in the abstract), which is still a priority among linguists today, rather than *la parole* (actual language behavior). In fact, there continues to be a need for a linguistics of *la parole*, which will, of course, also ultimately add to our understanding of *la langue*. Oral language in its natural form, and as discourse, is still by and large not taken seriously as a medium for study.

There is also little attention to written language in its natural form, and as discourse. Further, serious oral–written contrasts basic to schooling are ignored. Louis Hjelmslev (1961) views written language in itself as being worthy of analysis. Josef Vachek (1973) concurs and notes that there has been little understanding of written language as a separate system in its own right.

Speech as Primary

Since the turn of the century, it has been argued that it is use of the sound system that mediates meaning, and that sound—the ear—is essential to language processing. (See Sapir, 1921; Bloomfield, 1933; Jakobson, 1978; Jakobson & Waug ı, 1979.) The role of the spoken word in meaning is articulated as far ɔack as Socrates (Greene, 1951) and reiterated in various papers by scholars such as Havelock (1976). Without exception, these essays not only stress the importance of spoken language but also argue for the importance of speech in communication.

However, cogent arguments on why speech will not replace writing have been expressed (Sawyer, 1977), significant reservations about the primacy of speech are explicated by Scinto (1986) in his discussion of phonocentrism and its potential dangers for a balanced view of language. That language is primarily speech (a sound system), however, has been and continues to be a basic tenet in linguistics. But how so?

Under what conditions is sound necessary for meaning? At what level of language processing—orality or literacy—is sound a necessary ingredient? The analysis of sound has persisted at the phonological or orthographic level—in the examination of phoneme–grapheme relations— but how does sound influence syntactic, paragraph-level and even macrostructure processing and the meaning of a text that emerges line by line across stretches of ideas? This is barely touched.

Another line of work, conducted by rhetoricians, explores oral composing. Walter Ong, in his seminal publication *Orality and Literacy: The Technologizing of the Word,* points out that literacy, through nineteenth century America, was seen as serving primarily the needs of oratory: "Oratorical power and literacy style tended to be somewhat synonymous" (p. 1). At least up until the twentieth century, literacy instruction in schools consisted of formal oral composing. However, work in oratory and rhetoric has not been applied to theories of reading, text formation, and written discourse processing as we know them today.

Speech versus Writing

J. W. Gibson, Gruner, Kibler, and Kelly (1966, pp. 444–445) begin their essay on the differences and similarities between oral and written communication by noting:

> It appears to be generally accepted among language scholars that speaking is mankind's basic symbolic act and that writing is the super-structure built upon it. But some language scholars concerned with written communication do not take this theoretical condition into account when they treat writing and speaking as though the two modes were characterized by exactly the same qualities or when they ignore or devote limited attention to specifying the distinction between the written and oral response modes.

J. W. Gibson *et al.* (1966) note that researchers in the mid-1960s typically argue for similarity between speech and writing. They reviewed communication textbooks and found little study of the contrast between the two.

The differences between speech and writing have been studied for their influence on listening and reading comprehension (Goldstein, 1940). But most work has examined lexical or syntactic variation within the discourse—without attention to comprehension. Drieman (1962a, b), at the University of Amsterdam, conducted a quantitative and qualitative model study whereby eight university students in psychology wrote and spoke in monologue to a tape recorder. Color reproductions (after Renoir and nineteenth-century Dutch painter Weissenbruch) were used to stimulate discourse. Written language resulted in shorter messages, longer words, more attributive qualities, and more varied lexical choices. Similarly, J. W. Gibson *et al.* (1966) used a spoken–written contrast to study 45 speech students at two universities and found writing consisted of more multisyllabic words and an objective as opposed to a personal approach to language. DeVito (1967) found more abstract nouns in writing prepared by 10 university faculty. O'Donnell (1974) found more elaborate structural schemes (dependent clauses) in writing, including complex nouns and multiple predication (see also findings in Labov, 1986).

The research just discussed, while important for our understanding of oral and written language, is limited by small sample sizes, the use of university populations, and the topics and social situations used for speaking and writing. (See also similar remarks by Rubin, 1980.) Nevertheless, some of the findings hold up to more recent findings reported in this volume.

We have moved from viewing speech and writing as one and the same to considering them separate, dichotomous language systems, to be studied for their uniqueness. In some cases, however, the study of speech development is gaining new interest and has been reapplied to literacy. The influence of speech on (and in) writing is now being used to explain errors in reading and writing discourse, and oral composing is being related to written composing. Teachers of writing have told students to write as they would talk. Often dialogues and monologues are the source of written expression. And writing in speech is also said to emerge with literacy (see Lakoff, 1982, for discussion of the mingling of "speech in writing" and "writing in speech").

Speech in Writing

Robert de Beaugrande (1982) astutely cautions us in the application of speech to literacy. In his review of the history of psychology and language, he also notes parallelism in speech–writing research. He notes that dependent measures typically used in speech production research have been mistakenly transposed to writing research so that, for example, speech hesitations, rhythms, and errors have been associated with hesitations, pauses, and errors in writing. Beaugrande indicates two major flaws in the use of a speech model. First, this model assumes that *"The production process always works the same way"* (p. 234, Beaugrande's emphasis) and has consequently ignored variations arising from the differences in contexts. Second, *"pauses, hesitations, and errors may have a distinctive distribution in writing"* separate from that of speech (p. 234). To illustrate his points, Beaugrande (1982, 1983) entertainingly presents samples of speech characteristics—simple restarts, shifts from one topic to another, nonagreements, vagueness, recurrences, reusages—that were damaging when incorporated into writing by college-level writers reverting to speechlike behavior. These sorts of errors only create confusions for the reader—the counterargument that certainly "writing is not speech writ down."

Beaugrande is not alone in his recommendations. Havelock (1976, 1980), considering the origins of Western literacy, suggests that there may indeed be separate laws (or at least probabilities) for oral and written language, noting that "The laws of oral composition must first be grasped, if we are to understand the laws of literacy" (1976, p. 86). He also states that "Oral speech and written word are both acts, or represent acts, which seek to communicate. But the essential act of communication does not take place unless the speech is heard and the writing is read" (1976, p. 18). (See also Chafe, 1982, 1985, 1986; Danielewicz & Chafe, 1985.)

Speech in Reading

Not only is there uncertainty about the role of speech in writing, but also there is some debate in the literature as to the role of speech processes, and specifically recoding, in reading (Perfetti, 1985). Does the reader actually transform written language into a spoken form to access meaning? A review of scientific literature shows conflicting evidence. At least in skilled reading, speech recoding, for example, does not occur as a stage of processing prior to lexical access. However, Perfetti and others argue that speech processes can occur to aid memory and comprehension and may occur when reading is still not fully developed. Further study of speech processes in reading is needed (Kleiman, 1975; Levy, 1978; Perfetti, 1985; Perfetti & McCutchen, 1982).

Recently attention has been given to oral reading, in contrast to silent reading, in schools. Research supports the argument that these are not the same kinds of processes. The way in which teachers control and use oral reading in classrooms varies and is able to influence comprehension. Students also bring to the classroom different social and community beliefs about the value of reading aloud and the conditions under which oral reading should be used. For example, in the Middle East children are taught to read aloud a foreign language that they do not understand at all because a religious value is associated with the oral reading of language. Learning to read aloud has been a requirement for participation in synagogues in Europe and the United States. In schoolrooms in both Europe and the United States effective oral reading has also traditionally been a mark of effective comprehension, a matter that is now controversial.

THE SEARCH FOR LAWS OF LISTENING
AND READING COMPREHENSION

Research that considers listening and reading comprehension has taken on one of two perspectives. The first assumes that reading is analogous to listening, utilizing the same kind of underlying processes as listening. Consequently, the terms *listening* and *reading* have been used somewhat interchangeably in innumerable research reports with little distinction and often no reference to the type of language, oral or written, or the processes used. The second perspective is that reading requires use of the same skills as listening with the exception of decoding skills required for reading.

These two views have been influenced by listening and reading research that dates back to the early 1900s. This work suffers from several weaknesses: poor experimental designs, lack of sufficient control measures, and use of single dependent measures generally designed to test for perception rather than comprehension. These studies were often focused on the orthographic or phonological structure of language to the exclusion of higher-order language structures in natural speech and texts. Further, still more global issues—the context of the experiment, the type of oral discourse obtained, and social-situational factors, variables that we now consider so central—were often ignored. As Danks and End (this volume) so appropriately summarize, there are serious problems in making comparisons between listening and reading comprehension as many of the past experiments did.

Comparisons and contrasts are needed as, while there may be a high degree of overlap among the skills required for listening and reading comprehension, the fit is not perfect because each mode of input—by ear and by eye—requires special types of processing and skills. We believe that similarities and differences both need defining for school tasks.

Four volumes have made significant contributions to the listening and reading comparison and precede that which we include in this book. In 1972, James Kavanagh and Ignatius Mattingly edited *Language by Ear and by Eye: The Relationships between Speech and Reading.* This book sought to explain why most children acquire speech but have difficulty acquiring reading skill. It focused on perceptual aspects of speech and written language—orthography, speech perception, auditory coding—but did not address aspects of language processing and comprehension much beyond the phonological or orthographic code level.

Shortly thereafter, in 1974, Thomas G. Sticht *et al.* published *Auding and Reading: A Developmental Model,* providing an important and much needed historical review and compilation of listening and reading research. Some 44 studies were examined, 31 of which were summarized, that compared listening to reading. Sticht *et al.* concluded that the reading comprehension of written language was built upon ability to comprehend oral language plus decoding skills.

In 1979 and 1980 two volumes of research, *Processing of Visible Language*, were edited by Paul Kolers, Merald Wrolstad, and Herman Bouma (1979–1980). While both added to the study of oral-and-written-language processing, the second volume in particular gave greater emphasis to the nature of language in comprehension and explored interactions of person and computer and the characteristics of the physical and environmental factors that influence that interaction. Particular attention was given to the text and the writing system as these influence both perception and comprehension.

TECHNOLOGY AND ORAL AND WRITTEN LANGUAGE

The way in which we conceive of the contrasts that we have discussed thus far, that is, the way that we conceive of oral and written language, the processes of listening and reading, speaking and writing—or writing and reading—and the persons involved, suddenly take on new appearances as we consider advancements in technology. Although space limits our discussion of these advancements, not to consider them would be to provide an incomplete and inaccurate picture of the oral and written language and cognitive processes in which we have an interest for schools. As Ong predicts, technological advancements will certainly color the research about comprehending oral and written language, but they also will color what might actually occur in the way of classroom cognition and instruction through oral and written language.

New technology shapes the questions that researchers and teachers can ask today. To begin, the tape recorder permits analysis of speech products and processes that was not possible until recently. In fact, many linguists point to the multiple possibilities that now exist for the analysis of talk (and text) in ways that were not conceivable before the invention of the tape recorder. A range of talk, in locations and situations we may never have entered, now can be studied and discussed in schools. One need only turn to recent issues of such journals as *Discourse Processes* or *Text* for illustrations of these settings and analyses.

Transcribing machines enable us to process and analyze units of speech and to repeat that speech in ways we could not fathom before

their invention. However, the possibilities for understanding oral and written language processes expand even further with, of course, the use of computers.

Computers permit the production of a new kind of written language. Although it has not been extensively researched, the way in which written language is produced by computer operations may dramatically change not only the nature of writing as a process, but also the nature of language as an object. The computer permits rapid-fire writing in ways that the eye, the hand alone, and the human brain cannot. Spoken discourse (transcribed and placed on the computer) or written discourse typed onto a computer disk can be scanned at a controllable rate. In addition, this discourse can be examined by controlling and limiting the unit of language, such as word, clause, sentence, or paragraph, displayed. The on-line cognitive and motor processes used with written language for listening and reading can be monitored very systematically with such apparatus placed in a classroom research setting or classroom teaching situation.

Furthermore, we are developing computers that take dictation and "spit out" that dictation rapidly with correct spelling. This is particularly helpful for children not yet able to spell or for adults who could never spell and were inhibited as writers because of this weakness. When writers are able to talk their text into a computer, speech errors may suddenly appear in writing. But other things may also happen. Writing, as some linguists and computer experts suggest, may change form and become more speechlike, more like a talking text than we now know, but yet not "speech writ down." There is also the possibility that what will emerge will be a "friendlier" text than could or would be produced by the pen or typewriter. If we succeed in building computers that produce speech, we will be able to speak to and receive messages from a computer in natural spoken language, an event we dared not envision one decade ago. Some forecasts surrounding the fifth-generation Japanese computers indicate that computers will also be capable of "seeing"—i.e., will have vision of words and pictures, even a human stereo vision. Finally, there is already the possibility of computer adaptation to audience and possibilities of language translation. Certain heuristics would allow the system to treat a query from a high school physics student differently than that from an experienced physicist. Already, there is machine translation of a Spanish newspaper into English.

In the case of writing research, the written language that children, adolescents, or adults can manipulate on the computer in schools suddenly takes on new forms and possibilities as well (Daiute, 1985b; Frase, 1986; Wresch, 1987). With writing at the computer and voice feedback as a "scaffold" (i.e., voice production as an intermediary in the writing process), children may begin to develop faster and greater understanding of the relationship(s) between oral and written language and listening and reading, speaking and writing possibilities and limits for communication. As some research is beginning to show, this new technology will be particularly helpful for emergent writers and readers (Lehrer, Levin, DeHart, & Comeaux, 1986). Not only young children beginning to read and write, but also adolescents, learners of English as a second language, and adults with limited literacy proficiency may come to find new understanding of the oral and written relationships that were once so hard to uncover and single-handedly reinvent. Increase in use of personal home computers will contribute to development of oral and written language.

One last piece of technological equipment, electronic message systems, warrants mention. These systems have recently come to be in vogue in both school writing projects and business communication. Electronic message systems demonstrate how texts draw from both oral and written language, further calling into question the traditional dichotomy of oral and written language that we discussed earlier in this chapter. Electronic mail is speech given to a machine, but, like writing, it can be composed, edited, and leave a record. Business communication and school writing uses this to replace spoken language and the telephone. It may actually represent a new channel of communication, demonstrating an interactive relationship between speech and writing.

The way in which we conceive of the development of oral and written language (and the course that development might take) suddenly changes as one introduces the new technology that we have briefly outlined here. Relatedly, how we provide instruction for oral and written language learning will also change in conception. These new possibilities for teacher understanding of oral and written language for student learning in schools will need to be further explored, in light of the ideas expressed here and in light of discussion that follows.[8]

THE PRESENT VOLUME

This volume is composed of a range of chapters that build on the past work that we have summarized. The following chapters contain similar points of view but also differences of opinion. Our purpose here is to present these differences of opinion in the hope that they will stimulate further discussion and critical exploration of the issues involved.

Below we identify some of the key themes and highlight issues and contrasts treated in the volume.

Spoken versus Written Language

In the first part of the volume similarities and differences between spoken and written language are examined and new perspectives offered for considering this contrast.

Michael A. K. Halliday introduces the collection by calling for greater attention to spoken language. He calls for the development of an oral grammar, which he suggests will ultimately contribute to our understanding of the workings of language in written communication. While spoken and written language seem to differ in significant ways, they contain a "mixed variety of features" and there are "elements characteristic of both types."

However, speech and writing do represent different textures, and "it is as if they were the product of a different weave, with fibres of a different yarn." Halliday argues that certain speech may actually be more complex than we have envisioned. (See this in relation to other chapters in this volume that suggest speech is easier.) Halliday indicates "The more natural, un-self-monitored the discourse, the more intricate the grammatical patterns that can be woven." However, he cautions us to consider how we view and measure complexity. In the case of lexical density, speech may appear as the simpler of the two, but in the case of grammar, speech may be more complex than writing. In sum, Halliday says, "Spoken and written language . . . tend to display different KINDS of complexity; each of them is more complex in its own way."

In order to understand the variety of language usages, a grammar of spoken language is needed. "Such a grammar will help us understand not only oral language in speech, but also orality in writing" and "the strictly LINGUISTIC 'deviations' of casual conversation are mainly systematic features that would not seem deviant if we had a grammar that took into account the specifically 'spoken' resources of the linguistic system." Grammars, however, evolved solely for the interpretation of written language, and "instead of merely tinkering with them to adapt them to speech, we actually may need to back off and start anew with a different approach in order to develop a new model for oral grammars" (Michael A. K. Halliday, personal communication, April 27, 1983). Such an oral grammar would be valuable for understanding spoken *and* written language and their modes of meaning. Another point made here, and expressed elsewhere by linguists, is that such an approach is useful because as it advances, written language is becoming and may, in fact, with time, continue to slip into a more "process- and speechlike" form. Several chapters in this book consider specific structures and patterning of language in oral and written discourse. Different patterns of language displayed in oral and written discourse may represent different uses of language and, concomitantly, different ways of knowing and reasoning. There has been limited study of linguistic patterns in spontaneous and extended discourse. The research is scanty and much of the work that does exist is scattered in not readily available dissertation studies or technical reports that require translation, synthesis, and application to comprehension research. Finally, when patterns are identified, their function in the broader sense of a communication task and situations remains virtually unexplored. Findings about the influence of language patterns and meaning have also been contradictory and inconclusive.

In Chapter 3, Wallace Chafe and Jane Danielewicz provide much needed examples of the oral and written contrast using school-based and real-world-based discourse. They begin their essay with an important conclusion from their research: "There can be no doubt that people write differently from the way they speak." To support this contention, they compare four types of discourse produced by each of their 20 adult subjects in natural contexts. Type–token ratios (the number of different types of words per total number of words) were obtained for particular patterns found in each discourse. These researchers investigated conversation (dinner talk); university lectures; and two kinds of writing, informal (letters) and academic (essays). They examined lexical choices, levels of vocabulary, clause constructions, sentence structure, and differences within and across oral and written language. They note ". . . varying proportions of linguistic features surface as both spoken and written language are used in different circumstances." It must be noted that their conclusions about the complexity of oral and written language differ markedly from those expressed by Halliday in Chapter 2. For Chafe and Danielewicz, written language proves to be more complex than oral language.

Several investigators have asked subjects to produce ideas in spoken and written language (Kroll, 1977; Beaugrande, 1983; Chafe, 1985; Heath, 1986; Labov, 1986) in order to understand the nature of these language forms. For example, Horowitz and Davis (1984) examined second graders' use of speech versus writing in a persuasive task to an intimate target audience—parents. The research showed no differences in organizational structures across oral and written discourse, since differential conventions have likely not yet been learned by this sample of subjects; similar subarguments and types of social appeals emerged in both modes. However, there were fewer words and more limited ideas in written language than in oral language, suggesting some limits in putting ideas into writing. In Chapter 12, Perfetti notes that "It's not that . . . children's linguistic knowledge is not considerable. Rather, it's that much of what they know about linguistic forms is rather tentative. They can demonstrate competence in one situation but not another." Contrasts between a given child's spoken and written language enables one to study the learner's command and perception of language under each form and the type of arguments or discourse strategies used with spoken and written language, and can provide direction for literacy instruction in these language systems. It may also show exactly what children can do with lexical and rhetorical forms in a given register or with a given target audience and task.

In Chapter 2, Michael A. K. Halliday provides illustrations of several linguistic features in spoken and written samples of language—lexical density, the number and types of clauses, the organization of the complex clause, use of nominals (see also Chafe and Danielewicz, Chapter 3; Perfetti, Chapter 12)—and demonstrates how these operate in samples of spoken and written language. Halliday's entire discussion of nominals (the formation of a noun from a verb) contrasts sharply with Watson and Olson's ideas, especially when Halliday argues that they are often ambiguous and when Watson and Olson argue that they are key to explicit, positive definition and the very pinnacle of language development. This difference of opinion is significant, as Chafe and Danielewicz show that nominalization occurs more frequently in academic writing than in conversations, lectures, and letters.

Rosalind Horowitz, Chapter 4, discusses the limits of our theoretical and empirical knowledge of the structural dimensions of oral and written discourse and the processing of that discourse. Horowitz considers specific rhetorical structures, attribution (list–structure), adversative (compare–contrast), covariance (cause–effect), and response (problem–solution), thought to be characteristic of academic expository discourse. She examines their effect on the comprehension and processing of text by ninth graders and university freshmen. Horowitz finds that contrary to what has been reported elsewhere in theoretical and experimental literature, these patterns do not work in the same way across readers of various age groups and grades and across text topics. This experiment and the analysis of rhetorical structures in discourse leads Horowitz to a social-psychological approach to text structures and to consideration of still more global dimensions of discourse such as is being treated in the study of scientific discourse. The way in which science information is translated to particular audiences, including the public sector, is a matter needing attention. Finally, the study suggests that the coordination of form with content does not occur a priori to the writing of a text. It emerges as part of the act of writing and discovery of the grammar of a text.

The way in which we characterize the relationship between spoken and written language and the processes of speaking and writing is of more than academic interest. The approach adopted has important pedagogical ramifications.

For example, in the case of speech and writing, if some of the same linguistic or organizational structures appear in planned speech and in writing, students might benefit from speech activities (oral composing) which introduce these structures prior to writing (written composing). If written structures are of a more complex and varied nature—as some believe—separate instruction will need to be designed to highlight these forms in written discourse and will need to be used to develop manipulation and control of these more complex structures. Similarly, if the spoken word is the same as the written word, vocabulary instruction should cross discourse forms (Hall, Nagy, & Linn, 1984).

Further, if the processes for designing an effective speech (pre-text planning, oral composing, redesigning, revising, evaluating, and giving the speech) are the same as in writing, similar steps can be addressed and used with oral composing as with written composing in schools (Faigley, Cherry, Jolliffe, & Skinner, 1985).

However, if speech and writing differ as processes and products because they serve different functions for the individual interlocutors, the community, and cultures involved, knowledge of how to converse or compose orally may not be sufficient for composing in the written code. Likewise, knowledge of how to process oral language may not be sufficient for processing written language, and knowledge of how to process interpersonal listener-oriented language (intended to maintain interpersonal relationships) may not be sufficient for processing message-oriented (idea-centered) language (Brown, 1977, 1982). For example, a proposal of marriage is usually given orally in many communities, in an informal register; the bride-to-be might raise queries about a prospective mate were it given in formal writing. A contract of sale for a new house is, however, given in written legal form so that it can hold up in a court proceeding and under the eye of a judge, should that become necessary. (See Stubbs, 1980, 1982, 1986, for more excellent examples.)

Furthermore, what we deem an error of language in text writing may be considered correct in speech.

Speech Processing in Writing

Speech that enters into writing may be viewed as an error. In fact, writing experts emphasize that poor writers have not yet learned to remove hedges, redundancies, restarts, vagueness, or ellipses that are acceptable in conversation. However, the skilled writer knows how to convert writing into a language form that reads as smoothly as speech, that is speechlike, but is not the same as speech (Labov, 1986). The most readable forms of writing are suited to the eye; they employ right branching and keep the reader moving at a steady pace and rhythm from left to right as opposed to left branching, which is characteristic of a formal prose that requires regressive eye movements and bottom-up reading.

Listening versus Reading Comprehension

Listening and reading, speaking and writing have been in competition for attention over time. Historically, scholarly attention to listening has fallen by the wayside and has largely been neglected in most accounts of literacy and schooling. It is assumed listening develops "naturally" with increased schooling and that it requires little attention or relating to growth in the other language arts.

The importance of listening, however, has recently been expressed in *Becoming a Nation of Readers: The Report of the Commission on Reading* (Anderson *et al.*, 1985) where it has been noted that listening comprehension can be a significant predictor of reading comprehension and achievement at later grades. The research cited indicates that children who are good listeners in kindergarten and first grade are likely to become good readers by the third grade. Moreover, what is striking is that the role of listening in comprehension is even stronger at later grades. Good fifth grade listeners are likely to become good learners in high school. More specifically, this nationwide study in the United States showed listening comprehension in fifth grade to be "the best predictor of performance on a range of aptitude and achievement tests in high school, better than any other measure of aptitude achievement in the fifth grade" (p. 30).

If listening comprehension is indeed a reliable predictor of later reading comprehension and school achievement, the mutual aspects of listening and reading need to be identified. If listening comprehension is not a reliable predictor of later reading comprehension and school achievement, those aspects uniquely associated with reading comprehension need to be identified, so that they can be taught. How we view the relationship(s) between listening and reading will, then, determine what discourse types students listen to in order to read, when and how long students listen to school discourse, and how listening is used as an aid to prepare for reading or for follow-up to reading.

The single comprehension process hypothesis has prevailed in the literature and may be described in the following manner: Listening and reading comprehension show similar cognitive processing. The fluent reader is characterized as decoding print to the phonological representation and then processing the phonological representation as though it were coming through an auditory channel. The Gibson group at Cornell University has posited a single comprehension process. They characterize the task of the reader as one of translating graphemes to phonemes; then, after decoding to speech has been accomplished, comprehension processes associated with speech comprehension are brought to bear.

Not only has it been posited that there is similarity in listening and reading at the phonological level, recent research also shows similarity in sentence and discourse-thematic level processing. David Townsend, Caroline Carrithers, and Thomas Bever, in Chapter 7, demonstrate that there are indeed mutual comprehension processes used in listening and reading for individuals of a particular level of reading ability. Their studies of skilled and average middle-school and college readers extend the findings of other researchers that indicate that deficits in reading skill are accompanied by deficits in listening skills. Their findings are consistent with research reported by Sticht and associates (1974) which indicates that by grade 7–8, reading and listening become more alike and that ultimately reading comprehension exceeds listening comprehension.

The work by Townsend, Carrithers, and Bever reported here also extends previous research by discussion of the processes used by skilled and less-skilled average readers, a contrast seldom explored by reading researchers, but quite important for schooling. They find that middle-school skilled and average reader comprehension is dependent upon the extent to which subjects process clauses internally. These skilled and less-skilled readers differ primarily in sentence-level processing. However, at the college level, comprehension is defined by the extent to which subjects integrated propositions, with the more-skilled reader showing greater sensitivity to discourse-thematic relations and specifically to written signals that influence reader expectations. These researchers base their suggestions for reading instruction on the type of processes they found used and their reader's basic knowledge of language at different ages and reading ability levels.

Relatedly, Charles A. Perfetti, Chapter 12, uses Amos Tversky's theory of asymmetry in perception to demonstrate graphically how speech and print come to have more common than different components and are ultimately interdependent. The degree of relationship depends in part on the level of analysis, according to Perfetti. He notes that formal aspects of speech and print are different when different registers are involved (consistent with Halliday and others), but are similar when a single register is involved (see also Danks and End, Chapter 9). Acquiring literacy entails a shift in register knowledge and use. Following the acquisition of literacy, the processing of print and speech have more common than different components (comparable to research findings by Townsend *et al.*). Further, the relation of listening to reading comprehension may vary depending upon the experiences of the reader and the reader's stage in the development of literacy, a relationship that Sticht would support and that deserves added research with a range of discourse types.

Joseph H. Danks and Laurel J. End, in Chapter 9, note that listening and reading comprehension research has frequently been based on the assumption that listening and reading are invariant processes. Consequently, empirical studies have looked for overall similarities and differences. These researchers, unlike other contributors to this volume, provide a review of the literature and analyses which proceed from the premise that reading and listening (like writing and speaking) are flexible processes that vary with reader and listener purposes, type and difficulty of text, and task demands. Thus, they indicate that it may be possible to devise experimental situations that result in listening and reading as functionally identical, but such situations may not be typical of everyday discourse processing. Rather than take a wholistic approach, Danks and End believe that there are many subsets of processing strategies. They describe in some detail five subprocessing components and how they operate in listening and reading and lead us to a multicomprehension process hypothesis.

Peter Schreiber, Chapter 8, posits that reading comprehension tends to be more difficult than listening comprehension because prosodic features (such as pitch, stress, and juncture) that we ordinarily pick up in the syntactic processing of speech are not found in written language. Schreiber demonstrates that intonation, stress, and especially duration play a prominent role for children in demarcating syntactic constituents. On sentences with normal prosody, children perform like adults. However, on sentences with misleading prosody, children and adults perform differently. Children follow the prosody, while adults follow the syntactic structure. It thus appears that 6-, 7-, and 8-year-old children, beginning to read, are more sensitive to and reliant on prosody than adults and with development may somehow lose this sensitivity.

Schreiber's chapter may have special implications for classroom reading instruction, suggesting that there may be some value in considering how prosodic features are or are not represented in written language. Schreiber's chapter may also be important for the study of oral reading by students or teacher storybook oral reading. It is possible that students acquire certain knowledge about the reading process from the way in which oral reading is practiced and modeled in the classroom.

The theoretical perspectives treated in this volume and the literature at large are, once again, of more than academic interest. Depending upon the theoretical view we accept as correct, there are important pedagogical ramifications. For example, if the single comprehension hypothesis is indeed correct, then all we need to do is to teach reading until the student attains a specified degree of fluency, usually by Grade 3, and then we can discontinue teaching reading. The language experience approach (where children dictate stories that the teacher writes on the blackboard) would remain valid. That is, it would be regarded as useful to write oral language on the blackboard to show students how the spoken language is represented in print and to give students practice reading their own speech. On the other hand, if the comprehension of oral and written language is different and involves multicomprehension processes (as several of these chapters suggest) utilizing varied subsets of comprehension strategies (depending upon the situational context), we would continue to teach reading beyond Grade 3 because it may vary from spoken language and under different conditions (e.g., texts and tasks). In this instance, the language that is spoken is not the same register as that which is written. Therefore, in the language experience approach, the language printed on the blackboard becomes significantly different from that spoken by the child. In sum, these chapters would suggest that if the relationship between speech and writing is to be properly presented, the kind of comparison we propose here must be considered by both theoreticians and classroom practitioners.

S. Jay Samuels, Chapter 10, demonstrates how listening and reading comprehension must be contrasted and compared, not simply for academic reasons, but for diagnostic purposes. He systematically considers listening and reading by using an interactive model of inside-the-head and outside-the-head factors that influence comprehension. He identifies some of the difficulties that diagnosticians may experience in their decision making and offers a two-part plan for diagnosis using this perspective.

According to Samuels, in the analysis of listening comprehension, the diagnostician must consider multiple inside-the-head factors—the student's intelligence, language facility, background knowledge, speech register awareness, and metacognitive strategies—and outside-the-head factors—the discussion topic, speaker awareness of audience, clarity and speaker effectiveness, contextual cues which support the speaker, kinesics, and motivation.

In the case of analysis of reading comprehension, the diagnostician must consider inside-the-head factors of the student—intelligence, decoding ability, background knowledge and schema, text structure, knowledge of anaphoric terms, metacognitive strategies, language facility, graphic literacy, motivation, and attention—and outside-the-head factors—quality of instruction, text topic, conventions of print, clarity of writing style, text readability, text format, and time given for reading comprehension. Samuels stresses that it is only through a recognition of the interaction between inside-the-head and outside-the-head factors that effective evaluation of comprehension can take place.

The Function of Context

The chapters in this volume also point to differences of opinion associated with the nature and function of context in oral and written language, reading and writing, speaking and listening. It has been long agreed that context plays an important role in these language acts. Context has been a topic of concern dating back to Plato. Contextual factors are thought to be important factors which interact with readers and texts. However, the nature of context and how context functions in different types of reading and listening tasks or in varieties of writing and speaking acts, such as found in schools, remains unclear.

The important point to be made here is that how we conceptualize the nature of context clearly influences how we view the production of oral and written language and the processes of reading and listening, and how we might teach for these.

Rita P. M. Watson and David R. Olson, Chapter 11, and Olson in other publications (see, e.g., Olson, 1977, 1980) offer a different angle: they indicate there is context in oral discourse, but context is missing in school-literate text. Thus, word meaning takes on different dimensions in oral and written language. Further, because there is a clear-cut, visible context in oral discourse, cohesion of message is expressed through nonverbal measures—facial expressions, distance between speakers, gestures, etc. However, written discourse may require explicit linguistic cues, since the nonverbal information is missing and these cues must be learned and properly interpreted. The research by Murphy (1986) on the comprehension of deictic terms in oral and written language makes similar arguments. See also Rubin (1980) on deixis.

Charles A. Perfetti, in Chapter 12, presents arguments that are consistent with the Watson and Olson line of thinking. Perfetti argues that reading, at least for a beginning reader, is decontextualized. He indicates that the beginning reader is dependent upon the form of the language for meaning. For reading, the printed sentences hold the meaning. For speech, meaning is said to lie outside of the propositions, in the nonverbal exchanges—e.g., eye contact, gestures, physical positions—between interlocutors.

Scinto (1985, 1986) expresses arguments similar to those given by Watson and Olson and by Perfetti. He indicates that a scholarized written text in school is decontextualized and results in a psychologically different form of meaning from other kinds of texts.

However, Martin Nystrand emphatically refutes this interpretation and argues that written text is not autonomous. Through his discussion of the doctrine of autonomous text in Chapter 6 (also Nystrand, 1986), he argues that written text contains qualitatively different contextual factors (consistent with Street, 1984). The task of the reader is to understand how context is represented by way of written language in school text and to work with the forms in which context is marked or inferred for a given text type and discourse community. It is likely that the functional differences between oral and written language result in differences in language form (e.g., discourse organization) and use of context.

In the case of reading, one might note that the author is not present. There are words on a page, but no author to give rhythm and emphasis, no author to see, to ask, and to share control of the discourse. In writing there is no reader present, no audience to give "yea or nay" to the ideas, to question, and to call for immediate clarification and elaboration. Perhaps the writer's audience is always a fiction, as was proposed by Ong (1975). Readers and writers must infer a context, although meaning is never fully in the language. This requires use of past knowledge, experiential bases, and social-cognitive and social-situational models (van Dijk & Kintsch, 1983; van Dijk, this volume). When the text is less explicit than one might desire, the reader's memory and knowledge system are taxed. When the text is more explicit, the reader may lack certain knowledge and concepts will, nevertheless, still be instantiated.

We must recognize several levels of context: first, the context in which text is produced; second, the context in which the writer intended that the text be used (an ideal context); and third, the context in which the reader actually uses a text (a real context). Language in each context may function differentially and require different processing strategies and skills.

Further, a context may be given by a text or may be chosen or created by the reader. If chosen or created by the reader, it is based on information outside of the text that a reader brings to bear on the text, for example, a model, a scientific or intuitive hypothesis, anecdotal memories, cultural assumptions, beliefs and value systems. While readers of the same linguistic community may converge on the same language, there are still individual differences in the representation of events and the models brought to bear in discourse processing (see van Dijk, Chapter 5). Frequently a mismatch between context and discourse does occur in school settings. Work is needed on how skilled learners find or create an appropriate context that creates a mutual cognitive environment.

Once again, the way in which a context is perceived or accessed is of more than academic interest. The perspective one adopts about the nature or function of context in oral and written language influences the practices one will adopt in the teaching of reading and writing, or for that matter, listening and speaking. If there is indeed no context or limited context in written language, the writer is presumably dependent on the reader's context or ability to reconstruct a context. If context can be created through text language to some extent at least (e.g., through explicit rhetorical structure), writers may need to provide the context and readers will need to seek out the cues (e.g., rhetorical structure and signals, lexicon, and syntax) that explain or suggest the context in which the text was written and should be read.

Teun A. van Dijk, Chapter 5, indicates that we cannot theorize about oral and written language without considering context and the mental models of context that we hold. Van Dijk demonstrates the role of episodic models in discourse processing and offers some explanation as to how meaning is achieved when context in text and talk is limited or missing. He argues that there are social-situational events that become cataloged, so to speak, as representative of a category of events in memory. Van Dijk argues that such models in memory play an important role in discourse processing especially in the development of beliefs, attitudes, and opinions about a subject and are critical in particularly ethnic discourse production. These episodic models may be also particularly important in listening and reading (see also Danks and End, Chapter 9).

Sound and Meaning

There has been limited theory or research on the development of sensitivity to the temporal dimensions, that is, sound and rhythm, of spoken and written language. Yet the transition from orality to literacy, beginning with infancy and stretching to adulthood, entails an ability to transcribe elements of sound and rhythm (pitch, stress, pauses, expression) found in oral language to written language. With development, children eventually learn to read orally with the proper intonation, stress, fluency, and meaning and to "hear" the "movement" of ideas in a discourse through an "inner voice" during silent reading. Havelock (1976), as well as many linguists, is of the opinion that "any language owes its basic existence to an arrangement of sounds, not script" (p. 12).

Apprenticeships in Listening and Reading

An apprenticeship is a tutelage under a master teacher or expert who is willing to take on a learner at a workbench. In order to learn, children and adults alike must become apprentices. An apprenticeship in listening to and reading from a variety of text types and registers is necessary for learning in various domains of knowledge (Horowitz, in progress). Britton makes a similar suggestion. According to Britton, not only the reader but also the writer must know the sound of text. "How else can he come to hear an inner voice dictating to him the story [narrative or explanatory-type] he wants to produce? An apprenticeship of listening to others will enable him later to be aware of the rhythms of written language in the course of his own silent reading" (Britton, 1982, p. 167).

The possibility of apprenticeships (spontaneous and formalized) using various discourse types at the side of parent, caregiver, teacher, peer, or expert warrants exploration. The apprenticeship model would entail gradations of listening and reading under the guidance of a skilled model and using oral and written language across the continuum of language in a given domain of knowledge. More on this will need to be discussed elsewhere.

But what kinds of listening activities can infants, children, adolescents, or low-literate adults benefit from that will influence growth not only in concepts of print but also in reading and writing? Schreiber, Chapter 8, shows what children know about prosody that adults may not know. It cannot be assumed that the child's ear for sound is the same as the adolescent's or adult's ear for sound. With added research, we will begin to identify how knowledge about sound and meaning interacts and changes with development in the mind of the learner. Peter Schreiber's chapter is one step in that direction.

Acquiring and Extending Literacy

The closing section of this volume considers the acquisition and development of literacy in the schooling process. Scholars are attempting to determine how literacy is acquired, i.e., how reading and writing, in

particular, are acquired and what stages of development children naturally go through with or without formal instruction. Desperately needed
is a theory of literacy, one which accounts for the acquisition and extension of reading and writing knowledge in relation to orality—accounting
for development both inside and outside school. Several chapters of this
book attempt to describe what is involved in shifting from oral to written
language in schools (Chafe & Danielewicz; Perfetti; Stotsky; Watson &
Olson), but there are a variety of practices in schools employing different kinds of spoken and written language that have yet to be researched
and that we simply know little about.

School discourse represents what must be characterized as a specialized use of speech and writing, and concomitantly, a specialized kind of
listening and reading. Academic discourse in schools may be dependent
on a decontextualized language, as some researchers note. However,
once again it is possible that there is a context present, expressed in a
qualitatively different way. Students may acquire entry into this specialized use of discourse in some upper-class homes, even at dinner talk, or
in talk among friends, while others for various reasons may not have
this opportunity and the necessary contexts or social situations.

Rita P. M. Watson and David R. Olson, Chapter 11, propose that
comprehension of written language in schools marks a change in the
way lexical items are understood, used, and learned. The preliterate
child (like the preliterate society) learns words and their definitions
through real-world contexts and through objects and actions. School
contexts, however, teach word meaning, they argue, by representing
meaning in the structure of the language itself. The formal school-based
definition is a new kind of meaning achieved with literacy. Definitions
given in school follow a particular syntax, contribute to an autonomous
language—permit generalizability across contexts and occasions of use
and permit development of concepts and theorizing. Scinto (1986), following this line of thinking, says schooling requires use of a "schooled
discourse" that is objective, depersonalized, and divorced from immediate experience. The argument, thus, is that the oral culture through
which meaning is achieved in school is different from the oral culture of
the child. It is possible that there are multiple oral cultures that many
children know in our society, some of which may prepare children for or
overlap with school definitions and others that may not.

Another view of the acquisition of and extension of literacy in schools
is offered by Charles A. Perfetti in Chapter 12. For the child beginning to
read, reading is more similar to speech than vice versa. With gradual
development of literacy, speech takes on a new form and becomes more
like print (a literacy in orality). (See also similar remarks in Ehri, 1984.)

Perfetti gives graphic examples to illustrate possible changes in the similarities and differences between speech and print processing. According to Perfetti, linguistic meaning may not exist until children actually read, in a sense does not exist in preliterate speech.

According to Perfetti (and consistent with Sticht *et al.*, 1974; Sticht, 1979; Sticht & James, 1984), listening comprehension initially exceeds reading comprehension. Reading and listening become more alike as children gain experience with print. Knowledge of speech is said to be enhanced by literacy instruction: "Through reading the child may really come to appreciate the truly expressive power of language."

Sandra Stotsky, in Chapter 13, points to a serious gap in the oral and written contrasts. Following an extensive review of the literature, she finds no systematic account of the development of written language (consistent with Scinto, 1986). However, she finds and describes two major theories of the development of written language. These two theories are important because they suggest particular research paradigms and pedagogical practices. The first theory, traditional and long held, is that reading and writing development are influenced and limited by speech development: "What the reader understands aurally sets a ceiling on, or gates, what can be understood in written texts." Reading cannot influence writing according to this theory, and writing cannot influence speech. This model is one that would support oral language practices in the schools as a means to not only facilitate but to extend written language development.

The second theory suggests something different. Oral and written language differ in origin, purpose, and nature, although exactly how they differ needs elaboration in the literature. Written language can influence oral language. Reading and writing can influence each other. Written language can be more complex than oral language. What one has written can become a text to listen to. The reading and writing of academic discourse requires study and is different from the natural, often unstructured, language of the home.

Stotsky's views of the second theory are consistent with research by Vygotsky (1962, p. 98), who notes: "Our investigation has shown that the development of writing does not repeat the developmental history of speaking. Written speech is a separate linguistic function, differing from oral speech in both structure and mode of functioning. Even its minimal development requires a high level of abstraction."

Finally, Stotsky argues that at some point reading is learned and literacy is extended through practice in reading. This theory is particularly important for the upper grades of schooling, as it suggests that oral practice may not be sufficient or even helpful at this level. This means that the relationship between processes must be considered by grade from beginning learner to adulthood. The questions of when and how oral language training will aid written language are only touched upon here and must be explored further.

CAVEATS AND CRITIQUES

Comprehending Oral and Written Language begins to explore contrasts between oral and written language that are vital to school literacy, comprehension, and learning in schools. Certain caveats related to these contrasts must be expressed at the onset:

1. Oral and written language represent different ways of communicating. They represent different ways of knowing. While there are similarities, it is the differences between these forms of communication that have not been fully researched. Oral and written language do not constitute unitary constructs. There is much variation between oral and written modes and codes.

2. Oral and written language serve different functions and purposes in a discourse community, in time and space. They utilize different contexts. Writing is not simply talk or speech written down.

3. Each form influences and may interact with the other across human development. Speech may exist in writing. Written forms may emerge in speech.

4. The forms and functions of oral and written language may also overlap; thus, there is formal speech and informal writing.

5. The role of language as a mediational device in comprehension remains unexplored in most cognitive science accounts of schooling and in many discourse analysis accounts of texts. Not only is the language of oral and written discourse ignored, its function in controlling and establishing parameters for meaning in various language environments remains largely unexplored.

6. Knowledge about oral and written language development will contribute to a theory of language development, cognition, and literacy for schools.

7. A theory of written language development will need to account for early writing development to higher-level academic prose production and discourse of other institutional and work settings.

8. Understanding will require analysis of both oral and written language and comprehension processes and products associated with each. We have virtually only begun to touch the surface in formulating

the contrasts between speaking and writing, listening and reading, essential for a theory of composing and comprehending and essential for literacy.

9. Speech has typically been given priority or, like listening, totally left out of the account of written discourse. The study of writing as extended discourse is a recent phenomenon and the contrast of spoken and written discourse or listening and reading comprehension of discourse was not possible until the past decade.

10. The processes used in converting spoken forms to written forms and written forms to spoken must be addressed in light of schooling practices.

11. There is a need for study of the mingling of oral and written language and processes as these often do not exist in forms as pure as we suggest. We are moving toward a redefinition of and integrated theory of speaking and writing, listening and reading.

12. Cognitive and linguistic analysis of oral and written discourse must be related to social-cultural issues.

13. Extended discourse in a variety of registers, by various readerships, and put to a variety of uses must be addressed.

CONCLUSION

The chapters in this book pose difficult questions. They offer insights about oral and written language and primarily listening and reading comprehension.

Research is needed which characterizes individual and social group differences in the comprehension, processing strategies, and meaning systems derived from and represented by oral and written language and used in listening and reading, speaking and writing. A number of the chapters begin to consider social-situational and contextual dimensions of oral and written language comprehension.

These chapters offer insights about the relationships between oral and written comprehension. If indeed knowledge of oral language development can influence knowledge of written language development or if oral composing can to some extent contribute to written composing and comprehending, it would seem useful to further investigate orality in relation to literacy. A turn of attention to oral language—to children's dyadic conversations, to parent–child and teacher–child discourse, to practice in a range of oral registers used in composing, to speech practices and listening tasks in the schools and homes, to new kinds of talk in relation to text in classrooms and the listening to and oral and silent reading of various registers—warrants investigation. In addition, the study of the interaction of speech in reading or speech in writing may add substantial information to how we define not only oral language but also to what we can come to expect of literacy and schooling.

NOTES

[1] *Comprehending Oral and Written Language* was first conceived as a symposium, organized by the editors of this book and held at the 26th International Reading Association Annual Convention in New Orleans, Louisiana. At that symposium, papers were presented by researchers on the reading process, working in the United States. These included "An Overview of Comprehending Oral and Written Language" by Rosalind Horowitz, "A Comparison of Processing Strategies for Reading and Listening" by Joseph H. Danks, "Developmental Stages in Listening and Reading Comprehension" by Thomas G. Sticht, "Comprehension of Oral and Written Expository Texts" by S. Jay Samuels, "Reading to Learn and Listening to Learn" by Richard C. Anderson, "Language, Speech, and Print" by Charles A. Perfetti, and "Cognitive Processes Unique to Written Language" by John T. Guthrie. Using varied perspectives, this panel discussed similarities and differences in the comprehension of oral and written language in an individual's development toward literacy. Our audience consisted of classroom teachers, reading consultants and supervisors, graduate students, and reading and language researchers. It was our opinion that the theme presented and ideas discussed had not been sufficiently treated in the literature but were rich enough to deserve greater attention and wider dissemination beyond that which could be afforded at such a symposium. Thus, we solicited formal papers from panel members with the intent that they be published as part of a volume on *Comprehending Oral and Written Language*. Because there were still a number of scholars working in other fields and in Europe whose theory and research were relevant to this book, additional manuscripts were solicited and are included.

[2] We are using the phrases **oral and written language, speech and writing,** and **spoken and written language** somewhat synonymously to refer to systems of communication worthy of comparison and contrasts. Often these phrases are used to refer to the formal dimensions of language, i.e., language as an object as opposed to a process, although we are probably more interested in the processing of language. In our review of the literature we found no clear-cut distinctions between these phrases, although we looked for them. Nor did various linguists that we informally consulted offer particular distinctions. However, there may be some preferences in terminology, depending on the traditions found in the respective fields of research. **Oral and written language** has traditionally been used by scholars in the language arts, in English education, and by many in English departments to refer to conversation as opposed to written language and interpersonal communication as opposed to textual communication. **Speech and writing** and **spoken and written language** have traditionally been used by linguists or by scholars with a linguistics bent, including speech-communication researchers, who are particularly concerned with the actual sound and rhythm of speech (i.e., the prososdic features of language such as pitch, stress, pause, and intonation) and with the relationships between patterns of sound and meaning.

[3] The phrase **speaking and writing** is used in this chapter to refer to language as a process and the actual production of discourse. Some attention has been given to this contrast, but, as noted above, it has been limited. More work is needed from the angle of discourse analysis and text production. Knowledge of the manner in which text is pro-

duced should be valuable for understanding the comprehension of text providing we do not neglect the language. Oral and written language forms and as systems of meaning warrant study as they function in speaking and writing and listening and reading processes (Kroll & Vann, 1981; Cambourne, 1981).

[4] In this chapter, oral language primarily refers to natural conversation and does not include oral literature. Written language, as used here, primarily refers to expository discourse and not written literature. Conversational speech is a baseline against which other forms of language can be compared.

Some researchers are beginning to treat the relationships between oral and written language from the perspectives of learners at particular ages and stages of development. For a case in point, see Emilia Ferreiro (1985) which explores preschool children's viewpoints of these relationships. Findings are drawn from studies carried out in Buenos Aires, Venezuela, Geneva, Switzerland, and Monterrey and Mexico City, Mexico. Mead and Anne Campbell (1986) extend the discussion of written language by adding tests of oral language of the young adult, 21 to 25 years of age, in the United States. Mead and Campbell conclude their paper by noting that specific task assessment is necessary for studying oral–written relationships and that these relationships are more complex than we often note.

In sum, the results suggest that individuals who demonstrate limited literacy proficiency also demonstrate limited oral-language skills. It therefore appears to be naive to think that individuals demonstrating low literacy proficiency can talk their way through life. Those who demonstrate higher levels of literacy proficiency are more likely to also demonstrate higher oral-language proficiency. However, even among those with basic literacy skills there are some who have difficulty performing important oral tasks. (p. 42)

[5] Despite the contributions of the above work (and that cited in this chapter), there is little research to turn to for the kinds of oral–written language comparisons and concomitantly for the discourse comprehension contrasts that we have in mind. For a thorough review of the research contrasting spoken and written language since the 1920s see Akinnaso (1982). We thank Lester Faigley at The University of Texas at Austin for calling this to our attention. See also Chafe & Tannen (1987) for another excellent review.

[6] There is not one shift from oral to written language, but many shifts, as there are innumerable variations of oral language. Speech is used for a wide range of functions. However, written language tends to serve a more limited, rather specialized function at the more formal end of a continuum, including primarily institutional and occupational uses.

[7] Tannen (1980, 1982a, 1982b) has proposed a continuum of discourse with oral at one end and written at the other. This work has been followed by a discussion of oral and literate "strategies" that operate in spoken and written narratives. Tannen (1985) indicates that differences in language result not so much from oral versus written language as from the degree of personal involvement typical of conversation contrasted with the lack of personal involvement typical of exposition, where the emphasis is on message or content. This is very consistent with the ideas of Gillian Brown (1982) on spoken language. Brown refers to spoken language as a primarily listener-oriented interpersonal speech and argues there is also an "idea" language or message-oriented speech that schools have typically not treated. Message-oriented speech is not explicitly taught in schools but is essential for a range of tasks in a literate society.

[8] An excellent review of work by leading United States and Japanese computer experts in major computer research centers and their prognostications for the future is given in "friendly text" in *Invoking Tomorrow's Computers. A Mosaic Special Issue* (National Science Foundation, 1984; see also Metzer, 1984; Cromie & Edson, 1984).

ACKNOWLEDGMENTS

This chapter was prepared with the assistance of a National Academy of Education Spencer Fellowship awarded to Rosalind Horowitz for 1985–1988. Appreciation is extended to both the National Academy of Education and the Spencer Foundation for their support of this work.

This chapter was prepared with the research assistance of Anna Budzinski and Charles Thurston, both at The University of Texas–San Antonio.

Suggestions and comments on this chapter were made by Wallace Chafe at The University of California–Santa Barbara, Martin Nystrand at The University of Wisconsin–Madison, and Sandra Stotsky, Harvard University.

REFERENCES

Akinnaso, F. N. (1982). On the differences between spoken and written language. *Language and Speech, 25*(Part 2), 97–125.

Anderson, R. C., Hiebert, E. H., Scott, J. A., Wilkinson, I. A. G., with contributions from members of the Commission on Reading, The National Academy of Education, The National Institute of Education, & The Center for the Study of Reading. (1985). *Becoming a nation of readers: The report of the commission on reading, 1985*. Washington, DC: U.S. Department of Education.

Applebee, A. N., Langer, J. A., Mullis, I. V. S. (1986, November). *The writing report card. Writing achievement in American schools* (Report No. 15-W-02). Princeton, NJ: National Assessment of Educational Progress.

Beaman, K. (1984). Coordination and subordination revisited: Syntactic complexity in spoken and written narrative discourse. In D. Tannen (Ed.), *Coherence in spoken and written discourse* (pp. 45–80). Norwood, NJ: Ablex.

Beaugrande, R. de (1982). Psychology and composition: Past, present, and future. In M. Nystrand (Ed.), *What writers know: The language, process, and structure of written discourse* (pp. 211–267). New York: Academic Press.

Beaugrande, R. de (1983). Linguistic and cognitive processes in developmental writing. *International Review of Applied Linguistics in Language Teaching, 21*(2), 125–144.

Bereiter, C., & Scardamalia, M. (1981). From conversation to composition: The role of instruction in a developmental process. In R. Glaser (Ed.), *Advances in instructional psychology* (Vol. 2, pp. 1–64). Hillsdale, NJ: Erlbaum.

Bloomfield, L. (1933). *Language*. New York: Holt.

Borgh, K., & Dickson, P. (1986, April). *The effects on children's writing of adding speech synthesis to a word processor*. Paper presented at the American Educational Research Association, San Francisco.

Britton, J. (1982). Spectator role and the beginnings of writing. In M. Nystrand (Ed.), *What writers know: The language, process, and structure of written discourse* (pp. 149–169). New York: Academic Press.

Brown, G. (1977). *Listening to spoken English*. London: Longman.

Brown, G. (1982). The spoken language. In R. Carter (Ed.), *Linguistics and the teacher* (pp. 75–87). London: Routledge & Kegan Paul.

Buchmann, M. (1983). *Argument and conversation as discourse models of knowledge use* (Occasional Paper No. 68). East Lansing: Michigan State University Institute for Research on Teaching.

Cambourne, B. (1981). Oral and written relationships. A reading perspective. In B. M.

Kroll & R. J. Vann (Eds.), *Exploring speaking–writing relationships. Connections and contrasts* (pp. 82–98). Urbana, IL: National Council of Teachers of English.

Carnegie Forum on Education and the Economy and the Task Force on Teaching as a Profession. (1986). *A nation prepared: Teachers for the 21st century.* Washington, DC: Author.

Chafe, W. L. (1982). Integration and involvement in speaking, writing, and oral literature. In D. Tannen (Ed.), *Spoken and written language: Exploring orality and literacy* (pp. 35–53). Norwood, NJ: Ablex.

Chafe, W. L. (1985). Linguistic differences produced by differences between speaking and writing. In D. R. Olson, N. Torrance, & A. Hildyard (Eds.), *Literacy, language, and learning* (pp. 105–123). London: Cambridge University Press.

Chafe, W. (1986). Writing in the perspective of speaking. In C. R. Cooper & S. Greenbaum (Eds.), *Studying writing. Linguistic approaches* (pp. 12–39). Beverly Hills, CA: Sage.

Chafe, W. & Tannen, D. (1987). The relationship between written and spoken language. *Annual Review of Anthropology, 16,* 383–407.

Clifford, G. J. (1984). Buch und lesen: Historical perspectives on literacy and schooling. *Review of Educational Research, 54*(4), 472–500.

Cromie, W., & Edson, L. (1984). Before they can speak, they must know. In *Invoking tomorrow's computers. A Mosaic special issue. Mosaic 15*(1), 29–35.

Daiute, C. (1985a). Do writers talk to themselves? In S. W. Freedman (Ed.), *The acquisition of written language* (pp. 133–159). Norwood, NJ: Ablex.

Daiute, C. (1985b). *Writing & computers.* Reading, MA: Addison-Wesley.

Danielewicz, J., & Chafe, W. (1985). How "normal" speaking leads to erroneous punctuating. In S. W. Freedman (Ed.), *The acquisition of written language* (pp. 213–225). Norwood, NJ: Ablex.

Danks, J. H. (1980). Comprehension in listening and reading. Same or different? In J. Danks & K. Pezdek (Eds.), *Reading and understanding* (pp. 1–39). Newark, DE: International Reading Association.

Danks, J. H., Bohn, L., & Fears, R. (1983). Comprehension processes in oral reading. In G. B. Flores d'Arcais & R. J. Jarvella (Eds.), *The process of language understanding* (pp. 193–223). New York: Wiley.

DeVito, J. A. (1967). Levels of abstraction in spoken and written language. *Journal of Communication, 17,* 354–361.

Drieman, G. H. J. (1962a). Differences between written and spoken language: An exploratory study. Part I: Quantitative approach. *Acta Psychologica, European Journal of Psychology, 20*(1), 36–57.

Drieman, G. H. J. (1962b). Differences between written and spoken language: An exploratory study. Part II: Qualitative Approach. *Acta Psychologica, European Journal of Psychology, 20*(2), 78–100.

Duranti, A. (1986). Framing discourse in a new medium. Openings in electronic mail. *Quarterly Newsletter of the Laboratory of Comparative Human Cognition, 8*(2), 64–71.

Duranti, A., & Brenneis, D. (1986). The audience as co-author [Special issue]. *Text, 6*(3), 239–347.

Edmondson, W. (1981). *Spoken discourse. A model for analysis.* New York: Longman.

Ehri, L. C. (1984). How orthography alters spoken language competencies in children learning to read and spell. In J. Downing & R. Valtin (Eds.), *Language awareness and learning to read* (pp. 119–147). New York: Springer-Verlag.

Eimas, P. D. (1986). The perception of speech in early infancy. In *Language, writing and the computer. Readings from Scientific American* (pp. 17–23). New York: Freeman.

Eisenstein, E. L. (1968). Some conjectures about the impact of printing on Western society and thought: A preliminary report. *Journal of Modern History, 40,* 9–56.

Eisenstein, E. L. (1981). Some conjectures about the impact of printing on Western society and thought: A preliminary report in H. J. Graff, *Literacy and social development in the West. A reader* (pp. 53–68). London: Cambridge University Press.

Eisenstein, E. L. (1985). On the printing press as an agent of change. In D. R. Olson, N. Torrance, & A. Hildyard (Eds.), *Literacy, language, and learning* (pp. 19–33). London: Cambridge University Press.

Emerson, C. (1983). The outer word and inner speech: Bakhtin, Vygotsky, and the internalization of language. *Critical Inquiry, 10*(2), 245–264.

Emig, J. (1978). Hand, eye, brain: Some "basics" in the writing process. In R. Cooper & L. Odell (Eds.), *Research on composing. Points of departure* (pp. 59–71). Urbana, IL: National Council of Teachers of English.

Faigley, L., Cherry, R. D., Jolliffe, D. A., & Skinner, A. H. (1985). The classroom as a discourse community. In *Assessing writers' knowledge and processes of composing* (pp. 90–99). Norwood, NJ: Ablex.

Ferreiro, E. (1985). The relationship between oral and written language. The children's viewpoints. In M. M. Clark (Ed.), *New directions in the study of reading* (pp. 83–94). London: Falmer Press.

Fox, B. A. (1986). Local patterns and general principles in cognitive processes: Anaphora in written and conversational English. *Text, 6*(1), 25–51.

Frase, L. T. (1986, April). *Creating intelligent environments for computer use in writing.* Paper presented at a symposium at the American Educational Research Association Annual Meeting, San Francisco.

Freeman, N. H., & Cox, M. V. (Eds.). (1985). *Visual order. The nature and development of pictorial representation.* London: Cambridge University Press.

Frith, U. (1979). Reading by eye and writing by ear. In P. A. Kolers, M. E. Wrolstad, & H. Bouma (Eds.), *Processing of visible language* (pp. 379–390). London: Plenum Press.

Gelb, I. J. (1963). *A study of writing* (2nd ed.). Chicago: University of Chicago Press.

Gibson, J. J. (1966). *The senses considered as perceptual systems.* Boston: Houghton.

Gibson, J. W., Gruner, C. R., Kibler, R. J., & Kelly, F. J. (1966). A quantitative examination of differences and similarities in written and spoken messages. *Speech Monographs, 33,* 444–451.

Glushko, R. J. (1981). Principles for pronouncing print: The psychology of phonography. In A. M. Lesgold & C. A. Perfetti (Eds.), *Interactive processes in reading* (pp. 61–84). Hillsdale, NJ: Erlbaum.

Goldstein, H. (1940). *Reading and listening comprehension at various controlled rates.* Unpublished doctoral dissertation, Teachers College, Columbia University, New York.

Gottlieb, G., & Krasnegor, N. A. (Eds.). (1985). *Measurement of audition and vision during the first year of postnatal life.* Norwood, NJ: Ablex.

Graves, M. F. (1986). Vocabulary learning and instruction. In E. Z. Rothkopf (Ed.), *Review of research in education* (pp. 49–89). Washington, DC: American Educational Research Association.

Greenberg, M. (1983). *Biblical prose prayer.* Berkeley: University of California Press.

Greene, W. C. (1951). The spoken and written word. *Harvard Studies in Classical Philology, 60,* 23–59.

Greenfield, P. M. (1984). *Mind and media: The effects of television, video games, and computers.* Cambridge, MA: Harvard University Press.

Gruner, C. R., Kibler, R. J., & Gibson, J. W. (1967). A quantitative analysis of selected characteristics of oral and written vocabularies. *Journal of Communication, 17,* 152–158.

Hall, N. S., Nagy, N. E., & Linn, R. (1984). *Spoken words: The effects of situation and social group on oral word usage and frequency.* Norwood, NJ: Erlbaum.

Halliday, M. A. K. (1978). *Language as social semiotic: The social interpretation of language and meaning.* Baltimore: University Park Press.

Halliday, M. A. K. (1985). *An introduction to functional grammar.* Baltimore: Arnold.

Havelock, E. A. (1976). *Origins of western literacy* (Monograph Series No. 14). Toronto: Ontario Institute for Studies in Education.

Havelock, E. A. (1980). The coming of literate communication to western civilization. *Journal of Communication, 30,* 90–98.

Heath, S. B. (1986, March). *Writing re-structures consciousness.* Paper presented at the Conference on College Composition and Communication, New Orleans.

Hjelmslev, L. (1961). *Prolegomena to a theory of language* (F. J. Whitfield, Trans.). Madison: University of Wisconsin Press.

Hockett, C. F. (1958). *A course in modern linguistics.* New York: Macmillan.

Hockett, C. F. (1960). The origin of speech. *Scientific American, 203,* 89–96.

Horowitz, R. (1973). *A summary and analysis of recent studies of parent–child interaction with implications for language development.* Unpublished master's thesis, University of Minnesota, Minneapolis.

Horowitz, R. (1987). The text in the context of teaching. In H. Aristar-Dry, G. E. Cook, & M. Martinello (Eds.), *Teaching Effectively at The University of Texas at San Antonio* (pp. 49–54). San Antonio: University of Texas at San Antonio.

Horowitz, R. (1987, August). *Discourse organization in oral and written language: Critical contrasts for literacy and schooling.* Paper presented at the 8th World Congress of Applied Linguistics, The University of Sydney, Sydney, Australia.

Horowitz, R. (in preparation). Apprenticeships in listening and reading.

Horowitz, R., & Davis, R. (1984, July). *Oral and written persuasive strategies used by second graders.* Paper presented at the Third International Congress for the Study of Child Language sponsored by the University of Texas at Austin and the International Association for the Study of Child Language. Austin.

Jakobson, R. (1978). *Six lectures on sound and meaning.* Cambridge, MA: MIT Press.

Jakobson, R., & Waugh, L. R. (1979). *The sound shape of language.* Bloomington: Indiana University Press.

Jorm, A. F., & Share, D. L. (1983). Phonological recoding and reading acquisition. *Applied Psycholinguistics, 4,* 103–147.

Juel, C., & Holmes, B. (1981). Oral and silent reading of sentences. *Reading Research Quarterly, 16,* 545–568.

Kaestle, C. F. (1985). The history of literacy and the history of readers. In E. Gordon (Ed.), *Review of research in education.* Washington, DC: American Educational Research Association.

Kavanagh, J. E., & Mattingly, I. (Eds.). (1972). *Language by ear and by eye: The relationships between speech and reading.* Cambridge, MA: MIT Press.

Kirsch, I. S., & Jungeblut, A. (1986). *Literacy: Profiles of America's young adults* (Report No. 16-PL-02). Princeton, NJ: National Assessment of Educational Progress.

Kleiman, G. M. (1975). Speech recoding in reading. *Journal of Verbal Learning and Behavior, 14,* 323–339.

Kolers, P. A., Wrolstad, M. E., & Bouma, H. (Eds.). (1979–1980). *Processing of visible language* (Vols. 1 and 2). London: Plenum Press.

Kroll, B. (1977). Combining ideas in written and spoken English. In E. O. Keenan & T. L. Bennett (Eds.), *Discourse across time and space. Southern California Occasional Papers in Linguistics, 5,* 69–108.

Kroll, B. M., & Vann, R. J. (Eds.). (1981). *Exploring speaking–writing relationships. Connections and contrasts.* Urbana, IL: National Council of Teachers of English.

Labov, W. (1986, March). *Oral discourse and the demands of literacy.* Paper presented at the Conference on College Composition and Communication, New Orleans.

Lakoff, R. T. (1982). Some of my favorite writers are literate: The mingling of oral and literate strategies in written communication. In D. Tannen (Ed.), *Spoken and written language. Exploring orality and literacy* (pp. 239–260). Norwood, NJ: Ablex.

Lehrer, R., Levin, B. B., DeHart, P., & Comeaux, M. (1986, April). *Voice feedback as a scaffold for writing: A comparative study.* Paper presented at the American Educational Research Association, San Francisco.

Lemke, J. L. (1985). *Using language in the classroom.* Victoria, Australia: Deakin University Press.

Levinson, S. E., & Liberman, M. Y. (1986). Speech recognition by computer. In *Language, writing, and the computer. Readings from Scientific American* (pp. 97–109). New York: Freeman.

Levy, B. A. (1978). Speech processing during reading. In A. M. Lesgold, J. W. Pellegrino, S. D. Fokkema, & R. Glaser (Eds.), *Cognitive psychology and instruction* (pp. 123–151). New York: Plenum Press.

McCutchen, D. (in press). Children's discourse skill: Form and modality requirements of schooled writing. *Discourse Processes.*

McLane, J. B. (1981). *Dyadic problem solving: A comparison of child–child and mother–child interaction.* Unpublished doctoral dissertation, Northwestern University, Chicago.

Mead, N. A., & Campbell, A. (1986, April). *Profiles for literacy: Oral-language proficiency.* Paper presented on the National Assessment of Educational Progress (NAEP) Young Adult Literacy Assessment at the American Educational Research Association, San Francisco.

Metzer, N. (1984). To find the way forward. In *Invoking tomorrow's computers. A Mosaic special issue. Mosaic 15*(1), 3–9.

Murphy, S. (1986). Children's comprehension of deictic categories in oral and written language. *Reading Research Quarterly, 21*(2), 118–131.

Nagy, W. E., & Anderson, R. C. (1984). How many words are there in printed school English? *Reading Research Quarterly, 19,* 304–330.

National Assessment of Educational Progress. (1985). *The reading report card. Progress toward excellence in our schools: Trend in reading over four national assessments, 1971–1984.* (Report No. 15-R-01). Princeton, NJ: Author.

National Science Foundation. (1984). *Invoking tomorrow's computers. A Mosaic special issue. Mosaic 15*(1).

Nystrand, M. (1982). Rhetoric's "Audience" and linguistics' "Speech Community": Implications for reading. In *What writers know. The language, process, and structure of written discourse* (pp. 1–28). New York: Academic Press.

Nystrand, M. (1986). *The structure of written communication: Studies in reciprocity between writers and readers.* Orlando, FL: Academic Press.

O'Donnell, R. (1974). Syntactic differences between speech and writing. *American Speech, 49,* 102–110.

Ohmann, R. (1972). Speech, literature, and the space between. *New Literary History, 4,* 47–63.

Olson, D. (1977). Oral and written language and the cognitive processes of children. *Journal of Communication, 27,* 1–4, 10–26.

Olson, D. (1980). Some social aspects of meaning in oral and written language. In D. R. Olson (Ed.), *The social foundations of language and thought: Essays in honor of Jerome S. Bruner* (pp. 90–108). New York: Norton.

Olson, D. (1985). Computers as tools of the intellect. *Educational Researcher, 14*(5), 5–7.

Ong, W. J. (1975). The writer's audience is always a fiction. *PMLA, 90,* 9–21.

Ong, W. J. (1982). *Orality and literacy. The technologizing of the word.* New York: Methuen.

Perfetti, C. A. (1985). Speech processes in skilled reading. In *Reading ability* (pp. 52–67). New York: Oxford University Press.

Perfetti, C. A., & McCutchen, D. (1982). Speech processes in reading. In N. Lass (Ed.), *Speech and language: Advances in basic research and practice* (Vol. 7, pp. 237–269). New York: Academic Press.

Poole, M. E., & Field, T. W. (1976). A comparison of oral and written code elaboration. *Language and Speech, 19*, 305–311.

Quinn, C. N., Mehan, H., Levin, J. A., & Black, S. D. (1983). Real education in non-real time: The use of electronic message systems for instruction. *Instructional Science, 11*, 313–327.

Rabin, Ch. (1986). The discourse status of commentary. In C. R. Cooper & S. Greenbaum (Eds.), *Studying writing: Linguistic approaches* (pp. 215–225). Beverly Hills, CA: Sage.

Resnick, D. P. (Ed.). (1983). *Literacy in historical perspective*. Washington, DC: Library of Congress.

Resnick, D. P., & Resnick, L. B. (1977). The nature of literacy: A historical explanation. *Harvard Educational Review, 47*(3), 370–385.

Rosenberg, B. A. (1985, July). *The oral tradition*. Paper presented at Questions of Orality and Literacy: A Tribute to Walter J. Ong, S. J. A symposium honoring Walter J. Ong, S. J., at Rockhurst College, Kansas City, MO.

Rubin, A. (1980). A theoretical taxonomy of the differences between oral and written language. In R. J. Spiro, B. C. Bruce, & W. F. Brewer (Eds.), *Theoretical issues in reading comprehension. Perspectives from cognitive psychology, linguistics, artificial intelligence, and education* (pp. 411–438). Hillsdale, NJ: Erlbaum.

Ruddell, R. B., & Haggard, M. R. (1986). Oral and written language acquisition and the reading process. In H. Singer & R. B. Ruddell (Eds.), *Theoretical models and processes of reading* (3rd ed., pp. 63–80). Newark, DE: International Reading Association.

Sapir, E. (1921). *Language: An introduction to the study of speech*. New York: Harcourt.

Saussure, F. de (1916). *Cours de linguistique générale*. Lausanne: Payot. [English translation by W. Baskin, *Course in general linguistics*. New York: Philosophical Library, 1959]

Savin, H. B. (1972). What the child knows about speech when he starts to learn to read. In J. F. Kavanagh & I. G. Mattingly (Eds.), *Language by ear and by eye. The relationships between speech and reading* (pp. 319–326). Cambridge, MA: MIT Press.

Sawkins, M. W. (1971). *The oral responses of selected fifth-grade children to questions concerning their written expression*. Unpublished doctoral dissertation, State University of New York, Buffalo.

Sawyer, T. M. (1977). Why speech will not totally replace writing. *College Composition and Communication, 28*(1), 43–48.

Schallert, D. L., & Kleiman, G. M. (1979, June). *Some reasons why teachers are easier to understand than textbooks* (Reading Education Tech. Rep. No. 9). Urbana: University of Illinois at Urbana–Champaign, Center for the Study of Reading.

Scheffler, I. (1985). *Of human potential. An essay in the philosophy of education*. Boston: Routledge & Kegan Paul.

Schmandt-Besserat, D. (1986). The earliest precursor of writing. In *Language, writing and the computer. Readings from Scientific American* (pp. 31–40). New York: Freeman.

Scinto, L. F. M. (1985). Text, schooling, and the growth of mind. In E. Mertz & R. J. Parmentier (Eds.), *Semiotic mediation: Sociocultural and psychological perspectives* (pp. 203–218). Orlando, FL: Academic Press.

Scinto, L. F. M. (1986). *Written language and psychological development*. Orlando, FL: Academic Press.

Staton, J., Shuy, R., Kreeft, J., & Reed, L. (in press). Oral basis of written language acquisition. Topic continuation in dialogue as an aid to student writing. In *Interactive writing in dialogue journals*. Norwood, NJ: Ablex.

Stedman, L. C., & Kaestle, C. (1987). Literacy and reading performance in the United States, from 1880 to the present. *Reading Research Quarterly, 22*(1), 8–46.

Steiner, G. (1978). The distribution of discourse. In *On difficulty and other essays* (pp. 61–94). New York: Oxford University Press.

Sticht, T. G. (1979). Applications of the Audread model to reading evaluation and instruction. In L. B. Resnick & P. A. Weaver (Eds.), *Theory and practice of early reading* (Vol. 1, pp. 209–226). Hillsdale, NJ: Erlbaum.

Sticht, T. G., Beck, L. J., Hauke, R. N., Kleiman, G. M., & James, J. H. (1974). *Auding and reading. A developmental model.* Alexandria, VA: Human Resources Research Organization.

Sticht, T. G., & James, J. H. (1984). Listening and reading. In P. D. Pearson, R. Barr, M. L. Kamil, & P. Mosenthal (Eds.), *Handbook of reading research* (pp. 293–317). London: Longman.

Street, B. V. (1984). *Literacy in theory and practice.* London: Cambridge University Press.

Stubbs, M. (1980). *Language and literacy. The sociolinguistics of reading and writing.* London: Routledge & Kegan Paul.

Stubbs, M. (1982). Written language and society: Some particular cases and observation. In M. Nystrand (Ed.), *What writers know* (pp. 31–55). New York: Academic Press.

Stubbs, M. (1986). *Educational linguistics.* Oxford: Blackwell.

Szwed, J. F. (1981). The ethnography of literacy. In M. F. Whiteman (Ed.), *Writing: The nature, development & teaching of written communication: Vol. 1. Variation in writing: Functional & linguistic–cultural differences* (pp. 13–23). Hillsdale, NJ: Erlbaum.

Tannen, D. (1980). Spoken/written language & the oral/literate continuum. *Proceedings of the 6th Annual Meeting of the Berkeley Linguistic Society,* pp. 207–218.

Tannen, D. (1982a). The oral/literate continuum in discourse. In D. Tannen (Ed.), *Spoken and written language. Exploring orality and literacy* (pp. 1–16). Norwood, NJ: Ablex.

Tannen, D. (1982b). Oral and literate strategies in spoken and written narratives. *Language, 58,* 1–21.

Tannen, D. (1984). *Conversational style: Analyzing talk among friends.* Norwood, NJ: Ablex.

Tannen, D. (1985). Relative focus on involvement in oral and written discourse. In D. R. Olson, N. Torrance, & A. Hildyard (Eds.), *Literacy, language, and learning* (pp. 124–147). London: Cambridge University Press.

Vachek, J. (1973). *Written language: General problems and problems of English.* The Hague: Mouton.

van Dijk, T. A. (Ed.). (1985). *Handbook of discourse analysis* (Vol. 1). London: Academic Press.

van Dijk, T. A., & Kintsch, W. (1983). *Strategies of discourse comprehension.* New York: Academic Press.

Venezky, R. L., Kaestle, C. F., & Sum, A. M. (1987, January). *The subtle danger: Reflections on the literacy abilities of America's young adults* (Report No. 16-CAEP-01). Princeton, NJ: National Assessment of Educational Progress.

Vygotsky, L. (1962). *Thought and language.* Cambridge, MA: MIT Press.

Vygotsky, L. (1978). *Mind in society: The development of higher psychological processes.* Cambridge, MA: Harvard University Press.

Wardaugh, R. (1985). *How conversation works.* New York: Blackwell in association with André Deutsch.

Wertsch, J. V. (1980). The significance of dialogue in Vygotsky's account of social, egocentric, and inner speech. *Contemporary Educational Psychology, 5,* 150–162.

Wertsch, J. V. (1985). *Vygotsky and the social formation of mind.* Cambridge, MA: Harvard University Press.

Wresch, W. (Ed.). (1987) *Practical guide to computer uses in the English language arts classroom.* Englewood Cliffs, NJ: Prentice-Hall.

PART **I**

THE LANGUAGE OF SPOKEN AND WRITTEN DISCOURSE

Chapter **2**

Spoken and Written Modes
of Meaning

M. A. K. Halliday

SPOKEN LANGUAGE AND EDUCATION

It seems to me that one of the most productive areas of discussion between linguists and educators in the past quarter century has been that of speech and the spoken language. Twenty-five years ago, when I launched the "Linguistics and English Teaching" project in London, which produced *Breakthrough to Literacy* and *Language in Use,* it was still rare to find references to the place of spoken language in school, or to the need for children to be articulate as well as literate. Dell Hymes had not yet introduced "communicative competence"; the words *oracy* and *orality* had not yet entered the field (Andrew Wilkinson's *Some Aspects of Oracy* appeared in 1967); David Abercrombie (1963/1965) had only just published his "Conversation and Spoken Prose." Language, in school, as in the community at large, meant written language.

The word *language* itself was hardly used in educational contexts. In the primary school, there was reading and writing; in the secondary school there was English, which meant literature and composition. Not that a classroom was a temple of silence; but the kind of spoken language that had a place, once a pupil had got beyond the infant school, was prepared speech: reading aloud, drama, debating—language that was written in order to be spoken, or at least was closely monitored in the course of its production. Spoken language in its natural form, spontaneous and unselfconscious, was not taken seriously as a medium of learning.

Among linguists, by contrast, the spoken language had pride of place. One learnt in the first year of a linguistics course that speech was logically and historically prior to writing. The somewhat aggressive tone

COMPREHENDING ORAL AND WRITTEN LANGUAGE

Copyright © 1987 by Academic Press, Inc.
All rights of reproduction in any form reserved.

55

with which linguists often proclaimed this commitment did not endear them to educators, who sensed that it undermined their authority as guardians of literacy and felt threatened by a scale of values they did not understand, according to which English spelling was out of harmony with the facts of the English language—whereas for them it was the pronunciation that was out of step, being a distorted reflection of the reality that lay in writing.

The linguists' professional commitment to the primacy of speech did not, however, arise from or carry with it an awareness of the properties of spoken discourse. It arose from the two sources of diachronic phonology (the study of sound change) and articulatory phonetics (the study of speech production), which came together in twentieth century phonological theory. This was an interpretation of the system of speech sounds and of the phonological properties of the stream of speech; it did not involve any attempt to study the grammar and semantics of spoken as distinct from written language. As early as 1911, in his discussion of functional variation in language, Mathesius (1911/1964) was referring to "how the styles of speech are manifested in the pronunciation of language, in the stock of words, and in syntax" (p. 23), and to "the influence of functional styles on the lexical and semantic aspects of speech" (p. 24); and it is clear that "speech" for him (*parole*) did encompass both spoken and written varieties. But it was not until the 1950s, with the appearance of tape recorders, that natural speech could become the object of systematic study. The notion of "spoken text" is still not easily accepted, as can be seen from the confusion that prevails when spontaneous speech is reduced to writing in order to be analysed.

Spoken language came to figure in educational discussions in the context of language in the classroom: the language used by teachers to structure, direct and monitor their students' progress through the lesson. But the emphasis was on verbal strategies rather than on the text as a document; the investigators of the fifties and early sixties were not concerned with the particular place of spoken language in the learning process. It was assumed, of course, that students learnt by listening; but the expository aspects of the teacher's language were given little attention, while the notion that a student might be using his own talk as a means of learning was nowhere part of the picture. Probably it would have been felt that the principal means of learning through the spoken language was by asking questions; but studies of the early seventies (e.g., the Toronto research reported in *Five to Nine*) revealed that students seldom do ask questions—not, that is, while they are occupying their student role (i.e., in class). It is the teachers that ask the questions; and when they do so, both question and answer may be somewhat removed from the patterns of natural dialogue.

COMPLEXITY OF NATURAL SPEECH

Already half a century earlier Franz Boas (1911/1963) had stressed the unconscious character of language, unique (as he saw it) among the phenomena of human culture. Boas' observation was to be understood in its contemporary context as a characterization of the language system (*langue*); not that, writing in 1911, he could have read Saussure's *Course in General Linguistics*, any more than Mathesius could have done; but the unconscious was in the air, so to speak, and playing a critical role in the conception of systems as regularities underlying human behaviour. But Boas may also have had in mind the unconsciousness of the behaviour itself: the act of speaking (*acte de parole*) as an unconscious act. The lack of conscious awareness of the underlying SYSTEM, and the difficulty that people have in bringing it to consciousness, are things which language shares with other semiotic systems—for example, social systems like that of kinship; what is unusual about language is the extent to which even the MANIFESTATION of the system, the actual process of meaning, remains hidden from observation, by performer and receiver alike. In that respect talking is more like dancing, or even running, than it is like playing chess. Speaker and listeners are of course aware that the speaker is speaking; but they are typically not aware of what he is saying, and if asked to recall it, not only the listeners but also the speaker will ordinarily offer a paraphrase, something that is true to the meaning but not by any means true to the wording. To focus attention on the wording of language is something that has to be learnt—for example if you are studying linguistics; it can be a difficult and somewhat threatening task.

About 30 years ago, as a result of being asked to teach English intonation to foreign students, I began observing natural spontaneous discourse in English; and from the start I was struck by a curious fact. Not only were people unconscious of what they themselves were saying; they would often deny, not just that they HAD said something I had observed them to say, but also that they ever COULD say it. For example, I noticed the utterance *it'll've been going to've been being tested every day for the past fortnight soon*, where the verbal group *will have been going to have been being tested* makes five serial tense choices, present in past in future in past in future, and is also passive. This passed quite unnoticed by both the speaker and the person it was addressed to; yet at the time it was being seriously questioned whether a simple verb form like *has been being tested*, which one can hear about once a week, could ever occur in English. Five-term tense forms are, predictably, very rare—one can in fact make a reasonable guess as to how rare, on the basis of observed frequencies of two- and three-term tense forms together with the constraints of the tense system; but they are provided for within the resources of the spoken language. Another instance I observed was *they said they'd been going to've been paying me all this time, only the funds just kept on not coming through.*

Other things I noted regularly included present in present participial non-finites like *being cooking* in *I never heard you come in—it must have been with being cooking;* marked thematic elements with reprise pronoun, as in *that poor child I couldn't get him out of my mind;* and relatives reaching into dependent clauses, such as *that's the noise which when you say it to a horse the horse goes faster.* These are all systematic features that people are unaware that they incorporate in their speech, and often deny having said even when they are pointed out; or at least reject as unsystematic— after "I didn't say it," the next line of defence is "well it was a mistake." But of course it was not a mistake; it was a regular product of the system of spoken English.

But perhaps the most unexpected feature of those early observations was the complexity of some of the sentence structures. Here are two examples from recordings made at the time:

(i)   *It's very interesting, because it fairly soon is established when you're meeting with somebody what kind of conversation you're having: for example, you may know and tune in pretty quickly to the fact that you're there as the support, perhaps, in the listening capacity—that you're there, in fact, to help the other person sort their ideas; and therefore your remarks, in that particular type of conversation, are aimed at drawing out the other person, or in some way assisting them, by reflecting them, to draw their ideas out, and you may tune in to this, or you may be given this role and refuse it, refuse to accept it, which may again alter the nature of your conversation.*

(ii)   *The other man who kicks is the full-back, who usually receives the ball way behind the rest of his team, either near his line or when somebody's done what the stand-off in the first example was doing, kicked over the defenders; the full-back should be able then to pick it up, and his job is usually to kick for touch—nearly always for touch because he's miles behind the rest of his side, and before he can do anything else with the ball he's got to run up into them, before he can pass it, because he can't pass the ball forward, and if he kicks it forward to another of his side the other man's automatically off-side.*

       And you get a penalty for that, do you, the other side?

       Depending on whether it's kicking or passing forward. Passing forward—no, it's a scrum. If you kick it forward and somebody else picks it up that will be a penalty.

       And if not, if the other side picks—

       If the other side picks it up that's all right; but the trouble is this is in fact tactics again, because you don't want to put the ball into the hands of the other side if you can avoid it because it's the side that has possession, as in most games of course, is at an advantage.

Examples such as these were noteworthy in two respects. One was that they embodied patterns of parataxis (combining with equal status) and hypotaxis (combining with unequal status) between clauses which could run to considerable length and depth. The other was that they were remarkably well formed: although the speaker seemed to be running through a maze, he did not get lost, but emerged at the end with all brackets closed and all structural promises fulfilled. And this drew attention to a third property which I found interesting: that while the listeners had absorbed these passages quite unconsciously and without effort, they were difficult to follow in writing.

Lexical Density

These two examples have been around for a long time; so let me turn to some recent specimens taken from recordings made by Guenter Plum to whom I am indebted for drawing them to my attention. In these spontaneous narratives Plum regularly finds sequences such as the following:

1A *I had to wait, I had to wait till it was born and till it got to about eight or ten weeks of age, then I bought my first dachshund, a black-and-tan bitch puppy, as they told me I should have bought a bitch puppy to start off with, because if she wasn't a hundred percent good I could choose a top champion dog to mate her to, and then produce something that was good, which would be in my own kennel prefix.*

This displays the same kind of mobility that the earlier observations had suggested was typically associated with natural, unselfconscious speech—which is what it was. I asked myself how I would have expressed this in writing, and came up with two rewordings; the first (1B) was fairly informal, as I might have told it in a letter to a friend:

1B *I had to wait till it was born and had got to about eight or ten weeks of age; that was when I bought my first dachshund, a black-and-tan bitch puppy. By all accounts I should have bought a bitch puppy at the start, because if she wasn't a hundred percent good I could mate her with a top champion dog and produce a good offspring—which would carry my own kennel prefix.*

My second rewording (1C) was a more formal written variant.

1C *Some eight or ten weeks after the birth saw my first acquisition of a dachshund, a black-and-tan bitch puppy. It seems that a bitch puppy would have been the appropriate initial purchase, because of the possibility of mating an imperfect specimen with a top champion dog, the improved offspring then carrying my own kennel prefix.*

The aim was to produce a set of related passages of text differing along this one dimension, which could be recognized as going from "most likely to be spoken" to "most likely to be written." How such variation actually correlates with difference in the medium is of course problematic; the relationship is a complicated one, both because written/spoken is not a simple dichotomy—there are many mixed and intermediate types—and because the whole space taken up by such variation is by now highly coded: in any given instance the wording used is as much the product of stylistic conventions in the language as of choices made by individual speakers and writers. Here I am simply moving along a continuum which anyone familiar with English usage can readily interpret in terms of "spoken" and "written" poles.

The kind of difference that we find among these three variants is one that is often referred to as a difference of "texture," and this familiar rhetorical metaphor is a very appropriate one: it is as if they were the product of a different weave, with fibres of a different yarn. But when we look behind these traditional metaphors, at the forms of language they are describing, we find that much of the difference can be accounted for as the effect of two related lexicosyntactic variables. The written version has a much higher lexical density; at the same time, it has a much simpler sentential structure. Let us examine these concepts in turn.

The *lexical density* is the proportion of lexical items (content words) to the total discourse. It can be measured in various ways: the ratio of lexical items either to total running words or to some higher grammatical unit, most obviously the clause; with or without weighting for relative frequency (in the language) of the lexical items themselves. Here we will ignore the relative frequency of the lexical items and refer simply to the total number in each case, providing two measures (Table 2.1): the number of lexical items (1) as a proportion of the number of running words, and (2) as a proportion of the number of clauses. Only non-embedded clauses have been counted (if embedded clauses are also counted, then each lexical item occurring in them is counted twice, since it figures in both the embedded and the matrix clause—i.e., both in the PART, and in the WHOLE of which it is a part). The figures are given to the nearest decimal.

As Jean Ure showed in 1969 (Ure, 1971), the lexical density of a text is a function of its place on a register scale which she characterized as

TABLE 2.1
Lexical Density of Texts 1A, 1B,
and 1C

	(1) Lexical items	(2) Running words	(1:2)	(3) Clauses	(1:3)
1A	23	83	1:3.6	13	1.8:1
1B	26	68	1:2.6	8	3.3:1
1C	25	55	1:2.2	4	6.3:1

running from most active to most reflective: the nearer to the "language-in-action" end of the scale, the lower the lexical density. Since written language is characteristically reflective rather than active, in a written text the lexical density tends to be higher; and it increases as the text becomes further away from spontaneous speech.

Jean Ure measured lexical density as a proportion of running words; but as is suggested by the figures given above, if it is calculated with reference to the number of clauses the discrepancy stands out more sharply. Thus in the example given above, while the number of lexical items remained fairly constant and the number of running words fell off slightly, the number of clauses fell steeply: from 13, to 8, to 4. In other words, the lexical density increases not because the number of lexical items goes up but because the number of non-lexical items—grammatical words—goes down; and the number of clauses goes down even more.

Let us attempt a similar rewording the other way round, this time beginning with a passage of formal written English taken from *Scientific American*:

2A *Private civil actions at law have a special significance in that they provide an outlet for efforts by independent citizens. Such actions offer a means whereby the multiple initiatives of private citizens, individually or in groups, can be brought to bear on technology assessment, the internalization of costs and environmental protection. They constitute a channel through which the diverse interests, outlooks and moods of the general public can be given expression.*
The current popular concern over the environment has stimulated private civil actions of two main types.

2B is my attempt at a somewhat less "written" version; while 2C is another step nearer to speech:

2B *Private civil actions at law are especially significant because they can be brought by independent citizens, so enabling them to find an outlet for their efforts. By bringing these actions, either as individuals or in groups, private citizens can regularly take the initiative in assessing technology, internalizing costs and protecting the environment. Through the use of these actions as a channel, the general public are able to express all their various interests, their outlooks, and their moods.*
Because people are currently concerned about the environment, they have been bringing numerous private civil actions, which have been mainly of two types.

2C *One thing is especially significant, and that is that people should be able to bring private civil actions at law, because by doing this independent citizens can become involved. By bringing these actions, whether they are acting as individuals or in groups, private citizens can keep on taking the initiative; they can help to assess technology, they can help to internalize costs, and they can help to protect the environment. The general public, who want all kinds of different things, and who think and feel in all kinds of different ways, can express all these wants and thoughts and feelings by bringing civil actions at law.*
At present, people are concerned about the environment; so they have been bringing quite a few private civil actions, which have been mainly of two kinds.

TABLE 2.2
Lexical Density of Texts 2A, 2B,
and 2C

	(1) Lexical items	(2) Running words	(1:2)	(3) Clauses	(1:3)
2A	48	87	1:1.8	5	9.6:1
2B	48	101	1:2.1	12	4.0:1
2C	51	132	1:2.6	17	3.0:1

Table 2.2 shows the relative lexical density of the three variants of Text 2. Again, the number of lexical items has remained fairly constant; the variation in lexical density results from the increase in the total number of words—which means, therefore, in the number of grammatical words. This, in turn, is related to the increase in the number of clauses— where, however, the discrepancy is again much more striking.

Grammatical Intricacy

We have characterized the difference in general terms by saying that written language has a higher lexical density than spoken language; this expresses it as a positive feature of written discourse and suggests that writing is more complex, since presumably lexical density is a form of complexity. Could we then turn the formulation around, and express the difference as a positive characteristic of spoken language? To say that spoken discourse has more words in it, or even more clauses, does not seem to convey anything very significant about it. We need to look at how the words and clauses are organized.

Let us consider a shorter example of a pair of texts related in the same way, one "more written" (Text 3A), the other "more spoken" (Text 3B). I have constructed these so that they resemble the originals of Texts 1 and 2; but they are based on a natural example occurring in two texts in which a person had described the same experience twice over, once in speech and once in writing.

	More "written":		More "spoken":
3A	*Every previous visit had left me with a sense of the risk to others in further attempts at action on my part.*	3B	*Whenever I'd visited there before I'd end up feeling that other people might get hurt if I tried to do anything more.*

The first version (3A) is one sentence, consisting of one clause: a "simple sentence" in traditional grammar. The second version (3B) consists of

TABLE 2.3
Notational Conventions for the Clause Complex[a]

Logical-semantic relations		Interdependencies	
Category	Symbol	Category	Symbol
expansion: { elaborating	=	parataxis	1 2 3 . . .
extending	+	hypotaxis[b]	α β γ . . .
enhancing	x		
projection: { idea	'		
locution	"		

[a] For details of analysis see Halliday (1985, pp. 192 ff.).
[b] Hypotaxis is not equivalent to embedding, which is a constituency (not a "tactic") relation; see Table 2.4.

four clauses (assuming that *ended up feeling* and *tried to do* are each single predicators); but these too have to be transcribed as one sentence, since they are related by hypotaxis—only one has independent status. These four clauses form what is called in systemic grammar a *clause complex* (for analysis and notation see Table 2.3):

Whenever I'd visited there before	^{x}β
I'd end up feeling	α α
that other people might get hurt	α 'β α
if I tried to do anything more	α β ^{x}β

The structural representation of this clause complex is given in Figure 2.1. The lower lexical density of Text 3B again appears clearly as a function of the number of clauses. But the significant factor is not that this text consists of four clauses where Text 3A consists of only one. It is that Text 3B consists of a CLAUSE COMPLEX consisting of four clauses. The clauses are not strung together as one simple sentence after another;

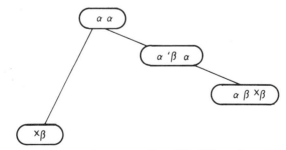

FIGURE 2.1. Structural representation of Text 3B as clause complex.

they are syntactically related. Looked at from the point of view of the sentence structure, it is the spoken text that appears more complex than the written one. The spoken text has a lower degree of lexical density, but a higher degree of grammatical intricacy.

Let us return to Text 1, in its original spoken form (Text 1A). This consisted of 13 clauses. However, these 13 clauses were not strung out end to end; they were constructed into a small number of clause complexes of mixed paratactic and hypotactic construction: arguably just one clause complex throughout. Here is its interpretation as one clause complex:

1 1	*I had to wait*
1 =2 α	*I had to wait*
1 2 ×β 1	*till it was born*
1 2 β +2	*and till it got to about eight or ten weeks of age*
×2 α	*then I bought my first dachshund, a black-and-tan bitch puppy*
2 ×β α	*as they told me*
2 β "β α α	*I should've bought a bitch puppy*
2 β β α ×β	*to start off with*
2 β β ×β α 1 α	*because . . .*
2 β β β ×β	*if she wasn't 100% good*
	. . . I could choose a top champion dog
2 β β β α 1 ×β	*to mate her to*
2 β β β α ×2 α	*and then produce something that was good*
2 β β β α 2 +β	*which would be in my own kennel prefix*

Sequences of this kind extend to a considerable length and depth in parataxis and hypotaxis. A typical pattern is one in which both these kinds of "taxis," or interdependency, occur, with frequent alternation both between the two and also among their various subcategories, as in the example here. The relationships between successive pairs of clauses in Text 1A are set out in Table 2.4.

Other examples from the same source but from different speakers show similar patterns; there are, obviously, individual differences (including perhaps in the preference for one or other type of interdependency), but the same free-flowing intricacy is noticeable all the time, as in Texts 4–6:

4 *Roy was always interested in dogs and unfortunately he'd never had the opportunity to have a dog of his own, just because of circumstances—where he lived and what not, and so I bought him a Shepherd pup, which was supposedly, you know, pure-bred Shepherd, but unfortunately people sold it because it didn't have papers with it, so it was a "pup."*

5 *Now how I got a German Shepherd was that I worked with a veterinary surgeon, as I've told you before, and there used to be a lady that brought her Shepherds along to the clinic and I used to admire them greatly, and she said, "Well," she said, "if you get married I'll give you one as a wedding present," so immediately I bustled around looking for someone to marry so I could get a Shepherd given to me for a wedding present, you see, so that's how that worked out—*

TABLE 2.4
Clause Complex Relationship in Text 1A

Clause number	Symbol	Type of interdependency	Logical–semantic relation	Marker
1–2	=2	parataxis	elaborating : repetitive	(tone concord)
2–3	ˣβ	hypotaxis	enhancing : temporal	*till*
3–4	+2	parataxis	extending : additive	*and*
4–5	ˣ2	parataxis	enhancing : temporal	*then*
5–6	ˣβ	hypotaxis	enhancing : causal	*as*
6–7	"β	hypotaxis	projecting : locution	—
7–8	ˣβ	hypotaxis	enhancing : purpose	*to*
8–9	ˣβ	hypotaxis	enhancing : causal	*because*
9–10	ˣβ	hypotaxis	enhancing : conditional	*if*
10–11	ˣβ	hypotaxis	enhancing : purpose	*to*
11–12	ˣ2	parataxis	enhancing : temporal	*and then*
12–13	+β	hypotaxis	extending : additive	*which*

well, not quite! However I got my Shepherd and he was my first dog, mainly because I was a youngster I always wanted a dog but I lived with grandparents who wouldn't have dogs or cats and I was a very frustrated animal lover at that stage of the game, so as soon as I got out on my own I sort of went completely berserk!

6 *So we rang up the breeder, and she sort of tried to describe the dog to us, which was very hard to do over the phone, so we went over to have a look to see what they were like, and we bought Sheba, because at that stage Bob was away a lot on semitrailers with the army and it used to get quite bad with the exercises—you'd have prowlers and perverts through the married quarters, so if we, you know, got a dog, which we could do because it didn't matter what sort of dog anyone had, it'd bark and they wouldn't bother us.*

Types of Complexity

Two distinct points need to be made here, and both of them run counter to received attitudes towards spoken language. One is that speech is not, in any general sense, "simpler" than writing; if anything, it is more complex. There are, of course, many different kinds of complexity, and we have already noted one measure—lexical density— whereby speech will appear as the simpler of the two. But the patterns we have been illustrating, which are the patterns of the organization of the clause complex, referred to above as *grammatical intricacy*, would seem to be at least as central to any conception of complexity; and in this respect, speech appears as the more complex. The "syntactic complexity expected in writing," with which Deborah Tannen (1982) introduces her discussion of oral and literate strategies, does not turn out to be a characteristic of written discourse.

Of course, there are many other variables. Some writers achieve considerable intricacy in the structure of the clause complex; it can be learnt and consciously developed as a style. Some forms of spoken discourse, on the other hand, militate against it: rapid-fire dialogue presents no scope for lengthy interdependencies—complex semantic patterns can be construed BETWEEN interactants, but usually without being realized in syntactic terms. And the categories of "written" and "spoken" are themselves highly indeterminate—they may refer to the medium in which a text was originally produced, or the medium for which it was intended, or in which it is performed in a particular instance; or not to the medium at all, but to other properties of a text which are seen as characteristic of the medium. So it is important to indicate specifically which variable of discourse is being referred to, when one variety is being said to display some distinctive characteristic.

My point here is to question the assumption that written language is syntactically more complex than spoken, and to suggest that, as far as one particular kind of syntactic complexity is concerned—the intricacy (I do not want to call it "structure" because that assumes a particular interpretation) of the sentence or "clause complex"—this is more a characteristic of the most unconscious spontaneous uses of language. The more natural, un-self-monitored the discourse, the more intricate the grammatical patterns that can be woven. Usually, this kind of discourse will be spoken, because writing is in essence a more conscious process than speaking. But there are self-conscious modes of speech, whose output resembles what we think of as written language, and there are relatively spontaneous kinds of writing; spoken and written discourse are the outward forms that are typically associated with the critical variable, which is that of consciousness. We can use the terms spoken and written LANGUAGE, to refer to the idealized types defined by that variable.

Spoken and written language, then, tend to display different KINDS of complexity; each of them is more complex in its own way. Written language tends to be lexically dense, but grammatically simple; spoken language tends to be grammatically intricate, but lexically sparse. But these *buts* should really be *ands*, because the paired properties are complementary, not counterexpectative. It is hard to find a form of expression which will show them to be such; I have usually had recourse to metaphors of structure versus movement, saying for example that the complexity of written language is crystalline, whereas the complexity of spoken language is choreographic. The complexity of spoken language is in its flow, the dynamic mobility whereby each figure provides a context for the next one, not only defining its point of departure but also setting the conventions by reference to which it is to be interpreted.

With the sentence of written language, there is solidarity among its parts such that each equally prehends and is prehended by all the others. It is a structure, and is not essentially violated by being represented synoptically, as a structural unit. With the clause complex, of spoken language, there is no such solidarity, no mutual prehension among all its parts. Its mode of being is as process, not as product. But since the study of grammar grew out of writing—it is when language comes to be written down that it becomes an object of study, not before—our grammars are grammars of the written language. We have not yet learnt to write choreographic grammars; so we look at spoken language through the lens of a grammar designed for writing. Spoken discourse thus appears as a distorted variant of written discourse, and not unnaturally it is found wanting.

For example, Chafe (1982) identifies a number of regular differences between speech and writing; writing is marked by more nominalization, more genitive subjects and objects, more participles, more attributive adjectives, more conjoined, serial and sequenced phrases, more complement clauses, and more relative clauses; all of which he summarizes by saying, "Written language tends to have an 'integrated' quality which contrasts with the fragmented quality of spoken language" (p. 38).

The general picture is that of written language as richly endowed, while speech is a poor man's assemblage of shreds and patches. But Chafe has described both speech and writing using a grammar of writing; so it is inevitable that writing comes out with positive checks all round. Not that he has no pluses on the spoken side: speech is said to have more first person references, more speaker mental processes, more *I mean*s and *you know*s, more emphatic particles, more vagueness like *sort of*, and more direct quotes—all the outward signs of language as interpersonal action. Chafe summarizes them as features of "involvement" as opposed to "detachment"; but they are items of low generality, and negative rather than positive in their social value.

This leads me to the second point that, as I remarked above, runs counter to our received attitudes towards speech. It is not only that speech allows for such a considerable degree of intricacy; when speakers exploit this potential, they seem very rarely to flounder or get lost in it. In the great majority of instances, expectations are met, dependencies resolved, and there are no loose ends. The intricacy of the spoken language is matched by the orderliness of spoken discourse.

THE MYTH OF STRUCTURELESS SPEECH

Why then are we led to believe that spoken discourse is a disorganized array of featureless fragments? Here it is not just the lack of an interpretative grammar for spoken language, but the convention of observing spoken discourse that we need to take into account.

Speech, we are told, is marked by hesitations, false starts, anacolutha, slips and trips of the tongue, and a formidable paraphernalia of so-called performance errors; these are regularly, more or less ritually, cited as its main distinguishing feature. There is no disputing the fact that these things occur, although they are much less prevalent than we are asked to believe. They are characteristic of the rather self-conscious, closely self-monitored speech that goes, for example, with academic seminars, where I suspect much of the observation and recording has taken place. If you are consciously planning your speech as it goes along and listening to check the outcome, then you naturally tend to lose your way: to hesitate, back up, cross out, and stumble over the words. But these things are not a particular feature of natural spontaneous discourse, which tends to be fluent, highly organized and grammatically well formed. If you are interacting spontaneously and without self-consciousness, then the clause complexes tend to flow smoothly without you falling down or changing direction in the middle, and neither speaker nor listener is at all aware of what is happening. I recorded this kind of casual discourse many years ago when studying the language spoken to and in the presence of a small child, and was struck by its fluency, well formedness, and richness of grammatical pattern. Interestingly, the same feature is apparent at the phonological level: spontaneous discourse is typically more regular in its patterns of rhythm.

However, while the myth of the scrappiness of speech may have arisen at the start from the kind of discourse that was first recorded, it has been perpetuated in a different way—by the conventions with which it is presented and discussed. Consider, for example, Beattie (1983, p. 33):

> Spontaneous speech is unlike written text. It contains many mistakes, sentences are usually brief and indeed the whole fabric of verbal expression is riddled with hesitations and silences. To take a very simple example: in a seminar which I recorded, an articulate (and well-known) linguist was attempting to say the following:
>
> No, I'm coming back to the judgements question. Indeterminacy appears to be rife. I don't think it is, if one sorts out which are counterexamples to judgement.
>
> But what he actually said was:

No *I'm saying* I'm coming back to the judgements question (267) *you know there appear to* (200) *ah* indeterminacy (1467) appears to be rife. I don't think it is (200) *if one* (267) if one sorts out which one counterexamples (267) to judgement, I mean observing.

Here, the brief silences (unfilled pauses) have been measured in milliseconds and marked (these are numbers in brackets) and all other types of hesitation—false starts, repetitions, filled pauses and parenthetic remarks put in italics. It is these hesitations (both filled and unfilled) which dominate spontaneous speech and give it its distinctive structure and feeling.

In other words: when you speak, you cannot destroy your earlier drafts. If we were to represent written language in a way that is comparable to such representations of spoken language, we should be including in the text every preliminary scrap of manuscript or typescript, with all the crossings out, misspellings, redraftings and periods of silent thought; this would then tell us what the writer actually wrote. Figure 2.2 is a specimen.

Now, there are undoubtedly research purposes for which it is important to show the planning, trial and error, and revision work that has gone into the production of a piece of discourse: it can have both educational and clinical applications. This is as true of writing as it is of speech: written material of this kind has been used in neuropsychiatry for most of a century. But for many purposes the discarded first attempts are merely trivial; they clutter up the text, making it hard to read, and impart to it a spurious air of quaintness. What is much more serious, however, is that transcribing spoken discourse in this way gives a false account of what it is really like. It may seem a harmless piece of self-gratification for a few academics to present spoken language as a pathological phenomenon; one might argue that they deceive nobody but themselves. But unfortunately this is not the way. Just when we are seeing real collaboration between linguists and educators, and the conception of "language in education" is at last gaining ground as a field of training and research, it seems we are determined to put the clock back to a time when spoken language was not to be taken seriously and could have no place in the theory and practice of education.

Let us recapitulate the argument. Speech and writing as forms of discourse are typically associated with the two modal points on the continuum from most spontaneous to most self-monitored language: spontaneous discourse is usually spoken, self-monitored discourse is usually written. We can therefore conveniently label these two modal points "spoken" and "written" language. Spoken and written language do not differ in their systematicity: each is equally highly organized,

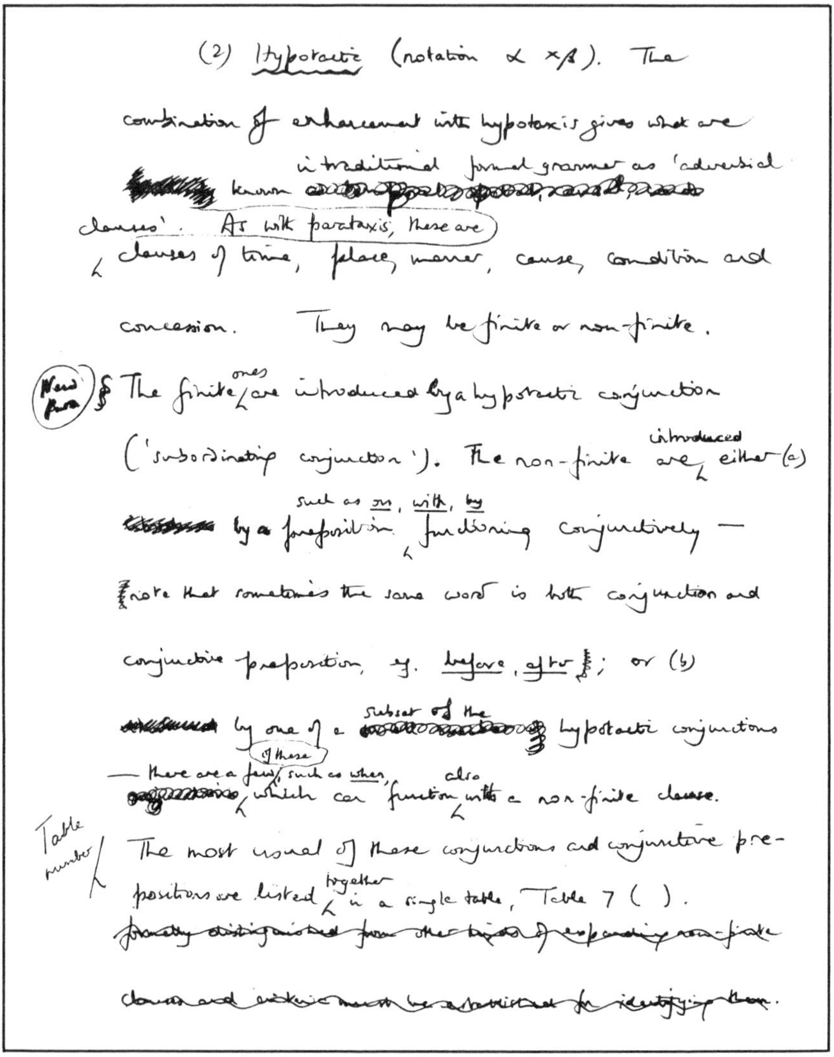

FIGURE 2.2   Written discourse.

regular, and productive of coherent discourse. (This is clearly implied once we recognize them both as "language.")

Discourse in either medium can be characterized by hesitation, revision, change of direction, and other similar features; these tend to arise when attention is being paid to the process of text production. Since highly monitored discourse is typically written, these features are actu-

ally more characteristic of writing than of speech; but because most
written text becomes public only in its final, edited form, the hesitations
and discards are lost and the reader is shielded from seeing the process
at work. Where they are likely to remain in is precisely where they occur
least, in the more spontaneous kinds of writing such as personal letters.
(Not all discourse features that are regarded as pathological, or assigned
negative value, are of this self-monitoring kind. One form of discourse
that has received a lot of critical attention is casual conversation, where
the well-recognized characteristics are those of turn-taking, such as in-
terruptions and overlaps. But the strictly LINGUISTIC "deviations" of
casual conversation are mainly systematic features that would not seem
deviant if we had a grammar that took into account the specifically
"spoken" resources of the linguistic system.)

Spoken and written language do differ, however, in their preferred
patterns of lexicogrammatical organization. Neither is more organized
than the other, but they are organized in different ways. We have already identified the principal variable. Spoken language tends to accommodate more clauses in the syntagm (to favour greater "grammatical
intricacy"), with fewer lexical items in the clause. Written language
tends to accommodate more lexical items in the clause (to favour greater
"lexical density"), with fewer clauses in the syntagm. (This does not
imply, of course, that the AVERAGE number of clauses per clause complex
will be greater in spoken language, because there may also be a tendency towards very short ones, especially in dialogue. It would be better
to say that the greater the intricacy of a clause complex the more likely it
is to be a product of spontaneous speech.) We must now return to this
distinction in order to look through and beyond it.

A CLOSER LOOK AT THE DIFFERENCE

Let us illustrate with another passage of written discourse (Text 7):

7   *Thus the sympathetic induction of people into a proper and deep understanding of what*
     Christianity is about should not be bracketed simply with the evangelizing aim to which I
     referred earlier. It is not absolutely incompatible with that aim, however, for the following
     reason. What counts as indoctrination and the like depends upon a number of criteria, to do
     with the degree to which a teacher fails to mention alternative beliefs, the tone of voice used, the
     lack of sympathy for the criticisms levelled at Christianity or Humanism and so on. A dogmatic
     teacher or lecturer differs from an open one. The non-dogmatic teacher may be tepid; the open
     one may be fervent. Fervour and indifference are not functions of closedness and openness.
     (Smart, 1968, p. 98)

This has the high lexical density that is typical of written language: 52
lexical items, 8 clauses, density 6.5 (ignoring embedded clauses; if em-

bedded clauses are counted, then 66 lexical items, 19 clauses, density 4.7). Let us make this explicit by setting it out clause by clause:

> clause complex boundary |||
> clause boundary ||
> embedded clause   [ ]
> lexical items shown in **boldface**

||| *Thus the* **sympathetic induction** *of people into a* **proper** *and* **deep understanding** *of* [*what* **Christianity** *is about* | *should not be* **bracketed simply** *with the* **evangelizing aim** [*to which I* **referred earlier**| · ||| *It is not absolutely* **incompatible** *with that* **aim,** *however, for the* **following reason.** ||| [*What* **counts** *as* **indoctrination** *and the like* | **depends** *upon a number of* **criteria,** || *to* **do** *with the* **degree** [*to which a* **teacher fails** *to* **mention alternative beliefs** |, *the* **tone** *of* **voice** [**used** |, *the* **lack** *of* **sympathy** *for the* **criticism** [**levelled** *at* **Christianity** *or* **Humanism** | *and so on.* ||| *A* **dogmatic teacher** *or* **lecturer differs** *from an* **open** *one.* ||| *The* **non-dogmatic** *teacher may be* **tepid;** || *the* **open** *one may be* **fervent.** ||| **Fervour** *and* **indifference** *are not* **functions** *of* **closedness** *and* **openness.** |||

To see how this lexical density is achieved, we can look at the first clause. After the cohesive *thus*, it begins with a nominal group *the sympathetic induction of people into a proper and deep understanding of what Christianity is about*. The Head is *induction;* the Postmodifier consists of a series of alternating embedded prepositional phrases and nominal groups, mainly one inside the other, and ending with an embedded clause:

> | *the sympathetic induction* [*of* [*people*]] [*into* [*a proper and deep understanding* [*of* [[*what*] ⟨*Christianity* | *is*⟩ *about* |]]] |
> group or phrase boundary |
> embedded group or phrase   [ ]
> enclosed elements   ⟨ ⟩
> (the prepositional phrase *what . . . about* is discontinuous, the items *Christianity* and *is* being enclosed within it)

This nominal group contains a large amount of lexical information; and if we take this passage as a whole we find that out of the 52 lexical items the only ones that do NOT occur in nominal groups are *bracketed, simply, depends, do,* and *differ*. It is a characteristic of written discourse that most of the lexical information is encoded in nominal form: that is, in nominal groups, with their structure potential of Head (typically a noun or adjective), Premodifier (typically adjectives and nouns), and Postmodifier (typically embedded phrases and clauses, which then have further nominal groups inside them).

Not every instance of a nominal group has a complex structure, of course; the remaining ones in this passage range from

| *the lack* [*of* [*sympathy* [*for* [*the criticisms* ‖ *levelled* | *at* [*Christianity or Humanism*] ‖]]]] |

which like the first one involves considerable embedding, to simple nominal groups such as *tepid, the open one, fervour and indifference*. But it is the potential for extended structures of this kind which enables the nominal group to take over the main burden of the lexical content of the discourse.

So while spoken English is marked by intricacy in the clause complex, written English is marked by complexity in the nominal group. Since the lexical items have to go somewhere, lexical density is accompanied by its own characteristic resources within the grammar. The key factor is the structure of the nominal group; and within that, the critical resource is that of embedding, because of its open-endedness—the recursive function which generates sequences like

implicit [*in* [*the argument* [*about* [*the necessity* [*of* [*the parahistorical approach* [*to* [*religious studies*]]]]]]]] (Smart, 1968, p. 98)

If now we construct a more "spoken" variant of one of the long nominal groups taken from Text 7, we might arrive at something like the following:

‖   *people can be sympathetically persuaded* α
‖   *so that they understand properly and deeply* $^{\times}\beta\alpha$
‖   *what Christianity is about*   ‖ $\beta'\beta$

where the structure is α $^{\times}\beta\alpha$ $\beta'\beta$. In place of the embedding, which is a nominalizing device, we have hypotaxis, which is a form of interdependency between clauses; and this points up the difference between the two variants.

This difference is obscured, on the other hand, if the grammar fails to distinguish between embedding and **hypotaxis**. Traditional grammar lumped them together, under the heading of subordination, and treated them both as **embedding** (noun clause, adjectival clause, adverbial clause). In other words, being a grammar of written language, it recognized only the category that was characteristic of written language. This ambiguity is in fact still present in the concept of embedding, which is why I have often employed the term **rank shift** to refer just to embedding in the strict sense, and so distinguish it from the interdependency relation of hypotaxis, where one element is dependent on another but is not a constituent of it. Hypotaxis is more like parataxis than it is like embedding; and both are characteristic of spoken rather than written language. So in order to do justice to the particular mode of organization of both spoken and written discourse, the grammar needs to distinguish between the constituency relation of embedding, or rank shift, where one element is a structural part of another, and the dependency relation of "taxis," where one element is bound or linked to another but is not a part of it. Either of these relations can be reduced to a form of the other one, but only at the cost of distorting the nature of discourse.

The distinction between embedding and hypotaxis—between, for example, *the conviction* [*that he failed*] / [*of failure*] and *was convinced* ‖ *that he had failed;* or between *the effect* [*of such a decision*] *would be* [*that no further launchings could take place*] and *if they decide that way* ‖ *no further . . .*—is an important one; but it is really an instance, and a symptom, of a more general and fundamental divergence. As always, when we talk about these phenomena, and when we illustrate them, they will appear as dichotomies: either this way or that. As always, however, at least in the present context (but also in most issues that have to do with language), they must be seen as tendencies—more or less continuous variation along a line, but with most actual instances (most texts, in this case) tending towards one pole or the other. The divergent tendency that is manifested in the distinction of hypotaxis and embedding is one that can be expressed in terms of the familiar opposition of process and product. Written language represents phenomena as if they were products. Spoken language represents phenomena as if they were processes (see the discussion in Martin, 1984).

In other words: speaking and writing—each one makes the world look like itself. A written text is an object; so what is represented in writing tends to be given the form of an object. But when one talks, one is doing; so when one talks about something, one tends to say that it happened or was done. So, in Text 3 above, the written variant tells the story in nouns: *visit, sense, risk, attempt, action;* whereas the spoken version tells it in verbs: *visited, ended up feeling, might get hurt, tried to do.*

This is to look at it from the point of view of the writer or speaker. For reader or listener, there is a corresponding difference in the way the discourse is received. To the reader, the text is presented synoptically: it exists, spread out on the page. So the reader is predisposed to take a synoptic view of what it means; behind it is a tableau—like the pictures from which writing originally evolved. But when one is listening, the text reaches one dynamically: it happens, by travelling through the air. So the listener is predisposed to take a dynamic view of what it means; behind it is a film, not a picture.

GRAMMATICAL METAPHOR

Where then in the linguistic system do spoken and written discourse diverge? A language, if it is not written down, consists of three interrelated subsystems: a semantic system (meanings), coded into a lexicogrammatical system (wordings), recoded into a phonological system (sounds). A language that has a writing system has an alternative form of expression: visual symbols as well as sounds. In such a language, a written text could, in principle, be a spoken text that has been written down ("transcribed"); here the written version is a transcoding of something that has already been coded in sound. Most writing is not like this. Secondly, a written text could be an alternative EXPRESSION of a given wording: in this case meanings are coded as words and structures ("wordings"), which are then expressed EITHER in sound OR in writing. If this was the norm, there would be no systematic difference between spoken and written texts; the medium would not be a significant register variable. But there are such differences; so, to some extent at least, spoken and written discourse must represent alternative WORDINGS. In this case, meanings are coded either as "speakable wordings" or as "writeable wordings," the former appropriate to the dynamic nature of the text process, the latter appropriate to the synoptic nature of the text product. This is the sort of interpretation we have been offering.

But is it the whole story? There is still a fourth possibility—that speech and writing can diverge already at the semantic level, so that spoken and written discourse embody different meanings. Is there any sign that this can happen? It would of course be only a very partial effect; no one has suggested that the two derive from different semantic systems (or even two different lexicogrammatical systems, for that matter). But we should consider the possibility that there is some flowback into the meaning.

Consider the last sentence of Text 2, in its original written form (2A):

> The current popular concern over the environment has stimulated private civil actions of two main types.

We "translated" it into something more speechlike as:

> At present, people are concerned about the environment; so they have been bringing quite a few private civil actions, which have been mainly of two kinds.

But this could be wrong; it may have meant:

> At present, people are concerned about the environment; so there have been mainly two kinds of action being brought by private citizens.

There is no way of deciding: BY REFERENCE TO THE SPOKEN VERSION, the written version is simply ambiguous. Compare the following, also from a written text:

A further complication was the 650-ton creeper cranes poised above the end of each 825-foot arm.

Does this mean

Above the end of each 825-foot arm there were poised 650-ton creeper cranes, and they made the work more complicated.

or does it mean

. . . and this made the work more complicated.

(i.e., not the cranes, but the fact that they were poised where they were)? Another example is

Slavish imitation of models is nowhere implied.

This could be reworded either as *it is nowhere implied that models have been slavishly imitated,* or as *. . . that models should be slavishly imitated.*

Examples of this kind could be added to indefinitely; they arise because nominal constructions fail to make explicit many of the semantic relations that are made explicit in clause structure. Written discourse conceals many local ambiguities of this kind, which are revealed when one attempts a more "spoken" paraphrase.

But the final sentence of Text 2 illustrates another significant feature of written language, which can be seen in the wording *popular concern over the environment has stimulated private civil actions.* We reworded this as *people are concerned about the environment, so they have been bringing private civil actions.* The original is one clause with the verb *stimulate* representing the Process; in other words, the thesis is encoded as a single happening, and what happened was that A brought about B. But A and B are themselves nominalized processes. The meaning of *stimulate* here is as in *pruning stimulates growth.* The spoken version represents the thesis as two distinct processes, linked by a relation of cause; cf. *if the tree is pruned, it will grow.*

Here one kind of process has been dressed up by the grammar to look like a process of a different kind—or, in this instance, two processes, one mental and one material, have been dressed up as one which is neither. This coding of a semantic relation BETWEEN two processes as if it was THE single process is very common in writing; the sentence immediately preceding Text 2A contained another example of the same thing, here with the verb *leads to:*

A successful tort action leads to a judgment of damages or an injunction against the defendant company.

But this is just one type of a more general phenomenon, something that I call **grammatical metaphor** (Halliday, 1985, chap. 10). Written language tends to display a high degree of grammatical metaphor, and this is perhaps its single most distinctive characteristic.

Here are three further examples of grammatical metaphor taken from various written sources, together with suggested rewordings which are less metaphorical:

Issue of the specially-coded credit cards will be subject to normal credit checking procedures.

> *'Credit cards have been specially coded and will be issued only when credit has been checked in the normal way.'*

Strong Christmas sales were vital to the health of the retail industry, particularly in the present depressed climate.

> *'Unless many goods were sold at Christmas the retail industry would not be healthy, particularly when the economy is depressed as it is now.'*

He also credits his former big size with much of his career success.

> *'He also believes that he was successful in his career mainly because he used to be big.'*

In all these examples **nominalization** plays a significant part, as it does in many types of grammatical metaphor; so it is perhaps worth stressing that nominalization is well motivated in English. It is not simply a ritual feature that has evolved to make written language more ambiguous or obscure; like the passive, which is another feature whose functions are widely misunderstood, nominalization is an important resource for organizing information. Take the example *youth protest mounted*, which is not a headline but a complete sentence from a feature article. We might reword this as *more and more young people protested*, or *young people protested more and more*; but the only way to get the combination of *youth* and *protest* as the Theme of the clause is by means of a nominalization (not necessarily such a laconic one; it might have been *the protests of the young people*, but this is still a nominalizing of the process). So while there is a price to be paid, in that the information being conveyed may become mildly (and sometimes severely) ambiguous, there is also a payoff: more choice of status in the discourse. In terms of systemic theory, there is a loss of ideational information, but a gain in textual information. This of course favours the specialist: you need to know the register. If you do not know the register you may misinterpret the thesis, so the fact that it is highly coded as a message is not very helpful to you; but if you do know it you will select the right interpretation automatically, and the additional "functional sentence perspective" is all tax-free profit.

Some nominalizations of course cannot be denominalized, like *private civil actions at law* or *an injunction against the defendant company*. These are abstractions that can enter into the structure of a clause—civil actions can be brought, an injunction can be issued—but cannot themselves be coded as finite verbs. Much of our environment today consists of such abstract entities and institutions; their representation in nominal form is no longer metaphorical—if it ever was—and they have become part of our ideology, our way of knowing about the world we live in. Patterns of this kind invade the spoken language and then act as infiltrators, providing cover for other metaphorical nominalizations—which are still functional in speech, but considerably less so, because spoken language has other resources for structuring the message, such as intonation and rhythm.

Grammatical metaphor is not confined to written language: quite apart from its tendency to be borrowed from speech into writing, there are specific instances of it which seem clearly to have originated in speech—most notably the pattern of lexically empty verb with the process expressed as "cognate object" (Range) as in *make a mistake* 'err', *have a bath* 'bathe', *give a smile* 'smile'. But in its principal manifestations it is typically a feature of writing. Writing—that is, using the written medium—puts distance between the act of meaning and its counterpart in the real world; so writing—that is, the written language—achieves this distance symbolically by the use of grammatical metaphor. It is often said that written discourse is not dependent on its environment; but it would be more accurate to say that it creates an environment for itself (see Nystrand, this volume), and this is where it depends on its metaphorical quality. If I say *technology has improved*, this is presented as a message; it is part of what I am telling you. If I say *improvements in technology*, I present it as something I expect you to take for granted. By objectifying it, treating it as if it was a thing, I have backgrounded it; the message is contained in what follows (e.g., . . . *are speeding up the writing of business programmes*). Grammatical metaphor performs for the written language a function that is the opposite of foregrounding; it backgrounds, using discourse to create the context for itself. This is why in the world of writing it often happens that all the ideational content is objectified, as background, and the only traces of process are the relations that are set up between these taken-for-granted objects. I recall a sentence from the O.S.T.I. Programme in the Linguistic Properties of Scientific English (Huddleston, Hudson, Winter, & Henrici, 1968) which used to typify for us the structures found in scientific writing:

> The conversion of hydrogen to helium in the interiors of stars is the source of energy for their immense output of light and heat.

WAYS OF KNOWING AND LEARNING

In calling the written mode metaphorical we are of course making an assumption; in fact each mode is metaphorical from the standpoint of the other, and the fact that the spoken is developmentally prior—the individual listens and speaks before he reads and writes—while it means that the language of "process" is LEARNT first, does not guarantee that it is in any sense "closer to reality." It might be a hangover from an earlier stage of evolution, like the protolanguage that precedes the mother tongue. But personally I do not think so. I am inclined to think the written language of the future will go back (or rather forward) to being more processlike; not only because the traditional objectlike nature of written discourse is itself changing—our reading matter is typed into a memory and fed to us in a continuous flow as the lines follow each other up the screen—but also because our understanding of the physical world has been moving in that direction, ever since Einstein substituted space-time for space and time. As Bertrand Russell expounded it in 1925 (1977, p. 54),

> We are concerned with *events*, rather than with *bodies*. In the old theory, it was possible to consider a number of bodies all at the same instant, and since the time was the same for all of them it could be ignored. But now we cannot do that if we are to obtain an objective account of physical occurrences. We must mention the date at which a body is to be considered, and thus we arrive at an *'event'*, that is to say, something which happens at a given time.

Meanwhile, grammatical analysis shows spoken and written English to be systematically distinct: distinct, that is, in respect of a number of related tendencies, all of which combine to form a single package. But it turns out to be a semantic package: the different features that combine to distinguish spoken and written discourse can be shown to be related and encompassed within a single generalization, only when we express this generalization in semantic terms—or at least in terms of a functional, meaning-oriented interpretation of grammar. Speech and writing will appear, then, as different ways of meaning: speech as spun out, flowing, choreographic, oriented towards events (doing, happening, sensing, saying, being), processlike, intricate, with meanings related serially; writing as dense, structured, crystalline, oriented towards things (entities, objectified processes), productlike, tight, with meanings related as components.

In their discussion of the comprehension and memory of discourse, Hildyard and Olson (1982, p. 20) suggested that meaning is PRESERVED in different ways by speakers and listeners:

> Readers and listeners may tend to extract different kinds of information from oral and written statements. Listeners may tend to recall more of the gist of the story and readers may recall more of the surface structure or verbatim features of the story.

In other words, the listener processes text largely at the level of meaning, the reader more, or at least as much, at the level of wording. But this is specifically a function of the medium in which the text is received, rather than of the linguistic features of the code that lies behind it. The notion of different ways of meaning implies, rather, that there are different ways of knowing, and of learning. Spoken and written language serve as complementary resources for acquiring and organizing knowledge; hence they have different places in the educational process. Teachers often know, by a combination of intuition and experience, that some things are more effectively learnt through talk and others through writing. Official policy usually equates educational knowledge with the written mode and commonsense knowledge with the spoken; but teachers' actual practice goes deeper—educational knowledge demands both, the two often relating to different aspects of the same phenomenon. For example: definitions, and structural relations, are probably best presented in writing; demonstrations of how things work may be more easily followed through speech. The two favourite strategies for describing the layout of an apartment, reported in the well-known study by Linde and Labov (1975), would seem to exemplify spoken and written modes of symbolic exploration. We may assume that speech and writing play different and complementary parts in the construction of ideologies (Hasan, 1986), since each offers a different way of knowing and of reflecting on experience.

Considerations of this kind are an essential element in any linguistic theory of learning. The development of such a theory is perhaps the most urgent task of educational linguistics; and certain components of it can already be recognized: (1) the child's construction of language, from presymbolic communication through protolanguage to the mother tongue; (2) the processing of new meanings into the system; (3) the interaction between learning elements that are ready coded and learning the principles of coding; (4) the relation between system and process in language; (5) the unconscious nature of linguistic categories; (6) the social construction of reality through conversation; (7) linguistic strategies used in learning; (8) the development of functional variation, or registers; (9) the relation between everyday language and technical language; and (10) the development of generalization, abstraction, and metaphor. The absence of any general theory of learning based on language has been a significant gap in educational thinking and practice. This provides an important context for our current concern, since the complementarity of spoken and written language will certainly be a central issue in any learning theory which has language as its primary focus.

REFERENCES

Abercrombie, D. (1963). Conversation and spoken prose. *English Language Teaching, 18*(1). (Reprinted in *Studies in phonetics and linguistics* (Language & Language Learning, Vol. 10, pp. 1–9). London: Oxford University Press, 1965.)

Beattie, G. (1983). *Talk: An analysis of speech and non-verbal behaviour in conversation.* Milton Keynes: Open University Press.

Boas, F. (1911). *Introduction to the Handbook of American Indian Languages (Bulletin of the Bureau of American Ethnology,* Vol. 40, No. 1). Washington, DC: Smithsonian Institution. (Reprinted with Foreword by C. I. J. M. Stuart. Washington DC: Georgetown University Press, 1963.)

Chafe, W. L. (1982). Integration and involvement in speaking, writing and oral literature. In D. Tannen (Ed.), *Spoken and written language: Exploring orality and literacy* (Advances in Discourse Processes, Vol. IX, pp. 35–54). Norwood, NJ: Ablex.

Doughty, P. S., Pearce, J. J., & Thornton, G. M. (1971). *Language in use.* London: Arnold (for the Schools Council).

Halliday, M. A. K. (1985). *Introduction to functional grammar.* London: Arnold.

Hasan, R. (1986). The ontogenesis of ideology: an interpretation of mother child talk. In T. Threadgold *et al.* (Eds.), *Semiotics, ideology, language* (Sydney Studies in Society and Culture, Vol. 3, pp. 125–146). Sydney: Sydney Association for Studies in Society and Culture.

Hildyard, A. & Olson, D. R. (1982). On the comprehension and memory of oral vs. written discourse. In D. Tannen (Ed.), *Spoken and written language: Exploring orality and literacy* (Advances in Discourse Processes, Vol. IX, pp. 19–34). Norwood, NJ: Ablex.

Huddleston, R. D., Hudson, R. A., Winter, E. O., & Henrici, A. (1968). *Sentence and clause in scientific English* (O.S.T.I. Programme in the Linguistic Properties of Scientific English, Final Report). London University College, Communication Research Centre.

Hymes, D. H. (1971). Competence and performance in linguistic theory. In R. Huxley & E. Ingram (Eds.), *Language acquisition: Models and methods.* London & New York: Academic Press.

Linde, C. & Labov, W. (1975). Spatial networks as a site for the study of language and thought. *Language, 51,* 924–939.

Mackay, D., Thompson, B., & Schaub, P. (1970). *Breakthrough to literacy.* London: Longman (for the Schools Council).

Martin, J. R. (1984). Process and text: two aspects of human semiosis. In J. D. Benson & W. S. Greaves (Eds.), *Systemic perspectives on discourse: Selected theoretical papers from the Ninth International Systemic Workshop.* Norwood, NJ: Ablex.

Mathesius, V. (1911). O potenciálnosti jevů jazykových [On the potentiality of the phenomena of language]. *Proceedings of the Czech Academy of Sciences, Philosophy and History Section.* (English trans. in J. Vachek (Ed.), *A Prague school reader in linguistics* (pp. 1–32). Bloomington, IN: Indiana University Press, 1964.)

Russell, B. (1925). *ABC of relativity.* London: Allen & Unwin. (3rd rev. ed., F. Pirani (Ed.), 1977.)

Smart, N. (1968). *Secular education and the logic of religion.* London: Faber & Faber.

Tannen, D. (1982). Oral and literate strategies in spoken and written narrative. *Language, 58,* 1–21.

Ure, J. N. (1971). Lexical density and register differentiation. In G. E. Perren & J. L. M. Trim (Eds.), *Applications of linguistics: Selected papers of the Second World Congress of Applied Linguistics, Cambridge, 1969* (pp. 443–452). London: Cambridge University Press.

Wilkinson, A. M. (Ed.) (1966). *Some aspects of oracy.* London: National Association for the Teaching of English.

Chapter 3

Properties of Spoken
and Written Language

Wallace Chafe
Jane Danielewicz

INTRODUCTION

There can be no doubt that people write differently from the way they speak. Current interest in the nature of the differences between "orality" and "literacy" was stimulated by Jack Goody and Ian Watt (1968), who combined the insights of an anthropologist and a literary scholar to give us a perspective on the consequences of literacy. In linguistics, Josef Vachek (1973) brought together the results of his and the Prague School's pioneering concern for the special nature and importance of written language. In educational psychology, David Olson (1977) explored the consequences of the essayist tradition in writing. These classic writings, and a number of other works which have been appearing with increasing frequency, have signaled the end to a period in which the systematic study of language was dominated by Leonard Bloomfield's dictum to the effect that "writing is not language, but merely a way of recording language by means of visible marks" (Bloomfield, 1933, p. 21).

The range of viewpoints and findings has continued to expand. A brief but representative cross-section of recent works might include the volumes written or edited by Kroll and Vann (1981), Scribner and Cole (1981), Tannen (1982a), and Ong (1982). Volumes like these show a concern for a range of topics which includes the kinds of language that are produced in speaking and writing, the cognitive and social reasons why spoken and written language may differ, the uses people make of

COMPREHENDING ORAL AND WRITTEN LANGUAGE

speaking and writing, and the different effects spoken and written language may have on the way people think. Our own earlier work (Chafe,
1982, 1985, 1986) tried to identify more precisely the differences to be
found in the kinds of language which are used by speakers and writers,
and we speculated on underlying causes for those differences. These
earlier reports of ours were restricted to a comparison of what we sup-
posed were two extremes of "spokenness" and "writtenness": conversational speaking at the one extreme and academic writing at the other.

It has always been clear, however, that neither spoken language nor
written language is a unified phenomenon. Far from there being one
single kind of language that people speak and one other kind that they
write, each of these two modes itself allows a multiplicity of styles. But,
beyond that, there is a great deal of overlap between speaking and
writing, in the sense that some kinds of spoken language may be very
writtenlike, and some kinds of written language very spokenlike (Tannen, 1982b). In examining varied samples of spoken and written language, one may even be led to wonder whether that distinction makes
any sense at all, or whether there are just many varieties of a language
which are available to its speakers, most or all of which varieties may be
either spoken or written depending on the circumstances.

Certainly there are a number of factors responsible for differences in
the kinds of language a person may use. And certainly one of these
factors is the matter of whether the language is produced with the
mouth and received with the ear, or whether it is produced with the
hand and received with the eye. We look here at some of the differences
in language which seem to have much to do with that difference in how
it is produced and received. At the same time we look at how some of
the uses to which language is put interact with the spoken–written
distinction. The context of language use, the purpose of the speaker or
writer, the subject matter of what is being said or written—these are
some of the other factors which influence the form language takes. It is
instructive to notice that the many languages which have never been
written at all also exhibit different styles—sometimes radically different
styles—which are used for different purposes (see in this connection
Chafe, 1981). Writing increases the ways in which language can be used
and adds significantly to the linguistic repertoire. But of course aspects
of written style may be borrowed by speakers when it suits them, just as
aspects of spoken style may be borrowed by writers. In what follows we
take particular note of the varying proportions of linguistic features
which surface as both spoken and written language are used in different
circumstances.

Our observations come from a project in which we collected four
kinds of language from each of 20 adults.[1] All of them were either

professors or graduate students at the University of California at Berkeley or the State University of New York at Albany. Our reason for investigating styles of language among this very specialized population was that we wanted to compare four specific kinds of language that are produced in the course of a person's normal activities. Academic people happen to produce these four kinds quite naturally. We refer to the four as conversations, lectures, letters, and academic papers.

The conversational samples were taken from tape recordings of casual talk which took place during, immediately preceding, or immediately following an informal dinner in one of our homes. Each subject was invited separately to a dinner, with the understanding that the conversation was to be tape-recorded. From each of the resulting several hours of taped conversation, we selected a portion consisting of at least 100 "intonation units" produced by that subject. An intonation unit can be thought of for the moment as a single clause, but its nature is discussed more fully below. We selected a portion of the tape during which the speaker in whom we were interested did most of the talking. As a result, most of the samples consist of one or more narratives of personal experiences. We transcribed these portions, recording not only the words uttered but also disfluencies, laughter, and, in a minimal way, intonation. We then proceeded to code these samples for the features which are discussed below.

The lecture samples were taken from tape recordings of these same professors or graduate students speaking to classes—in all cases small classes addressed under relatively informal circumstances. That is, we did not record formal lectures presented to large audiences. Again we selected at least 100 intonation units from each recorded sample, trying to choose a portion that was representative of the subject's lecturing style. We transcribed and coded these samples in the same manner as the others.

The samples of letters consisted of informal letters written by the same professors or graduate students to relatives, friends, or colleagues. In the end we found these materials to be somewhat less satisfying than the other three types, for several reasons. They were harder to obtain in the first place, since the subjects differed in their eagerness and ability to provide us with letters, and those who habitually do most of their informal communicating by telephone simply found it hard to come up with any. The samples also tended to be shorter than those of the other types, some of them consisting of fewer than 100 units. They also differed considerably in tone and purpose, and were in general less homogeneous than the other kinds of language we collected. In spite of these reservations, we believe that the letters represent a reasonable sample of the informal letter-writing style of academic people. We recopied each letter, dividing it into intonation units according to punctuation (discussed later), and coded it as we did the other materials.

Finally, the academic writing samples were excerpts from articles that had been written for academic journals or books. They were usually volunteered by their authors as representative of their academic writing styles. We selected portions of at least 100 intonation units each and processed them in the same manner as the other three kinds of language.

We found, not surprisingly, that these four styles of language—two of them spoken and two of them written—were quite different from each other. Some of the differences appeared to be caused only by the fact that the language was spoken or written. More often, there were additional factors of language use which interacted with the spoken–written distinction.

We begin by focusing on how speakers and writers choose words and phrases appropriate to what they want to say. The relevant point here is that speakers must make such choices very quickly, whereas writers have time to deliberate and even to revise their choices when they are not satisfied. As a result, written language, no matter what its purpose or subject matter, tends to have a more varied vocabulary than spoken. Another aspect of lexical choice is the style of the vocabulary items selected, the degree to which words and phrases are colloquial or literary. Here it is easily possible for lecturers to borrow from literary vocabulary, and for letter writers to colloquialize their product by drawing on the vocabulary of spoken language. The division between spoken and written language is therefore not as sharp in this respect, since the operative constraints are not associated with an inevitable factor such as speed of processing, but involve stylistic decisions which are easily transferable from one mode of language production to the other.

We turn next to the matter of how words are put together in clauses. We note that the relevant unit of spoken language appears to be the basically prosodic entity we have been calling an intonation unit, and this notion is explained. Intonation units are found to be longer in written than in spoken language, a fact that can again be attributed to different processing constraints. Spoken intonation units are limited in size by the short-term memory or "focal consciousness" capacity of the speaker, and perhaps also by the speaker's awareness of the listener's capacity limitations. Writers are under no such constraints, and as a consequence they have a tendency to produce expanded intonation units. We go on to consider a few of the many devices writers use to create this expansion.

Next we pay some attention to the different ways intonation units are joined together to form sentences in spoken and written language. Spoken language relies to a large extent on a chaining technique, and avoids elaborate syntactic relations among clauses. We point out that intonation units appear to be the natural unit of speaking, whereas integrated, elaborated sentences have become the natural unit of writing.

We turn finally to features of language related to the social interaction which is natural to speaking, as contrasted with the social isolation which is inherent in writing. We distinguish between involvement with the audience, involvement with oneself, and involvement with concrete reality. We go on to show how detachment from these kinds of involvement is manifested in academic writing. We speculate that writing makes possible a kind of abstract thinking that is less normal in the conversational use of language, but that is not a necessary component of writing either.

We now proceed with a closer examination of these points. As we examine each in turn, it is helpful to keep in mind the distinction between those differences that exist because of differences in the speaking and writing processes themselves, and those differences that have arisen because of the varied contexts, purposes, and subject matters of both spoken and written language. We show how differences of this latter kind are more easily overridden when the uses of speaking and writing overlap.

VARIETY OF VOCABULARY

One thing that speakers and writers alike must do is choose words and phrases that will express what they have in mind. They must find the vocabulary to convey their thoughts. We assume there is a discontinuity between what people have in mind and the language they use to express it. What is going on in people's heads does not always translate automatically into appropriate words and phrases. Knowledge of a language includes knowledge of a huge repertoire of lexical options that can be used for referring to the objects, states, and events which people may have occasion to talk about. As people construct language, they constantly have to choose among these options in ways they hope will communicate appropriately what they are thinking. It would thus appear that the choice of effective ways of saying things must call for the expenditure of some cognitive effort.

Of interest here is the fact that writing provides more time, and ultimately more resources, for this effort. The way we choose words and phrases in speaking and the way we choose them in writing are not the same processes at all. Speaking is done on the fly, while writing is both slow and editable. When we speak we have little time to choose our words, and once we have uttered them, they have been uttered. If we are not satisfied, we may try to revise what we have said, but too much fumbling is harmful to effective communication, and in any case our fumbling is laid bare for all to hear. When we write, we can produce language at whatever pace we wish. We can take hours, if we need to, to find an appropriate word. And there is no need to remain committed to the first lexical choices we make. Whatever words and phrases we may initially decide on, we are free to revise them again and again until they satisfy us. We have the leisure to dip into the rich storehouse of literary vocabulary, searching for items that will capture nuances which, if we were speaking, we would not have time to bother with. And this whole editing process is hidden from the eventual consumer of our language, to whom we can pretend that the aptness of our choices flowed naturally from our pen, typewriter, or word processor.

As a consequence of these differences, speakers tend to operate with a narrower range of lexical choices than writers. Producing language on the fly, they hardly have time to sift through all the possible choices they might make, and may typically settle on the first words that occur to them. The result is that the vocabulary of spoken language is more limited in variety. A mechanical measure of this difference is the type/token ratio of words: the number of different words in a sample divided by the total number of words in that sample. As a simple illustration, the first sentence in this paragraph contains 19 word tokens but only 17 word types, since the words *a* and *of* both occur twice. The type/token ratio of this one sentence is thus 17/19, or .89. It should be noted that such a ratio decreases as the number of words in a sample increases, so that the ratio just given cannot be compared with those given for our complete samples in Table 3.1. It can be seen from Table 3.1 that written language consistently shows a higher ratio than spoken, and that both styles of speaking (conversations and lectures) have lower type/token ratios, and thus less lexical variety, than both styles of writing (letters and academic papers).

TABLE 3.1
Type/Token Ratios

Conversations	.18
Lectures	.19
Letters	.22
Academic papers	.24

It is of some interest that the ratio in lectures is about the same as that in conversations. It appears that the necessarily rapid production of spoken language consistently produces a less varied vocabulary, regardless of the kind of speaking involved. Thus there seems to be a limit on the lexical variety a speaker can produce under any circumstances, a limit which cannot be overridden by a change in context or purpose. In speaking one always has to choose words quickly. In writing, with or without editing, one always has more time for choice. In other words, the constraints inherent in the speaking and writing processes are dominant here and are not overridden by different uses of the two.

There is evidence that speakers are aware of their limitations in choosing lexical items which adequately convey what they have in mind. An indication of such awareness is the use of hedges like *sort of* or *kind of*, as in the following examples:

(1) . . . *And* . . . *she was still young enough so I . . I just . . was able to put her in an . . uh—sort of . . . sling . . I mean one of those tummy packs . . you know.* (conversation)

(2) *A— —nd the graduate students are* **kind of** *scattered around.* (conversation)

(3) . . . *Um* . . . *I'm* **sort of** *I'm paraphrasing a little bit.* (lecture)

(4) . . . *So* . . . . *this one is* **kind of** *typical.* (lecture)

Such expressions suggest that, although these speakers settled quickly on the lexical choices *sling, scattered around, paraphrasing,* and *typical,* they were not completely satisfied with these ways of expressing things (cf. Lakoff, 1975). The speaker of (1), for example, indicated with *sort of* that what she was thinking of was not a typical sling, as she subsequently confirmed with her switch to *tummy pack* as a possibly better choice. Table 3.2 shows the distribution of hedges among our four kinds of language. The figures show the mean number of occurrences per thousand words in each sample. These figures are not large for any of the four styles, but there is a clear difference between the two spoken styles, where the incidence of hedges was identical, and the two written styles, where hedges were hardly present at all.

TABLE 3.2
Hedges

Conversations	4
Lectures	4
Letters	1
Academic papers	0

Type-token ratios and the use of hedges both have to do with the adequacy with which words express people's underlying intentions. Another, similar feature is the degree of referential explicitness. Speakers not only have less time to choose vocabulary, but they also cannot or do not take the time to be as explicit about what they are referring to. A symptom of this kind of vagueness is the use of third person neuter pronouns, usually *it*, *this*, or *that*. Typically, the antecedent of a pronoun has been spelled out in an earlier noun phrase. Sometimes, however, and especially in speaking, there is no such clear antecedent:

(5)   *And they have been arguing* (laugh) *about this for . . . I don't know!*
        . . At least 15 years or so.
        . . . . And . . . it seems like a fairly fruitless debate. (lecture)

The pronoun *it* in the last line refers to what was talked about in the two preceding lines (the 15-year-long argument), but that antecedent was never spelled out in an explicit noun phrase. Similarly, the pronoun *this* in the last line of (6) refers to the entire situation described in the lines above it:

(6)   *. . . The fact that they're not . . . alike,*
        . . . shows that . . . language . . m . . . can . . forces an assignment
        . . . of one of those objects . . . as reference point,
        . . with respect to the other object,
        . . . so the second object . . acts as reference point,
        . . . I'm calling it the ground object,
        . . . a— —nd the first one is relatively figure to it,
        . . . its . . . path . . or site . . . is characterized with respect to it.
        *. . . **This** happens in time as well.* (lecture)

Likewise, the pronoun *that* in the last line of (7) refers to the idea that husbands and wives would understand each other and have much in common, again an idea scattered over the preceding lines:

(7)   *. . . And I picked husbands and wives because I thought*
        . . . first of all
        . . . we would think that husbands and wives would understand each other.
        . . . if anybody can.
        . . . Because they live together,
        and they . . . have so much in common.
        *. . . Um although **that** often turns out not to be the case.* (lecture)

In Table 3.3 we see the distribution of such uses of pronouns in our

TABLE 3.3
Inexplicit Third Person Reference

Conversations	24
Lectures	22
Letters	11
Academic papers	4

four types of language, again listed in terms of the mean number of occurrences per thousand words. It can be seen that this phenomenon too is almost equally present in both styles of spoken language, whereas its frequency is considerably lower in either style of writing. In academic papers there are very few examples of it.

We have suggested, then, that the degree of richness of vocabulary, as measured by the type-token ratio, is limited by the rapidity of production of spoken language, whereas the added time and the editing possibilities allowed by writing increase the variety of lexical choice. And we have noted that there exists here a relatively pure difference between speaking and writing, one little influenced by the particular kinds of speaking or writing involved. There is here, in other words, a processing constraint which cannot easily be overridden by other factors. The same is true of certain related features, including the use of both hedges and inexplicit third person neuter pronouns. With regard to all these features relevant to adequacy of vocabulary, there is a sense in which written language might be thought to be a superior vehicle, just because it provides more time for a subtle and explicit packaging of thoughts. On the other hand, speaking has the advantage of providing a more direct expression of ongoing thought processes. For listeners, as well as for us as investigators, speaking makes available a more direct window on the mind in action.

LEVEL OF VOCABULARY

So far we have dwelled on the fact that speakers have less time than writers to choose lexical items adequate to what they want to convey. We need now to pay attention to the fact that speakers and writers do not choose from the same supply, that the store of words and phrases used in conversations is not the same as that used in formal writing, for example, and in general that spoken and written vocabularies are partially different. Many, perhaps all, languages have several levels or registers which are used for different purposes and in different situations.

Japanese, for example, is well known for dictating somewhat different lexical choices depending on the relative social status of the interlocutors. Many languages have ritual vocabularies which are different from those used in ordinary conversation. (How many times do we use the English word *merciful* outside of ritual contexts?) It is not surprising that languages with a long written tradition should have developed partially different vocabularies for speaking and writing. Not only does spoken language use a smaller repertoire, but the spoken and written repertoires contain somewhat different items.

There may be various ways in which such differences have arisen, but probably a common way is through differing rates of lexical change, spoken language being in general more innovative and written language more conservative. Thus, the spoken vocabulary of a language is likely to contain both new words and new senses of old words that are not present in the written vocabulary. At the same time the written vocabulary is likely to have retained older words and older senses of words which have passed out of spoken use. New uses, originating in the spoken language, may eventually enter the written vocabulary and become perfectly at home there. Samuel Johnson thought that the word *civilization* was not properly literary, but we would hardly make such a judgment today.

Perhaps spoken language compensates for its restricted lexical variety by assigning a premium to freshness. For example, the colloquial way of saying that something is good or desirable has changed from decade to decade—or even from year to year—through a series of words like *swell, cool, neat, far out,* and *awesome.* Speakers seem unwilling to let such a concept be expressed by a word that is stale and thus engage in a never-ending process of vocabulary replacement. Freshness of vocabulary is of less value in writing, where the important thing is to have a fixed stock of many subtly different items to choose from. Spoken language achieves richness through constant change within a limited range of choices; written language achieves it through broadening that range.

For our purposes, if we disregard slang, profanity, and professional jargon, lexical items in our samples of English fall into three classes: colloquial, literary, and neutral. There are certain items like *kid, bike, figure out,* and *bunch of* which occur quite naturally in casual spoken language, but which are generally out of place in writing unless the writer is trying to imitate speaking. There are other items like *ascertain, optimal, despite,* and *constitute* which are typically used in writing, but which sound out of place in speaking. Most vocabulary items, on the other hand—like *house, run, show,* and *try*—are neutral to this distinction, being equally at home in both spoken and written language. English speakers appear to be well aware of these differences and to be able to judge with considerable agreement the class to which a particular item belongs. Three of us have made such judgments with respect to the data under discussion here. Table 3.4 shows the number of occurrences per thousand words of distinctly literary or distinctly colloquial vocabulary.

It should be noticed that the distribution here is different from that which we saw in Tables 3.1–3.3. There the major, if not the only, difference was between speaking and writing. The purpose of the speaking or writing was only minimally, if at all, significant. Now we are looking at a distribution where there is a continuum from conversations at one extreme to academic papers at the other. Lectures and letters fall somewhere between, and there is less of a difference between these spoken and written varieties than there is within the two kinds of speaking, or within the two kinds of writing. It may be that differences in level of vocabulary had their genesis in the different uses of speaking and writing, but they are obviously not constrained by the speaking and writing processes themselves. There is nothing in the nature of speaking which prevents a speaker from using literary vocabulary, and nothing in the nature of writing which prevents a writer from using colloquial vocabulary. The level of word choice can be varied in whatever ways speakers and writers find appropriate to their contexts, purposes, and subject matters. Hence the fact that colloquial and literary vocabulary are equally present in lectures. Hence also the fact that letters, but not academic papers, have a fairly large colloquial component.

There is another feature whose use is much like the use of colloquial vocabulary. Spoken language commonly employs contractions like *it's*, *I'm*, and *don't*. Such items are rare in academic written language, as shown in Table 3.5, where their distribution can be seen to be similar to that shown for colloquial vocabulary in Table 3.4, except that there is a greater difference between lectures and letters. Thus, evidently, the constraints on speaking versus writing play a somewhat stronger role in

TABLE 3.4
Literary and Colloquial Vocabulary

	Literary vocabulary	Colloquial vocabulary
Conversations	8	27
Lectures	19	18
Letters	25	16
Academic papers	46	1

TABLE 3.5
Contractions

Conversations	37
Lectures	29
Letters	18
Academic papers	0

the use of contractions, with both kinds of spoken language showing significantly more of them than either kind of written language. If we put that difference aside, contractions can be regarded as further examples of innovative spoken vocabulary, innovations which the most formal kind of written language avoids altogether, but which more casual writing is more willing to accept.

To summarize what we have found so far, choosing lexical items is partly a matter of choosing aptly and explicitly, partly a matter of choosing the appropriate level. In the first case, the deliberateness and editability inherent in writing lead to a more richly varied, less hedged, and more explicit use of words. Speakers are so strongly constrained by their need to produce language rapidly and by their inability to edit, that they are unable to imitate the lexical richness and explicitness of writing even when, as in lecturing, such qualities would be especially valued. In the second case, although the separate histories of spoken and written language have led to partially divergent vocabularies, it is not as hard for speakers to borrow liberally from the written lexicon, or conversely for writers to borrow from the spoken. Thus lectures are more literary than conversations, and letters more conversational than academic papers. The constraints are not imposed by cognitive limitations, but by judgments of appropriateness.

CLAUSE CONSTRUCTION

Language consists of more than words, and there is more involved in speaking and writing than deciding which words to use. The obvious next question is how speakers and writers combine words and phrases into clauses. Do they form clauses in partially different ways, and, if so, are such differences imposed inevitably by the speaking and writing processes? Or are speakers and writers easily able to cross the boundary between spoken and written language when they find it appropriate, as we saw them able to do in choosing between colloquial and literary levels of vocabulary?

Instead of basing our discussion on clauses purely and simply, we have found it more realistic to proceed in terms of a slightly different kind of unit. One of the most noticeable and consistent properties of casual spoken language is that it is produced in relatively brief spurts. Although we have sometimes called these spurts "idea units" (see especially Chafe, 1980, for further discussion), here we will use the term *intonation unit*. The prototypical intonation unit has the following properties: (1) it is spoken with a single, coherent intonation contour, (2) it is followed by a pause, and (3) it is likely to be a single clause. Although the majority of intonation units are clauses, some contain an entire verb-complement construction while others are no more than a prepositional phrase, or even just a noun phrase, or a syntactic fragment of some other kind.

We have speculated on the cognitive basis of intonation units. It is fruitful to consider them the linguistic expression of that particular knowledge on which a speaker is focusing his attention at the moment. We can say that an intonation unit expresses what is in the speaker's short-term memory, or "focus of consciousness," at the time it is produced. Intonation units thus provide evidence as to the nature and capacity of focal consciousness. It seems that, under normal conditions, a speaker does not, or cannot, focus attention on more information than can be expressed in about six words. It seems, furthermore, that the syntax of intonation units must be kept fairly simple, and that attempts to achieve any very high degree of syntactic complexity are likely to cause trouble: hesitations, false starts, repetitions, and other verbal disfluences (Pawley and Snyder, 1976).

The following is an example of conversational language presented with each intonation unit on a separate line. Sequences of two or three dots indicate pauses:

(8)   . . . *I just this year have . . . dropped down to teaching half time.*
       . . . *Which is what I've always wanted.*
       . . . *You know I'm happy about it.*
       . . . *It's a . . . terribly long commute,*
       . . . *a— —nd now I'm just going two days a week.*
       . . . *And just teaching one course a quarter.*
       . . . *Cause the regular . . . teaching load for us is six courses a*
       year.

We assume that written language has a covert prosody which is analogous to that of spoken language: that both writers and readers assign pitch, stress, and pauses to language as they write and read it. We assume also that an important aspect of this prosody is the assignment

TABLE 3.6
Words per Intonation Unit

Conversations	6.2
Lectures	7.3
Letters	8.4
Academic papers	9.3

of intonation unit boundaries to written language. We assume, finally, that these boundaries are at least reasonably well indicated by punctuation. We are currently studying the extent to which the "punctuation units" of writing can be identified with the intonation units of speaking, but for the purposes of the present discussion we will simply equate the two. Thus, when we use the term *intonation unit* with reference to writing we will be referring to stretches of language between punctuation marks.

Table 3.6 shows the increase in intonation unit size, measured in terms of words per intonation unit, which takes place as we move from conversations to lectures, then to letters, and finally to academic papers.

The difference between the two spoken language types on the one hand and the two written types on the other is what we might expect. Writing frees writers from the constraint which keeps down the size of spoken intonation units. They need not limit the production of language to what can be focused on at one time, but can spend an indefinite amount of time constructing intonation units of any size. Writing frees intonation units from the limitations of short-term memory.

It is interesting to speculate on why a writer should keep intonation units within the bounds of about 9 words. Two answers have occurred to us. One is that written intonation units are a carryover from spoken language. Since spoken language has been with the human race for so long, and since it is still the kind of language we use most of the time, it is not surprising that it should influence the form of written language. But another factor may be a writer's sensitivity to the task of a reader. Suppose that a reader reads written language in more or less the same way that a hearer hears spoken language—that intonation units are a significant unit not only of production, but also of comprehension. If that is true, then writers most concerned with the readability of their product may provide their readers with moderately sized intonation units because they know intuitively that language so packaged will be easier to process. The four intonation units of (9) approximate those of spoken language. The principal intonation unit of (10) is much longer, and possibly less readable for that reason:

(9)   *There are exceptions to this general rule, and they are related to festivals of the winter solstice and death. Christmas ritual focuses upon the Virgin Mary, who is synonymous with the moon in their belief.*

(10)   *Thus, subjects can better recognize the shape of an average chair and give more consistent and detailed accounts of what a chair is and how one interacts with a chair than they can when asked to perform similar tasks with respect to the superordinate category furniture.*

Lectures show a mean intonation unit length of 7.3 words, only slightly higher than conversations. It would seem that the cognitive constraint which limits the size of spoken intonation units is difficult to overcome. Although there are some properties of academic writing which academic lecturers successfully borrow—literary vocabulary as well as other features discussed below—lecturers are unable to transcend very far the limitations on intonation unit formation imposed by the capacity of focal consciousness.

Letters show a mean intonation unit length of 8.4 words, midway between lectures and academic papers. They represent, then, a mixture of the limits characteristic of spoken language and the expansiveness allowed by writing. We might think of letter writers as language producers who take some advantage of the possibilities allowed by writing, but who are not interested in carrying these possibilities as far as academic writers. One reason for their restraint may be that letter writers typically write faster and with less editing than academic writers, and thus do not take the time necessary to expand intonation units to the same degree. Another reason may be that they try to maintain the casualness of spoken language, realizing that shorter intonation units make for easier reading.

In summary, we have identified clauselike units of spoken language which we have called intonation units. We have found that these units are relatively brief in casual spoken language, and have attributed their brevity to the fact that speakers can focus their consciousness on only a limited amount of material at one time. Since writers do not have to produce language on the fly as speakers do, they are freed from this constraint. As a consequence, written language which has undergone much planning and editing, as represented here by academic writing, shows intonation units that are markedly longer. Academic speaking, on the other hand, characteristically produces intonation units which are only slightly longer than those of casual speaking, a fact which suggests that the cognitive limitation on the size of spoken intonation units is difficult to overcome. Letter writers produce intonation units of intermediate length, avoiding the extreme of academic writing and aiming at something closer to spoken language.

There are many linguistic devices whose effect is to increase the size of intonation units; these are used more by writers than by speakers. Here we discuss only a few of the more common of them, considering how they are distributed among our four kinds of language and attempting to draw some conclusions from those distributions. There are three such devices which are used much more frequently than any others: prepositional phrases, nominalizations, and attributive adjectives. All three occur with considerable frequency in all four of the kinds of language we collected, a fact which suggests that there are no strong cognitive constraints limiting their use. On the other hand, they are unusually frequent in academic writing, where they are by far the favorite ways for academic writers to expand the size of intonation units. They occur with approximately equal frequency in lectures and in letters.

The following examples show how academic writing often piles prepositional phrase upon prepositional phrase:

(11)   *Language change has occurred when the utterances **of** some members **of** that community have characteristics demonstrably different **from** those **in** utterances **of** previous generations.*

(12)   *In order to account for the use **of** linguistic features **by** certain speakers **in** prolonged interaction, I taped two and a half hours **of** naturally occurring conversation **among** six participants **at** a dinner **in** 1978.*

The distribution of prepositional phrases in our data is shown in Table 3.7, in terms of the number of occurrences per thousand words. The fact that they are used so commonly, even in conversations, suggests that they are easy to use—that they exact no very high price in terms of cognitive capacity. Conversationalists, however, are much less apt to construct prepositional phrase sequences like those seen in (11) and (12), and are more apt to rely on prepositions which form close constructions with verbs, or even to construct idea units which consist of nothing but

TABLE 3.7
Prepositional Phrases

Conversations	53
Lectures	88
Letters	91
Academic papers	117

prepositional phrases. The following sequence exemplifies both of these tendencies:

(13)   *so he took us to some lake,*
        . . . in Quebec,

The first idea unit is built around the memorized sequence *take (someone) to (somewhere).* The second shows the speaker giving full attention to a prepositional phrase to the exclusion of anything else.

These observations suggest that it would be rewarding, not just to count occurrences of prepositional phrases, but to examine more closely how they are used in different kinds of language. We have not yet undertaken such a study, except to examine occurrences of prepositional phrase sequences—two or more such phrases juxtaposed within the same intonation unit. The occurrences of such sequences per thousand words are shown in Table 3.8. Their predominance in academic writing is obvious, and again it is of interest that they are equally frequent in lectures and in letters.

Assuming that prepositional phrases are relatively easy to use, why should they occur with equal frequency in lectures and letters? We suggest that the lack of cognitive strain must make it possible for lecturers to use them more or less effortlessly, thereby mimicking written academic style. Still, the fact that lecturers are speaking and not writing prevents them from using prepositional phrases as abundantly as academic writers. Conversely, letter writers, writing more quickly and mimicking conversational style, do not make as much use of prepositional phrases as academic writers, but the extra time available to writers of any kind allows even letter writers to use them more than conversationalists. Thus the opposite goals and constraints of lecturers and letter writers lead to an almost identical result.

A second favorite device used by writers for increasing the length of intonation units is nominalization, the formation of a noun from a verb, as with the words *representation, determinant,* and *performance* in the following examples:

(14)   *It is at this level of language that the **representation** of space is explored here.*

TABLE 3.8
Prepositional Phrase Sequences

Conversations	6
Lectures	14
Letters	14
Academic papers	22

TABLE 3.9
Nominalizations

Conversations	27
Lectures	56
Letters	55
Academic papers	92

(15)   *If processing is a crucial **determinant** of memory **performance**,*

Nominalizations are a principal means whereby a single clause can be constructed from what might otherwise have been several clauses. For example, in place of (14) a conversationalist might have said something about *how people represent space*, increasing the number of intonation units by adding one based on the verb *represent*. The distribution of nominalizations is similar to that of prepositional phrases, though they are slightly less frequent, as shown in Table 3.9.

Many words which originated as nominalizations have become standard items of the academic vocabulary, without which academic writers would be unable to say the kinds of things they like to say. Such words then become easy for speakers to use as well. If an academic speaker uses a word like *categorization* or *development*, for example, it may not be to coalesce into a larger intonation unit a nominalization of the verbs *categorize* or *develop*, but simply to refer to a well-established technical concept. It is possible that the concepts of categorization or development would not have arisen historically without the possibilities provided by writing. However, the current use of such nouns by speakers no longer shows a productive act of nominalizing, but only the use of a technical term. It may be for this reason that the occurrence of nominalizations is relatively high in spoken language, and especially high in lectures, where again we see a convergence with the frequency in letters.

A third device of a similar sort is the preposed or attributive adjective, two occurrences of which can be seen in (16).

(16)   *It allows an **unambiguous** manipulation within the **semantic** level.*

Although they are less common, attributive nouns play a similar role. An example is the noun *target:*

(17)   *Subjects searched for instances of **target** categories.*

The distribution of attributive adjectives and nouns together is shown in Table 3.10. There is little difference between these figures and those given in Table 3.9 for nominalizations, and similar explanations may apply.

TABLE 3.10
Attributive Adjectives and Nouns

Conversations	23
Lectures	56
Letters	55
Academic papers	77

To summarize: (1) prepositional phrases, nominalizations, and attributives are commonly used devices in all kinds of language; (2) they are especially frequent in academic writing; and (3) they occur with equal frequency in lectures and in letters. Since they are so frequent in language of every sort, they must be easy-to-use grammatical devices which place no undue cognitive strain on the language producer. Since they are especially frequent in academic writing, they must lend themselves especially well to the kind of intonation unit expansion which takes place in that style. And since they occur with equal frequency in lectures and letters, the opposing goals of lecturers to imitate academic prose and of letter writers to imitate conversation must converge on a single result.

These three are not the only devices whose effect is to increase the length of intonation units. There are a number of others, less frequent, which show a distribution more like that in Table 3.6, and which thus help to contribute to the overall greater length of intonation units in letters as opposed to lectures. One is the use of *and* to conjoin two elements into a compound phrase, as in the following:

(18)   . . . *slang for patients reflects responses to their **suffering and illness*** (paper)

(19)   *(she) . . . tried to help the children **focus and structure*** *their discourse.* (paper)

Although it would not seem particularly difficult to accomplish conjoining of this kind, the facts are that speakers do not do it nearly as often as writers and that academic writers do it three times as often as conversationalists, as shown in Table 3.11.

TABLE 3.11
Conjoining

Conversations	8
Lectures	12
Letters	18
Academic papers	24

TABLE 3.12
Participles

Conversations	5
Lectures	6
Letters	11
Academic papers	24

A similar distribution is found in the use of present and past participles.[2] Both types may occur either preposed or postposed. Thus, in (20) we find a preposed present participle, and in (21) a preposed past participle:

(20)   It was a **recurring** classroom activity.

(21)   **Bowed** oscillations can begin in two ways.

In (22) we find a postposed present participle, and in (23) a postposed past participle.

(22)   Cult activity **originating** in the hamlets is atypical.

(23)   Where they still embody the properties **denoted** by the words which refer to them,

The pooled distribution of these four kinds of participles is shown in Table 3.12. Here we see a distribution similar to that in Table 3.11, except that language other than academic writing makes considerably less use of participles, and lecturers fail to use them much more than conversationalists.

To summarize this entire section, a principal way in which written language differs from spoken is in the greater length of written intonation units. Intonation units are expanded with a variety of devices, among the more common of which are prepositional phrases, nominalizations, and attributive adjectives and nouns. Less frequently used devices are the conjoining of words with and, and participles of several kinds and uses. All of these intonation unit expansion devices are much more frequent in academic writing than in conversations, with lectures and letters being of intermediate frequency. None of these devices is cognitively difficult, but combining them in quantity evidently requires the extra time and care available to a writer.

SENTENCE CONSTRUCTION

Conversational spoken language consists in large part of intonation units joined together in a chain, very often with the coordinating conjunction and linking them together. In other words, there is a strong

TABLE 3.13
Coordination

Conversations	34
Lectures	21
Letters	12
Academic papers	4

tendency for casual speakers to produce simple sequences of coordinated clauses, avoiding the more elaborate interclausal relations found in writing. Elaborate syntax evidently requires more processing effort than speakers can ordinarily devote to it. The following is a typical example of clause coordination in conversational language:

(24)   . . . *And there was two women,*
hiking up ahead of us,
. . . and you sort of got to a rise,
and then the lake was kind of right there where we were gonna . . .
camp.
. . . And the two of them,
. . got to the rise,
and the next minute,
. . . they just . . . fell over,
totally.

A simple way to measure the degree of coordination in a language sample is by counting the coordinating conjunctions (usually *and,* less often *but* or *so*) which are located at the beginnings of intonation units. We can express this measure as the percentage of intonation units which begin in this way. The percentages for our data are shown in Table 3.13. Conversational spoken language thus exhibits by far the largest amount of intonation unit coordination, but even lectures show twice as much as letters. Papers show very little in comparison with the other styles. It appears that spoken language of any kind tends to chain clauses together significantly more often than any kind of written language, and that academic writers avoid this practice considerably more than others.

As a speaker proceeds with the chaining of intonation units, every so often he will end one of these units with the kind of falling pitch associated with the end of a sentence. The function of sentences in spoken language is problematic, but speakers appear to produce a sentence-final intonation when they judge that they have come to the end of some coherent content sequence (Chafe, 1980). What produces this coherence may vary from one instance to the next. It is difficult to predict when a speaker will decide that a chain of intonation units worthy of recognition as a complete sentence has been produced. Speakers are sloppy in this respect, often producing a sentence-final intonation before they mean to, or neglecting to produce one when they should. Premature sentence closures are often followed by afterthoughts; delayed ones give the effect of run-on sentences. The following example is typical:

(25)   . . . *And she said . . . um– . . . she said . . . um– . . . I got*
         my degree at Harvard,
         . . *and one of the things we had to do,*
         . . . *was– to read.*
         . . . *Constantly she said.*
         I read,
         . . . *eight hours a day.*
         . . *For four years.*
         . . . *And I read everything.*
         . . *She said.*
         And t . . to graduate from Harvard,
         . . . *one of the things we had to do was type.*
         . . . *A paragraph.*
         . . *We had to . . . we had to date it,*
         . . *we had t . . tell who wrote it,*
         .. . . *and she said not only . . do I know*
         . . . *she said I'm I'm trained to detect . . . minute . . switches in*
         style.

Sentences in written language are better planned than this, giving evidence of the time and effort that went into their construction. We have been led to the conclusion that intonation units are the natural unit of speech, their content and structure dependent on the capacity of short-term memory, whereas sentences have become the major unit of writing. Writers have time to give thought to how much they want to put into a sentence—how best to sculpt it into a complex, integrated whole, as in the following:

(26)   *A novelist's insistence on the referential function of her work's*
         language is, at least in part, always necessarily divided against
         itself (as the deconstructionist critics show) because that insistence
         stems, paradoxically, from an awareness of the novel's fictionality.

One piece of evidence for this difference between spoken and written sentences is the fact that in conversational language the largest number of sentences consist of one word, a slightly smaller number of two words, and so on, with a gradual tailing off to a small number of sentences with a length of 100 words or more. Although the mean length of spoken sentences is 18 words, this figure has no special significance. There is no reason to think that speakers have any stake in producing sentences approximately 18 words long. Academic writing, in contrast, shows a relatively normal distribution of sentence lengths centered around a mean of 24. We take this as an indication that writers possess an intuitive concept of "normal sentence length" which speakers do not have.

In summary, speakers chain intonation units together, often connecting them with *and*, stopping occasionally to insert a sentence-final falling pitch which often turns out to have been a mistake. Writers connect intonation units in more complex ways, sculpting them into planned sentences which, in spite of deliberate variability in length, tend toward a mean length of about 24 words. Intonation units are the natural units of speaking, sentences the natural unit of writing, presumably because writers have the leisure to perfect the complex and coherent sentence structures which speakers are moving too fast to produce.

INVOLVEMENT AND DETACHMENT

So far we have looked at properties of speaking and writing which can be attributed to differences in the two activities and specifically to the rapidity and evanescence of speaking as opposed to the deliberateness and editability of writing. Another, equally important difference has to do with the relation between the producer of the language and the audience. In most spoken language an audience is not only physically present, but also has the ability to respond with language of its own. For writers, the audience is usually unseen and often unknown. Spoken language contains indications of the speaker's involvement with the audience, as well as of the speaker's involvement with himself, and furthermore of his involvement with the concrete reality of what is being talked about. Much written language, on the other hand, lacks involvement of any of these three kinds, and is apt to show indications of the writer's detachment from the audience, from himself, and from concrete reality. However, linguistic features of involvement and detachment are not cognitively, but contextually, determined. They can, therefore, be overridden when the context is appropriate. They do not necessarily divide spoken language from written, and we will see that it is possible for some written language to be more spokenlike than any spoken language in these respects.

One obvious measure of involvement with an audience is the occur-

TABLE 3.14
Involvement with the Audience

	Responses	*you know*
Conversations	9	11
Lectures	2	2
Letters	0	0
Academic papers	0	0

rence of language which responds to something just said by another person. For example:

(27)   (*Would you do that?*)
        . . . *Yeah . . I think I would.*

(28)   (*Beatrice said that?*)
        . . . *That's what I thought she said.*

Another such measure is the occurrence of the phrase *you know*, with which a speaker attempts to reassure himself that he is getting through to the listener without explicitly requesting confirmation of that fact (Ostman 1981):

(29)   *So you can't . . . **you know** . . fudge in some styrofoam . . or something like that.*

(30)   *Only this all takes . . **you know** . . ten minutes to . . . to compose,*

The distribution of both interactional responses and *you know* in our four styles of language is shown in Table 3.14. For obvious reasons such devices hardly occur at all in either kind of written language, but they are also relatively rare in lectures, whose language, though it may occasionally be interactional, is more often monologic.

A different kind of involvement is explicit concern with oneself, an obvious measure of which is the use of first person pronouns (*I, me, my, mine, we, us, our,* and *ours*). The following examples are both from letters:

(31)   *I could be telling you the same things in person.*

(32)   *As you can see, **my** difficulty with writing extends not only to its phrasing but also to its timing.*

Table 3.15 shows the occurrence of first person pronouns in the four kinds of language. They occur very little in academic writing, a fact which must be due in part to their deliberate discouragement in that

TABLE 3.15
First Person Pronouns

Conversations	48
Lectures	21
Letters	57
Academic papers	4

medium, but in part also to the fact that academic writing usually has a subject matter which excludes much talk about oneself. The most interesting finding shown in Table 3.15, however, is that personal letters show more ego involvement than any of the other kinds of language studied here. While first person reference is high in conversations, and even present to a significant degree in lectures, it is by far the highest in letters. If people have a natural inclination to talk about themselves, it is apparently in letters that they have the best opportunity to do so, being freed of whatever inhibitions might be imposed by the immediate presence of an interlocutor. The use of first person pronouns is thus not necessarily a feature which differentiates spoken from written language, but rather a feature which the absence of a direct audience may even foster when the circumstances are right. At the same time, as we can see from the figure for academic papers, writing can create a context in which maximum suppression of one's own identity is possible.

There are numerous linguistic indications of involvement with concrete reality. One that occurs frequently and with an interesting distribution is the use of temporal and spatial adverbs and adverbial phrases. Elements of this kind locate the people and events being talked about in specific time and space. We interpret their use to be one important manifestation of a speaker or writer's involvement with the reality of his subject matter, as opposed to a stance of abstract detachment. Note the occurrence of temporal and locative adverbial elements in the following examples, again from letters:

(33)   *I applied for this postdoc **last March**,*

(34)   *It looks like life is going to really be nice **in Akron**.*

The distribution of such elements in our data is shown in Table 3.16. They present a picture much like that of Table 3.15, where the least frequent occurrence is in academic writing and the most frequent in letters. Thus, like involvement with oneself, involvement with specific time and space is not a feature which necessarily differentiates spoken from written language, but rather something which is suppressed in one

TABLE 3.16
Adverbial Expressions

	Locative adverbials	Temporal adverbials
Conversations	14	16
Lectures	11	10
Letters	19	22
Academic papers	6	8

kind of writing while it is exaggerated in another. Although such involvement may be characteristic of spoken language, and something written language can and often does suppress, there is no processing constraint which prevents it from surfacing and even from predominating in writing when the context is appropriate.

We use the term *detachment* as the opposite of *involvement*. Instead of showing a concern for the concrete aspects of language interaction and for concrete reality, features of detachment show an interest in ideas that are not tied to specific people, events, times, or places, but which are abstract and timeless. We have looked at several features which we take to be manifestations of such detachment. They predominate in academic writing, where they represent the opposite side of the coin from the involvement features just discussed.

Involved language tends to favor clauses whose subjects refer to specific concrete persons, usually persons who perform some concrete action or are in some concrete state. Detached language uses clauses whose subjects refer to abstractions. For example (from academic papers):

(35)   *This suggestion* finds some support in studies of children's "egocentric speech."

(36)   *Educational settings* are rich in such situations.

The two subjects, *this suggestion* and *educational settings*, illustrate the kinds of abstractions typical of such language. The distribution of abstract subjects in our data is shown in Table 3.17. As might be expected, their occurrence is lowest in conversations, but it is almost as low in letters, whose penchant for concreteness we have already noticed. While lectures show a higher degree of this kind of abstractness, they do not approach the frequency to be found in academic writing.

A similar feature, though less common throughout our samples, is the use of passive constructions. The use of a passive allows a writer to

TABLE 3.17
Abstract Subjects

Conversations	21
Lectures	38
Letters	25
Academic papers	48

avoid mentioning any concrete doer, and in that way to treat an event in a more abstract fashion. Even when an agent is mentioned, a passive construction shows less concern for concrete people doing concrete things, in that it gives subject status to things (usually abstractions) which have something done to them. (37) and (38) are examples from academic papers.

(37)   *The resonance complex **has been studied** through experiments with an electronic violin.*

(38)   *This tendency **has been remarked upon** by other researchers.*

By far the largest number of passives occurred in our samples of academic writing, as shown in Table 3.18. There were very few in conversations, and only a modest number in either lectures or letters. It would seem that the passive construction provides a device that academicians find especially suited to their purpose, while no one else is especially fond of it.

Still another indication of detachment is the use of words which express the probability of some generic statement being true. We have found that academic writers are particularly fond of expressions which indicate that things happen, in general, a certain proportion of the time, but not necessarily always—words like *normally, usually, primarily, principally,* and *virtually.* Such words are academic hedges, by which the writer escapes blame for instances which fail to correspond to this generalization. For example,

(39)   *Correction is **usually** thought of as being only a matter of stopping and saying part of your sentence over differently.*

TABLE 3.18
Passives

Conversations	3
Lectures	9
Letters	7
Academic papers	22

TABLE 3.19
Indications of Probability

Conversations	4
Lectures	7
Letters	6
Academic papers	10

(40)   *The contour used **primarily** by the white children was a gradually*
        rising contour.

Such expressions occur noticeably more often in academic writing than
elsewhere, as shown in Table 3.19.

   In summary, different kinds of language show different degrees of
involvement and detachment. Involvement with one's audience is obviously an important aspect of conversations. It is a minimal feature of
lectures, and is lacking in any kind of writing. Involvement with oneself,
though conspicuous in conversations also, is present to an even greater
degree in letters, a fact which suggests that letters provide the best
forum of all for egocentrism. Involvement with concrete reality, as measured in terms of temporal and locative adverbs, shows a similar pattern. Letter writers have the time for such expression and lack the inhibitions against it shown by academic writers. Academic writing shows
various manifestations of detachment from concrete reality, including
maximum use of abstract subjects, of passives, and of probabilistic gen-
eralizations.

CONCLUSION

   Language users, whether they are speakers or writers, have certain
variable resources available to them. Every speaker or writer possesses a
repertoire of devices which are combined in varying mixtures depending on the context, the purpose, and the subject matter of language use.
In other words, language adapts to its varying environments. It may be
useful for us to summarize the varying characteristics of spoken and
written language as they have appeared in this survey.

   Conversationalists, first of all, employ a relatively limited vocabulary,
and they are inclined to hedge their lexical choices and to be referentially
inexplicit. They make considerable use of colloquial words and phrases.
They create relatively brief intonation units, which they chain together,
stopping every so often to make a sentence boundary which is not

always well justified in terms of topical coherence. They interact with their audiences, show ego involvement, and talk frequently about specific times and places. These properties are appropriate to language that is produced rapidly in an environment where the immediate presence of the audience plays an important role.

Academic lecturers speaking in relatively informal contexts employ an equally limited vocabulary, also use hedges, and are also referentially inexplicit. Their use of literary vocabulary is somewhat greater than that of conversationalists. They are, however, only slightly more able to extend the length of intonation units, and they are no more able than conversationalists to cope with syntactically elaborate sentences. They interact slightly with their audiences, but not nearly as much as conversationalists. They make some use of first person and concrete spatio-temporal references, though not as much as either conversationalists or letter writers. Conversely, they show some degree of detachment, but not as much as academic writers. This is a mixed kind of language, still controlled by the constraints of rapid production, but striving after some of the elegance and detachment of formal writing.

Letter writers use a more varied vocabulary, are sometimes inexplicit, but use hedges very rarely. They use a moderate number of colloquial words and contractions, but at the same time a greater number of literary items. Their intonation units are intermediate in length between conversationalists and academic writers, and their sentences tend to be better formed. They show a greater degree of involvement with themselves and with concrete reality than any other language users within the range that we have studied. Their degree of detachment is not much greater than that of conversationalists. This is a kind of language which takes some advantage of what the deliberateness of writing allows, but which also maintains, and in some respects even surpasses, the casualness and involvement of speech.

Academic writers represent for us the extremes of what writing permits. Their vocabulary is maximally varied, and they avoid both hedges and inexplicit references. Their writing is maximally literary, with almost no colloquial items or contractions. Their intonation units are maximally long, with frequent use of all the devices by which intonation units can be expanded. Their sentences show a tendency toward an ideal length and are maximally coherent. They show little involvement with themselves, or with concrete reality, and on the contrary make the greatest use of devices signaling detachment. This kind of language represents a maximum adaptation to the deliberateness and detachment of the writing environment.

This chapter has dealt only with the most frequent of the linguistic features we have examined. We will have more to say in the future about various other features whose occurrence is less pervasive. Beyond that, we need to emphasize that the four types of language we have discussed here are only four out of many. We expect in the future to deal with literary and journalistic language, for example, and also with several styles of spoken and written language produced by third- and sixth-grade children. Our preliminary findings have suggested that as children learn to write, they first learn to slough off the most positive features of spoken language, those which we have presented here under the heading of involvement, so that there is a stage at which their writing can best be characterized as bland. Only later do they begin gradually to gain proficiency in handling the positive features of written language, above all the elaboration of sentences. It will be interesting to see how well this two-stage sequence of writing acquisition is supported by additional data.

In the meantime, we hope to have provided a start toward a better understanding of the ingredients of language which both speakers and writers use in differing combinations for different purposes. A general hope is that dissemination of research of this kind will lead teachers to recognize more clearly not only that writing and speaking are very different activities, but also that the kinds of language which result from these activities are very different too, and that there are good cognitive and social reasons for such differences. We hope to have provided some specific clues to what the linguistic differences are, as well as to the factors which are responsible for them.

NOTES

[1] We also collected roughly parallel samples from 20 third graders and 20 sixth graders, but they will not be discussed here. This project was sponsored by Grant G-80-0125 from the National Institute of Education. We are grateful to Pamela Downing for her valued assistance and advice.

[2] We exclude here the use of participles in progressive and perfect constructions like *he is writing* and *he has written*, as well as in passive constructions like *it has been written*.

REFERENCES

Bloomfield, L. (1933). *Language*. New York: Holt.
Chafe, W. (1980). The deployment of consciousness in the production of a narrative. In W. Chafe (Ed.), *The pear stories: Cognitive cultural, and linguistic aspects of narrative production*. Norwood, NJ: Ablex.

Chafe, W. (1981). Differences between colloquial and ritual Seneca, or how oral literature is literary. In A. Schlichter, W. Chafe, & L. Hinton (Eds.), *Reports from the survey of California and other Indian languages* (No. 1). Berkeley: University of California, Department of Linguistics.

Chafe, W. (1982). Integration and involvement in speaking, writing, and oral literature. In D. Tannen (Ed.), *Spoken and written language: Exploring orality and literacy*. Norwood, NJ: Ablex.

Chafe, W. (1985). Linguistic differences produced by differences between speaking and writing. In D. R. Olson, A. Hildyard, & N. Torrance (Eds.), *Literacy, language, and learning: The nature and consequences of reading and writing*. London: Cambridge University Press.

Chafe, W. (1986). Evidentiality in English conversation and academic writing. In W. Chafe & J. Nichols (Eds.), *Evidentiality: The linguistic coding of epistemology*. Norwood, NJ: Ablex.

Goody, J., & Watt, I. (1968). The consequences of literacy. In J. Goody (Ed.), *Literacy in traditional societies*. London: Cambridge University Press.

Kroll, B. M., & Vann, R. J. (Eds.). (1981). *Exploring speaking–writing relationships: Connections and contrasts*. Urbana, IL: National Council of Teachers of English.

Lakoff, G. (1975). Hedges: A study in meaning criteria and the logic of fuzzy concepts. In D. Hockney, W. Harper, & B. Freed (Eds.), *Contemporary research in philosophical logic and linguistic semantics*. Dordrecht, Netherlands: Reidel.

Olson, D. R. (1977). From utterance to text: the bias of language in speech and writing. *Harvard Educational Review, 47*, 257–281.

Ong, W. (1982). *Orality and literacy: The technologizing of the word*. London: Methuen.

Ostman, J.-O. (1981). *You know: A discourse-functional approach*. Amsterdam: Benjamins.

Pawley, A., & Snyder, F. (1976, August). Sentence formulation in spontaneous speech: the one-clause-at-a-time hypothesis. Paper presented at the First Annual Congress of the Linguistic Society of New Zealand, Auckland.

Scribner, S., & Cole, M. (1981). *The psychology of literacy*. Cambridge, MA: Harvard University Press.

Tannen, D. (Ed.). (1982a). *Spoken and written language: Exploring orality and literacy*. Norwood, NJ: Ablex.

Tannen, D. (1982b). Oral and literate strategies in spoken and written language. *Language, 58*, 1–21.

Vachek, J. (1973). *Written language*. The Hague: Mouton.

PART **II**

PROCESSING STRATEGIES: RHETORICAL, SOCIAL-SITUATIONAL, AND CONTEXTUAL CONSTRAINTS

Chapter **4**

Rhetorical Structure in Discourse Processing

Rosalind Horowitz

INTRODUCTION

Theoretical and experimental work to characterize the structure of discourse, specifically the role of rhetorical structures in discourse comprehension, has received considerable attention in both the United States and Europe since the mid-1970s. Although scholarship on this theme has gained in momentum and rhetorical structures have been treated as a significant component in theoretical accounts of discourse, (see, e.g., van Dijk and Kintsch, 1983), as we approach the twenty-first century it must be recognized that the study of discourse structure—albeit of oral or written language—remains very much in a state of infancy.

The rhetorical structures in which we are interested in this chapter are the highest-order organizational patterns in a discourse hierarchy of information. These include the patterns of *attribution* (list structure, including attributes and examples), *adversative* (compare–contrast, including examination of alternatives), *covariance* (cause and effect), and *response* (problem and solution). These structures are foregrounded by signal words which function as signposts for each of the organizational patterns: for attribution, *first, in addition;* for adversative, *however, nevertheless;* for covariance, *the cause, the effect,* and for response, *the problem, the solution.*

This chapter is dedicated in loving memory to my mother Fannie (Fayge) Hartman Horowitz (b. Lipnick, Russia, 1905 and d. Minneapolis, Minnesota, 1985) who was truly a queen. A pillar of strength and wisdom, she shared in the joys and tensions of this work to the last days of her life.

The study of these rhetorical structures is an important area of inquiry for a number of reasons. One finds in the literature on expository prose considerable attention to these elements of language as critical organizational devices. These structures have been viewed as aids to the discovery and invention of argumentation. They have been a significant part of the teaching, learning, and thinking of the orator dating back to classical times. More important for our purposes here, writers use these elements of language to establish semantic relations, at the clause, sentence, and paragraph level or higher. The rhetorical structures are presumed to provide synthesis of form and content for the reader and to contribute to the predictability and interpretation of explanatory discourse.

Above all, the study of rhetorical structures cuts across the discussion of a number of questions and issues associated with the study of discourse processes at large. Our knowledge about the uses and limitations of these structures influences the way in which we approach the discourse that we use and witness in nearly all walks of life, including that which we process through the media or press, through computers, as well as in various institutional settings—be it legal, medical, or educational. This work has a special significance because of the possibilities it affords for the way in which we develop oral and written discourse in the classroom and for how we select and use texts in schools.

This chapter operates from the premise that the rhetorical structure of discourse must be further explored from a social perspective, as a sociolinguistic component in models of oral and written discourse processing. The point to be made in this chapter, through theoretical discussion and empirical evidence, is that these structures interact with other linguistic, cognitive, and social-contextual factors associated with discourse comprehension. It is not their singular effect, it will be argued, but rather their interaction with other discourse features, and above all, their variability that is in most need of explanation.

These structures, or similar features, have captured the attention of modern rhetoricians—oral and written composition specialists—interested in the effects of discourse on audiences (see, e.g., D'Angelo, 1975, 1979; Brooks & Warren, 1958; Clark & Delia, 1979; Connors, Ede, & Lunsford, 1984; Dick, 1964; Kopperschmidt, 1985; G. Levin, 1981; Perelman, 1982; Perelman & Olbrechts-Tyteca, 1969; Toulmin, 1958), and have also received attention by linguists interested in the effects of speech communities on language uses (Grimes, 1975; Longacre, 1976, 1983) and the nature of discourse structure (Anderson, 1982; Batalova, 1977; Hinds, 1979; Hoey, 1983, 1986; Jordan, 1980, 1984; Kaplan, 1982; Kučera, 1980; N. Levin, 1979; Litteral, 1972; Petöfi & Sözer, 1983; Winter, 1983), by literary theorists (Barthes, 1970; Fowler, 1981; Uspensky, 1973), by reading researchers, educational psychologists (Calfee & Curley, 1984; B. J. F. Meyer, 1975, 1982; Meyer & Rice, 1984), by psychologists, and indirectly by artificial intelligence experts interested in theories of comprehension (Bock, 1982; Bock & Brewer, 1985; Brewer, 1980; Flammer & Kintsch, 1983; Garnham, 1981; Kieras, 1980; Kieras & Bovair, 1981; Kintsch, 1982, 1984; Kintsch & Yarbrough, 1982; Lesgold *et al.*, 1979; Thorndyke, 1978).

Despite the proliferation of work from so many different fields, we know little about the effects and uses of these structures in oral or written discourse of the schools. Yet, a legacy of work in rhetoric and composition has provided us with numerous axioms and typologies, i.e., categories of arguments, for the design of discourse. For example, in schools rules exist about such matters as the preferred types, placements, and combinations of certain arguments in speaking or writing. One need only turn to a high school or college freshman composition handbook to find what sound like rather definitive statements indicating where and how a thesis statement should be used and under which conditions it should be placed at the beginning, middle, or end of a discourse. In addition, the cognitive and affective appeal rhetorical structures have on listener–audiences are often treated in these speech-communication and written-composition handbooks. These handbooks form the basis for speech or writing instruction and, indirectly or directly, reading instruction. Above all, I argue that clearly more is at stake here than the type or placement of a structure. Decisions about structure ultimately influence decisions about thinking, ways of knowing, and the different realities that readers or writers construct.

Given the above, research is needed which examines how particular rhetorical structures are used as strategies to facilitate academic comprehension or everyday discourse understanding (Freedman & Calfee, 1984). Work is needed that examines how these structures are used by specific populations in our society and that considers the use of rhetorical structures across the continuum of oral and written discourse and the continuum of listening and reading tasks.

Researchers have begun to consider the effect of rhetorical structures on reading comprehension and learning from texts in the schools. This work has demonstrated that rhetorical structures influence comprehension and that good readers use these structures in school learning. We know that poor readers are not aware of and do not use these structures in school learning. However, there are a number of questions that remain unanswered that we begin to treat in this chapter: What effect do the rhetorical structures have on the comprehension and processing of discourse? Do some rhetorical structures more effectively influence comprehension over others? Do particular rhetorical structures differentially influence comprehension across ages and grades? Do listeners and readers utilize rhetorical structures for the processing and synthesis of discourse differently? Do speakers or writers operate from certain social and cognitive networks of options that listeners or readers must recognize and use in discourse processing?

This chapter examines the effect of select rhetorical structures in discourse comprehension and processing and begins to explore a number of the above questions. The chapter is, accordingly, divided into the following two sections. The first is a theoretical and historical account of the study of these elements of language. I consider the move from a structural to a functional approach to language, the architecture of text, terminology used in the literature, and the way in which rhetorical structures can contribute to the synthesis of form and meaning. I only touch upon a number of complex questions that will need to be pursued in more detail elsewhere, but that inform the research to follow.

In the second part I discuss a research experiment which investigated the different effects of rhetorical structures on comprehension. While there has been considerable theoretical and descriptive discussion of these features, there has been limited investigation of their role in comprehension by school populations.

FROM A STRUCTURAL TO A FUNCTIONAL APPROACH TO WRITTEN LANGUAGE

Although there are many schools of language study, two primarily epistomological frameworks dominate the literature and influence research on rhetorical structures in discourse processing. The prevailing view of language in the twentieth century has been and continues to be one of formal structuralism. Saussure (1916) believed language could be studied synchronically as a self-contained, autonomous discipline through examination of interrelationships and permutation of linguistic forms, without attention to diachronics, i.e., language variation over time and space.

Saussure coined the term *la langue* to refer to a set of rules about a language and language competence, and *la parole* to refer to single concrete examples of the rules of *la langue* and actual performance or use of these rules. Attention in the linguistic literature has persisted at the level of *la langue*. Scholarship by Bloomfield (1933) and others followed this line of thinking, creating a bifurcation between these two dimensions of language, one that is presumably, to some extent, being eroded and redefined.

Additionally, linguistic research, particularly in the United States from the 1950s onward, has emphasized the sentence as a self-contained unit of language and as the primary object of study. The focus has been on a grammar, that is, a set of rules, a formal logic, derived from a model, where the organizing concept has been structure (e.g., the work of Harris, Chomsky, Katz, and Fodor). This has not only been the approach used to study sentences, it has also become the approach used in the study of text language and grammar. That is, in some of the work, we see theoretical aspects associated with phonology inappropriately applied to other components of the language system such as sentences or texts (see Moore & Carling, 1982, for similar remarks).

Structuralism has been a topic of great discussion and debate in books and seminars in the humanities and social sciences. For example, Kurzweil (1980) surveys the different ways structuralism has been treated across Europe in specific disciplines such as anthropology, history, and literature, and points out that it is the failure of structuralism that prepared the ground for poststructural thinking. As part of a series of cross-disciplinary seminars held at the University of Minnesota, Liberman (1980) noted, "During the past fifty years people have been trying to apply methods of phonology to grammar and semantics with varying degrees of success" (p. 8). He explained that at the level of acoustics and articulation, the study of language as a discrete, self-contained system may, in part, work, but he also argued that this has nothing to do with the act of communication and the message itself. (See similar remarks by Nystrand, this volume.)

Scientific research on texts is a mere decade old in the United States. It has focused on the logical analysis of how structures work with the intent of establishing a classification system that will hold across linguistic situations. Such work has been misguided. It has operated from the mistaken assumption of the invariance of language, but Beaugrande (1985) correctly observes, and many of us concur, that this invariance is essentially a fiction.

> In real communication, an element is classified not by what it is in the linguist's scheme, but by what it does, that is, by its function in the processing of the participant. A single element may have several functions, and a single function may be assigned to several elements. Thus what we need is not grander, more elaborate lists of elements, but an account of how elements are selected and defined during ongoing processes. (p. 49)

Linguistics has also been dominated by an individualist ideology; Halliday (1978) observes that the angle of reasoning has been typically from the "language outwards" rather than from the social order "into language." Recognizing this neglect, a second epistomological orientation has emerged, calling for a functional approach to spoken and written language. This approach, influenced by the work of eminent linguists such as J. R. Firth, Louis Hjelmslev, and more recently proponents of systemic theory, is concerned with the systematic functions and uses of language by specific social and cultural groups. Particular attention has been given to the interaction and dialectic between writer and reader and speaker and listener by way of language and within natural contexts. Theoretical papers and volumes with this view show that language and texts grow out of human needs to construct, negotiate, and interpret meaning for an audience and the personal intentions of a speaker or writer. They are ultimately processed from listener or reader cultural perspectives. In essence, the speaker and writer and listener and reader roles are being studied in relation to one another and are moving us toward an integrated theory of language processes and products. (See recent volumes on systemics by Benson & Greaves, 1985a, 1985b; Halliday, 1985, and also this volume; Horowitz & Samuels, this volume; Nystrand, 1982, 1986.)

Moreover, several scholars who employ a functional and revisionist approach to language theoretically characterize how the rhetorical structures, in which we are interested, might evolve in discourse production. Barthes (1970) pointed out that it is the social structure that generates semiotic tensions, rhetorical styles, and text genres that writers produce and readers process. Halliday (1978) states that the rhetorical structure of discourse or text has its origin in the social structure and context of situation, and finally, Beaugrande (1980) indicates that a text only becomes coherent when there is connectivity between text knowledge and world knowledge. Despite these theories, we have little research that treats oral or written discourse interpretation from a functional approach, taking into account the angle of production and the social-contextual perspectives suggested here.

The Architecture of Text

Hierarchical Dimensions of Text

It is essential that we discuss the comprehension of oral and written discourse with attention to the way texts are produced and structured. The examination of text from a production and structural angle presents a number of new considerations including the notion of strategic choice. This concept is an integral part of my definition of text. I draw from Halliday (1975) who notes:

> Let us use the word *text* to refer to any instance of language that is operational (as distinct from citational) . . . in some living context of use. Let us then conceive of text as choice. The text represents a selection within various sets of options; what is said presupposes a background of what might have been said but was not. In linguistic terms, it presupposes a paradigmatic environment. . . . we can conceive of text not as 'what is said' but as 'what is meant,' still in the environment of what might have been. . . . A text represents a pattern of selection within a meaning potential. (pp. 10–11)

The processing and comprehension of text has been viewed as primarily the recall of ideas or propositions from a textbase, without consideration of the design and structural dimensions of language patterns. However, philosophical essays increasingly point to the selective choice and use of patterns of language in particular contexts. According to M. Meyer (1983), textual meaning is not strictly a cognitive matter; it is also a rhetorical matter. Meaning is based on questions and answers that are expressed through the production of language patterns. The importance of rhetorical form is expressed by Cummings, Herum, and Lybbert (1971) and Parret (1980), who stress the use of repetitive patterns (e.g., reiteration of a clause) establishes cohesion and form. While traditional work in psychology has held that the surface forms are only briefly remembered following language processing, or are not remembered at all (Jarvella, 1977), both theory and research now emphasize the surface structure is not only used in discourse processing, but is also remembered (Fine, 1985). Along with this attention to language patterns has come some attention to the hierarchical nature of the structures used to build written language.

Limited Knowledge of Written Language

Because the study of written language is relatively new, there is limited knowledge available about the way *strategic choices* are made and function in the hierarchical patterning of written language.

Vachek (1973) reminds us that "the latter half of the nineteenth century, as well as the first three decades of the twentieth century, showed very little understanding for written language viewed as a system 'in its own right' " (p. 9). There is hardly reference to written discourse but rather reference to writing as spelling, the graphophonemic aspects of language. Saussure (1916) indicates that "the only raison d'etre of 'writing' (*écriture*) is to 'represent language,' i.e., to serve as a means of putting down or transcribing 'spoken utterances.' The 'written word' is even accused of 'usurping the principal part' which should be played by the spoken word" (Saussure, cited in Vachek, 1973, p. 10).

In conclusion, Saussure (1916), Sapir (1921), Bloomfield (1933), and Hockett (1958), four scholars representing three different generations of linguists, excluded written language from their domain of language study.

Contrasts between Spoken and Written Language

Contrasts between the structural nature of spoken and written language are likewise recent undertakings. For example, Hockett (1958) argues that "speech and writing are merely two different manifestations of something fundamentally the same" (p. 4). It must be highlighted that rhetoric historically has told us little about the way in which a given structure might function under these different language systems and the different modalities. There has been some argument for the superstructure status of writing, and the myth has prevailed that written language is more complex than spoken language (Halliday, 1986).[1] Consequently a number of questions remain open for scholarly investigation. These questions will need to be tackled using real-world and school-world texts: Do the highest-order rhetorical structures function differently in oral and written language? Do rhetorical structures in written language have the potential of exerting influence on cognitive development and learning in ways that are distinct from those of oral language structures? Is the architecture of written discourse, namely its structural and hierarchical dimensions, markedly different than that of oral discourse, e.g., in conversations, formal or informal speeches, commentaries, critiques, monologues, dyadic exchanges, and group exchanges? As Vachek (1973) notes, the structural correspondence of what he calls the two language "norms" remains undefined.

A History of Rhetorical Structures

The rhetorical structures that we examine in this chapter have been treated in the literature under a variety of terms, depending upon the field or perspective of the scholar. These terms are important because they imply different approaches to language, language analysis, and discourse processing.

Theory dating back to Aristotle's *Rhetoric* (1954) included discussions of 28 enthymeme topics, referred to as *topoi*, i.e., common topics or commonplaces, which were strategic approaches to be applied to specific oral compositions. These were extended by Cicero in the *Topica* (1949) to include logical categories of definition, partition, comparison, analogy, antecedent, cause–effect, genus and species, and nonlogical categories. Stump (1978) notes that the concept of *topoi* and their role in discourse has undergone significant change and reinterpretation over time (see Hill, 1884). Traditional treatments of *topoi* have been unconnected to broader issues of discourse or theories of discourse processing as we know them. Typically *topoi* have been used to generate the writing of discourse types and genres and have been related to rhetorical structures of explanatory text.

The rhetorical structures discussed in this chapter have also been characterized as *text-forming structures* (Halliday & Hasan, 1976). These are structures that are presumed to be responsible for shaping a discourse and for establishing cohesion (Hoey & Winter, 1986; Horowitz, 1986; Winter, 1982). Research examining the effect of signal words has not yet isolated the conditions under which these features contribute to comprehension, but theoretical vocabulary analysis (see, e.g., Winter, 1977) argues forcefully for their central role in discourse formation and processing.

Van Dijk (1980) uses still another term, *schematic superstructures*, to refer to global forms of discourse and the conventions that writers use to structure a composition of a particular genre (e.g., narratives, persuasive arguments, or experimental research reports). Schematic superstructures show the relationships between propositions in a text and also constrain and establish guidelines for the processing of a text. They are defined by recursive rules and specific transformations that may be culturally determined (see van Dijk, 1980, pp. 107–132, for further discussion of these structures). *Macrostructures* are the global meanings of discourse that are represented by superstructures. Considerable theoretical discussion has taken place to describe the formation of a macrostructure. In the model of text comprehension presented by Kintsch and van Dijk (1978) and later in van Dijk and Kintsch (1983), the formation of a macrostructure is characterized as a basic part of the reading process. More recently, Guindon and Kintsch (1984) demonstrate that subjects form the macrostructure of a text as part of the comprehension process during reading and not just in response to certain task demands. However, language users, like other artists, e.g., painters, musicians, or architects, may not always be conscious of how these structures come to be used in comprehension or interpretation.

This chapter focuses on the concept of *rhetorical predicates*, defined by Grimes (1975) and B. J. F. Meyer (1975) as elements of text that connect sentences and paragraphs to give prose its overall organization and form. These elements establish patterns of semantic relationships among ideas in a text. As defined by Grimes, rhetorical predicates may appear at many levels of a text hierarchy of information, linking lexical propositions and lower-level rhetorical propositions. The rhetorical predicates examined in this chapter are the highest-order elements of a discourse content structure. B. J. F. Meyer (1975) and associates have referred to these as *top-level structures* and have conducted empirical research that demonstrates their influence on text comprehension.

Concurrent with work in linguistics and discourse analysis is another set of terms used by cognitive scientists. One finds the concept of *frames* introduced in this literature. As treated by Minsky (1975), a frame is a structure in memory which influences comprehension. While Tannen (1979) and others have considered the frame as represented in the surface structure of discourse, more recently the focus is on the frame as a linguistic mental representation, mental model, or a social-experiential event in memory (Goffman, 1974; Garnham, 1981; van Dijk & Kintsch, 1983; van Dijk, 1977, also this volume), interacting with semantic meaning from text, and vital to the way we conceptualize text. A frame is a top-down macrostate supplying global hypotheses about what is to come in the text. A rhetorical predicate may be conceived of as a frame which exists in memory for a particular text and structures the arguments and processing of that text. One may, for example, think of a trip to Disneyland by employing cause–effect frames that give the before, during, and after events and, thereby, create a mental model of "Disneyland adventures."

In sum, in surveying the ways in which rhetorical structures have been viewed, we find three separate representations of these structures: a surface representation in text, a representation in memory, and a social-situationally based representation, also in text or memory. Each approach allows us to gain a qualitatively different kind of insight into discourse processing.

The Synthesis of Form and Content

As conceived theoretically (Grimes, 1975; Longacre, 1976), rhetorical predicates in discourse should have some effect on the synthesis of form and content in speaking and writing or listening and reading. In the case of the listening and reading contrast, few studies that have compared listening and reading have controlled for the rhetorical structure in the discourse to ascertain whether it functions differently for listeners and readers, and when so. It is possible that these structures operate differently across oral and written discourse, and across formal and informal registers. For instance, they may be more necessary for certain registers in formal written discourse comprehension than for informal oral discourse comprehension, or for certain social situations. For example, the taking of notes by a student during a lecture would be greatly enhanced if the global structure of the lecture were made explicit by an instructor on the blackboard and translated into a form one could actually see and rescan.

It may be hypothesized that the listener of formal prose, such as in schools, is under the gun—obligated to process what is often fleeting information promptly in order to obtain the form and gist (what van Dijk, 1980, calls the *macrostructure*) within a certain time limit. The tempo of speech, be it conversation or a lecture, may be a critical factor for the listener. But the spatial presentation of written discourse, whether it be a chapter or a syllabus, may be a particularly critical factor in reading. It is possible that in formal reading, such as is in school reading, the structure will be reread, or instantiated if not present in the text, making the synthesis of the form and content more easily obtainable than in listening. One might argue that this synthesis results in the formation of a "main idea" or "gist" of text.

Important work has begun to examine such possibilities. For example, Schreiber (this volume) shows how young children use the prosodic features of language in listening. Rhythm, tone, pauses, pitch, and vocal cues or other paralinguistic elements may aid the listener but may not be readily available in formal reading in schools. Townsend, Carrithers, and Bever (this volume) show there is greater sensitivity to discourse-thematic relations with development, and show that similar cognitive processes operate under reading and listening with this development. However, Hron, Kurbjuhn, Mandl, and Schnotz (1985) indicate that the formation of a macrostructure "should be accomplished more easily in reading, because the reader can reconstruct the inferential processes far more independently" than the listener (p. 4). With a popular scientific text, reading reproduction was better than listening reproduction. Hron *et al.* found signals (cues associated with the global, rhetorical structures) aided both listeners and readers, but were less effective over time for listeners than readers.

Hron *et al.* conclude that signals employed typically in texts should be included with difficult oral discourse, as these should facilitate macro-processing and the construction of macrostructures. They make their recommendation for the use of "text signals" in oral news reporting or educational lectures.

While some signaling is regarded as desirable for both oral and written formal language, it may not be desirable or necessary for other kinds of oral or written discourse comprehension, and some research has shown it clearly does not effect comprehension. One can also think of various instances where too many signals are sheer interferences, as in the reading of legal documents, where too many uses of *thus* and *therefore* may only confound matters. Future research will need to tease apart conditions for the necessity of signals.

The Match between Form and Content

The task facing the composer of text is similar to that of the composer of music: to present content in a form which follows and supports the ideas expressed. From a pragmatic standpoint, the match between form and content should ensure efficient and effective understanding. But how is this match achieved? One might look into the experiences of various artists.

In a letter of 1878, the musician, Tchaikovsky, indicates:

> I never compose in the *abstract;* that is to say, the musical thought never appears otherwise than in a suitable external form. In this way I invent the musical idea and the instrumentation simultaneously: . . . Only after strenuous labour have I at last succeeded in making the form of my compositions correspond, more or less, with their contents. (Tchaikovsky, 1878/1970, p. 59)

Similarly, the architect–artist struggles with form and content relationships.

> The ultimate object of design is form. . . . problem begins with an effort to achieve fitness between two entities: the form in question and its context. *The form is the solution to the problem; the context defines the problem.* In other words, when we speak of design, the real object of discussion is not the form alone, but the *ensemble* comprising the form *and* its context. Good fit is a desired property of this ensemble which relates to some particular division of the ensemble into form and context. (Alexander, 1964, pp. 15–16, italics added)

Alexander goes on to provide a variety of metaphors associated with design and the psychological establishment of form.

> There is a wide variety of ensembles which we can talk about like this. . . . The ensemble consisting of a suit and tie is a familiar case in point; one tie goes well with a certain suit, another goes less well. Again, the ensemble may be a game of chess, where at a certain stage of the game some moves are more appropriate than others because they fit the context of the previous moves more aptly. The ensemble may be a musical composition—musical phrases have to fit their contexts too: think of the perfect rightness when Mozart puts just *this* phrase at a certain point in a sonata. (Alexander, 1964, p. 16).

The experiment which follows begins to consider the themes treated in this section: (1) the match between form and content, (2) the differences between reading and listening, and (3) the role of rhetorical structures in comprehension by school populations.

THE EXPERIMENT: EFFECTS OF RHETORICAL PREDICATES IN DISCOURSE PROCESSING

Paratactic versus Hypotactic Structures

Linguists have divided discourse structures into two categories, **paratactic** and **hypotactic**. These two categories have been analyzed as they function in oral and written discourse (Halliday, this volume). Linguists have typically associated hypotaxis with the compactness of written language and parataxis with the looseness of oral language, although such contrasts seem superficial and restrictive (Hudson, 1984).

An emphasis on hypotactic structure has also been carried to the classroom where study of the adversative structure (compare–contrast, a hypotactic structure) is a significant part of writing instruction. Freshmen composition in universities, for example, routinely includes the writing and reading of compare–contrast essays.

Below I identify characteristics and examples of paratactic and hypotactic rhetorical predicates relevant to the research to be described, drawing from the theoretical work of Grimes (1975).

Paratactic rhetorical predicates dominate all of our subarguments in a coordinate fashion; they involve two semantic subtrees in a symmetric relation. The second subtree is coordinated with, and largely taken from, the first (Grimes, 1975, p. 210).

Attribution (list–structure) is typically a paratactic rhetorical predicate. See Figure 4.1 for an example.

Response (problem–solution) is a paratactic rhetorical predicate, as its problem argument and solution argument are placed at the same level of the text hierarchy; the second solution argument is taken from the first.

Covariance (cause–effect) is another paratactic rhetorical predicate used in the research. See Figure 4.3 for examples.

Hypotactic rhetorical predicates place some ideas at a superordinate level and others at a subordinate level. They relate subarguments to the superordinate, dominating, center statement. Hypotaxis, according to Grimes (1975), is characterized by subordination rather than parallel arguments, implies classification, and may be essential to written language.

Adversative (compare–contrast) is a hypotactic rhetorical predicate. The favored view is placed at a higher level than the opposed view in the text hierarchy of information. These arguments, therefore, are not equally weighted. See Figure 4.2 for an example.

A neutral rhetorical predicate is described by Grimes (1975) as the most common rhetorical predicate in text; this can assume either a paratactic or hypotactic form depending upon its relationship to the remainder of the text and the context in which this structure is placed. Grimes indicates that whether a neutral predicate is taken as paratactic or hypotactic depends upon the author's decisions in the area of staging. In the experiment to be described, attribution (list–structure, collection) is a neutral rhetorical predicate. In one text, "Body Water," it has a paratactic form, as the list of items included in the text are placed at an equal level with one another and the items are unrelated to one another. In a second text, "Social Spiders," attribution (list–structure, collection) has a hypotactic form, as one list item is given prominence and serves as a link to the remainder of the text. It should be noted that both types of

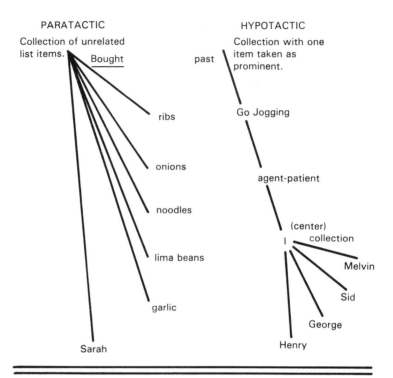

ATTRIBUTION
List-Structure
Collection

PARATACTIC
Collection of unrelated
list items.

Bought

ribs

onions

noodles

lima beans

garlic

Sarah

past

HYPOTACTIC
Collection with one
item taken as
prominent.

Go Jogging

agent-patient

(center)
collection

I

Melvin

Sid

George

Henry

| Sarah bought ribs, onions, noodles, lima beans, and garlic. Some of these items could be used to make a European stew. | I went jogging with Henry, George, Sid, and Melvin. We did a mile and a half. |

FIGURE 4.1.   Neutral rhetorical predicates.

attribution use a list format,[2] and that little is known about the effects of either of these forms of attribution on discourse processing and comprehension. [See Figure 4.1 for examples of the two types of attribution, as treated by Grimes.]

The following rhetorical predicates were examined in the research to be discussed:[3]

Attribution: A predicate that relates a collection of attributes to an event or an idea in a list-type format. Figure 4.1 shows an example of this type.

ADVERSATIVE

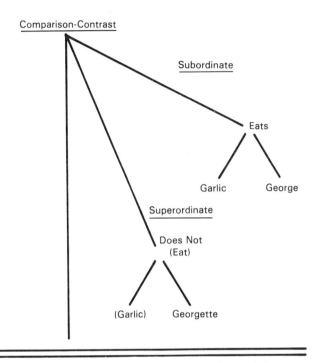

Although George eats garlic, Georgette does not (eat garlic).

FIGURE 4.2. Hypotactic rhetorical predicate.

Adversative: A predicate that relates a favored view to an opposed view. See Figure 4.2.

Covariance: A predicate that relates an antecedent to a consequent. See Figure 4.3.

Response: A predicate that relates a problem to a solution. See Figure 4.3.

The experiment reported in this chapter draws on the theoretical literature on paratactic and hypotactic structures found in rhetoric and linguistics. In that literature, these structures are not given equal status. Rhetoricians have historically made strong claims, as have linguists, regarding the power of certain rhetorical structures. For instance, Perelman and Olbrechts-Tyteca (1969), in their historical review of types

RESPONSE   COVARIANCE

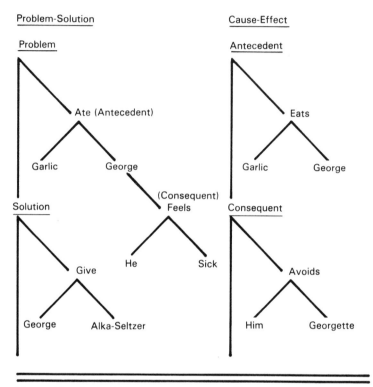

(The problem is that) George ate   (The cause of the break-up is that)
the garlic. He feels sick.   George eats garlic.

(The solution is to) give him   (The result is that) Georgette
Alka-Seltzer.   avoids him.

FIGURE 4.3. Paratactic rhetorical predicates.

of argu ̄nents in discourse, have characterized the hypotactic structure as the "argument par excellence." This point of view has persisted in the literature.

The hypotactic construction is the argumentative construction par excellence. Auerbach considers it to be characteristic of Greco-Roman literature in contradistinction to the paratactic construction favored in Hebrew culture. Hypotaxis creates frameworks, constitutes the adoption of a position. It controls the reader, forces him to see particular relationships, restricts the interpretations he may consider, and takes its inspiration from well-constructed legal reasoning. Parataxis leaves greater freedom and does not appear to wish to impose a particular view point. (p. 158)

The research presented in this chapter was designed to test claims in the literature that the adversative pattern (a hypotactic structure) would have significantly greater influence on discourse processing and recall over the other rhetorical structures treated in the literature.

Several questions were posed within the context of previous theory and recent research:

Would the advantage of the adversative pattern reported by Meyer & Freedle (1979, 1984) for graduate students persist with students at several levels of schooling? With secondary students and university freshmen?

Subjects tested in the Meyer and Freedle study listened to "Body Water." Would these findings persist with reading tasks? This seemed important given growing evidence that we should not automatically equate reading and listening tasks (Horowitz & Samuels, 1985; Hron et al., 1985; see also other chapters in this volume: Danks & End; Samuels; Perfetti).

Would a rhetorical predicate be necessary for the "Body Water" passage, and with upper-grade readers? Meyer and Freedle, as well as other researchers of these structures, did not include a control text, one without a rhetorical predicate.

Would findings persist with another text topic and content and with a text calibrated to "Body Water?" Meyer and Freedle's "Body Water" text had been used in several other studies. Additional texts were needed to confirm their findings.

Would there be an interaction between rhetorical predicate and passage? Contra to Meyer and Freedle, it was posited that a rhetorical predicate might be better suited to a particular text and context and that these structures would be selected on the basis of content and message intention, rather than the presumed powerful effects of one pattern. In conclusion, some patterns simply might not be a good fit to some texts (see Alexander, 1964, and discussion in the first part of this chapter).

Experimental Study of Rhetorical Predicates

Despite the interest in these structural elements, actual scientific tests of the effects of rhetorical predicates on different listener and reader audiences have been limited (Horowitz, Piché, & Samuels, 1981; Horowitz, 1982a, 1982b, 1983, 1984a, 1984b, 1985a, 1985b; B. J. F. Meyer, Brandt, & Bluth, 1980; Meyer & Freedle, 1979, 1984; Roen & Piché, 1984;

Urquhart, 1976). Constructs extraneous to the text have more often been the focus of attention than the rhetorical elements of text (Bartlett, 1978; Brandt, 1978; Elliott, 1980; Slater, Graves, & Piché, 1985). There is little information available about how upper-grade readers process expository discourse with and without rhetorical structures before the intervention measures are applied. Since a number of researchers have begun to examine ways of teaching students to be aware of and to use these structures in learning tasks (see, e.g., Reder, 1985), further information about what effects they have in discourse processing is needed.

The Meyer and Freedle Study

At the time of my research, only one study had been undertaken to contrast the effects of the four rhetorical predicates on reader recall of expository discourse holding passage constant. B. J. F. Meyer and Freedle (1979, 1984) conducted an important study where they contrasted the effects of the four rhetorical predicates using the by-now quite familiar loss of body water passage.[4] The subjects ($N = 44$) were graduate students, teachers enrolled in an introductory research course in Western Connecticut State College. They listened to tape recordings of these passages. This research demonstrated significant differences in the recall of passages organized by the rhetorical predicates. Specifically, graduate students produced greater recall of texts organized by an adversative (compare–contrast) and covariance (cause–effect) structure than with texts organized by attribution (list–structure). Surprisingly, response (problem–solution) fell between the two categories of structures and was rejected by the graduate students as a viable solution, and appropriate structure, for problems posed in the passage. Subjects who listened to the response passage opted instead for another higher-order rhetorical predicate.

In the 1984 report of this research, a second experiment was added, whereby another group of graduate students who were teachers ($N = 55$) was asked to rate the four texts on difficulty for learning. The content of the body water text was not judged as more suited to one rhetorical predicate.

Experimental Design

Overview.   Two large experiments were conducted. The two experiments included 397 subjects and resulted in a total of 894 immediate and 7-day delayed recall protocols of 10 passages. In Experiment I ($N = 219$, 438 protocols) we tested for the effect of the four rhetorical predicates on immediate, 7-day delayed recall and probed recall, and tested for reader judgment of the texts used in the research one week following the reading. In addition, reader use of rhetorical predicates in the written recalls was scored and reading time recorded. In Experiment II (N = 178, 356 protocols) we tested for the effects of select positioning of rhetorical predicates on recall with the expectation that the placement of rhetorical predicates in the surface structure would influence recall. Experiment II employed the same multiple dependent measures as used in the first experiment (Horowitz, 1982b). Due to space limitations, only portions of Experiment I are reported herein.[5]

A 5 × 2 × 2 fixed factorial design was used in Experiment I. Independent variables were four rhetorical predicates—attribution (list–structure), adversative (compare–contrast), covariance (cause–effect), response (problem–solution)—and a control condition (a text with no higher-order rhetorical predicate); two expository text topics ("Body Water" and "Social Spiders"); and subjects at two levels of formal schooling (9th and 13th graders).

Sample. There were 219 subjects, 120 ninth graders and 99 university freshmen. Ninth graders ($\bar{x}$ age = 14.7 years) were students in a primarily middle-class suburb of Minneapolis, Minnesota. Administrators indicated that approximately 65% of the school population was college bound. Based on the Gates-MacGinitie Reading Comprehension Test (Level E, Form 3M), it was apparent that they were skilled readers and were reading well above grade level ($\bar{x}$ = 11.19, range 7.0–13.0).

A second sample of students ($\bar{x}$ age = 20.14 years) enrolled in freshmen composition classes, Composition 1001 and 1002 in the English Department at the University of Minnesota, participated in the study. The freshmen participating in this research were on the average not coming directly from high school. Students who identified themselves as freshmen had completed a mean of 29.54 credits, ranging from 3 to 83 postsecondary quarter credits. The mean verbal score on the PSAT, or a PSAT equivalent score for 77% of the freshmen subjects was 41.7.

Procedures. The procedures followed were the same as those used in the Meyer and Freedle study (1979, 1984), except that subjects in this experiment read rather than listened to the passages under consideration. Each subject was randomly assigned to a treatment condition and read one of 10 passages, since previous research had shown evidence of practice effect when subjects read more than one passage. Subjects were informed in advance that they would be asked to recall all that they could remember from the passage. A Hunter Digital Klockcounter, Model 120C, was used to measure reading time in seconds. The goal was to use reading time as an index of processing differences. Students recalled the texts in writing immediately following reading. There was no time limit for the reading or the writing tasks. Seven days later, without advance notice, a second recall was procured and subjects responded to six Likert scales that required that they rate the passages on several criteria.

Texts. "Body Water." The various versions of the body water passage used in the Meyer and Freedle listening experiment were used in this research. The body water texts were two to three paragraphs ranging from 109 to 144 words, from seven to nine sentences, depending upon the predicate manipulation. The original source of this passage is unknown.

"Social Spiders." In addition, a second scientific passage on social spiders was used in the research. This was an edited version of content from "Unraveling the Top Arachnid" a National Science Foundation (1978) publication. The passage described the sociability of particular spider groups as a means for studying behavior in various environments.

"Social Spiders" was edited to resemble "Body Water" along multiple criteria. As was the case with "Body Water," it contained from seven to nine sentences, depending on the predicate manipulation. "Social Spiders" was two to three paragraphs, ranging from 109 to 145 words. Rhetorical predicates were placed in the same locale as in "Body Water." The passages were scored using the Meyer (1975) prose analysis system. The number of idea units and hierarchical levels in the passage's semantic structure were determined on the basis of this system. These passages differed in two important respects: "Body Water" contained 58 target idea units, while "Social Spiders" contained 88 target idea units. The passages did not have a similar number or type of hierarchical structures.

"Social Spiders" was organized by a response (problem-solution) rhetorical predicate. Additional rhetorical predicates were created as possible organizers of the information. The topic was intended to be unfamiliar, following the recommendation in previous research (Brandt, 1978) that such a text would force readers to rely on the structure for meaning. The texts used in this research are included in the Appendix. The semantic structures of these texts may be found in Horowitz (1982a). Table 4.1 presents the various types of rhetorical structures treated in this research. Table 4.2 identifies characteristics of each of the texts.[6]

Results

Scoring of Recalls. Using the content structures for "Body Water" and the content structures developed for "Social Spiders," two colleagues assisted the experimenter in scoring 438 protocols. An intraclass correlation formula (Ebel, 1951) was used to ensure reliability. Reliability for proportion of target idea units immediately recalled for "Body Water" was .91 and for "Social Spiders" was .93. Scores for 219 immediate recalls are reported here, although delayed recalls do not depart from immediate recalls.

Proportion of Target Idea Units Recalled. An ANOVA was performed on three factors, rhetorical predicate, passage, and grade, using proportion of target idea units recalled as the dependent measure. Contrary to previous findings by B. J. F. Meyer and Freedle (1984), no main effect for rhetorical predicate was found. However, an interaction between rhetorical predicate and passage was found $F(4, 199) = 2.63$, $p = .035$. Figure 4.4 depicts this significant interaction with grades com-

TABLE 4.1
Text Patterns

Rhetorical predicate	Type of structure	Degree of structure
Control condition (no rhetorical predicate)	No overall organizing pattern	No higher-order rhetorical pattern
Attribution (list-type structure)	Linear form	Some structure
Covariance (cause–effect)	Hierarchical	**Complex structure.** *Paratactic form*: Predicate parts of equal weight and parallel to one another. Superordinate to text
Response (problem–solution)	Hierarchical	Same as complex structure above
Adversative (comparison–contrast)	Hierarchical	**Complex structure.** *Hypotactic form:* Predicate parts of unequal weight—one predicate part superordinate and another part subordinate. Superordinate to text

TABLE 4.2
Text Characteristics for "Body Water" and "Social Spiders"

	Attribution		Adversative		Covariance		Response		Control	
	BW	SS	BW	SS	BW	SS	BW	SS	BW	SS
Number of paragraphs	3	3	2	2	2	2	2	2	2	2
Number of words	141	141	141	142	141	141	144	145	109	109
Number of sentences	8	9	7	8	7	8	7	8	6	7
Number of words in rhetorical predicates	32	32	32	33	32	32	35	36	0	0
Number of idea units in rhetorical predicates	10	10	10	12	10	10	10	12	0	0
Number of target paragraph words	109	109	109	109	109	109	109	109	109	109
Number of words in Paragraph A	42	42	42	42	42	42	42	42	42	42
Number of words in Paragraph B	67	67	67	67	67	67	67	67	67	67
Number of idea units in target paragraphs	58	88	58	88	58	88	58	88	58	88
Text structure	List-structure, Paratactic Hypotactic		Hypotactic		Paratactic		Paratactic		No higher-order rhetorical structure	
Discourse force	To inform		To inform		To inform		To inform		To inform	
Explanation relation link between paragraphs 1 & 2	No	No	Yes	Yes	Yes	Yes	Yes	Yes	No	No
Lexical cohesion reference (repetition of major referent)	Yes	Yes	Yes	Yes	Yes	Yes	Yes	Yes	Yes	Yes

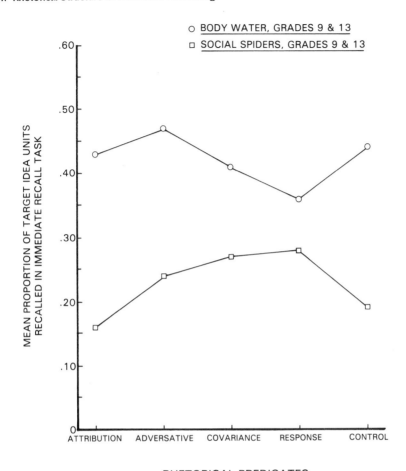

RHETORICAL PREDICATES

FIGURE 4.4. Significant interaction between rhetorical predicate and passage for mean proportion of target idea units recalled, grades combined.

bined. Table 4.3 provides mean proportion of target idea units recalled by rhetorical predicate and passage in immediate recall task. Figure 4.5 illustrates this interaction with grades separated. Table 4.4 provides mean proportion of target idea units recalled by rhetorical predicate, passage, and grade in immediate recall tasks.

Following the ANOVA, post-hoc analyses were conducted which included ten Bonferroni t-tests. In order to avoid a Type 1 error, t needed to equal 2.80 and α was set at .005. An alpha of .005 was arrived at by dividing .05 by 10 (the total number of contrasts). Contrasts were designed to compare recall of texts with no higher-order structure (con-

TABLE 4.3
Target Idea Units Recalled by
Rhetorical Predicate and Passage in
Immediate Recall Task

	Body Water		Social Spiders	
Rhetorical predicate	M	SD	M	SD
Attribution	.43	(.16)	.16	(.11)
Adversative	.47	(.18)	.24	(.14)
Covariance	.41	(.16)	.27	(.17)
Response	.36	(.13)	.28	(.12)
Control	.44	(.16)	.19	(.11)

trol), some structure (list-format), complex structure (covariance, response) and more complex structure (adversative). (See Table 4.1.) These contrasts treated "Body Water" and "Social Spiders" separately, and combined and separated grades.

Significant results emerged. Below is only a brief discussion of findings with text topics separated and grades combined. For a more complete discussion of rhetorical predicates contrasted, see Horowitz (1982a).

1. Control and attribution functioned in much the same way. There were no significant differences for "Body Water" or "Social Spiders," with grades combined or separated, suggesting that a text with list-structure functioned like one with no higher-order structure. This was consistent with theoretical literature.

2. When text recalls from control and attribution passages were compared to other presumably more complex structured passages (adversative, covariance, and response), there were no significant differences for "Body Water." However, for "Social Spiders" the presumably more complex structures were significantly more effective in facilitating recall than control and attribution structured texts ($p = .001$).

3. Similarly, response was significantly more effective than control and attribution for "Spiders" ($p = .005$) but not for "Body Water" with grades combined or separated.

4. Relatedly, *covariance, response,* and *adversative* were more effective organizational structures than *attribution* for "Social Spiders" ($p = .004$), but not for "Body Water."

Additional contrasts focused on the different effects of the single response and the adversative structures. We expected that the response

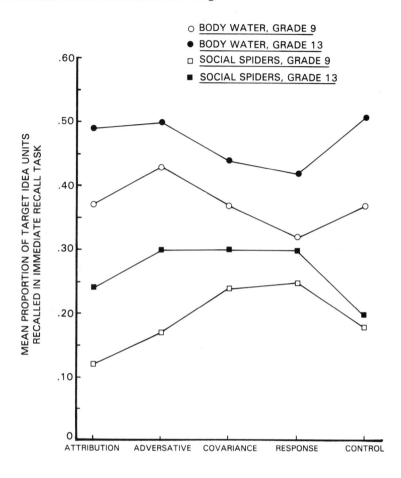

RHETORICAL PREDICATES

FIGURE 4.5. Significant interaction between rhetorical predicate and passage for mean proportion of target idea units recalled, grades separated.

structure would be a better fit for "Social Spiders" than the other structures.

1. Response was significantly less effective than control and resulted in the lowest mean recall for "Body Water" ($t = 1.75$, $df = 51$, $p < .05$). Meyer and Freedle, as noted, also found that this response rhetorical predicate resulted in poor recall, and they indicate that this structure was inappropriate for the text and their sample. However, response was significantly more effective than control for "Social Spiders" ($t = 2.25$,

TABLE 4.4
Target Idea Units Recalled by Rhetorical Predicate, Passage,
and Grade in Immediate Recall Task

	Body Water				Social Spiders			
	9th		13th		9th		13th	
Rhetorical predicate	*M*	*SD*	*M*	*SD*	*M*	*SD*	*M*	*SD*
Attribution	.37	(.15)	.49	(.16)	.12	(.07)	.24	(.12)
Adversative	.43	(.20)	.50	(.15)	.17	(.09)	.30	(.15)
Covariance	.37	(.18)	.44	(.15)	.24	(.16)	.30	(.19)
Response	.32	(.13)	.42	(.12)	.25	(.09)	.30	(.14)
Control	.37	(.16)	.51	(.14)	.18	(.11)	.20	(.12)

$df = 41$, $p < .05$) and resulted in the highest mean recall for that text. Likert scales ratings confirm that the spiders passage was a highly unfamiliar topic. Where topic is highly unfamiliar there is likely to be greater need for a higher-order rhetorical predicate. It is also possible that this structure was simply a better match to the text.

2. Adversative also functioned differentially by text. Unlike data reported by Meyer and Freedle (1979, 1984), the adversative was not better than attribution for "Body Water" with the present population ($t = .90$, $df = 42$, $p > .05$), but adversative was significantly better than attribution for "Spiders" ($t = 2.0$, $df = 42$, $p < .05$). In sum, the effects of rhetorical predicates were not the same across texts.

Reading Rate. An ANOVA was performed on the three key factors using number of words read per minute as a dependent measure. Only a main effect for grade was significant, with, as would be expected, 13th graders reading at a faster rate than 9th graders ($p = .006$). These results confirmed that, for this population, rhetorical predicates were not differentially influencing discourse processing, as measured by reading time.

Likert Scale Tasks. Readers were asked to judge the texts, one week later, on six scale items. This part of the study was designed to assess reader judgments of the passage across age-grades. An ANOVA was performed on the three factors—rhetorical predicate, passage, grade— on each of the six Likert scales, using the scale options 1–5 (with 1 as negative to 5 as positive) as a dependent measure. Where the ANOVA resulted in significant difference, this was followed by simple *t*-tests. Table 4.5 provides the six Likert scales used in the research.

TABLE 4.5
Likert Scales

Questions associated with text processing posed to 9th and 13th graders:

1. Text comprehensibility and difficulty: "How difficult was this text for you to read and understand?"
Very difficult	Somewhat difficult	Average difficult	Not too difficult	Easy
1	2	3	4	5
2. Memorability: "How difficult was this text for you to remember?"
Very difficult	Somewhat difficult	Average difficult	Not too difficult	Easy
1	2	3	4	5
3. Prior knowledge: "How much background knowledge do you think you had in this area?"
Very little	Some	Average amount	Good amount	Quite a lot
1	2	3	4	5

Questions associated with rhetorical dimensions of text posed to 9th and 13th graders:

4. Staging of main line of argument: "How clear was the main line of thought or argument of the text?"
Unclear	Somewhat clear	Clear	Quite clear	Very clear
1	2	3	4	5
5. Text cohesiveness: "How cohesive was the text that you read?"
Not cohesive	Somewhat cohesive	Cohesive	Quite cohesive	Very cohesive
1	2	3	4	5
6. Text organization: "How well organized do you think the text was that you read?"
Not organized	Below average	Average	Above average	Very well organized
1	2	3	4	5

Rhetorical Predicates. For the most part, the rhetorical predicates of interest in this research did not influence subject judgments of the texts. This is consistent with findings by Faigley and Meyer (1983) who report college freshmen viewed top level structure as less important than other factors, in this case, a time element in the classifying of texts. A main effect on Likert #5 (text cohesiveness) for rhetorical predicate emerged ($p = .009$). Post-hoc t-tests indicated that the adversative texts, when compared to control texts, were judged as more cohesive ($t = 2.09$, $df = 64$, $p < .05$).

Passages. Scale items indicated that the two texts were judged as significantly different on the basis of every measure used including comprehensibility and difficulty, memorability, prior knowledge, clarity of main line argument, cohesiveness, and organization (each t-test $p = .01$).

Grade Differences. Although there were not age-grade differences in the proportion of idea units produced in a text recall, the 9th and 13th graders judged the texts differently. The Likert scale revealed the following:

1. An interaction between passage and grade on memorability revealed that 13th graders perceived their texts as being different in memorability while 9th graders did not ($t = 4.66$, $df = 75$, $p = .01$); 9th graders judged the memorability of "Body Water" and "Social Spiders" as the same. The 9th graders may not have yet acquired the ability to distinguish the potential degree of memorability of these expository passages.

2. An interaction between passage and grade revealed that 9th and 13th graders saw themselves as having different amounts of prior knowledge for the two texts. Ninth and 13th graders saw their prior knowledge for "Social Spiders" as about the same but differed in their judgments of their background knowledge for "Body Water" (13th graders indicated greater prior knowledge for "Body Water" than did 9th graders ($t = 2.73$, $df = 87$, $p = .01$).

3. Finally, 9th graders judged the texts as more organized than 13th graders ($p = .018$). It is possible that their view of text organization may not have been as differentiated as the 13th grade subjects in this study.

Conclusions

In summary, the following were major findings:

1. Contrary to previous research by Meyer and Freedle, replication here with "Body Water" and a second passage, "Social Spiders," controlled for readability and select text features, revealed no main effect for rhetorical predicate. Although some theoreticians and researchers have posited the saliency of particular organizational patterns in influencing text recall, arguments for the advantage of particular patterns, i.e., the hypotactic structure, may be premature and incomplete.

2. The use of a control passage was found to be as effective as a text cast with a higher-order rhetorical predicate (e.g., attribution for "Body Water"). This was the case with idea units recalled in Likert scale #5, where readers did not differentiate the main line of argument with a rhetorical predicate present or absent. This suggests that under certain conditions, skilled readers, and particularly university freshmen, may be able to induce their own higher-order structure and may not need these rhetorical predicates. This may, however, not be the case with younger, less-skilled readers who have not acquired the ability to produce their own structure.[9]

3. The effect of a rhetorical predicate was found to covary with the textual context in which it was placed and by text topic. Some rhetorical predicates were found to increase recall—with some texts—but others must be regarded as inappropriate matches to text and even interferences.

4. Findings reported by Meyer and Freedle using a listening mode were not replicated in a reading mode. It is possible that findings reported in a listening condition may not so readily transfer to a reading condition as has been assumed.

5. This work supports the notion that the topic and content of text should be considered more carefully in prose recall research. It is possible that rhetorical structures as those studied here may be optimally reflected in different constellations of topics and text types, but this is something that we know little about.

6. This research demonstrates that study of reader judgment of expository texts warrants further consideration. It also demonstrates that there are important age-grade differences in readers' judgments of texts. This finding is consistent with views that the perceptions that readers may have of a text represent important data for understanding the development of expository discourse processing.

Discussion of the Experiment

This research provided an assessment of the function of an element thought to be a critical feature of written expository discourse. Although rhetorical structures have received considerable attention in theoretical and descriptive work, arguments advanced regarding the advantage of some structures, while intuitively appealing, remain speculative and are not supported by this study.

The results of the present study may be further explained by considering rhetorical predicates under the aegis of features of cohesion and surface structure connectives. They may help readers achieve coherence. However, skilled readers may not always need these structures since these readers have a repertoire of rhetorical patterns that are stored in memory and that can be applied to a text when a rhetorical predicate is not present. Thus, it may be the case that some higher-order rhetorical predicates in short well-organized passages like those studied here are simply surface reflections of overall conceptual integration without any independent function. They may facilitate and integrate information up to a point, but they are not always essential for the integration of relations to occur.

Moreover, in my extension of the Meyer and Freedle study I found that no one structure was consistently more effective than another structure in facilitating recall and that at least 9th graders were not more aware of one structure over another. The effect and awareness of structure is contingent upon the topic and content of the passages being used in the research and the task at hand. The question is not which structure is better or more useful for readers at particular grades, but which structures students are more aware of and capable of using given particular text topics, author goals, and reader intentions. Since no control condition was used in the Meyer and Freedle work, it is difficult to know whether the structures studied were actually needed as an overall organizational pattern.

This research, like other experimental research, has its limitations. The texts which are organized by the rhetorical predicates are two-to-three paragraphs long and not full texts (see work on paragraph structures by Crothers, 1972). We cannot generalize that the findings here would repeat themselves with longer texts and other topics or content.

Differences between the results of the present study and the Meyer and Freedle study may be due to still other factors. The present research used a new population. There was also a new passage and the rhetorical predicates were placed in a qualitatively different linguistic environment. Moreover, the texts here were read silently, rather than heard. It is possible that the oral reading of the Body Water passage in the Meyer and Freedle study resulted in certain interpretation of the rhetorical predicates and the text. Through accentuation of prosodic features of text (pitch, stress, and pauses) the rhetorical structures may be varied—highlighted or deemphasized—by an oral reader (as has been shown by McLendon, 1982). For example, an oral reading of a text may influence the prominence given a rhetorical structure and this may in turn influence the prosody of the remaining discourse and the overall intent of the passage. These are, of course, matters that require empirical testing, particularly in light of the uses of oral reading in elementary and secondary school classrooms, not to mention other settings such as family story telling or reading, oral readings of reports in work settings, e.g., court reports, or oral reading in various other social, religious, or communal arrangements. In the case of classrooms, teacher or student oral readings may influence the meaning obtained from any given text in some rather distinct ways, thus hearing these texts may not be the same as reading these texts.

However, similar conclusions which show that organizational patterns may be suited to specific reader and listener audiences and topics and do not consistently work the same way were reached in studies by Schnotz (1984) and Bingham (1986), and the limits of cohesive devices such as these have been stressed by Doyle (1982) and others.

In sum, this research suggests that we must go beyond the study of main effects of rhetorical structures on reader comprehension. It is the interaction of these structures with other elements of discourse and social-contextual factors, not main effects, that warrants further research, and will prove most promising to researchers interested in language and discourse processing.

TOWARD A SOCIAL–PSYCHOLOGICAL THEORY OF RHETORICAL STRUCTURE IN DISCOURSE PROCESSING

In future work, we must look at rhetorical structures in relation to three kinds of textual considerations.

Intratextual factors (the structure in relation to text context). The rhetorical structures of interest here must be related to the message with which they are associated and the remaining linguistic structures of a given oral and written discourse. They are an organic outgrowth of the specific architecture, i.e., hierarchical structure, of a given discourse, and they interact with other linguistic features of discourse in sometimes rather subtle and unconscious ways which may not always be systematically observed and scientifically measured given the tools that we have available in the field of discourse processing.

Intertextual factors (the relationship of a text to other texts, including oral or written discourse). The rhetorical structures will need to be related to constellations of discourse and content domains of knowledge. In retrospect, there is reason to believe that "Body Water" and "Social Spiders" grow out of different constellations of registers, genres, discourse domains, and goals. Student judgments of the texts support this. That is, the quantitative analysis of the Likert scales provides evidence of disparate domains. Similarly, qualitative information, collected informally following the research indicated that many readers responded to the texts as representative of different social worlds and functions. "Body Water" was interpersonally identified with by our adolescent and college readers with a common lay interest in athletics. "Social Spiders" was representative of the domain of social psychology that many adolescents in 9th as well as 13th grades know nothing about and would not or could not enter. In fact, the 9th graders in this study could not make predictions about the passage and commented on their lack of familiarity with the topic of this text.

Extratextual factors. How the rhetorical structures emerge as a result of social-contextual factors should be of interest to researchers. How do these texts come about and come to be processed given the social, political, and situational climate and parameters of a reader or witer's discourse community? Work on the comprehension and interpretation or composition of texts must consider the "social meaning" instantiated in linguistic structures, a more broadly based social-interactive model of reading is much needed. (See similar recommendations in Blom & Gumperz, 1972; Bruce, 1981; Cicourel, 1980; Lemke, 1985.)[10]

There are a number of questions to be explored about the social-psychological factors that influence the production of written discourse and in turn the comprehension and interpretation of discourse. For instance, Bazerman (1984) argues that scientific discourse is subject to nonscientific considerations which can and should be studied. In his research, he examined the background surrounding a physicist's writings and demonstrates that despite what we might believe, even a quantum physicist is subject to external influences (extratextual factors) including past knowledge, belief systems, and ideologies that contribute to an author's thinking and writing in science.

Moreover, a number of recent reports have raised serious questions about the design and translation of scientific information for a general, nonscientific public, as in the case of the population and texts used in the present research. For one, Fahnestock (1986) discusses the issue of translation and presentation of scientific facts and the "rhetorical life" such facts lead as they are reported and repeated in different texts and for different reader–listener audiences. (See also Fahnestock & Secor, 1983, for a discussion of uses of *topoi* in scientific discourse.) *Mosaic,* the source of "Social Spiders," attempts to translate findings from scientific research and the scientific sector to the general public. The present study shows that, at least for our sample, that translation will influence meaning depending upon the match between rhetorical structure and text and the age of the subjects and the social-psychological knowledge from which they process the rhetorical structures and texts.

In conclusion, this chapter suggests that greater understanding of the functions and uses of the rhetorical structures across discourse content, across social and cultural groups, and modes of presentation is desperately needed. We have worked toward a characterization of texts, but there is now clearly a need for characterization of contexts and situations-of-use of discourse by the specific social groups found in or historically neglected by schools.

ACKNOWLEDGMENTS

This chapter was completed with the support of a National Academy of Education Spencer Fellowship awarded to the author for 1985–1988. I am grateful to both the National Academy of Education and the Spencer Foundation for this award. The experimental research reported here was supported by a University of Minnesota Graduate School Fellowship, a Wesley E. Peik Scholarship awarded by the College of Education's Special Grants Committee of the University of Minnesota, and by the Center for Research in Learning, Perception, and Cognition at the University of Minnesota. These grants are gratefully acknowledged.

Some of the content included in this chapter was presented at the American Educational Research Association Conference, Los Angeles, California, as part of a Symposium on Text Design: Text Features and Cognitive Outcomes, April 16, 1981; the National Reading Conference, Clearwater, Florida, December 22, 1982; the International Reading Association Conference, Anaheim, California, May 5, 1983; the Texas Council of the International Reading Association Conference, Corpus Christi, Texas, March 2, 1984; and the American Educational Research Association Conference as part of a symposium: Context as a Research Issue in Writing and Reading, Chicago, April 4, 1985. I am grateful for the comments and discussions provided on these occasions and by many colleagues.

I am indebted to Gene L. Piché and S. Jay Samuels, both at the University of Minnesota, for their suggestions and support throughout the research. I thank Martin Nystrand at the University of Wisconsin–Madison and Teun A. van Dijk at the University of Amsterdam for reading the manuscript and offering valuable remarks. None of the forementioned individuals, or those identified below, however, is responsible for the final product and the points of view expressed herein.

A number of insights noted in this chapter were influenced by papers heard at the 32nd Annual Georgetown University Round Table on Languages and Linguistics, Analyzing Discourse: Text and Talk, Washington, DC, March 19–21, 1981.

NOTES

[1] It is possible that the hierarchical nature of certain written formal registers may require that the text be viewed rather than heard, for certain written formal registers may be hierarchically structured so that they would exceed capacity for processing and memory were the text read orally to an audience or even given in a spoken, formal language. Students, for whatever reasons, deprived of the mental exercise of unraveling complex hierarchical dimensions of written formal registers (a case in point may be legal written discourse or persuasive writing), may be lacking linguistic and cognitive experience which stretches their intellectual capacities. It is also possible that once such written language is understood and worked through, skills will transfer to the processing of written language that is spoken or to spoken, formal language (see Perfetti, this volume, for some related arguments).

However, we simply know very little about the hierarchical dimension of various formal registers, written or spoken, about the development of skill with these registers under various school or real-world tasks. Halliday persuasively argues that it is mistaken to assume speech is less complex structurally than writing. Rather, he argues that they are qualitatively different forms of language. However, other researchers proport that written language is more complex structurally (Chafe, this volume; Ochs, 1979). However, only a limited corpus of speech or writing to permit the necessary comparisons has been collected. Acquisition of a rich corpus of spoken and written language, and of a variety of registers, is needed and will provide challenging data for future research comparisons.

2 Since the work of Grimes, Halliday has defined hypotaxis somewhat differently. For Halliday (1985, also this volume), hypotaxis is a pattern that realizes the basic relation of dependence. Rather than assume that hypotaxis is characterized by subordination and embedding and is strictly characteristic of written language, Halliday uses hypotaxis to refer to dependence relations and thereby considers this structure as a viable possibility in both written and spoken language. This is important because it would suggest that spoken language can be more complex than we have typically envisioned it to be.

Following Halliday (1985, p. 195), parataxis and hypotaxis each have a primary and secondary clause. In parataxis the primary clause is initiating and equal to the secondary clause, which is continuing. In hypotaxis, the primary clause is dominant and the secondary clause is dependent.

	Primary clause	Secondary Clause
Parataxis	1 (initiating)	2 (continuing)
Hypotaxis	α (dominating)	β (dependent)

Moreover, subordination is limited to written discourse, while dependence may occur in spoken or written language: In subordination, one element is a structural part of another, e.g., *the conviction that he failed*. Dependence occurs when one element is bound or linked to another but is not part of it, e.g., *was convinced/that he had failed*.

3 The rhetorical predicates examined in the present research are 4 of the 20 rhetorical predicates identified in the discourse and predicate classification system developed by Grimes (1975). That system was influenced by work in a number of areas including rhetorical theory, literary theory and criticism, Biblical exegesis, and by various branches of linguistics including Kenneth Pike's work on tagmemics and the Functional Sentence Perspective of the Prague School of Linguistics.

4 B. J. F. Meyer, Freedle, and Walker (1978) examined the effect of the four rhetorical predicates on the listening recall of graduate students who were teachers. This report was later revised as the B. J. F. Meyer and Freedle study (1979). A final report was published as B. J. F. Meyer and Freedle (1984) and has proven to be an important contribution to the literature on discourse organization and comprehension.

5 Experiment I tested for immediate recall, 7-day delayed recall, probed recall, and use of rhetorical predicate in recall, as was done in the Meyer and Freedle study. A more detailed statistical report of Experiments I and II is to be published in a scientific journal. See Horowitz (1982a) for more details associated with Experiment I and Horowitz (1982b) for details associated with Experiment II.

6 I thank Bonnie J. F. Meyer at Arizona State University for providing me with detailed specifications of the 1979 Meyer and Freedle "Body Water" passages and for her review of experimental procedures used in that study and the passages and content structures that were used in the present study.

7 Wayne H. Slater at the University of Maryland and Duane H. Roen at the University of Arizona scored the recall protocols of the subjects who participated in this study. Statistical assistance was provided by Matthew McGue and Dennis McGuire, both at the University of Minnesota.

8 Two other studies are significantly related to this work. They also examined the effect of rhetorical predicates on expository discourse comprehension and processing. Roen and

Piché (1984) examined rhetorical predicate interaction with microstructural elements and found no advantage in discourse processing for one rhetorical predicate over another using reading time as a dependent measure. Similarly, Slater, Graves, and Piché (1985) examined their interaction with structural organizers and found no advantage for one rhetorical predicate over another.

According to Ong (1982), historically the development of western civilization progressed from use of paratactic to hypotactic constructions. The list structure was used in formulaic learning and as a memory device. Little research, however, points to individual development in use of these structures.

[9] In this study freshmen performed better than I would have expected with the texts organized by a list-structure. This is contrary to findings by other researchers who demonstrate that the list produces low recall. I argue that given certain social-psychological factors that enter into comprehension, the list may be an effective and even desirable structure. In the case of college freshmen, they may have conditioned themselves to recall by list—lectures, notes, and texts. Lists may have a special cognitive possibility. As we take them in we may have conditioned ourselves to rehearse them for certain uses and thus a list may actually create unity and coherence.

[10] The methods of inquiry best suited to a social-psychological study of written language have yet to be delineated. There presently is much concern about the best quantitative and qualitative approaches to be applied to such research. There are many complex and thought-provoking philosophical questions that are beyond the scope of this chapter. If the social factors suggested here are to be addressed in the literature, new methods are desperately needed for the analysis of discourse comprehension and processing. A number of articles in the *Educational Researcher* during 1985–1986 address epistemological issues that are relevant to a variety of fields, including a social-psychological study of written language, for example, Smith and Heshusius (1986a). This essay calls for continued discussion and examination of the debate between quantitative and qualitative research paradigms and is followed by "Some Comments on Keeping the Quantitative–Qualitative Debate Open" (Miller, 1986) and a "Rejoinder" (Smith and Heshusius, (1986b). It is only through such debate that new methodological approaches will evolve and the study of discourse and comprehension will advance.

APPENDIX: EXPERIMENTAL TEXTS*

Body Water

Attribution (list-structure):

SEVERAL ASPECTS OF THE LOSS OF BODY WATER WILL BE DISCUSSED. FIRST, the loss of body water is frequently required by athletic coaches of wrestlers, boxers, judo contestants, karate contestants, and 150-pound football team members so that they will attain specified body weights. These specified weights are considerably below the athletes' usual weights.

---

* Subjects in this research group read texts without this pattern of capital letters and italics. The words set in all capital letters represent the rhetorical structure, with the nonitalic portion explicitly signaling that rhetorical structure.

SECOND, *THE LOSS OF BODY WATER SUSTAINED BY A 150-POUND IN-DIVIDUAL EACH DAY IS THREE PINTS OF WATER.*
THIRD, loss of body water impairs cardio-vascular functioning limiting work capacity. More specifically, a loss of three percent of body water impairs physical performance and a loss of five percent results in heat exhaustion. Moreover, a loss of seven percent of body water causes hallucinations. Losses of ten percent or more of body water result in heat stroke, deep coma, and convulsions; if not treated death will result.

Adversative (compare-contrast):
The loss of body water is frequently required by athletic coaches of wrestlers, boxers, judo contestants, karate contestants, and 150-pound football team members so that they will attain specified body weights. These specified weights are considerably below the athletes' usual weights.

IN CONTRAST TO ACTION TAKEN BY COACHES *LOSS OF BODY WATER FOR ATHLETES IS STRONGLY CONDEMNED BY THE AMERICAN MEDICAL ASSOCIATION. THEY CONDEMN LOSS OF BODY WATER* DUE TO THE FACT THAT THE loss of body water impairs cardio-vascular functioning limiting work capacity. More specifically, a loss of three percent of body water impairs physical performance and a loss of five percent results in heat exhaustion. Moreover, a loss of seven percent of body water causes hallucinations. Losses of ten percent or more of body water result in heat stroke, deep coma, and convulsions; if not treated, death will result.

Covariance (cause–effect):
IT IS TRUE THAT the loss of body water is frequently required by athletic coaches of wrestlers, boxers, judo contestants, karate contestants, and 150-pound football team members so that they will attain specified body weights. These specified weights are considerably below the athletes' usual weights.

AS A RESULT, *TRAGEDIES ARE UNWITTINGLY CAUSED BY THE COACHES REQUIRING THIS LOSS OF BODY WEIGHT IN THESE SITUATIONS. THESE TRAGEDIES OCCUR* DUE TO THE FACT THAT THE loss of body water impairs cardio-vascular functioning limiting work capacity. More specifically, a loss of three percent of body water impairs physical performance and a loss of five percent results in heat exhaustion. Moreover, a loss of seven percent of body water causes hallucinations. Losses of ten percent or more of body water result in heat stroke, deep coma, and convulsions; if not treated, death will result.

Response (problem–solution):
A SERIOUS PROBLEM IS the loss of body water frequently required by athletic coaches of wrestlers, boxers, judo contestants, karate contestants, and 150-pound football team members so that they will attain specified body weights. These specified weights are considerably below the athletes' usual weights.

A SOLUTION TO THIS PROBLEM *IS IMMEDIATE DISMISSAL BY SCHOOL BOARDS OF ATHLETIC COACHES WHO REQUIRE LOSS OF BODY WATER. THIS STEP MUST BE TAKEN* DUE TO THE FACT THAT THE loss of body water impairs cardio-vascular functioning limiting work capacity. More specifically, a loss of three percent of body water impairs physical performance and a loss of five percent results in heat exhaustion. Moreover, a loss of seven percent of body water causes hallucinations. Losses of ten percent or more of body water result in heat stroke, deep coma, and convulsions; if not treated, death will result.

Control (no higher-order rhetorical predicate):
The loss of body water is frequently required by athletic coaches of wrestlers, boxers, judo contestants, karate contestants, and 150-pound football team members so that they will attain specified body weights. These specified weights are considerably below the athletes' usual weights.

Loss of body water impairs cardio-vascular functioning limiting work capacity. More specifically, a loss of three percent of body water impairs physical performance and a loss of five percent results in heat exhaustion. Moreover, a loss of seven percent of body water causes hallucinations. Losses of ten percent or more of body water result in heat stroke, deep coma, and convulsions; if not treated, death will result.

Social Spiders

Attribution (list-structure):
SEVERAL APPROACHES USED BY SCIENTISTS STUDYING SOCIAL BEHAVIOR WILL BE DISCUSSED. FIRST, scientists studying human social behavior find that people are individualistic and that it is difficult to predict their responses—at cocktail parties, football games or in apartments. Specifically, factors that explain human cooperation or competition in these places are difficult to identify.

SECOND, *SOME 30-YEAR PRACTICING SCIENTISTS USE CERTAIN SPIDERS TO LEARN ABOUT WHAT INFLUENCES THE MENTAL HEALTH OF PEOPLE.*

THIRD, scientists find that social spiders provide a model for clues to the evolution of social behavior in all species. Some scientists explore the chemistry, vibrations and touch used by social spiders to communicate. Others examine spider spacing on communal webs. They find that Mexican spiders cooperatively build a web for thousands of adults. Ultimately, these findings may be applied to human social life in schools, airports or hospitals.

Adversative (compare-contrast):
Scientists studying human social behavior find that people are individualistic and that it is difficult to predict their responses—at cocktail parties, football games or in apartments. Specifically, factors that explain human cooperation or competition in these places are difficult to identify.

IN CONTRAST TO SCIENTISTS WHO STUDY HUMANS, *THERE ARE OTHER SCIENTISTS WHO ELECT TO STUDY SPIDERS. THEY STRONGLY REJECT THE ARGUMENT THAT ALL SPIDERS ARE ANTISOCIAL* BECAUSE some spiders are social; and these scientists find that social spiders provide a model for clues to the evolution of behavior in all species. Some scientists explore the chemistry, vibrations and touch used by social spiders to communicate. Others examine spider spacing on communal webs. They find that Mexican spiders cooperatively build a web for thousands of adults. Ultimately, these findings may be applied to human social life in schools, airports or hospitals.

Covariance (cause–effect):

IT IS TRUE that scientists studying human social behavior find that people are individualistic and that it is difficult to predict their responses—at cocktail parties, football games or in apartments. Specifically, factors that explain human cooperation or competition in these places are difficult to identify.

AS A RESULT, *SOME SCIENTISTS HAVE INVESTED LIFETIME CAREERS, AS MUCH AS 30 YEARS, EXPLORING SPIDER SOCIAL BEHAVIOR. THIS INVESTMENT HAS BEEN MADE* BECAUSE OF THE FACT THAT scientists find that social spiders provide a model for clues to the evolution of behavior in all species. Some scientists explore the chemistry, vibrations and touch used by social spiders to communicate. Others examine spider spacing on communal webs. They find that Mexican spiders cooperatively build a web for thousands of adults. Ultimately, these findings may be applied to human social life in schools, airports or hospitals.

Response (problem–solution):

A SERIOUS PROBLEM IS that scientists studying human social behavior find that people are individualistic and that it is difficult to predict their responses— at cocktail parties, football games or in apartments. Specifically, factors that explain human cooperation or competition in these places are difficult to identify.

A SOLUTION TO THIS PROBLEM *IS TO SHIFT TO ANOTHER SPECIES FOR RESEARCH—SOCIAL SPIDERS. THIS STEP SHOULD BE TAKEN BY MORE SCIENTISTS INTERESTED IN PEOPLE* BECAUSE OF THE FACT THAT scientists find that social spiders provide a model for clues to the evolution of behavior in all species. Some scientists explore the chemistry, vibrations and touch used by social spiders to communicate. Others examine spider spacing on communal webs. They find that Mexican spiders cooperatively build a web for thousands of adults. Ultimately, these findings may be applied to human social life in schools, airports or hospitals.

Control (no higher-order rhetorical predicate):

Scientists studying human social behavior find that people are individualistic and that it is difficult to predict their responses—at cocktail parties, football games or in apartments. Specifically, factors that explain human cooperation or competition in these places are difficult to identify.

Scientists find that social spiders provide a model for clues to the evolution of behavior in all species. Some scientists explore the chemistry, vibrations and touch used by social spiders to communicate. Others examine spider spacing on communal webs. They find that Mexican spiders cooperatively build a web for thousands of adults. Ultimately, these findings may be applied to human social life in schools, airports or hospitals.

REFERENCES

Alexander, C. (1964). *Notes on the synthesis of form.* Cambridge, MA: Harvard University Press.

Anderson, J. (Ed.). (1982). *Language form and linguistic variation.* Amsterdam: Benjamins.

Aristotle. (1954). *"The Rhetoric" and "The Poetics" of Aristotle* (W. R. Roberts and I. Bywater, Trans.). New York: Modern Library.

Barthes, R. (1970). L'ancienne rhétorique. *Communications,* p. 16.

Bartlett, B. J. (1978). *Top-level structure as an organizational strategy for recall of classroom text.* Tempe: Arizona State University.

Batalova, T. (1977). On predicative–relative relations of text-forming units. *Style, 11* (4), 375–390.

Bazerman, C. (1984). The writing of scientific non-fiction. Contexts, choices, constraints. *Pre/Text, 5*(1), 39–74.

Beaugrande, R. de (1980). *Text, discourse, and process: Toward a multidisciplinary science of text.* Norwood, NJ: Ablex.

Beaugrande, R. de (1985). Text linguistics in discourse studies. In T. A. van Dijk (Ed.), *Handbook of discourse analysis: Vol. 1. Disciplines of discourse* (pp. 41–70). New York: Academic Press.

Benson, J. D., & Greaves, W. S. (Eds.). (1985a). *Systemic perspectives on discourse: Vol. 1. Selected theoretical papers from the 9th International Systemic Workshop.* Norwood, NJ: Ablex.

Benson, J. D., & Greaves, W. S. (Eds.). (1985b). *Systemic perspectives on discourse: Vol. 2. Selected applied papers from the 9th International Systemic Workshop.* Norwood, NJ: Ablex.

Bingham, A. B. (1986). Readers' and listeners' use of cohesive ties in processing relational meaning. *Language Sciences, 8*(1), 49–61.

Blom, J. P., & Gumperz, J. J. (1972). Social meaning in linguistic structure. In J. J. Gumperz & D. Hymes (Eds.), *Directions in sociolinguistics* (pp. 407–434). New York: Holt.

Bloomfield, L. (1933). *Language.* New York: Holt.

Bock, J. K., & Brewer, W. F. (1985). Discourse structure and mental models. In T. H. Carr (Ed.), *The development of reading skills. New Directions for Child Development* (No. 27, pp. 55–75). Jossey-Bass Social & Behavioral Sciences Series. San Francisco: Jossey-Bass.

Bock, J. K. (1982). Toward a cognitive psychology of syntax: Information processing contributions to sentence formulation. *Psychological Review, 89,* 1–47.

Brandt, D. (1978). *Prior knowledge of the authors' schema and the comprehension of prose.* Unpublished doctoral dissertation, Arizona State University, Tempe.

Brewer, W. F. (1980). Literary theory, rhetoric, and stylistics: Implications for psychology. In R. J. Spiro, B. C. Bruce, & W. F. Brewer (Eds.), *Theoretical issues in reading comprehension: Perspectives from cognitive psychology, linguistics, artificial intelligence, and education* (pp. 221–239). Hillsdale, NJ: Erlbaum.

Brooks, C., & Warren, R. P. (1958). *Modern rhetoric.* New York: Harcourt.

Bruce, B. (1981). A social interaction model of reading. *Discourse Processes, 4*(4), 273–311.

Calfee, R. C., & Curley, R. (1984). Structures of prose in the content areas. In J. Flood (Ed.), *Understanding reading comprehension* (pp. 161–180). Newark, DE: International Reading Association.

Cicero, M. T. (1949). [*Topica*] (H. M. Hubbell, Trans.). Cambridge, MA: Loeb Classical Library, Harvard University Press.

Cicourel, A. V. (1980). Three models of discourse analysis. The role of social structure. *Discourse Processes, 3*(2), 101–131.

Clark, R. A., & Delia, J. G. (1979). *Topoi* and rhetorical competence. *Quarterly Journal of Speech, 65,* 187–206.

Connors, R. J., Ede, L. S., & Lunsford, A. A. (Eds.). (1984). *Essays on classical rhetoric and modern discourse.* Carbondale, IL: Southern Illinois University Press.

Crothers, E. J. (1972). *Paragraph structure inference.* Norwood, NJ: Ablex.

Cummings, D. W., Herum, J., & Lybbert, E. K. (1971). Semantic recurrence and rhetorical form. *Language and Style, 4,* 195–207.

D'Angelo, F. J. (1975). *A conceptual theory of rhetoric.* Cambridge, MA: Winthrop.

D'Angelo, F. J. (1979). Paradigms as structural counterparts of *topoi.* In D. McQuade (Ed.), *Linguistics, stylistics, and the teaching of composition* (pp. 41–51). Akron, OH: University of Akron Press.

Dick, R. C. (1964). *Topoi.* An approach to inventing arguments. *Speech Teacher, 13,* 313–319.

Doyle, A. (1982). The limitations of cohesion. *Research in the Teaching of English, 16,* 390–393.

Ebel, R. L. (1951). Estimation of the reliability of ratings. *Psychometrika, 16,* 407–424.

Elliott, S. N. (1980). *Effect of prose organization on recall: An investigation of memory and metacognition.* Unpublished doctoral dissertation. Arizona State University, Tempe.

Fahnestock, J. (1986). Accommodating science: The rhetorical life of scientific facts. *Written Communication, 3*(3), 275–296.

Fahnestock, J., & Secor, M. (1983). Grounds for argument: Stasis theory and the common and special *topoi.* In D. Zarefsky, M. O. Sillars, & J. Rhodes (Eds.), *Argument in transition: Proceedings of the third summer conference on argumentation.* Annandale, VA: Speech Communication Association.

Faigley, L., & Meyer, P. (1983). Rhetorical theory and readers' classification of text types. *Text, 3*(4), 305–325.

Fine, J. (1985). What do surface markers mean? Towards a triangulation of social, cognitive, and linguistic factors. In J. D. Benson & W. S. Greaves (Eds.), *Systemic perspectives on discourse: Vol. 2. Selected applied papers from the 9th International Systemic Workshop* (pp. 102–115). Norwood, NJ: Ablex.

Flammer, A., & Kintsch, W. (Eds.). (1983). *Discourse processing.* Amsterdam: North-/Holland.

Fletcher, C. R. (1983). *Surface forms, textbases and situation models: Recognition memory for three types of textual information.* Boulder, CO: University of Colorado.

Fowler, R. (1981). Cohesive, progressive and localizing aspects of text structure. In R. Fowler (Ed.), *Literature as social discourse. The practice of linguistic criticism* (pp. 58–79). Bloomington, IN: Indiana University Press.

Freedman, S. W., & Calfee, R. C. (1984). Understanding and comprehending. *Written Communication, 1*(4), 459–490.

Garnham, A. (1981). Mental models as representation of text. *Memory and Cognition, 9,* 560–565.

Goffman, E. (1974). *Frame analysis. An essay on the organization of experience.* Cambridge, MA: Harvard University Press.

Grimes, J. E. (1975). *The thread of discourse.* The Hague: Mouton.

Guindon, R., & Kintsch, W. (1984). Priming macropropositions: Evidence for the primacy of macropropositions in the memory for text. *Journal of Verbal Learning and Verbal Behavior, 23,* 508–518.

Halliday, M. A. K. (1975). Talking one's way in. A sociolinguistic perspective on language and learning. In A. Davies (Ed.), *Problems of language and learning* (pp. 8–33). London: Heinemann.

Halliday, M. A. K. (1978). *Language as social semiotic. The social interpretation of language and meaning*. Baltimore: University Park Press.

Halliday, M. A. K. (1985). *An introduction to functional grammar*. Baltimore, MD: Arnold.

Halliday, M. A. K. (1986). *Spoken and written language*. Victoria, Australia: Deakin University Press.

Halliday, M. A. K., & Hason, R. (1976). *Cohesion in English*. London: Longman.

Hill, D. J. (1884). *The elements of rhetoric and composition* (new ed.). New York: Sheldon.

Hinds, J. (1979). Organizational patterns in discourse. In T. Givón (Ed.), *Syntax and semantics: Vol. 12. Discourse and syntax* (pp. 135–157). New York: Academic Press.

Hockett, C. F. (1958). *A course in modern linguistics*. New York: Macmillan.

Hoey, M. (1983). *On the surface of discourse*. Boston: Allen & Unwin.

Hoey, M. (1986). Overlapping patterns of discourse organization and their implications for clause-relational analysis of problem–solution texts. In C. R. Cooper & S. Greenbaum (Eds.), *Studying writing: Linguistic approaches. Written Communication Annual: An International Survey of Research and Theory* (Vol. 1, pp. 187–214). Beverly Hills, CA: Sage.

Hoey, M., & Winter, E. (1986). Clause relations and the writer's communicative task. In B. Couture (Ed.), *Functional approaches to writing research perspectives* (pp. 120–141). Norwood, NJ: Ablex.

Horowitz, R. (1982a). *The limitations of contrasted rhetorical predicates on reader recall of expository English prose*. Unpublished doctoral dissertation, University of Minnesota, Minneapolis.

Horowitz, R. (1982b, January). *Staging of information in scientific text: Effects on reader–audience processing and recall. Paper presented at the meeting of the Southwest Educational Research Association, Austin, TX*.

Horowitz, R. (1983, December). The uses and limitations of rhetorical elements of expository texts. In *Expository text comprehension: Critical research issues*. Symposium conducted at the National Reading Conference, Austin, TX.

Horowitz, R. (1984a). Toward a theory of literacy. [Review of *What writers know: The language, process, and structure of written discourse*]. *Harvard Educational Review, 54*(1), 88–97.

Horowitz, R. (1984b). The application of literacy scholarship. A reply to Zorn. *Harvard Educational Review, 54*(4), 498–500.

Horowitz, R. (1985a). Text patterns, Part I. *Journal of Reading, 28*(5), 448–454.

Horowitz, R. (1985b). Text patterns, Part II. *Journal of Reading, 28*(6), 534–541.

Horowitz, R. (1986). [Review of *Towards a contextual grammar of English*]. *Instructional Science, 15*(2), 174–181.

Horowitz, R., Piché, G. L., & Samuels, S. J. (1981, April). The effect of contrasted rhetorical predicates on the recall and processing of expository English prose. In *Text Design: Text features and cognitive outcomes*. Symposium conducted at the American Educational Research Association Conference, Los Angeles.

Horowitz, R., & Samuels, S. J. (1985). Reading and listening to expository text. *Journal of Reading Behavior, 17*(3), 185–198.

Horowitz, R., Piché, G. L., & Samuels, S. J. (in preparation). The effect of contrasted rhetorical predicates on reader recall of expository English prose.

Hron, A., Kurbjuhn, I., Mandl, H., & Schnotz, W. (1985). Structural inferences in reading and listening. In G. Rickheit & H. Strohner (Eds.), *Inferences in text processing* (pp. 1–30). Amsterdam: North-Holland.

Hudson, R. (1984). *The higher-level differences between speech and writing* (Committee for

Linguistics in Education, Working Paper No. 3). London: University College, Department of Phonetics and Linguistics.

Jarvella, R. J. (1977). From verbs to sentences: Some experimental studies of predication. In S. Rosenberg (Ed.), *Sentence production: Developments in research and theory* (pp. 275–306). Hillsdale, NJ: Erlbaum.

Jordan, M. P. (1980). Short texts to explain problem–solution structures—and vice versa: An analytical study of English prose to show the relationship between clear writing and clear thinking. *Instructional Science, 9*(3), 221–252.

Jordan, M. P. (1984). *Rhetoric of everyday English texts.* Boston: Allen & Unwin.

Kaplan, R. (1982). *Contrastive rhetoric: Readers and writers and the "Discourse Compact."* Paper presented at the Seventh Annual Boston University Conference on Language Development, Boston.

Kieras, D. E. (1980). Initial mention as a signal to thematic content in technical passages. *Memory and Cognition, 8,* 345–353.

Kieras, D. E., & Bovair, S. (1981). *Strategies for abstracting main ideas from simple technical prose* (Tech. Rep. No. 10). Tempe: University of Arizona.

Kintsch, W. (1982). Text representations. In W. Otto & S. White (Eds.), *Reading expository material* (pp. 87–101). New York: Academic Press.

Kintsch, W. (1984). Approaches to the study of the psychology of language. In T. G. Bever, J. M. Carroll, & L. A. Miller (Eds.), *Talking minds: The study of language in cognitive science* (pp. 111–145). Cambridge, MA: MIT Press.

Kintsch, W., & van Dijk, T. A. (1978). Toward a model of text comprehension and production. *Psychological Review, 85,* 363–394.

Kintsch, W., & Yarbrough, J. C. (1982). Role of rhetorical structure in text comprehension. *Journal of Educational Psychology, 74*(6), 828–834.

Kopperschmidt, J. (1985). An analysis of argumentation. In T. A. van Dijk (Ed.), *Handbook of discourse analysis: Vol. 2. Dimensions of discourse* (pp. 159–168). New York: Academic Press.

Kučera, H. (1980). *Computational analysis of predicational structures in English.* Paper presented at the COLING Meetings, Tokyo.

Kurzweil, E. (1980). *The age of structuralism. Lévi-Strauss to Foucault.* New York: Columbia University Press.

Lemke, J. L. (1985). Ideology, intertextuality, and the notion of register. In J. D. Benson & W. S. Greaves (Eds.), *Systemic perspectives on discourse* (Vol. 1, pp. 275–294). Norwood, NJ: Ablex.

Lesgold, A. M., Roth, S. F., & Curtis, M. E. (1979). Foregrounding effects in discourse comprehension. *Journal of Verbal Learning and Verbal Behavior, 18,* 275–290.

Levin, G. (1981). *Prose models* (5th ed.). New York: Harcourt.

Levin, N. S. (1979, Winter). *The listing function.* Paper presented at the 1979 Annual Meeting of the Linguistic Society of America, Los Angeles.

Liberman, A. (1980). *Structuralism in linguistics.* Paper presented at a series of seminars, What is structuralism? An interdisciplinary perspective. Linguistics—Mathematics—Literature—Folklore—Anthropology—Psychology, under the auspices of the Minnesota Forum and University of Minnesota, Minneapolis.

Litteral, R. (1972). Rhetorical predicates and time typology in Anggor. *Foundations of Language, 8,* 391–410.

Longacre, R. E. (1976). *An anatomy of speech notions.* Lisse: de Ridder Press.

Longacre, R. E. (1983). *The grammar of discourse.* New York: Plenum Press.

McLendon, S. (1982). Meaning, rhetorical structure, and discourse organization in myth.

In D. Tannen (Ed.), *Georgetown University Round Table on Language and Linguistics 1981. Analyzing discourse: Text and talk* (pp. 284–305). Washington, DC: Georgetown University Press.

Meyer, B. J. F. (1975). *The organization of prose and its effects on memory.* Amsterdam: North-Holland.

Meyer, B. J. F. (1982). Reading research and the composition teacher: The importance of plans. *College Composition and Communication, 33*(1), 37–49.

Meyer, B. J. F., Brandt, D. M., & Bluth, G. J. (1980). Use of top-level structure in text: Key for reading comprehension of ninth grade students. *Reading Research Quarterly, 16*(1), 72–103.

Meyer, B. J. F., & Freedle, R. O. (1979). *Effects of different discourse types on recall* (Research Report No. 6). Tempe: Arizona State University, Department of Educational Psychology.

Meyer, B. J. F., & Freedle, R. O. (1984). Effects of discourse type on recall. *American Educational Research Journal, 21*(1), 121–143.

Meyer, B. J. F., Freedle, R. O., & Walker, C. (1978). *Effects of discourse type on the recall of young and old adults.* Tempe: Arizona State University.

Meyer, B. J. F., & Rice, G. E. (1984). The structure of text. In P. D. Pearson, R. Barr, M. L. Kamil, & P. Mosenthal (Eds.), *Handbook of reading research* (pp. 319–351). New York: Longman.

Meyer, M. (1983). The rhetoric of textuality. In *Meaning and reading: A philosophical essay on language and literature* (pp. 61–86). Amsterdam: Benjamins.

Miller, S. (1986). Some comments on keeping the quantitative–qualitative debate open [Letter to the editor]. *Educational Researcher, 15*(9), 24–25.

Minsky, M. (1975). A framework for representing knowledge. In P. H. Winston (Ed.), *The psychology of computer vision* (pp. 211–280). New York: McGraw-Hill.

Moore, T., & Carling, C. (1982). *Language understanding. Towards a post-Chomskyan linguistics.* New York: St. Martin's Press.

National Science Foundation (1978). Unraveling the top arachnid. *Mosaic 9*(6), 10–18.

Nystrand, M. (Ed.). (1982). *What writers know. The language, process, and structure of written discourse.* New York: Academic Press.

Nystrand, M. (1986). *The structure of written communication. Studies in reciprocity in writers and readers.* New York: Academic Press.

Ochs, E. (1979). Planned and unplanned discourse. In T. Givón (Ed.) *Syntax and semantics: Vol. 12. Discourse and syntax.* New York: Academic Press.

Ong, W. J. (1982). *Orality and literacy: The technologizing of the word.* New York: Methuen.

Parret, H. (1980). *Contexts of understanding.* Amsterdam: Benjamins.

Perelman, C. (1982). *The realm of rhetoric.* Notre Dame, IN: University of Notre Dame Press.

Perelman, C., & Olbrechts-Tyteca, L. (1969). *The new rhetoric: A treatise on argumentation.* Notre Dame, IN: University of Notre Dame Press.

Petöfi, J. S., & Sözer, E. (Eds.). (1983). *Micro and macro connexity of texts.* Hamburg: Buske Verlag.

Reder, L. M. (1985). Techniques available to author, teacher, and reader to improve retention of main ideas of a chapter. In S. F. Chipman, J. W. Segal, & R. Glaser (Eds.), *Thinking and learning skills* (Vol. 2). Hillsdale, NJ: Erlbaum.

Roen, D. H., & Piché, G. L. (1984). The effects of select text-forming structures on college freshmen's comprehension of expository prose. *Research in the Teaching of English, 18*(1), 8–25.

Sapir, E. (1921). *Language: An introduction to the study of speech.* New York: Harcourt.

Saussure, F. de (1916). Cours de linguistique générale. Lausanne: Payot. [English translation by W. Baskin, *Course in general linguistics*. New York: The Philosophical Library, 1959].

Schnotz, W. (1984). Comparative instructional text organization. In H. Mandl, N. L. Stein, & T. Trabasso (Eds.), *Learning and comprehension of text*. Hillsdale, NJ: Erlbaum.

Slater, W. H., Graves, M. F., & Piché, G. L. (1985). Effects of structural organizers on ninth grade students' comprehension and recall of four patterns of expository text. *Reading Research Quarterly, 20*(2), 189–202.

Smith, J. K., & Heshusius, L. (1986a). Closing down the conversation. The end of quantitative–qualitative debate among educational inquirers. *Educational Researcher 15*(1), 4–12.

Smith, J. K., & Heshusius, L. (1986b). Rejoinder to Miller [Letter to the editor]. *Educational Researcher, 15*(9), 25.

Stump, E. (Trans.). (1978). Boethius' *De topicis differentis*. Ithaca, NY: Cornell University Press.

Tannen, D. (1979). What's in a frame? Surface evidence for underlying expectations. In R. O. Freedle (Ed.), *New directions in discourse processing* (pp. 137–181). Norwood, NJ: Albex.

Tchaikovsky, P. I. (1878). Letters. In R. Newmarch, *Life and letters of Peter Ilich Tchaikovsky*. John Lane, 1906. In P. E. Vernon (Ed.), *Creativity* (p. 59). New York: Penguin Books, 1970.

Thorndyke, P. W. (1978). Pattern-directed processing of knowledge from texts. In D. A. Waterman & F. Hayes-Roth (Eds.), *Pattern-directed inference systems* (pp. 347–360). New York: Academic Press.

Toulmin, S. (1958). *The uses of argument*. New York: Cambridge University Press.

Urquhart, A. H. (1976). *The effect of rhetorical organization on the readability of study texts*. Unpublished doctoral dissertation,University of Edinburgh, Edinburgh.

Uspensky, B. (1973). *A poetics of composition: The structure of the artistic text and typology of a compositional form* (V. Zavarin & S. Wittig, Trans.). Berkeley: University of California Press.

Vachek, J. (1973). *Written language: General problems and problems of English*. The Hague: Mouton.

van Dijk, T. A. (1977). Semantic macro-structures and knowledge frames in discourse comprehension. In P. Carpenter & M. Just (Eds.), *Cognitive processes in comprehension* (pp. 3–32). Hillsdale, NJ: Erlbaum.

van Dijk, T. A. (1980). *Macrostructures: An interdisciplinary study of global structures in discourse, interaction, and cognition*. Hillsdale, NJ: Erlbaum.

van Dijk, T. A., & Kintsch, W. (1983). *Strategies of discourse comprehension*. New York: Academic Press.

Winter, E. O. (1977). A clause-relational approach to English text: A study of some predictive lexical items in written discourse. *Instructional Science, 6*, 1–92.

Winter, E. O. (1982). *Towards a contextual grammar of English*. London/Boston: Allen & Unwin.

Winter, E. O. (1983, April). *Two basic text structures in English*. Unpublished paper presented at the Hatfield Association of Applied Linguistics Discourse Conference. Hatfield, Herts, England.

Chapter 5

Episodic Models in Discourse Processing

Teun A. van Dijk

INTRODUCTION

In this chapter it is shown that models play an important role in both oral and written discourse processing. Although the term *model* has several other meanings, it will here exclusively be used to denote a specific kind of knowledge structure in memory.[1] In particular, the notion of model is intended here to account for the role of personal knowledge people have about real or imagined situations in the process of discourse production and understanding. In order to distinguish this notion from other uses of the term *model*, we speak of *situational models.* Such situational models are assumed to be representations of personal experiences and therefore are part of *episodic memory.* Episodic memory is the component of long term memory where people store particular information about each event or action—including verbal acts such as discourses—they have processed in short term memory. Since situational models are assumed to reside in episodic memory we also sometimes call them *episodic models.*

Expressions in natural language in general, and discourse in particular, may be used to refer to, or denote, something "in the world" or in some sociocultural context. Discourse is about objects or people, about their properties and relations, about events or actions, or about complex episodes of these, that is, about some fragment of the world which we call a *situation.* A model, then, is the cognitive counterpart of such a situation: it is what people "have in mind" when they observe, participate in, or hear or read about such a situation. Thus, a model incorporates the personal knowledge people have about such a situation, and this knowledge has been accumulated during previous experiences with such a situation. Each new piece of information about that situation may be used to extend and update the model we have in episodic memory. For instance, I thus have a model of "shopping on Saturday," including the locations, shops, shopowners, my actions of buying, and the things I buy. And similarly, I have a personal model of "going to work," including going to a particular university building, information about the form and layout of the building, people with whom I work, and the kinds of things I do. Such information in memory is necessary to plan my actions, to execute these actions in a specific order, and to understand what others are doing in such situations. In this chapter, however, we show that such models of situations are also crucial in the understanding of discourse, because understanding (or producing) a discourse not only involves grasping the meaning of a discourse, but also understanding what it is about. From the shopping and going-to-work examples mentioned above, we see that models may be formed and transformed (updated or changed) about repeated personal actions or events, but of course we may also have a model of one unique situation, such as "the car accident I had last year in France." Also, models may typically involve highly personal knowledge about situations, but part of this information may also be shared by others or even by a whole sociocultural group, as is the case for important political or historical events. In other words, the episodic knowledge we have about situations may be more or less unique or general, and more or less personal or social. One of the tasks of this chapter is to indicate the specific role of models in discourse processing with respect to other (more general and social) knowledge of the world.

The analysis of this kind of cognitive models takes place against the background of a more embracing theory of discourse processing, as it has in part been elaborated together with Walter Kintsch (van Dijk & Kintsch, 1983). I briefly summarize some of the major points of that theory, so that the specific role of models can be explained in relation to this previous work.

There is growing interest in linguistics, philosophy, logic, cognitive psychology, and artificial intelligence in the role of models in language and discourse understanding. Although all this work cannot be reviewed here in detail, a next section offers a brief perspective on this other work and at the same time indicates our specific position among these various model theories.

The central aim of this chapter, however, is to provide some systematic hypotheses about the functions and the structures of situational models in discourse processing. Several researchers have recognized the important role of models, but we hardly know what such models look like. Neither do we know in detail how models are formed, transformed, and actually used in processing discourse.

If people form models of situations in which they participate or read about, it seems plausible that they also build a model of the communicative situation they participate in when producing or understanding a discourse (or when engaging in a conversation). Clearly such models are of particular interest for us, and we therefore also briefly pay attention to this special role of context models.

Finally, situation models should not remain theoretical components in a discourse-processing theory, but also should describe and explain empirical phenomena related to speaking, writing, listening, or reading. However, we can here mention only little experimental evidence, or make suggestions for relevant experiments, that exhibit the structures and functions of models.

We assume that situation models are equally necessary in spoken and in written discourse. Only the strategies for their actual use may be somewhat different in these two modes of communication. Yet, since context models are about the communicative situation, the differences between written and spoken discourse processing need to be represented in such context models.

Many of the situations modeled in episodic memory are social situations. This means that we might be able to apply and extend some of the insights from neighboring disciplines such as social psychology and microsociology into the structures of social situations. And conversely, our cognitive approach to discourse understanding may at the same time establish an important link with the relevant issues related to interaction and communication in these other disciplines by devising a theory of episodic models that incorporate such social information. Indeed, we have taken models to be some kind of knowledge structure, but it goes without saying that we not only have knowledge, in the narrow sense, about situations, but also personal beliefs, opinions, attitudes, and emotions. However, here we can only briefly draw some conclusions from this assumption, so that our cognitive theory of discourse should be supplied with an important social dimension in further work about cognitive models.

The discussion in this chapter is rather informal, although systematic. This means that we cannot go into many technical details of logical or cognitive model theories. Also, space limitations prevent us from specifying all aspects of the role of models in discourse processing, so that we can address only the major issues involved. Finally, cognitive model theory is a very recent development, so that many of our assumptions should be seen as, maybe very plausible, working hypotheses. Future theoretical work and experimental research will need to specify the functions and roles of models in discourse processing. We do not repeat these final words about the limitations of this chapter in each section where such caution would be mandatory.

BACKGROUNDS: A STRATEGIC THEORY
OF DISCOURSE PROCESSING

Situational models play a role in a more complex theory of discourse and discourse processing, of which some central notions are briefly mentioned in this section.

This more general theory of discourse processing should first be understood against the background of a general movement in several disciplines, since the early 1970s, toward an account of more natural language data, such as speech acts, language use in the social context, and actual texts or conversations (for a survey of these developments see van Dijk, 1985; for introduction, see Coulthard, 1977; de Beaugrande & Dressler, 1981). Within linguistics, this recognition of the importance of discourse phenomena has led to the development of so-called text grammars (van Dijk, 1972, 1977), in which notions such as local and global coherence were spelled out, among other semantic relationships among sentences in a discourse. Thus, global coherence of a discourse was formulated in terms of macrostructures that represent the overall gist or the topics of a discourse (van Dijk, 1980a).

However, an adequate account of the semantics, and hence of the interpretation, of discourse, in which notions such as coherence or macrostructure are an integral part, cannot be given without a cognitive dimension. Parallel to work in psychology and artificial intelligence about the cognitive processing of discourse, a theory was developed by Kintsch and myself about the comprehension of discourse (van Dijk & Kintsch, 1978, 1983; Kintsch & van Dijk, 1975, 1978). The major features of this theory can be summarized as follows:

1. Discourse understanding primarily involves the construction, by the language user, of a semantic representation of the input discourse in the form of a *textbase,* consisting of a locally and globally coherent sequence of propositions.

2. This process of constructive interpretation takes place in short term memory, but due to the capacity limits of short term memory this process must take place cyclically: input clauses are interpreted as propositions, propositions are coherently linked together and then gradually

stored in episodic memory, after which new clauses can be interpreted, and so on.

3. The processes of local and global interpretation also need various kinds of presupposed knowledge, e.g., as organized in frames or scripts (Schank & Abelson, 1977) within the memory of language users.

4. The various processes involved in understanding are supervised by a *control system,* in which, for each point of the interpretation process, the relevant topics (macropropositions), the actual goals of the reader/listener, and information from now-operating knowledge scripts are represented.

5. Finally, in van Dijk and Kintsch (1983), we have stressed and demonstrated in much theoretical and experimental detail that the processes of comprehension have a strategic nature (rather than a structural, rule-governed nature): understanding is gradual, on-line, often makes use of incomplete information, requires data from several discourse levels and from the communicative context, and is controlled by individually variable goals and beliefs. Such a strategic theory is intended to be more flexible and should be a better approximation of what language users really do when understanding (or producing) a discourse.

We see that one result of understanding a text is a representation of the meaning of the text in (episodic) memory, in the form of a textbase. However, this is not enough. In van Dijk and Kintsch (1983), it was also shown that discourse understanding requires the kind of situational models we have mentioned in our introduction. Thus, besides a textbase we also need a particular knowledge structure, in the form of a situation model in episodic memory. The textbase in that case would represent the actual meaning of a text, and the model would represent the situation the text is about (referring to, or denoting). We enumerated many arguments to explain why a model needs to be postulated in addition to a textbase. In accordance with other work on models that we mention below, for instance, such models would allow us to account for many referential aspects of discourse, such as coreference (and pronoun understanding), and local coherence between propositions. In this way we were able to build into the cognitive theory earlier ideas from logical and linguistic approaches to the semantics of discourse (van Dijk, 1973, 1977), using notions such as reference, interpretation relative to "possible worlds" and (logical) discourse models. Yet, although we mentioned several crucial uses for cognitive situational models, we did not specify the strategic processes of model formation, transformation, and use, nor did we have an idea about the possible structures of such models. It is the task of this chapter to fill these gaps.

MODELS IN FORMAL SEMANTICS

The theory of models in cognitive psychology owes part of its inspiration to logic and linguistics, in particular to formal semantics. Also in formal semantics, models are constructions used to formulate interpretation rules for expressions in some formal or natural language. In that respect, formal models can be seen as abstract reconstructions of the world to which expressions may refer. Expressions, such as sentences, are interpreted relative to such a formal model. Besides an interpretation function, a model consists of a model structure, featuring, for instance, a set of individuals (objects, persons, etc.). A predicate such as *is sick* can then be interpreted as a subset of these individuals, viz., as the set of sick people. With this elementary picture of the world, formal semantics can specify truth conditions for sentences. In philosophy and logic, such truth conditions have often been identified with the meaning of sentences. Since the mid 1970s it has been shown, however, that in order to interpret many other aspects of natural language sentences, such as modalities, tenses, adjectives, deictic expressions (such as *I, you,* or *here*), or natural connectives, model structures should be much more complex. Thus, we may need a set of "possible worlds" (among which our own, historical world is a special member), times or locations, and contextual features such as speakers and their information sets (Hughes & Cresswell, 1968; Keenan, 1975; Guenthner & Schmidt, 1979).

For our discussion it is more relevant to point to an important limitation of this kind of formal semantics and its models: it only is designed to interpret isolated sentences, not discourse. In recent years, however, there has been a development toward the formulation of discourse models (Stenning, 1978; Nash-Webber, 1978, 1981; Kamp, 1981), after earlier work in linguistics about the formal semantics of discourse (van Dijk, 1973, 1977; Petöfi & Rieser, 1974), and after earlier suggestions by Karttunen (1975), introducing a notion such as "discourse referent." A discourse model should account for the fact that we do not just have a set of (unspecified) individuals, but a set of specifically described objects and persons, gradually introduced by the expressions of the text. Different expressions, thus, may refer to the same individual discourse referent, but we may find changes of time or location. Also, different speakers may be involved, as is the case in conversation. In other words, the interpretation rules and the necessary models become much more complex. They should, as it were, account for the dynamic nature of the gradually developing description of events and episodes. A model, thus, should permanently be updated, as should cognitive models.

It should be stressed, though, that formal models are merely highly abstract and reduced reconstructions of events and episodes, and we show below what else is needed in cognitive models in memory.

MODELS IN PSYCHOLOGY AND ARTIFICIAL INTELLIGENCE

Also in cognitive psychology and artificial intelligence, there has been increasing interest in the notion of episodic model. Thus, also inspired by ideas from logical semantics, and in order to account for specific problems of inference and the interpretation of pronouns, Johnson-Laird and collaborators have discussed the role of mental models (Johnson-Laird, 1983; Johnson-Laird & Garnham, 1980; Garnham, Oakhill, & Johnson-Laird, 1982; Garnham, 1981). That models play an essential role in the planning of our future actions, and that they allow us to use our past knowledge in such actions, has already been stressed earlier in psychology (e.g., by Craik, 1943; also quoted in Johnson-Laird, 1980). In this latter paper, Johnson-Laird argues at length that the meaning of sentences in natural language cannot simply be reduced to propositional representations, but that models are necessary:

> Mental models and propositional representations can be distinguished on a number of criteria. They differ preeminently in their functions: a propositional representation is a description. A description is true or false, ultimately with respect to the world. But human beings do *not* apprehend the world directly; they possess only internal representations of it. Hence a propositional representation is true or false with respect to a mental model of the world. In principle, this functional difference between models and propositions could be the only distinction between them: there need be nothing to distinguish them in form or content. . . . A model *represents* a state of affairs and accordingly its structure is not arbitrary like that of a propositional representation, but plays a direct representational or analogical role. Its structure mirrors the relevant aspects of the corresponding state of affairs in the world. (p. 98)

The last sentence in this quotation seems to suggest that there are differences, at least in form (propositions have arbitrary structure, and models may be analogical representations and be partly imagelike), and we may assume that there are also differences in content. Thus, the proposition "Last Saturday I went shopping" is conceptually much more simple than the complex personal knowledge structure, that is, the model, I have about such a situation. One of the uses Johnson-Laird (1980) sees for mental models is to explain specific inferences that may be drawn (or not) from sentences featuring spatial terms such as *to the right of.* One of his examples is that, if we say of people around a round table that if B is sitting to the right of A, and C to the right of B, the transitive nature of a predicate "to the right of" breaks down: the last person in the series would sit on the left of A, and not on the right. A mental model, which would capture an analogical (spatial) representation of reality, would faithfully show why the inference in this case does not hold. Indeed, as Johnson-Laird (1980, p. 104) also states, a model is not only based on information from the propositional representation, but also incorporates general knowledge and other relevant representations. In an experiment it was shown also that a (new) model was built up more easily if propositions describing dimensions of a spatial layout of objects are presented in a certain continuous order (Ehrlich, Mani, & Johnson-Laird, 1979). It was also assumed that models are easier to recall, whereas propositional recall would also display memory for verbatim structure.

Johnson-Laird (1983) elaborates these various ideas in more detail within a more embracing theory of meaning and interpretation in formal psychology. Although his notion of a mental model is close to our situational model concept, his illustrations are mainly within the framework of formal grammars of (isolated) sentences. One major reason for introducing the notion of models that both approaches share, however, is the importance of dealing with (co)reference in psychology. Whereas Johnson-Laird is more interested in inferences and reasoning, I here use the notion of situational model rather for the interpretation of discourse. Also, we pay more attention to the structures of models in terms of cognitive representations of situations, borrowing suggestions from other domains, such as social psychology and sociology. Finally, I hope to show in more detail the cognitive processes, such as interpretation strategies, involved in the use of models, and to make a distinction between ad hoc or particular models and more general models in episodic memory—which form the experiential basis for frames, scripts, or similar more abstract knowledge representations in semantic memory. Important, however, both for mental models and for situational models, is that they are distinguished from semantic representations of sentences or discourse.

Garnham (1981) seems to take one step further and assumes that these mental models are the representation of a text. The text meaning, its semantic representation, is only needed to form the model, and will after that no longer be necessary. As was shown also in van Dijk and Kintsch (1983), I assume that the propositional textbase, representing the meaning of a discourse, is not only used to construct (or to retrieve) an episodic situational model, but must be represented independently: we simply do have memory, at least for certain texts and contexts, for the specific different meanings of a text even if they are about the same situation. The ordering of the propositions in a story may be different, and yet describe the same situation. Such different meaning structures may have different pragmatic implications and be required in different social contexts of communication. This does not mean that because people also construct a model and use this for further inferences, they will not often confuse different descriptions for the same individual (Garnham, 1981, p. 561). Similarly, Garnham was able to show that for certain prepositions, as in the sentences *The hostess bought a mink coat from the furrier* or in *The hostess bought a mink coat in the furrier's*, people will tend to confuse the originally used prepositions in recognition tests and similarity ratings. This is the case if the respective sentences describe more or less the same situation, that is, if a model is used to retrieve the original information.

Foss (1982) uses the term *discourse model* to explain that for certain high-level propositions in such a knowledge structure, the priming effect of concepts remains constant during a stretch of the text, instead of rapidly decaying, as was assumed in earlier work on semantic priming. Foss argues that language users construct and update a semantic model "in which reside entities representing elements and relations in the world of a speaker" (p. 594). However, it is not quite clear here, as in similar work about the role of models in discourse understanding, what the precise difference is between a semantic representation and a model of a text. One could in this case easily explain the results of the experiments in terms of semantic macrostructures (topics) of a text. These also stay active during the understanding of the relevant fragment of a text (Kintsch & van Dijk, 1978; van Dijk & Kintsch, 1983; van Dijk, 1980a).

Finally, Fletcher (1983) presents some experimental evidence for a tripartite distinction in memory for discourse among the surface structure, the semantic (propositional) representation, and the situation model. Thus, distractor items are easier to reject if they are at variance with the model than those items that only differ from textbase propositions.

From this brief view of some relevant work, we may conclude that there is some convergence about the general hypothesis that in addition to a semantic representation of a discourse we also need a situation model in memory, and that such a model plays an important role in such tasks as making inferences, drawing pictures, recall, and recognition. Obviously, much more experimental evidence needs to be accumulated. Also the precise structures and functions, and the differences with textbases, should be spelled out in more detail. One line of future experimental work could investigate when and how information from situation models, that cannot directly come from or be inferred from the original propositional representation of a text, is used in later tasks. Systematic recall and recognition errors or confusions for textual information may be expected as soon as subjects use situation models as dominant retrieval bases (see below). These expectations are in accordance with earlier work such as the experiments by Bransford and his associates (see, e.g., Bransford & Franks, 1972).

In artificial intelligence, it has above all been the work of Roger Schank about scripts and the process of reminding that bears resemblance to our notion of a situation model (Schank, 1982). In the earlier work, scripts, taken as more general knowledge-representation formats (Schank & Abelson, 1977), were considered to be organized clusters of information about stereotypical events, such as eating in a restaurant, going to a party, or taking a bus ride. This kind of general information, which is largely socially shared, would be part of semantic long term memory. Yet, Schank (1982) later stresses that the knowledge we use for various tasks is primarily episodic: a script should rather be seen as the knowledge we have represented about some particular personal experience, as in the previously mentioned example of "my car accident last year in France." Only fragments of such scripts would have a more general nature; these are called Memory Organization Packages (MOPS). Thus, each train ride, which as a whole is unique, will contain some stereotypical episodes, such as buying tickets, getting into the train, and searching for a seat, and may therefore be represented as MOPS.

Schank's (personal) scripts and our situational models have been developed independently and from rather different perspectives. Yet, as episodic representations of personal episodes, they are very similar, especially in their relation to more general knowledge structures. The approach of my work with Kintsch, however, is formulated rather in terms of cognitive interpretation strategies (for discourse), and with the aim of providing an explicit cognitive semantics for coreference, coherence, and similar phenomena. We distinguish between particular models and generalized models, and further assume that models are built and searched for according to standard categorical structures, viz., a model schema. Finally, we would reserve a much more modest role for processes of reminding within the general framework of model retrieval strategies. As is shown in more detail below, models in our case are retrieved by conceptual structures in, e.g., the semantic representation of discourse, for instance macropropositions (themes), after having been inserted into the overall, monitoring control system. Future work will have to show whether and how various notions such as mental models, personal scripts, and situational models can be integrated into one theoretical framework for the representation of episodic knowledge and beliefs and for use in processes of understanding, representation, retrieval, updating and the processes relating episodic (personal) memory and semantic (social) memory.

MODEL STRUCTURES IN MEMORY

Before we are able to specify the functions of models in the processing of discourse, we should specify what such models look like. Suggestions for these internal structures of situational models in memory may be drawn from various sources in philosophy, psychology, linguistics, and the social sciences. Although in each case many technical and methodological problems are involved, we focus only on the major conclusions.

Situational Models versus Real Situations

If situational models in memory can be taken as cognitive reconstructions of the kind of world fragments we have called situations, the structure of such real situations may have some analogies with models. It is however an old insight in ontology and epistemology that the structure of "what there is" is closely related to "what we (can) know" about reality. Indeed, as Johnson-Laird (1983) points out: we only grasp reality via our models (see also Lippmann, 1922). This means that our intuitive, commonsense notions and categories used to interpret reality are in fact notions and categories that make up our models of reality. Thus, we usually distinguish between different, discrete entities, such as different objects or persons, and do not see reality as one continuous mass. Similarly, we distinguish different natural categories of such entities, such as tables, chairs, women, or theories. Also, individuals of some category may be seen as having certain properties or as being parts in some relation. And finally, individuals being assigned such properties or relations make up processes, events, or actions, that is, "facts" of some real or imagined situation. These various types of things also appear in the logical models encountered above. Yet there are also differences between real situations and their cognitive counterparts. For instance:

1. Since we cannot and need not know all facts of the world, cognitive models are typically fragmentary and incomplete.

2. Models may represent real situations at different levels of generality. Thus, we may globally represent in a model the complex action "John made a trip to Portugal," whereas in reality this action consists of

a highly complex and continuous sequence of events, actions, objects, and people, of which only a small subset appear in the model.

3. The concepts in a model are not arbitrary but reflect socially relevant interpretations of situations. For instance, the transmission of an object from one person to another in some social situation may be seen as "giving a present."

4. Apart from the social constraints on conceptualizations of situations, cognitive models are of course personal or subjective: the same situation may be interpreted in different ways, from different perspectives, and with individually different goals in mind, by different people.

These and other specific features of cognitive models have been formulated, sometimes in different terms, in several approaches in the social sciences, and we should take them into account in our theory of model structures in memory. And conversely, our cognitive model theory is intended as a systematic explanation of the well-known features of "understanding the world" mentioned above.

Language and Discourse

In our discussion about formal semantics we have seen that language use and discourse are also related to the world. Thus, we may describe situations in discourse and its sentences. Language users in that case express their interpretation of the world, their models, and we may assume that this expression is not arbitrary. Indeed, various functional grammars (Dik, 1978; Givón, 1979) stress that, for instance, syntactic structure is functionally related to underlying semantic representations (and to communicative acts). These are taken to consist of a predicate (often expressed by a verb phrase) and a number of arguments with different roles, such as agent, patient, instrument, or goal. Apparently, such functional categories show how we analyze the structure of action, for instance. In other words, syntactic and semantic categories tell us something about the makeup of our models of reality.

Similarly, discourse structures tell us something about our understanding of episodes, i.e., sequences of events or actions, as is the case for the respective sentences in a story. Overall macrostructures (topics), and their expression in, for instance, titles, show how we are able to represent higher-level, more abstract, structures of situations. These stories may feature conventional categories, such as a setting and a complication, that show how we can organize episodes in different categories. The same holds for the sentential and textual differentiation between foreground and background, or the special categories for time, place, or circumstances (van Dijk, 1977, 1980a). In other words, syntactic and semantic structures of sentences and discourses are not arbitrary; they reflect basic categories and structures of our cognitive models of reality.

Social Cognition and the Definition of Situations[2]

In social psychology and microsociology there has long been interest in the objective and subjective features of situations and their role in the understanding of interaction (for detailed reviews see Forgas, 1979; Argyle et al., 1981). In order to be able to participate in social situations, social members need models of such situations. These represent what traditionally has been called the "definition of the situation" (Thomas, 1928). Such models are accumulations of previous, biographically determined experiences of (similar) situations (Schutz, 1970).

Forgas (1979) in his review shows that most work on situations deals with holistic properties of situations, such as variations along dimensions such as pleasant vs. unpleasant, relaxed vs. formal, involved vs. uninvolved. How people are able to make such overall evaluations is not spelled out. He also shows that despite the many different taxonomies of situations, there are only a limited number (some 30) of basic everyday social situations.

Argyle et al. (1981) conclude from much theoretical work that social situations and their component interactions are analyzable into categories such as (1) persons and their properties, (2) social structures, such as status and role, (3) elements of interaction, such as friendliness, (4) relevant objects of attention, such as drinks or food at a party, (5) the environmental setting, such as boundaries, props, or spaces, and (6) rules and conventions that specify what actions may or must be performed in such situations. These elements systematically determine how people act and understand each other's actions.

This renewed research about the structures and the interpretation of (social) situations also has common historical sources with work on cognitive models. Thus, Lippmann (1922) in his book on public opinion not only provided important new ideas about the nature of social stereotypes (a notion introduced by him), or about the properties of news, but based his theoretical analysis of public opinion on a notion "pictures in our heads" that is similar to the notion of a situational model:

> For the real environment is altogether too big, too complex, and too fleeting for direct acquaintance. We are not equipped to deal with so much subtlety, so much variety, so many permutations and combinations. And although we have to act in that

environment, we have to reconstruct it on a simpler *model* [italics added] before we can manage with it. To traverse the world, men must have maps of the world. . . . The analyst . . . must begin, then, by recognizing the triangular relationship between the scene of action, the human picture of that scene, and the human response to that picture working itself out upon the scene of action. (pp. 16–17)

The very fact that men theorize at all is proof that their pseudo-environments, their interior representations of the world, are a determining element in thought, feeling and action. For if the connection between reality and human response were direct and immediate, rather than indirect and inferred, indecision and failure would be unknown. (p. 27)

These statements of a journalist of more than 60 years ago are still very pertinent today, and would not be out of place in a contemporary study of cognitive social psychology (except for the reference to "men" who traverse the world and theorize . . .). We also find early suggestions for the application of cognitive model theory in the study of social stereotypes and group representations to which we briefly turn at the end of this chapter.

Situation Schemata

Our final step in this section is to bring together the various suggestions discussed into a first sketch for a theoretical framework. The basic idea we propose is that people make use of so-called situation schemata to build situation models. That is, people make models all the time, and this process is not arbitrary, nor very much context dependent. Rather they use more-or-less stable categories for the kinds of things that should make up a situation model. This also means that people use effective strategies to build models (van Dijk & Kintsch, 1983), which implies that they analyze different situations in much the same way. Only the contents differ to make different models: the schematic skeleton of each situation is more or less invariant (although for some situations not all categories are always relevant). In Figure 5.1 we have made an attempt to put together the various situational categories we have met above. The terminal nodes of the schema are filled by sets of propositions, which again may be summarized by macropropositions.[3] This kind of schema is similar in several respects to schemata we find elsewhere in the literature (P. Brown & Fraser, 1979), especially in work about story structures, in which narrative structures are often identified with the structure of real world episodes (van Dijk, 1980b). Also, the schema is rather close to the functional structures underlying the semantic representations of sentences (Dik, 1978; Givón, 1979). Yet the difference with an actual representation of a particular discourse (the textbase) is that the model schema may take much information in its

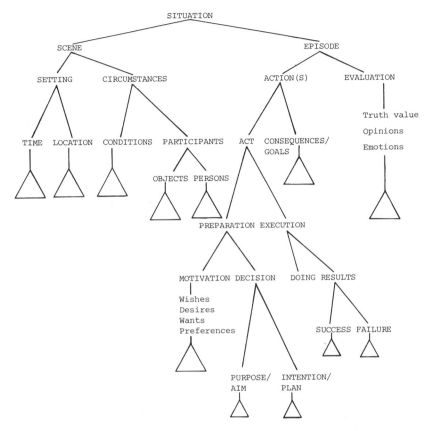

FIGURE 5.1. The schematic structure of a situational (action) model.

terminal categories that is not and need not be expressed in sentences or discourse, e.g., because it is presupposed general knowledge or personal episodic memories that are not relevant in a particular discourse. These differences between textbases and models are considered below.

Another feature of a situation schema is that for various of its component categories, such as (human) participants or action, people also have general knowledge schemata: they have intuitive theories of persons and of actions and, if relevant, these may become part of the model schema.

For reasons of simplicity we have assumed that the terminal nodes of model schemata are filled by propositional (macro-) structures. We have assumed earlier, however, that models need not only be propositional, but may also feature analogical information, such as the structural layout of locations, the spatial relations between objects, and configural properties of objects and persons (see Johnson-Laird, 1983, for a discussion). The schema merely shows that, whatever the kind of information about situations involved, people make systematic distinctions between, e.g., settings, circumstances, participants and their actions, or the various properties of these components. Finally, the schema allows us to assign overall properties to a situation, both at higher (macro-)levels, and lower (micro-)levels. A birthday party, as a whole, may be boring, and so may individual people at the party. In other words, beliefs and opinions of people can also be part of their modeling of situations. In the description of a situation, such beliefs and opinions might only appear indirectly, viz., in the form of specific stylistic choices of words, which would usually not be represented as special propositions in the textbase. Rather, the choice of, for instance, *hooligans* instead of *demonstrators* in a news story (see, e.g., Halloran *et al.*, 1970), would express an evaluative proposition that is part of the model the journalist has of the demonstration (see also van Dijk, 1987b,c).

Finally, we should of course allow for the possibility that models are complex, i.e., consist of other models. That is, within the overall situation of a birthday party, we may have the more specific "situation" of a fight or a fire, requiring its own time and circumstances, and its own subset of participants and events. Typically, the embedding situation may in that case function as some sort of background, e.g., in a circumstance category, for the foregrounded situation. More in general, we may assume that models are not just isolated knowledge structures in episodic memory, but are systematically linked along one or more categories or dimensions, such as "the time I visited California last year," or situations in which "Harry was a participant." Such links enable the combination or even fusion of particular models, but also the process of reminding as described by Schank (1982).

THE FUNCTIONS OF MODELS IN DISCOURSE COMPREHENSION

We started this chapter by assuming that models play an important role in discourse processing. More specifically, it was suggested that situational models provide the episodic knowledge base for the understanding of discourse. They are what a discourse is about. We have also seen that, when hearing or reading a discourse, people do not only construct its meaning in the form of a textbase, but at the same time they build or retrieve from memory a model which represents what they imagine of the situation the discourse is about. Although this assumption may seem plausible for several reasons, we still do not know exactly how this use of models takes place. In this section I try to specify some of these functions of situation models. Although models play a role in all kinds of information processing, such as in perception and action, I limit the discussion to discourse processing.

The Episodic Nature of Models

It has been assumed that situation models are part of episodic memory. This means, first of all, that they represent the personal experiences of people. Yet this criterion is still rather vague. Strictly speaking, we would in that case have models only of situations in which we have participated ourselves, at least as observers. We think that this condition is too strict, however, and we assume that we also may construct (and retrieve) models on the basis of indirect information, e.g., from stories or other discourses. If John tells us about a fight during a birthday party, we try to model that fight and that party much in the same way as if we had been there ourselves. This is possible because we have partial information about specific particulars from John's story, but we also have general frame or script knowledge about fights and parties, as well as our own previous experiences of parties, that is, personal party or even fight-at-party models. These various information sources allow us to make at least part of the model of the situation John is telling about. Obviously, if we had been at the party ourselves, our model would have been more complete. The same takes place, we assume, when people read or hear the news. Models that have been constructed about the same situation, such as the civil war in El Salvador or the Israeli invasion of Lebanon, on the basis of previous news items about these topics (and information from war scripts), are updated with new information (van Dijk, 1987b,c). The specific episodic nature of these models in this case resides in the fact that we will also represent when and where and by whom we were told about the new events (Tulving, 1983).

Particular and General Models

Situations are, by definition, unique. They embody events or actions that are defined by particular time and place parameters and a unique series of events or actions and their participants. This would also imply that our models of such situations would be unique. Again, we find this condition too strict. Of course, we do have unique models of unique experiences (or situations read about), and we are sometimes even able to retrieve such particular models from memory, for instance if they are about highly interesting or prominent situations in our lives, or if they are linked with deep emotions. In that case, new situations may indeed remind us of these specific occurrences.

However, such a theory of episodic models would not explain what seems to go on when we understand a discourse. Especially, we would like to make explicit what goes on in the process of updating our personal knowledge. We therefore make a distinction between particular and generalized models. A particular model is, indeed, the unique representation of a unique situation we are involved in or read or hear about. This unique model is constructed out of the following kinds of information: (1) fragments of general models we already have, (2) information from the present discourse/observations, (3) instantiated fragments of general semantic knowledge. In other words, each particular model is an ad hoc construction, a composition of other forms of knowledge. After discourse understanding, that particular model is seldom of any use anymore, however, and we assume that the new elements in this particular model are used to update the more general models we have. The information about a particular fight at a particular party may be used to update our personal knowledge about fights and parties. Only on some later occasions do we need the particular model, for instance when we want to tell a story about it. For most everyday situations, however, this uniqueness is not required. The respective situations of our everyday working, shopping, household, or seeing-friends activities hardly need be kept retrievable as particular instances. Rather, we combine information from the particular models into more general (but still personal!) models of such situations. In such cases, the general model is defined in terms of the same location, maybe same time periods, same participants, and same types of action or events. We abstract from irrelevant details of the circumstances or the actions. It should be stressed that such generalized models do not contain the same kind of general, stereotypical, knowledge as is usually represented in frames or scripts. This information is socially shared and is not about particular locations or participants, but only about general cultural properties of social situations, such as having drinks or giving presents at a birthday party. Such social scripts may provide part of the structure of general models, but only by substituting general terms by particular terms. In fact, our personal models may be rather different from the social scripts.

We make an even stronger assumption: general script information is only used through its instantiation in a general or particular model if people understand a situation or a discourse about it. If I model a birthday party I went to, I model the fact that I gave a present and that I had drinks or had a conversation with John. Formally speaking, then, scripts would at most define possible models. A script would define, socially speaking, what kinds of models we could call birthday parties. Our accumulated experiences of birthday parties, that is, our general model of such parties, may embody recurrent personal facts that are not at all present in the social script. If we use our personal models for the formation of social scripts, viz., in processes of social learning, then we will in general abstract from such specific personal experiences. We normalize our experiences by comparing them to those of others, e.g., when we understand and store their stories and their models of similar situations. Many episodic (general) models do not even have a corresponding script.

The fact that we may have personal models of unique events of course does not preclude the existence of socially shared knowledge about such events, especially when they have been communicated by the media. Many people have a personal model about the assassination of President Kennedy, often paired with specific contextual information (about when and where they heard that news; see R. Brown & Kulik, 1977), but personal models of unique events may be shared and thereby become social knowledge. In other words, not all social knowledge is frame- or scriptlike, as is the case for recurrent, stereotypical episodes in some culture. Interesting for our discussion is that this shared social knowledge about public events may be presupposed in discourse.

The Strategic Use of Models

Like all knowledge, models are used strategically during discourse processing (van Dijk & Kintsch, 1983). The strategies for the use of models are geared toward an effective use of relevant personal knowledge. For instance, in order to understand a story about a birthday party, we probably need not retrieve all we know about such parties, either socially or personally. Maybe only fragments of our models are necessary, depending on goals, text, and context. And we assumed above that in order to construct a particular model for the situation we are confronted with, it may be necessary to combine these various fragments into a new, ad hoc model. Let us try to specify these assumptions more systematically by enumerating the strategic moves people may go through when using models:

1. *Communicative context.* First, people participate in and understand the communicative context in which the discourse they read or hear should be interpreted, and therefore retrieve particular or general

models of similar previous contexts, e.g., a job interview or a lecture (see below). At this point it is relevant that communicative context models may as such be used to retrieve relevant situation models the discourse in such context may be about. For instance, a job interview model may be used to retrieve models of previous job interview experiences; reading the newspaper activates sociopolitical and public event models.

2. *Goals and interests.* More specifically, not only the type of communicative event but also our actual goals and interests may as such—that is without having yet read or heard the discourse—be used to activate or retrieve particular situation models. I may read the newspaper with the intention of getting new information about the latest developments in Central America, and such a specific goal may already have triggered my personal Central America models.

3. *Titles, announcements, and initial thematic sentences.* Expressions of fragments of the macrostructures (topics) of a discourse, e.g., in the title or the initial thematic sentences, are not only used to strategically set up the probable macrostructure of the text, but also to activate the relevant knowledge about the specific events. Thus, if a newspaper headline says *NEW FIGHTING IN LEBANON* we not only get a summary of new events, but also a powerful retrieval cue for our previous models about fighting in Lebanon.

4. *Sentences.* Understanding the respective sentences of a discourse takes place by the strategic construction of propositional schemata. These will be coherently linked, on line, with previous propositions, e.g., on the basis of conditional relations between facts or the identity of arguments. If no situational model fragment has been activated and retrieved by the context, our goals, or previous (macro-)information, the initial propositions of a text may do so. If the initial propositions provide new information, an appropriate model may be searched for and the new information be added to it. Coherence between the sentences, then, requires a match with local information in the model: if a conditional link is possible, we construct a conditional link between facts denoted. The same holds for the referential identity of discourse participants: does the current description fit the same person in the model we are now talking or reading about? Time, location, and circumstance categories in sentences and propositions will then monitor the possible continuity or changes in the respective episodes of the model.

5. *Monitoring.* The complex process of local and global understanding, the activation and retrieval of models and scripts or other knowledge, and the permanent match between text and communicative context needs to be monitored, viz., by a control system. This control system is fed with the macroinformation about the communicative con-

text, such as sort of communicative situation, genre of discourse, properties of the participants, as well as with the current goals or interests of the language user, and finally the current macroproposition for a fragment of the discourse. We assume that this control system keeps track of the general scripts that are now needed for processing in short term memory, as well as the current personal models needed or activated. It is this control system which is also responsible for the strategic combination of several situational models: it uses local information from short term memory or the textbase in episodic memory, and matches this with the overall context and goal information, as well as with general scripts, and then makes an effective hypothesis about the kinds of model fragments that should be searched for, activated, and how they should be combined.

6. *Updating*. Strategic model use does not imply that we need to activate all our personal knowledge about some situation, nor even that relevant information be activated all at once. Rather, the on-line nature of understanding would suggest that a particular model is built gradually, both from new information and from old models. This also allows that new information be added to the particular model at the precise points where this is relevant, and not in an arbitrary manner. Only in some cases may it be necessary to completely transform a previous model in such an updating process, e.g., when we see that we previously had completely misunderstood similar situations.

7. *Evaluation*. The interpretation of discourse seems to have two major components, viz., the construction of a coherent textbase and the construction of a particular model by transformations such as recombination of old model fragments and processes of updating. Yet, more is at stake. We may also want to evaluate both the incoming information and the possible or actual model transformations that this information would involve. For instance, we would want to know whether information is true or false. False propositions are of course represented in the textbase because they are part of what is said and what was meant, but they need not be taken up in the particular model if the information is inconsistent with information in the models we already have. We see that for the important decision regarding the truth or plausibility of sentences and discourses, we must have a cognitive theory involving episodic models.

Similarly, discourse is not merely evaluated for its truth value, but also for its relations with personal norms and values, that is, with respect to current opinions of the language user. Again, not only the discourse or the textbase may thus be evaluated (as good, bad, interesting, stupid, etc.), but also the facts it denotes. At several points in a particular model, then, the reader/hearer will assign personal values to participants, events, or acts. This is another reason why models are both essentially episodic and personal. In later stages we often do not remember details of a situation, but only our positive or negative evaluation of the situation or episode (Forgas, 1979). Bower (1980) has shown that associated moods alone may be sufficient to serve as retrieval cues in the selection of experiences that have been recorded in the same mood.

CONTEXT MODELS

It may be trivial to repeat that discourses are not produced or read or heard in a vacuum. They are an integral part of a communicative situation. We therefore assume that language users also make a model of the particular situation of which they are by definition a participant. Whereas situation models may be called semantic, such so-called context models are pragmatic and social. They are necessary, as we have seen above, in order to establish a coherent textbase, to define the discourse genre, to represent the goals or interests of the speech participants, and to keep track of established or locally negotiated social properties of the participants, such as status and roles. These conditions are necessary also to assign a pragmatic interpretation to the discourse, that is, to define what speech act is being performed: is this a threat, an assertion or a request? (van Dijk, 1981).

Context models are by definition particular: they are models of this specific communicative situation. Yet, on some occasions we may derive more general models from them, for instance models about important or difficult talks we had, or a model of when we heard or read an important discourse, such as a job interview, a lecture, or a news item on TV.

Since a specific discourse is part of a communicative context, we must assume that a representation of a text is part of a context model. Indeed, we sometimes may remember what was said (that is, part of the textbase) as well as how, when, and by whom it was said (Keenan, MacWhinney, & Mayhew, 1977). Discourse is an integral part of the context. It is not only about things, and therefore not only situational models are necessary to understand it. Discourses are themselves social actions that may be remembered in their own right. Such discourses may cause important changes in social relations and establish changes in social situations. A court trial, for instance, largely consists of situated discourses such as accusations (indictments), pleas, testimonies, interrogations, and judgments, which together may have important social implications. Hence it is often important that people construct context models of these communicative situations that have crucial consequences for their lives. We may even remember only a context model of a talk we had with somebody and not at all remember what we talked about (the situational model).

It is ultimately the context model that provides the typical episodic nature for a discourse and a particular situation model: it specifies when, where, and how we heard about some situation. Although we have made theoretical distinctions between a textbase and general or particular models in episodic memory, and between personal and social models, it should be realized that together with the context model here discussed our memory system is an integrated structure of these "sorts" of information. We have already seen that the representation of the discourse itself (textbase and surface structure) is part of the context model, and this context model is systematically related to the particular situational model now being constructed. In Figure 5.2 we show how these various memory models are related.

The context model also allows us to theorize about the differences between oral and written discourse (Rubin, 1980). Generally speaking, we assumed that models of the situation are formed and needed for the understanding of oral and written texts. Yet, the difference in communication mode may sometimes be relevant, and therefore needs to be represented in the context model. On some occasions we may still remember whether we have read or heard some information, or who said or wrote it. Also, in written discourse we may find various signals for the formation of textbases, macrostructures, and models that we do not have, as such, in oral discourse, such as typographical organization, headlines, types of printing. We have seen that in such cases the formation of macrostructures may be facilitated, as well as the retrieval of situation models.

Major differences between oral and written communication, however, should be sought in the strategic processes of production and understanding (Hildyard & Olson, 1982). Contrary to listening, reading allows personal speed in decoding, understanding, and the integration of knowledge. This means that people can reserve more time for the retrieval of personal models, or can activate more information from such models. The effects of this process may be conflicting though: it may lead to better understanding due to more extensive and more relevant model use, but uncontrolled activation of personal memories may also be confused with actual discourse and the now-relevant situation model information. On the other hand, the rich information from oral discourse (intonation, gestures, paraverbal acts) leads to a possibly more-differentiated context model, and hence to better recall of the communicative situation itself.

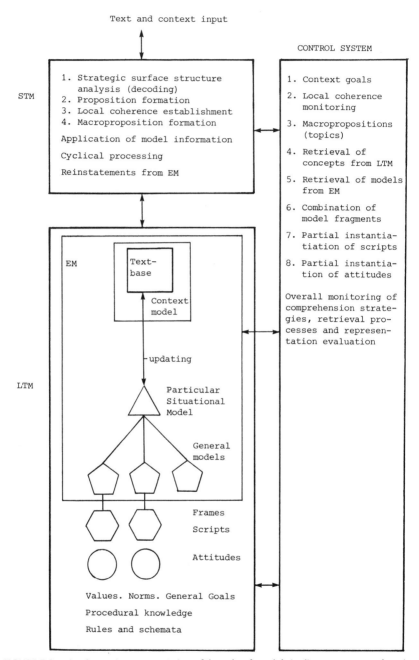

FIGURE 5.2.   A schematic representation of the role of models in discourse comprehension.

AN EXAMPLE: A NEWS ITEM AND ITS
ASSOCIATED MODELS

Although a full analysis of the relevant model knowledge required for the understanding of a simple text would probably cover most of the space of this chapter, we can only give some fragments of such an analysis. In Figure 5.3 we have copied and analyzed the beginning of a news item translated from a Dutch newspaper (*NRC-Handelsblad*, July 12, 1983). In the left column we find (in natural English, not formal notation) the information expressed by the text or part of the communicative context, and in the right column the assumed models that are activated, used, and updated during the reading process. Since there is no standard way of representing the many processes involved, our notation of the models, their contents, the retrieval steps, the updating, and the establishment of links within and across models, is ad hoc.

First we see that the context provides and activates some information about the kind of communication (newspaper), the kind of newspaper, and the consequences for the background ideology (conservative) that may be implicit in the news item. This may imply that only negative information will be given of leftist guerrilla movements.

The headline of the text and its underlying semantic representation provide the concepts that may be used to activate the major models of this text, viz., PERU and (ARMED) ATTACK. The particular model in that case is a combination of information from these two models together with information from the text: an attack has taken place in Peru. The models embody both general information about Peru and about armed attacks, as well as possible personal information, such as having friends in Peru for example. The information in Model A.c and d derives from recent news items in the press about guerrilla activities in Peru. This information may even trigger recent particular text and context models and hence a particular model about these guerrilla activities. The conventional categories of the ATTACK model, such as participants, goal, action, are partly filled in (updated) from the information in the textbase. That arms are used in the attack is part of our general model (and scripts) of attacks, but also presupposed by the new information in the title (*one killed*). The knowledge we have about Peru makes it plausible that it is a political action. The next sentences gradually fill in further information about these models: precise location (Lima, HQ of PAP), number of attackers, sort and number of victims, and arms used. Much information, however, may be used or inferred that is not expressed in the text, e.g., that Lima is the capital of Peru, that the attackers are opposed to the ruling PA party, and maybe even the evaluative opinion

Text   ONE KILLED IN PERU IN ATTACK AT PARTY BUREAU

During an attack by five armed men on the headquarters of the ruling Popular Action Party in Lima a woman was killed and thirty people were wounded. The police assumes that the attackers are members of the Maoist inspired guerrilla movement Sendero Luminoso.

About seven o'clock yesterday evening local time , the five men started to shoot with submachine guns and to throw bombs from cars at the building of Popular Action, where a meeting of the women's section had just begun.

Javier Alva Orlandini, secretary-general of the party, called the attack "the most barbarian" in the three years since the guerrilla-movement Sendero Luminoso started its activities.

Just before the attack other bombs had **exploded at fifteen** other places in the capital. There were no casualties there. (AP, AFP).

CONTEXT INFORMATION

1. Newspaper
2. Inside page, small article
3. International news

MODEL INFORMATION

1. MODEL: (DUTCH) NEWSPAPER
   a. conservative
2. Relatively unimportant international event
   a. social and political events

TEXTBASE FRAGMENTS

N.B. Information acquired from the textbase is in italics, also when already known. Relevant discourse/model referents are numbered (p1, p2,...) for co-reference.

3. MODEL A: PERU
   a. Country. LOCATION EVENTS   e. I have friends (k,m) in Peru.
   b. Northwest of South America   (MODELS k and m)
   c. Actual political troubles (from 1 and 2a)
   d. Guerrilla activities

4. MODEL B: ARMED ATTACK (news event, violent events in third world, from 1a).
   a. Participants: attackers(p1), attacked (p2)(victims: <u>one killed</u> (p3)).
   b. Goal: party bureau (buildingㅣp4)
   c. Action: attack
   d. Instruments: arms
   e. Reasons: political (from B.b. and A.c.)

4. Title
   One killed in Peru
   in attack at party bureau

186

5. Five armed men attacked the HQ of the ruling Popular Action Party in Lima.	5. MODEL B.a. Armed men (p1), five (p1) B.b. Party bureau = HQ(p4) Modifier: Popular Action Party (P5) Modifier: PAP part of government
6. One woman was killed and thirty people were wounded.	6. MODEL A: Lima: capital MODEL B: Location: Lima
7. The police assumes that The attackers are members of the Maoist inspired guerrilla movement Sendero Luminoso.	7. MODEL B.e.1.Attackers opposed to ruling party (from B.b.) 2.Attackers members of guerrilla? (from B.e. and A.c-d.)
8. About seven o'clock yesterday evening local time, the five men started to shoot with submachine guns and to throw bombs from cars at the building of Popular Action, where a meeting of the women's section had just begun.	8. MODEL B: Consequences: woman(p3), thirty of p2 wounded. B.e. Evaluative Modifier: Attackers are mean (kill women).

9. MODEL B: Reaction: Police action, declaration.

10. Model B.a.: (7.2. Confirmed?) and A.d.: Guerrilla: Sendero Luminoso: MODEL C.

MODEL C. SENDERO LUMINOSO

a. Guerrilla movement in Peru.   e. Recent article in newspaper
b. Maoist ideology (orthodox)   f. Spanish: Shining Path.
c. Have support from poor farmers   g. Are mean? (From B.e.)
d. Headed by ex-university professor   h. MODEL: NEWSPAPER information

11. MODEL B: Time: About seven o'clock, yesterday, local time (time in Peru)
    B.c.: started to shoot with submachine guns(p1)
          throw bombs (p1)
    B: Origin: from cars. (NB: repeated info in text about Target not here.Cf.4).

12. MODEL B: Circumstances: meeting of women's section of P5 had just begun.
    (women in the building: women(p3))
    (MODEL A.e.: MODELS k and m: Friends member of SL?(MODEL C))

FIGURE 5.3.   Sample analysis of a text, its textbase, and its situational model.

that those who attack defenseless women are bad people. Previous information in the press may have set up a next model, viz., about the guerrilla movement SENDERO LUMINOSO, which may trigger information not in the text, such as their (earlier) support from farmers. This lack of information in the text may tie in with the model we have about the particular newspaper (for details about news understanding see van Dijk & Kintsch, 1983).

Not represented here is of course the possible imagery we have about the situation: how does the action take place exactly? Did the men shoot from the cars, and how can they throw bombs from a (moving?) car? The same may be asked about the picture we have about a (party) building, in a town, etc.[4]

Most important, though, is that this example shows how fragments of models are retrieved by text cues, used, and updated.

EMPIRICAL EVIDENCE

If the notion of a situational model has any empirical relevance, we should at least try to experimentally test some of its more specific implications. Some experimental work is reviewed above, and of course there is much previous experimental work that could be reinterpreted in light of a model theory. Space limitations, however, do not allow a detailed examination of these experimental results in this chapter. We, therefore, only make some brief suggestions and formulate some tentative predictions.

1. A first general expectation is of course that if language users do not have a model of a situation, or have only a very fragmentary one, understanding of a discourse is generally impaired. This may imply slower reading times, less recall, more errors in recall or recognition, and other consequences of a lesser degree of understanding. Thus, stories about highly unusual experiences may be more difficult because we do not have a ready-made model or cannot construct a particular model as easily. This is typically the case for stories about events and actions in other cultures (Kintsch & Greene, 1979).

2. We may expect that certain properties of discourse facilitate or impair the construction of a particular model. This is typically the case for abstract texts, in which imagery of concrete persons, objects, events, or actions does not play a role (Paivio, 1971).

3. Discourse that provides a description of a situation may follow the canonical structure of a model and in that case it may be easier to con-

struct the model than when we have a transformed description of the situation (Mandler, 1978; Ehrlich *et al.*, 1979; Levelt, 1982; Jarvella & Klein, 1982).

4. If indeed a discourse is structurally rather different from the canonical structure of a model, it may make understanding more difficult but at the same time it may be easier to recognize the passages that do not have the canonical ordering. The same would hold for specific stylistic choices and rhetorical operations.

5. If particular models are assembled from fragments of other models, one should expect that if more models need to be retrieved and combined, it will take more time to understand a discourse. Also, recall may be less than with the description of one-model situations.

6. Especially after longer delays, people will increasingly tend to confuse specific textual information with model information. This effect will be enhanced as soon as they have read several texts about the same situation, as is the case for news in the paper (see also Bower, Black, & Turner, 1979).

7. If models play a role in the process of updating, we may expect that texts with much new information are more difficult to read, understand, or recall than those with much old model information, because in that case more constructive work must be done.

8. Models provide the background knowledge for the understanding of discourse. Hence, if models are more complete, a text may be more implicit and be relatively less coherent: we will find enhanced use of presuppositions and less explicit connectives or linking propositions.

9. If particular models have only an ad hoc function in the updating of more general models, it will be more difficult to retrieve these particular models than the (updated) general models.

10. We have assumed that general (social) scripts are used in discourse comprehension only through their instantiations in episodic models. This might mean that instantiated script fragments are better recalled than noninstantiated ones. However, we should also take into account the possibility that general, stereotypical knowledge is easier to retrieve than episodic models. We here need further exploratory evidence.

11. Models are formed not only on the basis of textual information, but also on the basis of the interpretation of real scenes and pictures. A series of experiments is necessary to explore the possible confusion of model information derived from text and information derived from other modes of comprehension (Schallert, 1980). It should also be experimentally possible to separate understanding and recall of textual information from model information.

Although we here have formulated some rather general predictions about the role of models, it will in general not be easy to precisely separate textbase information from information in particular models, general models, or scripts.[5]

Of course, empirical evidence for the cognitive reality of situation models need not come only from controlled experiments in the laboratory. On the contrary, data about the contents and the personal strategies of episodic models may be drawn from more natural expressions of such models, e.g., in self-reports, stories, or interviews. Access, assessment, and manipulation of the personal experiences that form our personal models indeed would be difficult to obtain in experimental conditions. There is much work on different methods, and these will precisely yield evidence about the contents, the structures, and the uses of personal models (Linton, 1975; Neisser, 1982; Whitten & Mauriello Leonard, 1981).

Finally, we should at least mention one interesting application of cognitive model theory. In our work in a project about ethnic prejudice in conversations about ethnic minorities in the Netherlands, it appeared that different kinds of prejudice and at the same time different strategies of expressing these (or not) in discourse closely correspond to the theoretical distinctions made between different kinds of models in this chapter (van Dijk, 1984, 1987a). Prejudices based on personal experiences, i.e., derived from models of the situation in some neighborhood, are different from the kinds of prejudices people derive from more general, social stereotype schemata about ethnic groups. However, personal prejudices are quickly extended from particular models to general models, or may be used as "evidence" of negative social attitudes.

Work on social cognition (see, e.g., Forgas, 1981) and its application in social stereotype research (Hamilton, 1981), also has given increasing attention to the important role of social representations of situations, persons, and groups. Notions such as schemata and scripts have been borrowed from psychology and artificial intelligence in order to model the structures and uses of stereotypical beliefs about minority groups. Our work suggests that, in addition to much more explicit representation formats and precise strategies of social information processing, situational models are also important to account for the formation and uses of ethnic beliefs and attitudes. Without the notion of a model, it is not clear how prejudiced people actually interpret interethnic situations and how they act in such situations. The lack of concrete personal experiences, such as encounters with minority group members, will urge people to "imagine" such experiences by constructing models "by default," i.e., by instantiating preestablished ethnic attitude schemata from semantic (social, shared) memory. Conversely, a single particular model of such an encounter may strategically be used to form general models and abstract attitude schemata about minority groups (for detail see van Dijk, 1987a).

We have given this example of work in progress not only because it shows the relevance of the notion of episodic model in other domains of psychology and sociology, or to account for a number of specific properties of prejudiced discourse, but also to stress the need for interdisciplinary integration in the further development of such a notion and to point to the possibility of making cognitive theories really useful in the analysis of pressing social problems.

CONCLUSIONS

We have shown that a cognitive theory of discourse processing needs a model theory. Models are cognitive representations in episodic memory of the situations discourses are about. They embody accumulated experiences of previous occasions with the same or similar things, persons, or events. We need them as an interpretation basis for discourse. Only with respect to such models can we evaluate discourse with respect to truth values, establish referential identity, and decide about the local and global coherence of discourse.

We have assumed that situational models are built up around a model schema, consisting of a limited number of categories people use to interpret situations. These schemata are then filled with concrete information we obtain about such a situation in different observational or communicative contexts. Discourse is usually processed in order to update existing models or to build new ones. Since discourses may be about different kinds of experiences at the same time, we often need to construct a new, particular, model from fragments of existing models. In this way, each particular model is constructed by (1) information from the discourse, (2) fragments of old models, and (3) instantiations from general knowledge (scripts).

Finally, it was shown that discourse understanding also requires the formation of particular context models, of which the actual discourse is an integrated part. Such context models not only provide the necessary social dimension for the text, but also serve as the proper episodic and communicative dimension of the situation models conveyed by discourse processing.

ACKNOWLEDGMENTS

I would like to acknowledge helpful critical comments on the first versions of this paper by Rosalind Horowitz, Philip Johnson-Laird, Alan Garnham, and Walter Kintsch. Remaining errors are my own. A lengthy discussion about the foundations of model structures has been reduced to a short summary. Presupposed knowledge of my earlier work and of other research on discourse processing has been kept to a minimum.

NOTES

[1] One confusion that should be avoided is that with the notion of model that roughly is equivalent to theory. In this chapter, a cognitive model is not a model (theory) of cognition, but a knowledge representation in memory.

[2] Especially in this section we cannot possibly do justice to the many suggestions about the sociocognitive aspects of situations and episodes that have been elaborated in decades of research. For details see Forgas (1979) and Argyle, Furnham, and Graham (1981). A useful reader with many papers from several disciplines about the notion of (social) situation is Furnham and Argyle (1981).

[3] These macropropositions are necessary in order to hierarchically organize the sometimes vast amounts of knowledge that may be accumulated during many previous experiences (including discourse) about the various categories of the schema, e.g., details about persons, objects, or actions we are confronted with regularly.

[4] Other newspaper accounts in the Dutch press, as well as the item in *The Guardian* of July 13, 1983, provide different details of the same event, and hence express and induce different models (which we may call **model variants** or **alternative models**) of the situation. Thus, *The Guardian* mentions that the attackers were led by a woman, that three people were killed, and that the attackers actually left their cars and entered the party building. Despite the exactness of the numbers in news stories (rhetorically used to signify credibility), the different agencies and papers seem to convey different models.

[5] This is rather a practical problem for controlled experimentation. This chapter however has shown that there are systematic differences in content, functions, and uses for these various knowledge/belief structures in memory, even if they are multiply interconnected. Since episodic memory not only stores episodes, and semantic long-term memory is not only semantic (and also features episode schemata), we suggest that it might make more sense to speak of **personal** and **social** memory, respectively.

APPENDIX

Rebels Blast Lima HQ*

LIMA: More than 15,000 police yesterday hunted for leftwing guerrillas who made a bloody bomb and submachinegun attack on the headquarters of the ruling Popular Action Party in what President Fernando Belaunde Terry said amounted to an act of war. Three people were killed and 32 wounded.

"Yes, gentlemen, war is what Peru is fighting," President Belaunde said in an emotional appearance at the headquarters after Monday night's attack. The party HQ is only 200 yards from the Civil Guard headquarters.

The country, he said, was passing through a grave hour—a reflection of growing government concern over escalating guerrilla actions and rebel ability to strike during a 60-day national emergency declared to fight terrorism.

The Civil Guard said the hunt for guerrilla suspects in and around the Peruvian capital had resulted in several arrests.

The guerrilla strike was the first made directly on people since the Maoist movement called Shining Path started fighting the government three years ago. The rebels also set off a dozen bombs elsewhere in Lima, causing brief power cuts.

Witnesses said that four or five guerrillas led by a woman burst into the unguarded two-storey building firing sub-machineguns and throwing at least four dynamite bombs. The guerrillas sped away in a waiting car.

The executive committee of Mr. Belaunde's party demanded the restoration of the death penalty.

President Belaunde abolished the death penalty except for wartime treason when he took office in 1980 after his election ended 12 years of military rule.—AP/Reuter.

* *The Guardian*, Wednesday, July 13, 1983.

Dode in Peru bij aanslag op partijbureau*

LIMA, 12 juli—Bij een aanval van vijf gewapende mannen op het hoofdkwartier van de regerende Volksactie-partij in Lima is een vrouw gedood en dertig mensen gewond. De politie vermoedt dat de daders van de aanslag lid zijn van de maoïstisch geïnspireerde guerrillabeweging Sendero Luminoso.

Omstreeks zeven uur gisteravond plaatselijke tijd begonnen de vijf mannen vanuit auto's met mitrailleurs te schieten en gooiden zij bommen naar het gebouw van Volksactie, waar juist een vergadering van de vrouwenafdeling was begonnen.

Javier Alva Orlandini, de secretaris-generaal van de partij, noemde de aanval "de meest barbaarse" in de drie jaar dat de guerrillabeweging Sendero Luminoso actief is.

Vlak voor de aanval waren op vijftien andere plaatsen in de Peruaanse hoofdstad bommen ontploft. Hierbij vielen geen slachtoffers. (AP, AFP)

* *NRC-Handelsblad*, Tuesday, July 12, 1983.

REFERENCES

Argyle, M., Furnham, A., & Graham, J. A. (1981). *Social situations*. London: Cambridge University Press.

Beaugrande, R. de, & Dressler, W. U. (1981). *Introduction to text linguistics*. London: Longman.

Bower, G. H. (1980). Mood and memory. *American Psychologist, 36,* 129–148.

Bower, G. H., Black, J. B., & Turner, T. J. (1979). Scripts in memory for text. *Cognitive Psychology, 11,* 177–220.

Bransford, J. D., & Franks, J. J. (1972). The abstraction of linguistic ideas. *Cognitive Psychology, 2,* 331–350.

Brown, P., & Fraser, C. (1979). Speech as a marker of situation. In K. R. Scherer & H. Giles (Eds.), *Social markers in speech.* London: Cambridge University Press.

Brown, R., & Kulik, J. (1977). Flashbulb memories. *Cognition, 5,* 73–99.

Coulthard, M. (1977). *Introduction to discourse analysis.* London: Longman.

Craik, K. (1943). *The nature of explanation.* Cambridge: Cambridge University Press.

Dik, S. (1978). *Functional grammar.* Amsterdam: North-Holland.

Ehrlich, K., Mani, K., & Johnson-Laird, P. N. (1979). *Mental models of spatial relations.* University of Sussex: Laboratory of Experimental Psychology.

Fletcher, C. R. (1983). *Surface forms, textbases and situational models. Recognition memory for three types of textual information.* University of Colorado, Boulder: Department of Psychology.

Forgas, J. P. (1979). *Social episodes.* New York: Academic Press.

Forgas, J. P. (Ed.). (1981). *Social cognition.* New York: Academic Press.

Foss, D. J. (1982). A discourse on semantic priming. *Cognitive Psychology, 14,* 590–607.

Furnham, A., & Argyle, M. (Eds.). (1981). *The psychology of social situations.* London: Pergamon.

Garnham, A. (1981). Mental models as representations of text. *Memory & Cognition, 9,* 560–565.

Garnham, A., Oakhill, J., & Johnson-Laird, P. N. (1982). Referential continuity and the coherence of discourse. *Cognition, 11,* 29–46.

Givón, T. (1979). *On understanding grammar.* New York: Academic Press.

Guenthner, F., & Schmidt, S. J. (Eds.). (1979). *Formal semantics and pragmatics for natural languages.* Dordrecht, The Netherlands: Reidel.

Halloran, J. D., Elliott, P., & Murdock, G. (1970). *Demonstrations and communication.* Harmondsworth, England: Penguin Books.

Hamilton, D. (Ed.). (1981). *Cognitive processes in stereotyping and intergroup behavior.* Hillsdale, NJ: Erlsbaum.

Hildyard, H., & Olson, D. R. (1982). On the comprehension and memory of oral vs. written discourse. In D. Tannen (Ed.), *Spoken and written language.* Norwood, NJ: Ablex.

Hughes, G. E., & Cresswell, M. J. (1968). *An introduction to modal logic.* London: Methuen.

Jarvella, R. J., & Klein, W. (Eds.). (1982). *Speech, place and action.* Chichester, England: Wiley.

Johnson-Laird, P. N. (1980). Mental models in cognitive science. *Cognitive Science, 4,* 72–115.

Johnson-Laird, P. N. (1983). *Mental models.* London: Cambridge University Press.

Johnson-Laird, P. N., & Garnham, A. (1980). Descriptions and discourse models. *Linguistics and Philosophy, 3,* 371–393.

Kamp, H. (1981). A theory of truth and semantic representation. In J. A. G. Groenendijk, T. Janssen, & M. Stokhof (Eds.), *Formal methods in the study of language.* Amsterdam: Mathematical Centre Tracts.

Karttunen, L. (1975). Discourse referents. In J. D. McCawley (Ed.), *Syntax and semantics* (Vol. 7). New York: Academic Press.

Keenan, E. L. (Ed.). (1975). *Formal semantics of natural language.* Cambridge: Cambridge University Press.

Keenan, J. M., MacWhinney, B., & Mayhew, D. (1977). Pragmatics in memory: A study of natural conversation. *Journal of Verbal Learning and Verbal Behavior, 16,* 549–560.

Kintsch, W., & Greene, E. (1978). The role of culture-specific schemata in the comprehension and recall of stories. *Discourse Processes, 1,* 1–13.

Kintsch, W., & van Dijk, T. A. (1975). Comment on se rappelle et on résume des histoires. *Langages, 40,* 98–116.

Kintsch, W., & van Dijk, T. A. (1978). Toward a model of text comprehension and production. *Psychological Review, 85,* 363–394.

Levelt, W. J. M. (1982). Linearization in describing spatial networks. In S. Peters & E. Saarinen (Eds.), *Processes, beliefs and questions.* Dordrecht, Netherlands: Reidel.

Linton, M. (1975). Memory for real-world events. In D. A. Norman & D. E. Rumelhart (Eds.), *Explorations in cognition.* San Francisco: Freeman.

Lippmann, W. (1922). *Public opinion.* New York: Harcourt.

Mandler, J. (1978). A code in the node: The use of a story schema in retrieval. *Discourse Processes, 1,* 14–35.

Nash-Webber, B. L. (1978). *A formal approach to discourse anaphora* (Tech. Rep.). Cambridge, MA: Bolt, Beranek & Newman.

Nash-Webber, B. L. (1981). Discourse model synthesis: Preliminaries to reference. In A. K. Joshi, B. L. Webber, & I. A. Sag (Eds.), *Elements of discourse understanding.* London: Cambridge University Press.

Neisser, U. (Ed.). (1982). *Memory observed: Remembering in natural contexts.* San Francisco: Freeman.

Paivio, A. (1971). *Imagery and verbal processes.* New York: Holt.

Petöfi, J. S., & Rieser, H. (1974). *Probleme der modelltheoretischen Interpretation von Texten.* Hamburg: Buske.

Rubin, A. (1980). A theoretical taxonomy of the differences between oral and written language. In R. J. Spiro, B. C. Bruce, & W. F. Brewer (Eds.), *Theoretical issues in reading comprehension.* Hillsdale, NJ: Erlbaum.

Schallert, D. L. (1980). The role of illustrations in reading comprehension. In R. J. Spiro, B. C. Bruce, & W. F. Brewer (Eds.), *theoretical issues in reading comprehension.* Hillsdale, NJ: Erlbaum.

Schank, R. C. (1982). *Dynamic memory.* London: Cambridge University Press.

Schank, R. C., & Abelson, R. P. (1977). *Scripts, plans, goals and understanding.* Hillsdale, NJ: Erlbaum.

Schutz, A. (1970). On phenomenology and social relations. In H. R. Wagner (Ed.), *Alfred Schutz on phenomenology and social relations.* Chicago: University of Chicago Press.

Stenning, K. (1978). Anaphora as an approach to pragmatics. In M. Halle *et al.* (Eds.), *Linguistic theory and linguistic reality.* Cambridge, MA: MIT Press.

Thomas, W. I. (1928). Situational analysis. The behavior pattern and the situation. In M. Janovits (Ed.), *W. I. Thomas on social organization and social personality.* Chicago: University of Chicago Press.

Tulving, E. (1983). *Elements of episodic memory.* London: Oxford University Press.

van Dijk, T. A. (1972). *Some aspects of text grammars.* The Hague: Mouton.

van Dijk, T. A. (1973). Text grammar and text logic. In J. S. Petöfi & H. Rieser (Eds.), *Studies in text grammar.* Dordrecht, Netherlands: Reidel.

van Dijk, T. A. (1977). *Text and context.* London: Longman.

van Dijk, T. A. (1980a). *Macrostructures.* Hillsdale, NJ: Erlbaum.

van Dijk, T. A. (Ed.). (1980b). Story comprehension. [Special issue]. *Poetics, 8,* (1/3).

van Dijk, T. A. (1981). *Studies in the pragmatics of discourse.* Berlin: Mouton.

van Dijk, T. A. (1983). Cognitive and conversational strategies in the expression of ethnic prejudice. *Text, 3,* 375–404.

van Dijk, T. A. (1984). *Prejudice in discourse.* Amsterdam: Benjamins.

van Dijk, T. A. (Ed.). (1985). *Handbook of discourse analysis.* (4 vols.). London: Academic Press.

van Dijk, T. A. (1987a). *Communicating racism: Ethnic prejudice in thought and talk.* Newbury Park, CA: Sage.

van Dijk, T. A. (1987b). *News as discourse.* Hillsdale, NJ: Erlbaum.

van Dijk, T. A. (1987c). *News analysis.* Hillsdale, NJ: Erlbaum.

van Dijk, T. A., & Kintsch, W. (1978). Cognitive psychology and discourse. Recalling and summarizing stories. In W. U. Dressler (Ed.), *Current trends in text linguistics.* Berlin: de Gruyter.

van Dijk, T. A., & Kintsch, W. (1983). *Strategies of discourse comprehension.* New York: Academic Press.

Whitten, W. B., & Mauriello Leonard, J. (1981). Directed search through autobiographical memory. *Memory & Cognition, 9,* 566–579.

Chapter **6**

The Role of Context in Written Communication

Martin Nystrand

INTRODUCTION

The common claim that written texts are "autonomous" and explicit compared to speech, which is "context-bound" and "fragmentary," is an oversimplification that misses the main point of one aspect of writing. A text is explicit not because it says everything all by itself but rather because it strikes a careful balance between what needs to be said and what may be assumed. The writer's problem is not just being explicit; the writer's problem is knowing what to be explicit about.

In this chapter I examine the fallacies of the doctrine of autonomous texts, showing how even the most formal of essays works *not apart from but in terms of its context of use.* These issues are relevant to psychologists and linguists concerned about the nature of text and discourse processes. These issues will also interest educators, who, as Watson and Olson (this volume) show, typically work from the premise that formal prose ought to work independently of its context and who accomplish this objective by teaching writing as a matter for preferred form rather than effective use.

THE DOCTRINE OF AUTONOMOUS TEXTS

A substantial body of thought, from Plato to the present, supports the notion that written and spoken language differ most with respect to the contexts in which each is created and must function. The essential argument is as follows: Writers, unlike speakers, do not produce language in the company of a language receiver. And written texts, unlike spoken, must function apart from the context of their production. Therefore, writing must differ fundamentally from speech. Specifically, written texts must be "autonomous" and "explicit" in order to function acontextually.

Plato was perhaps the first philosopher to consider the context of oral language. He especially distrusted the performances of bards and poets, who he believed appealed to the emotions rather than reason. The classicist Eric Havelock (1963, 1977) supports Plato's suspicions about oral language by arguing that the requirements for memorizing Homeric epics, as well as the conditions of their recitations, promoted the use of such oral mnemonic devices as prosodic organization, personal reference, concrete images, and narrative style. Goody and Watt (1968) contend that such logical language forms as syllogisms, propositions, and the elaboration of premises became possible only with the advent of writing and the availability of permanent text for inspection and review. In this view, writing made possible historical and literary criticism as well as modern systems of logic: The former enabled Herodotus to compare past and present claims whereas the latter enabled Plato and Aristotle to compare propositions. Sociolinguist Stubbs (1980) discusses written language in this regard when he notes the special role it plays in Sir Karl Popper's (1972) *Theory of World 3:* Writing makes possible objective knowledge which lies beyond the world of physical events (world 1) and beyond the world of experience and consciousness (world 2). Writing is that essential and ultimate path of language that leads its users to the archives of a knowledge which exists independently of the knowers, for example, in libraries.

These notions of written and spoken language have been amplified by psychologists. For example, Vygotsky (1962) notes how the basic cognitive processes of abstraction, generalization, and inference are favored by the propensity of written language for reflection and analysis: Writing is "the deliberate structuring of the web of meaning" (p. 100) and so enhances the analytic processes of "scientific concepts." Patricia Greenfield (1972), a developmental psychologist whose work has been influential among educators, concludes that schooling and literacy are the primary factors involved in the development of "context-free," abstract thought mainly because of the impact of written language on cognitive processes. By learning to write, she notes, students learn skills of critical analysis because of the requirements of written language for autonomous text. Snow (1983) outlines important similarities in both oral and written language development. Both, she concludes, require learning how to understand and produce decontextualized language, i.e., "growth in their ability to discuss the remote and the abstract" (p. 175).

A number of important studies have challenged this doctrine of autonomous texts by arguing that the proposed dichotomy of context-bound spoken utterance, on the one hand, and autonomous text on the other, is an oversimplification which obscures many important aspects of language. Tannen (1982), for example, shows that features which researchers have often identified as characteristic of each mode (for example, literary devices such as prosody and alliteration and oral devices such as rementions and assonance) are also found in the other mode. Lakoff (1982) shows that oral and written language influence each other historically and culturally. At the same time that writers of fiction have increasingly used quotation marks to personalize their writing and bring an emotional directness to their prose, she notes, many speakers have learned to indicate quotation marks with their fingers as a paralinguistic device. In a seminal study of the cognitive consequences of literacy, Scribner and Cole (1981) conclude that literacy per se contributes only marginally to cognitive development. They argue that literacy is not adequately understood as proficiency in decontextualized language. "Literacy is not simply knowing how to read and write a particular script but applying this knowledge for specific purposes in specific contexts of use" (p. 236).

Nonetheless, the doctrine of autonomous texts is fairly well established, and nowhere more so than among educators and in composition theory. Indeed, composition research distinguishes composition from writing a priori in precisely these terms (see, e.g., Bereiter & Scardamalia, 1981; Dillon, 1981; Hirsch, 1977; Kroll, 1981; Olson, 1977). Bereiter and Scardamalia's distinction is typical:

> Writing is use of the written medium and entails such skills as handwriting, spelling, and punctuation. People who could converse by passing notes back and forth to one another would be said to know how to write. If that were all they could do, however, they could not be said to know how to compose. . . . [Composition] involves producing . . . "autonomous text" . . . a coherent piece of language that can accomplish its rhetorical purpose without depending on context or on interaction between sender and receiver. One does not, in principle, need to know how to write in order to compose. Composing can be done by dictation. (1981, p. 3–4)

This contrast between context-bound utterance and autonomous text is often defined in terms of **exophoric** and **endophoric referencing** (Halliday & Hasan, 1976). Exophoric references "point away from" the text either to things in the speaking environment (e.g., *Put it here*) or to ideas which exist as presumed, shared knowledge and require no elaboration (e.g., *I don't believe it*). By contrast, endophoric references point to other parts of the text where they are elaborated, illustrated, or defined. Consider the following example:

(1)   *What we really need in our field is articulation of a comprehensive theory. This effort is complicated by the fact that so many researchers operate out of different and frequently incompatible assumptions.*

In these two sentences, *This effort* is an endophoric reference to something identified in the text itself, namely, *articulation of a comprehensive theory* in the previous sentence. Endophoric referencing is the chief way writers and speakers explain what they mean; and when editors and teachers ask a writer to be clear and explicit, they are typically requesting a more endophoric and less exophoric text.

THREE FALLACIES

It is true that written texts typically function in contexts other than those in which they were written. It does not follow from this premise, however, that in order to function, written texts must be "autonomous," "acontextual," and "explicit." Nor does it follow that those which are abbreviated,[1] e.g., notes, are uncomposed. There are three fallacies in such deductions. The first fallacy is confusing **situation of expression** with **context of use**. The fact that writers do not converse with readers face-to-face or that their texts speak independently of them does not mean that these texts are therefore "acontextual" and "autonomous." Rather, it means that unlike speech, where situation of expression and context of use are concurrent, written texts are composed for a **context of eventual use** (cf. Nystrand, 1986).

The second fallacy is confusing **fullness of meaning** with **explicitness of text**. Although it is true that difficult texts often benefit from revisions which clarify and elaborate key points, it does not follow that texts become categorically more meaningful as more of their references are elaborated. This is why legal documents do not necessarily mean the more for all their explicitness and why EXIT signs and grocery lists do not necessarily mean the less for all their crypticness. Moreover, the kind of effective elaboration which enhances, say, well-written technical manuals with ample explanations, illustrations, and definitions is neither random nor ubiquitous. Rather, it is planned and selective, dealing only with points requiring emphasis or clarification.

There is a subtle and important difference between an **elaboration** and a **complication of text.** For example, a particular part in the tax code that might be ambiguous and consequently difficult for tax attorneys may well be abstruse and hard in a very different way for the general tax-payer. That a given text can be ambiguous for some readers, and abstruse for others can easily be demonstrated by showing that high- and low-knowledge readers require qualitatively different revisions (Nystrand, 1986): tax attorneys require more details—elaborations of key points—whereas taxpayers need the main idea to relate all the details. The same endophoric text which works to clarify things for the attorneys works just the opposite to complicate things for the general taxpayer.

A well-written text communicates not because it says everything all by itself but rather because it strikes a careful balance between what needs to be said and what may be assumed. Clearly, what counts in effective composition is knowing how and when to be explicit, not simply being explicit.

The third fallacy is distinguishing written and spoken language in terms of autonomy of text. The doctrine of autonomous texts juxtaposes not spoken and written language but rather certain highly specialized uses of language, namely, literary composition and casual chatter. It is a skewed comparison, overlooking such examples of spoken language as lectures, seminar discussions, and college rap sessions; and such examples of writing as kit instructions and notes.[2] **Cohesion** results not when language is written but rather when language—both written and spoken—is put to particular uses, especially those uses which bridge discrepancies in writer–reader knowledge, as in expert-layman communication (Nystrand, Doyle, & Himley, 1986). Language is not composed *because* it is internally cohesive; language takes particular form when it is put to particular uses. To characterize written composition in terms of text structure is to put the structural cart before the functional horse (for more on this point, see Horowitz, 1982, and this volume).

To test the relationship between explicitness of text and fullness of meaning, Nystrand *et al.* (1986) elicited and compared oral and written speculations and reports from college students. For each sample, they also collected recall data. Using Halliday and Hasan's (1976) definition of endophoric references as their measure of explicitness, and holistically scored recall protocols as their measure of comprehension, they found the following: (1) The written speculations were significantly more endophoric than all other samples combined ($F = 28.69$; $p < .001$); (2) there was a statistically insignificant negative correlation between recall and proportion of endophoric references ($r = -.143$; $p > .05$); and (3) the written speculations were not any better recalled than the oral reports ($F = .0598$; $p > .05$) even though the written speculations and oral reports differed overwhelmingly in terms of proportion of endophoric references ($F = 19.52$; $p < .0001$).

Not only is the doctrine of the autonomous text specious. By excluding a priori important examples of written communication, this doctrine has fostered a number of misconceptions about the composing process, especially among educators. First, it has perpetrated the idea that certain uses of written language (viz., essays) not only can but ought to function rhetorically without any relationship to their context of use. As a corollary to this point, it has justified teaching writing as a matter of correct form rather than effective use. It has furthermore perpetrated the idea that there are some uses of written language (e.g., notes) that are acompositional. And it has promoted a categorical explicitness of text as an appropriate instructional objective.[3]

In order to examine the many problems with these sundry contentions, we now consider the composition of notes.

How Notes Are Composed

Notes and signs are typically informational (e.g., EXIT or "Gone to store—be home for dinner"), and their composition requires keeping in mind a number of critical informational factors having to do with who, what, when, where, and how: who the readers will be and what they will know at the time they discover the text; when the readers will read and, in the case of signs, how much time they will have to read; and where the readers are most likely to find the information (notes), or where the readers are most likely to be when they discover the information (signs). These situational variables are critical to text meaning, defining a window of semantic opportunity as it were: EXIT signs have no meaning except in relation to doors, and notes which are addressed to the person who delivers the milk must be placed next to empty bottles, etc. Children's notes are often amusing and uncommunicative because of their failure to take these factors into account, e.g., "Mom, I'll be home in a few minutes" (Gundlach, 1982).

If composition is a deliberate process of organizing language and thoughts in order to achieve a particular purpose or effect, then writing notes clearly qualifies. It certainly involves far more than "the mere basic skills" of handwriting, spelling, and punctuation. Composing notes requires the writer to make a great number of correct assumptions about context. Notes are no less composed simply because they are abbreviated. As with all composition, the writer must carefully *balance what is said,* i.e., the text, *against what need not be said.* And what need not be said, of course, depends on the actual context of use, i.e., who's reading, what they know when they read it, what they want to find out, and so on.

How Essays Communicate[4]

If notes are no less composed because they are cryptic and contextualized, essays are no more composed and "autonomous" because they are elaborately explicit. The composition of an essay is as much constrained by its context of eventual use as is the briefest grocery note. A good example of this point is Canadian psychologist David Olson's "From Utterance to Text: The Bias of Language in Speech and Writing" (1977), the seminal essay which argues the case for autonomous texts and is typically cited as the source of the doctrine. This essay was written for a very particular context of use, namely the forum of *The Harvard Educational Review,* a research journal for scholars with multidisciplinary interests in educational issues. So that the essay might function in this context of scholarly dialogue, argument, and reference, it is paginated; it is prefaced by an abstract; it is replete with footnotes, reference notes, and references; and it is appropriately formatted in such a way that the author's name and the title of the journal, along with volume, number, and date, appear on the title page of the essay. The publisher has made sure that these essential contextual factors accompany all future photocopies of the text.[5]

The author himself, moreover, contextualizes his argument by starting with an extensive literature review, reciting not only historical but also contemporary evidence from research in the structure of language, the nature of comprehension, the nature of logical reasoning, the acquisition of language, and the psychology of reading. The **argumentative purposes** of this review is obvious: the author hopes to show compelling reasons for his thesis. The **communicative function** is different, however: the review serves to establish **footing**[6]—shared knowledge of common ground with readers from which the author sallies forth with his main points. In this sense, the review functions like the question that begins a conversation, *You know that box I'm always talking about? Well . . .* or the *re:* of business correspondence or, indeed, the effective introduction to any essay: it works thematically by establishing a communicative footing and so initiating the communication (Nystrand & Himley, 1984).

THE STRUCTURE OF ARGUMENT VERSUS THE STRUCTURE OF COMMUNICATION

It is generally true that the British essayists Olson discusses proceed by explicating the many implications entailed by their premises in the manner of Locke's "An Essay Concerning Human Understanding," and that, for this reason, essays tend to be highly explicit. Yet if essays are more explicit than grocery lists, this explicitness is due to more than requirements of genre to state propositions. Reasoning by inference, deduction, demonstrations, and proof—particularly on topics new to readers—makes special demands on language, as well as on logical processes. These two kinds of demands require careful distinction if we are to understand what essayists do qua thinker compared to what essayists do qua writer.

It is essayist qua thinker whom we "charge with reasoning via unspecified inference and assumptions" "if unconventionalised or nonlinguistic knowledge is permitted to intrude" into the argument (Olson, 1977, p. 272). But it is the essayist qua writer whom we charge with incomprehensibility if complex new ideas and terms are inadequately contextualized in terms of shared, nonlinguistic knowledge. Indeed, any text which might succeed in eliminating all dependence on presupposed, world knowledge would be a very ambiguous and nonexplicit text—as unclear as any image which is all figure and no ground. The essayist qua thinker formulates "a small set of connected statements of great generality that may occur as topic sentences or paragraphs or as premises of extended scientific or philosophical treatise" (Olson, 1977, p. 269). By contrast, the essayist qua writer makes appropriate text segmentations, this indentation "functioning, as does all punctuation, as a gloss upon the overall literary process underway at that point" (Rodgers, 1966, p. 6). Endophoric referencing is important in terms of **exposition** because it is the way essayists spell out the implications entailed in their premises. Endophoric referencing is important in terms of **communication** because it is the major way writers contextualize new information and so maintain a balance of understanding between themselves and their readers.

In short, effective text analysis requires careful distinction between **the structure of argument** and **the structure of communication**.[7] As argument, Olson's essay works by stating explicit points and propositions. As communication, however, it works by juxtaposing these propositions with knowledge readers bring to the text. This reader knowledge is unstated, shared, given, and not necessarily propositional in nature. Hence, as important as the many explicit points that Olson makes are the many that are never stated. And this omission is surely no sin. To the contrary: Olson's thesis is clear because he strikes an effective balance between what needs to be said and what may remain unsaid. Were he elaborate in his treatment of the latter, his essay would be turgid, wordy, unclear; and we might rightly hold him in violation of the "contract" that underlies all communication from the briefest note to the longest treatise.

The contract which writers have with their readers requires them to attend to three different kinds of compositional tasks. First, they must establish footing by identifying common ground, as noted above. In addition, they must contextualize new information—buttressing those points of text which, if not treated, would threaten the established balance of discourse and shared knowledge. And finally (though not necessarily last), they must carefully mark relevant text boundaries to indicate conceptual, narrative, and other shifts, and to break the text into manageable information units.[8]

Olson's essay is clearly not just an autonomous text expliciting all the implications entailed by his general premise. We understand Olson's thesis largely as we do (1) because it appears in the context of a research journal and (2) because the argument concerns an idea which has a history (dating back at least to Plato), and which has been researched by scholars in many diverse fields of inquiry. The text of Olson's essay, like all well-written compositions, functions not because it is independent of its context of use but because it is so carefully attuned to this context.

THE ROLE OF CONTEXT IN WRITTEN COMMUNICATION

What, then, is the role of context in written communication? To begin, context of use in written communication is eventual, not concurrent with the production of discourse as with spoken language. For the most part, the writer's situation is irrelevant to actual text functioning. Where the writer composes, what might be viewed from the writer's window during the composing process, what music might have provided inspiration—all these aspects of the composer's situation while writing are functionally irrelevant. Pieces of writing do not function communicatively at the time of their creation; they only bear a potential for communication. Learning to write is precisely learning to create such a potential. This potential is realized, moreover, only when writer and reader finally come together by way of the text. It is this situation of the reader reading which defines context of use in written communication, for it is this moment precisely when the writer finally speaks to the reader and the text must do its communicative thing.

Let me pursue this argument a bit further before continuing, for it leads to insights about not only writing but also language generally. In both speaking and writing, communicative interaction takes place in a context of use, i.e., the situation in which the utterance or text functions and has meaning. In comparing the comprehension of oral and written discourse, however, it is important to note that context of use (or context of situation, Firth, 1957) is not the same as context of production (or context of utterance, Lyons, 1977). **Context of production** refers to the moment and situation of the text's creation by speaker or writer, whereas **context of use** refers to the occasion on which the text is actually processed by the hearer or reader. In speech, this distinction typically has no practical maning since the context of production and the context of use are inevitably identical. Hence, when I shout, *Watch out, it's going to fall!* the context of production and the context of use are one and the same, in this case the dangerous situation of a wobbly ladder which my addressee is obliviously climbing.

The context of use impinges as much upon the writer as the reader. As they write, writers pause often to review and frequently to repair what they have already composed. When done, they sometimes survey the results from the vantage point of their intended readers. In so doing, the writer momentarily becomes a reader, and the context of production temporarily becomes a context of use. As the writer "tries out the text" in this way, the text comes to have meaning and import. The writer decides that she has used enough examples or needs more reasons or a different reason or another paragraph or another beginning, and so forth and so on. Making the appropriate revisions and repairs, the writer, of course, returns to work in the context of production. Hence, we see that even during the composing process, ostensibly solitary and private, the writer is continuously negotiating and balancing what she wants to say with her own expectations as a reader, either real or imagined. Throughout the process, the context of use is the key factor in arbitrating these negotiations and regulates production at every turn.

Writing is obviously not interactive in the behavioral sense that writers and readers take turns as do speakers and listeners. But then spoken language is not interactive simply because the participants conspicuously take turns. Turntaking is not interaction except in a very superficial, behavioral sense. If sequential turntaking were interaction, then play acting, elevator talk, and a lot of religious ritual would be interaction. Turntaking is the way conversants *accomplish* interaction. But the interaction of interest is what the turntaking accomplishes, namely *an exchange of meaning or transformation of shared knowledge.*

Statisticians know the distinction I am making. They know that **interaction** refers not to the influence of two independent variables on each other but rather on how the two variables combine, or "interact," to produce a separate, joint effect. This joint effect is a new whole not equal to the sum of the parts; that is, the effects of the two variables are not additive. This is why the effects of coffee and whiskey on reaction time cannot be determined by simply adding the individual effects of each but only by determining the effect of their interaction. To put it another way, Placido Domingo and Teresa Stratas interact not because they influence each other but rather because in concert they render arias and duets.

Discourse is like this. When each conversant does certain things (e.g., takes turns), the result is the interaction of intelligible, meaningful conversation. And when writers do certain things and readers do certain other things, the result is the unique interaction of lucid, comprehensible text. This is why writing is no less interactive in either principle or practice than speech. As discourse, writing is nonetheless interactive even though the writer and reader may never meet or indeed even though the writer may be long deceased when the reader finds the text. So long as writers and readers collaborate in their complementary and reciprocal tasks of composing and comprehending, or as Rommetveit (1974, p. 63) puts it, so long as writers write on the premises of readers and readers read on the premises of writers, the result is communication and comprehension.

As we have seen, this point has been a source of considerable confusion in many comparisons of spoken and written language. The doctrine of autonomous texts, for example, defines context narrowly in terms of immediate context of production—mainly such paralinguistic features as gestures and quizzical looks. The actual context of situation for any communication, however, is far more rich and complex than the physical gestures of the conversants. Relevant factors include the nature of the audience, the medium, and the purpose of the communication. This is no less true for writing than speech. Business executives, for example, know all too well that the complete meaning of an interoffice memorandum frequently involves not just the typed text but myriad contextual details, including (1) why the communication is in writing; (2) who has received carbon copies, or *cc;* (3) who has not received copies; and especially (4) who though not "copied," is nonetheless a recipient of the "blind" carbon copy or *bcc* and is perhaps even the main reason for the memo.

It is true, of course, that written texts must function without benefit of hand gesture or eye contact. But it is a serious mistake to view the paralinguistics of speech as a categorical prerequisite to all communication. If **paralinguistics** refers to those phenomena that "occur alongside spoken language, interact with it, and produce together with it a total system of communication" (Abercrombie, 1967, p. 55), then written language may be said to have its own special resources in this regard. These resources, moreover, serve the essential paralinguistic purposes of **modulation** (superimposing upon a text a particular attitudinal coloring) and **punctuation** (marking boundaries at the beginning and end of a text and at various points within to emphasize particular expressions, and to segment the utterance into manageable information units) (Lyons, 1977). Quotation marks, for example, commonly indicate irony, skepticism, or critical detachment; and exclamation marks and underlining typically show emphasis. Sentence fragments can often be used to show emphasis, particularly at the ends of paragraphs. A more complex type of modulation is achieved when writers exploit readers' expectations for particular genres of written discourse. The classic example here is irony in Swift's "A Modest Proposal." Because it is in essay form, readers often assume the proposal is serious and the contents are meant to be taken literally.[9]

The increasing availability and sophistication of electronic wordprocessors substantially increase the range of such paralinguistic modulation available to professional, business, and academic writers. With capabilities previously available only in printers' shops, these machines now sit on many individual writers' desks. Included among these capabilities are the usual marks of punctuation, plus boldface, italics, hanging indents, offsets, and fonts of all sorts. The rhetorical impact of these typographic capabilities in this new setting is not yet clear, especially on writing tasks not usually published. For example, what sorts of correspondence and typescripts should and should not be formatted with justified right margins? Nonetheless, the possibilities of these systems for subtle modulations of text have not been lost on the office systems people, who routinely promote their products not only in terms of increased efficiency but also, and especially, enhanced corporate image. With only a few formatting commands, businesses can present themselves as Baskerville, Palatino, Futura, or Bold Roman. No doubt the day of the designer letter is upon us.

In addition to such possibilities for paralinguistic modulation, writers have access to a wide range of punctuation for marking syntactic, prosodic, and semantic boundaries. Consider the range of devices writers have for setting off particular expressions. A particular phrase that may be subordinated as a nonrestrictive clause with commas in

(2)   *Hostilities between countries in the Middle East, which are increasingly armed with weapons made in the USA, threaten to start a world war.*

may be further subordinated with parentheses in

(3)   *Hostilities between countries in the Middle East (which are increasingly armed with weapons made in the USA) threaten to start a world war.*

and may be subordinated further still by asterisking its referent (*countries in the Middle East*) and treating the phrase in a footnote. By contrast, setting the phrase off in dashes marks it with emphasis:

(4)   *Hostilities between countries in the Middle East—which are increasingly armed with weapons made in the USA—threaten to start a world war.*

The most significant mark of punctuation for use beyond the sentence, of course, is indentation and paragraphing. The paragraph (from Greek *para* 'beside' + *graphos* 'mark') was originally a symbol placed in the margin to indicate conceptual, narrative, and other shifts in the flow of discourse. The original notion persists in our transitive verb *to paragraph* (Rodgers, 1966). This treatment of paragraphing has recently been elaborated by Halliday and Hasan (1976), who see the paragraph as a"device introduced into the written language to suggest . . . periodicity":

> In principle, we shall expect to find a greater degree of cohesion within a paragraph than between paragraphs; and in a great deal of written English this is exactly what we do find. In other writing, however, and perhaps as a characteristic of certain authors, the rhythm is contrapuntal: the writer extends a dense cluster of cohesive ties across the paragraph boundary and leaves a texture within the paragraph relatively loose. And this itself is an instance of a process that is very characteristic of language altogether, a process in which two associated variables come to be dissociated from each other with a very definite semantic and rhetorical effect. Here the two variables in question are the paragraph structure and the cohesive structure. (pp. 296–297)

This approach to paragraphing has recently been operationalized by Bell Labs in its Writer's Workbench program, a collection of computer programs designed to aid writers in evaluating and modifying their texts (Gingrich, 1980).

RESEARCH ISSUES

What sorts of research issues are raised by the functionalist view of text presented here? What kinds of research are suggested which might be of interest to scholars in psychology, linguistics, discourse analysis, and education?

The expectation for reciprocity in discourse is important because it means that the shape and conduct of discourse is determined not only by what the speaker or writer has to say (speaker/writer meaning) or accomplish (speaker/writer purpose) but also by the joint expectations of the conversants that they should understand one another (producer–receiver contract). We may consequently view discourse generally as a form of social interaction whereby the conversants (writers and readers, speakers and listeners) negotiate common categorizations and mutual understandings. In talk this negotiation is comparatively conspicuous, manifesting itself in turntaking, querulous glances plus rephrasings, etc. In writing, however, this negotiation is more abstract: the writer must create a text that will effect an exchange of meaning in a context of eventual use, as we have seen, for example, future reference or personal communication. This is not to say, of course, that the aim of discourse is always substantive agreement, but only that the character and conduct of discourse are governed by the expectations of the conversants that they should understand one another. In making this point, I am making a distinction between *the practical purposes of discourse* and *the principles* which govern its functioning.

Research has barely begun on the ways in which written text accomplishes this interaction. Promising starts have been made by scholars working from Prague premises (see, e.g., Halliday, 1978; Scinto, 1986). Another promising line of research is work in discourse processes which has examined the effects of differentials in knowledge between writers and readers in terms of text processing (see, e.g., Voss, Vesonder, & Spilich, 1980; Harris, Begg, & Upfold, 1980; Johnson & Kieras, n.d.). Key issues in this research are:

1. What are a writer's text options for starting a text (establishing footing), as well as segmenting and elaborating text? When is enough enough? When should a writer say more? Are some organizations better than others? What principles of text functioning bear on these issues?

2. How do these text options work especially in terms of accomplishing interaction between writers and readers who are distinguished respectively by varying degrees of knowledge? Why are some text elaborations helpful while others are distractions and still others are complications (on this issue see Reder, 1982)? How do text options which provide category definition such as titles, paragraphing, and advanced organizers work with knowledgeable writers and unknowledgeable readers and vice versa?

3. Under what circumstances is interaction inhibited and texts unreadable?

4. What classroom conditions and activities best enhance children's chances to learn to exercise their text options? There is a substantial literature in English education (see, e.g., Moffett, 1968) which convinc-

ingly advocates the importance of peer conferencing as "the only way, short of tutorial, to provide individual students enough experience" (p. 12) in this regard. But in light of research into discourse production, the composing process, and classroom context, what can we now say about the impact of peer conferencing and other classroom practices in terms of the development and use of effective text options?

CONCLUSION

It is clearly a mistake to associate the spontaneity of casual talk with fragmented expression, and equally wrong to confuse elaborateness of text with fullness of meaning. The attempt to view writers as somehow disadvantaged because they are bereft of the paralinguistic resources of speech, moreover, is a misconception of written communication and is consistent with the traditional conception of writing as a defective representation of speech (Householder, 1971). What is missed by such confusions is how writing and speech work differently as language systems. If casual conversation with friends as well as notes to oneself are cryptic whereas formal inquiries to and from the Internal Revenue Service— either written or spoken—are comparably elaborate and explicit, this difference mainly means that the former *can* be more abbreviated while the latter *must* be more elaborated if coherence is to be maintained, messages are to be adequate, and communication assured. It does not mean that cryptic texts are necessarily "semantically inadequate" or unclear to the reader/hearer. And above all, it most definitely does not mean that written texts are autonomous whereas spoken utterances are context-bound. What it mainly means is that speech and writing work differently to maintain reciprocity and the underlying pact of discourse between conversants.

ACKNOWLEDGMENTS

The author thanks Margaret Himley and Charles Scott for their comments and suggestions regarding this chapter. This chapter is a revised and expanded version of The role of context in written communication, *The Nottingham Linguistic Circular*, 12 (1), 55–65, 1983.

NOTES

[1] The impression that speech is "fragmented" and writing is "compact" and "integrated" (see, e.g., Chafe, 1982; Chapter 3 this volume) may be partly phenomenological. In speech, planning processes and generated text are largely simultaneous and inseparable

whereas in writing, they always separate as soon as the composing is complete. As public behavior, speech presents itself not only as words spoken but also as a sequence of starts and restarts and pauses. By contrast, writing, which is private behavior, conceals hesitations and restarts, and presents itself only as the tidied up result, altogether detached from the process. Until recently, pauses in the writing process have not even drawn research interest (cf. Matsuhashi, 1982).

Also, it is important to recognize the bias of written language in the analysis of language, both written and spoken. Because both analyses are conducted via the written medium (actual written texts in the case of writing and written transcripts in the case of speech), the analyst typically enters the analysis as a *reader*. It should surprise no one that written texts seem "integrated" by comparison with written transcripts, which seem fragmented: speech is indeed fragmented by the very process of transcription, a process which written texts never undergo.

[2] Three important exceptions to this generalization are Stubbs (1982), Tannen (1982), and Wells (1981).

[3] One study which shows the extent to which the doctrine of autonomous texts is a pedagogical notion rather than a linguistic or rhetorical concept is Michaels (1981).

[4] For extended discussion of this section, see Nystrand *et al.* (1986).

[5] As more books are photocopied, alas, more publishers are printing the year of publication on the title page.

[6] Communicative footing is not to be confused with Goffman's (1979) **footing:** the speaker's stance toward the audience in face-to-face interaction.

[7] My distinction here between the structure of argument and the structure of communication is roughly parallel to Halliday's (1978) distinction between **ideational** and **textual functions** of language. The ideational has to do with the expression of content, the points and pieces of evidence that the author presents. By contrast, the textual has to do with the effective balance of given and new information, as well as the overall structure of the text as a recognizable essay.

[8] A typology of text footings, elaborations, and segmentations will be found in Nystrand and Himley (1984).

[9] Steinmann (1981) has written extensively on poetic effect in these terms.

REFERENCES

Abercrombie, D. (1967). *Elements of phonetics.* Edinburgh: Edinburgh University Press.

Bereiter, C., & Scardamalia, M. (1981). From conversation to composition: The role of instruction in a developmental process. In R. Glaser (Ed.), *Advances in instructional psychology* (Vol. 2). Hillsdale, NJ: Erlbaum.

Chafe, W. (1982). Integration and involvement in speaking, writing, and oral literature. In D. Tannen (Ed.), *Spoken and written language: Exploring orality and literacy.* Norwood, NJ: Ablex.

Dillon, G. (1981). *Constructing texts: Elements of a theory of composition and style.* Bloomington: Indiana University Press.

Firth, J. R. (1957). *Papers in linguistics, 1934–51.* NY: Oxford University Press.

Gingrich, P. (1980, April). *A measure of text cohesion.* Paper presented at the Annual Meeting of the American Educational Research Association. Chicago, IL.

Goffman, I. (1979). Footing. *Semiotica, 25,* 1–29.

Goody, J., & Watt, I. (1968). The consequences of literacy. In J. Goody (Ed.), *Literacy in traditional societies.* London: Cambridge University Press.

Greenfield, P. M. (1972). Oral and written language: The consequences for cognitive development in Africa, the United States, and England. *Language and Speech, 15,* 169–172.

Gundlach, R. (1982). Children as writers: The beginnings of learning to write. In M. Nystrand (ed.), *What writers know: The language, process, and structure of written discourse.* New York: Academic Press.

Halliday, M. A. K. (1978). *Language as social semiotic: The social interpretation of language and meaning.* Baltimore: University Park Press.

Halliday, M. A. K., & Hasan, R. (1976). *Cohesion in English.* London: Longman.

Harris, G., Begg, I., & Upfold, D. (1980). On the role of the speaker's expectations in interpersonal communication. *Journal of Verbal Learning and Verbal Behavior, 19,* 597–607.

Havelock, E. A. (1963). *Preface to Plato.* Cambridge, MA: Harvard University Press.

Havelock, E. A. (1977). *The origins of Western literacy.* Toronto: Ontario Institute for Studies in Education.

Hirsch, E. D., Jr. (1977). *The philosophy of composition.* Chicago: University of Chicago Press.

Horowitz, R. (1982). *The limitations of contrasted rhetorical predicates on reader recall of expository English prose.* Unpublished doctoral dissertation, University of Minnesota, Minneapolis.

Householder, F. W. (1971). *Linguistic speculations.* London: Cambridge University Press.

Johnson, W., & Kieras, D. (n.d.). *Representation-saving effects of prior knowledge in memory for simple technical prose.* Unpublished manuscript.

Kroll, B. (1981). Developmental relationships between speaking and writing. In B. Kroll & R. Vann (Eds.), *Exploring speaking–writing relationships: Connections and contrasts.* Urbana, IL: National Council of Teachers of English.

Lakoff, R. (1982). Some of my favorite writers are literate: The mingling of oral and literate strategies in written communication.In D. Tannen (Ed.), *Spoken and written language: Exploring orality and literacy.* Norwood, NJ: Ablex.

Lyons, J. (1977). *Semantics* (Vol. 1). London: Cambridge University Press.

Matsuhashi, A. (1982). Explorations in the real-time production of written discourse. In M. Nystrand (Ed.), *What writers know: The language, process, and structure of written discourse.* New York: Academic Press.

Michaels, S. (1981). "Sharing time": Children's narrative styles and differential access to literacy. *Language in Society, 10,* 423–442.

Moffett, J. (1968). *Teaching the universe of discourse.* Boston: Houghton.

Nystrand, M. (1986). *The structure of written communication: Studies in reciprocity between writers and readers.* Orlando: Academic Press.

Nystrand, M., Doyle, A., & Himley, M. (1986). A critical examination of the doctrine of autonomous texts. In M. Nystrand, *The structure of written communication: Studies in reciprocity between writers and readers.* Orlando: Academic Press.

Nystrand, M., & Himley, M. (1984). Written text as social interaction. *Theory into Practice, 23*(3), 198–207.

Olson, D. R. (1977). From utterance to text: The bias of language in speech and writing. *Harvard Educational Review, 47,* 257–281.

Popper, K. (1972). *Objective knowledge: An evolutionary approach.* London: Oxford University Press (Clarendon).

Reder, L. (1982). Elaborations: When do they help and when do they hurt? *Text, 2*(1/3), 211–224.

Rodgers, P. (1966). A discourse-centered rhetoric of the paragraph. *College Composition and Communition, 17,* 2–11.

Rommetveit, R. (1974). *On message structure: A framework for the study of language and communication.* London: Wiley.

Scinto, L. (1986). *Written language and psychological development.* Orlando: Academic Press.

Scribner, S., & Cole, M. (1981). *The psychology of literacy.* Cambridge, MA: Harvard University Press.

Snow, C. (1983). Literacy and language: Relationships during the preschool years. *Harvard Educational Review, 53*(2), 165–189.

Steinmann, M. (1981). Superordinate genre conventions. *Poetics, 10,* 243–261.

Stubbs, M. (1980). *Language and literacy: The sociolinguistics of reading and writing.* London: Routledge & Kegan Paul.

Stubbs, M. (1982). Written language and society: Some particular cases and general observations. In M. Nystrand (Ed.), *What writers know: The language, process, and structure of written discourse.* New York: Academic Press.

Tannen, D. (1982). Oral and literate strategies in spoken and written narratives. *Language, 58*(1), 1–21.

Voss, J. F., Vesonder, G. T., & Spilich, G. J. (1980). Text generation and recall by high-knowledge and low-knowledge individuals. *Journal of Verbal Learning and Verbal Behavior, 19,* 651–667.

Vygotsky, L. (1962). *Thought and language.* Cambridge, MA: MIT Press.

Wells, G. (1981). Language, literacy and education. In G. Wells (Ed.), *Learning through interaction: The study of language development.* Cambridge, England: Cambridge University Press.

PART III

PROCESSING STRATEGIES: PERCEPTUAL AND COGNITIVE DEMANDS IN LISTENING AND READING

Chapter **7**

Listening and Reading Processes in College- and Middle School-Age Readers

David J. Townsend
Caroline Carrithers
Thomas G. Bever

Language comprehension involves the formation of a meaningful mental representation from the perception of a physical linguistic stimulus. This chapter considers two issues regarding the language comprehension process. First, is the process different for spoken and printed language? Second, does the difference between skilled and average reading ability occur at the sentence level or at the discourse-thematic level?

We first examine the view that the comprehension process is different for reading and listening. We then review alternative theoretical approaches that make different assumptions about the types of processing which most highly covary with reading ability. In the third section, we present research that we have conducted with skilled and less-skilled readers in college and in middle school. Our goals were to determine whether less-skilled readers are also less skilled in listening and to determine how comprehension processes differ for skilled and less-skilled readers at the level of the sentence and at the level of the thematic relations among sentences. Our research indicates that comprehension processes are quite similar in reading and listening for individuals at a particular level of reading ability. Skilled and less-skilled readers in the middle school differ primarily in sentence-level processing, but in college, they differ primarily in discourse-thematic level processing. The most effective comprehension involves an interaction between sentence and discourse-thematic level processing.

THE NATURE OF THE STIMULUS

There are two obvious possibilities regarding the relation between reading and listening. (1) The linguistic stimulus is sufficiently different in the visual and auditory modalities that reading and listening comprehension processes are substantially different. On this view, reading and listening consist of independent sets of processes, and reading skill is independent of listening skill. (2) Aspects of language that are essential for comprehension are identical regardless of the form of the stimulus. On this view, reading and listening share many similar processes, and reading and listening skills covary.

A cursory examination of the reading comprehension literature provides the impression that comprehension processes are quite different in reading and listening. The bulk of the reading comprehension research has focused on how text is organized and how it relates to prior knowledge; such a program of research may isolate processing strategies which are more salient in reading than in listening. In contrast, auditory comprehension research has focused on the role of sentence structure in speech perception; again, such a program may isolate comprehension processes that are more salient in listening.

There are several differences between reading and listening that have fostered this split in emphasis in the two research traditions. The most obvious aspect of reading is the recognition of words from printed sequences of letters, which is not a part of listening comprehension. The opportunity for interaction between the sender and the receiver of a message is greater in speech than in printed language (Rubin, 1980). The transitory nature of the physical speech signal entails that the listener is more constrained by the order in which the sender transmits the message, and less free to backtrack or look ahead. Speech contains much richer prosodic cues to sentence structure and meaning than is provided by punctuation in printed language (Fries, 1962; see also Boomer, 1965; Cooper & Cooper, 1980; Danley & Cooper, 1979; Goldman-Eisler, 1972; Huggins, 1978; Sorenson, Cooper, & Paccia, 1978).

However, the two modalities do contain similar morphemic cues to the organization of word sequences into phrases and propositions. If both readers and listeners rely on such cues to propositions and their relations, comprehension processes in the two modalities will be similar.

The fact that artificial languages without syntactic markers are very difficult to learn (Green, 1979; Moeser & Bregman, 1972) suggests that both listeners and readers must rely on the patterns of such morphemes to provide an initial syntactic organization of messages.

Since morphemic and sequential cues to sentence structure and propositional meaning are a major feature of both spoken and printed language, the question of how reading and listening are related is partly a question of how much the physical differences between the two modalities influence the role of the proposition as a unit of perception. If word sequences that correspond to propositions are units of perception, it would appear a priori that sentence structure must be perceived, whether the stimulus is auditory or visual. Nevertheless, the permanence of the message and the relative dependence of the reader on prior knowledge might allow reading to bypass the proposition in forming a representation of text. If so, comprehension processes in reading and listening might differ substantially, and skilled and less-skilled readers might differ only in their reading comprehension. This leads us to review contrasting approaches to comprehension that emphasize either the perception of propositions or the perception of thematic relations between propositions.

TWO CONTRASTING THEORIES OF COMPREHENSION

Two general approaches to comprehension emphasize different levels of structural analysis. One approach, derived in large part from research on the perception of spoken sentences, concentrates on sentence-level analysis; it emphasizes the processes of organizing words into units of meaning and using morphemic and sequential cues to meaning. A second approach, derived from research on the comprehension and memory of printed text, concentrates on discourse-level analysis; it emphasizes the effects of text organization, the use of schemata, and the confirmation of expectations.

The question of the relation between reading and listening overlaps with the question of which of these theoretical approaches describes processes that are intrinsic to reading comprehension. If performance on listening tasks is related to reading ability, this would imply that similar comprehension processes are used in reading and listening. If sensitivity to the interrelations of propositional units of meaning is also related to reading ability, this would imply that language comprehension in general involves the kinds of propositional processing that have been isolated in speech perception.

Propositional Processing

Proposition Theory has focused on how listeners isolate phrases and the relations among phrases. Three activities in language perception are (1) isolating word groups that form natural units of meaning, most notably phrases and clauses, (2) integrating the meaning of each unit with what came before, and (3) formulating hypotheses about what might come after. Sequences of words that represent complete propositions are among the most important units of comprehension. For example, a surface structure clause functions as a unit during comprehension (see, e.g., Fodor, Bever, & Garrett, 1974). While hearing such a clause, the listener assigns potential syntactic/semantic organizations (Bever, Garrett, & Hurtig, 1973; Marslen-Wilson & Tyler, 1975); at its end, the listener fixes semantic roles to the words and phrases (Abrams & Bever, 1969) and integrates the resultant meaning with the representation of the preceding discourse (Townsend, 1983). When the listener determines a set of semantic roles within a clause and an interpretation for the whole clause and its role in discourse, memory for the exact words fades, freeing working memory for the words in the subsequent semantic unit (Caplan, 1972; Jarvella, 1971; Townsend & Bever, 1978).

Kleiman's (1975) model of reading corresponds in part to Proposition Theory. The reader retains words in a limited-capacity working memory until a complete syntactic–semantic unit is obtained. At this point, an interpretation of the words in working memory is stored in permanent memory, freeing working memory for the beginning of a new syntactic unit. Failure to segment syntactic units produces word-by-word segmentation (as exemplified in certain beginning readers, "word callers," according to Smith, Goodman, & Meredith, 1976) and a failure to comprehend the propositions in the text.

There is evidence that readers engage in syntactic processing of sentences. Reading comprehension improves when syntactic patterns correspond to common patterns in speech (Tatham, 1970). Readers spend more time reading and fixating on the last word of a clause (Aaronson, 1976; Mitchell & Green, 1978), presumably to integrate its meaning with what came before. The eye–voice span generally extends to the end of a major phrase, particularly for advanced readers (Gibson & Levin, 1975). Pauses in oral reading frequently occur at the ends of clauses (Goldman-Eisler, 1968, 1972). Other linguistic surface structure units such as noun phrase and verb phrase also elicit relatively large pauses in reading (Goldman-Eisler, 1972).

This evidence suggests that readers impose an initial grouping of words by using the kinds of morpheme- or sequence-sensitive phrase structure strategies that they use in listening. They might develop such strategies in listening by first relying on the intonation patterns of speech. As they become more experienced listeners (and readers), they can utilize perceptual strategies based on morphemic patterns alone. Such a view explains why inappropriate intonation has less effect on listening comprehension in skilled readers than in less-skilled readers (Oaken, Weiner, & Cromer, 1971).

The kinds of structural analyses identified in speech perception research differentiate readers of different levels of skill (Clay & Imlach, 1971; Cohen & Freeman, 1978; Denner, 1970; Fry, Johnson, & Muehl, 1970; Guthrie, 1973; Steiner, Weiner, & Cromer, 1971; Vogel, 1974; Weinstein & Rabinovitch, 1971). For example, Cromer (1970) has demonstrated that there are readers who are deficient in their comprehension of typically formatted printed materials but not in their comprehension of material that is formatted to emphasize major phrase structure groupings of words. Muncer and Bever (1984) showed that skilled readers are relatively less attentive to characteristics of printed words at the ends of clauses. Studies such as these suggest that reading involves the application of strategies developed independently in listening. From this point of view, reading deficits may be due to deficits in the application of strategies that the reader successfully applies during listening. However, less-skilled readers also differ from skilled readers in their use of cues to the relations between propositions even while listening (Goldman, 1976; Perfetti & Goldman, 1976). For example, Perfetti and Goldman (1976) found that less-skilled readers are not as sensitive to the structural distinctions between main and subordinate clauses. These studies suggest that reading deficits may be due to inefficient listening strategies that are transferred to reading (see also Durrell, 1969; Sticht, 1972).

Discourse-Thematic Processing

Schema Theory maintains that readers use expectations based on world knowledge (e.g., "scripts") and the organization of text to make inferences that connect propositions and to organize propositions in memory (Bartlett, 1932; Bower, Black, & Turner, 1979; Bransford & Johnson, 1973; Mandler & Johnson, 1977; Pearson & Spiro, 1982; Schank, 1982; Weaver, 1978). Note that Schema Theory presupposes that propositions are the units of meaning underlying texts. The question that is most relevant to understanding the relation between reading and listening is whether schematic knowledge is used to perceive sentences, thereby reducing the role of cues to sentence structure and propositional meaning. Evidence appears to support this claim of Schema Theory: Sentences that violate expectations take longer to read (Bower *et al.*, 1979; Duffy, 1983; Gibbs & Tenney, 1980; Townsend, 1983; see also

Abelson, 1981; Adams & Collins, 1979; Rumelhart & Ortony, 1977; Schank & Birnbaum, 1984; Tyler & Marslen-Wilson, 1977).

Such demonstrations, however, are also consistent with an "interactive" view that levels of representation interact primarily at those points at which descriptions at the two levels utilize a common "vocabulary" (Townsend & Bever, 1982). That is, text structure interacts most freely with sentence structure at the level of the proposition, which is the level of description that is common to text structure and sentence structure. On this interactive view, expectations derived from semantic context and preceding text structure influence the integration of propositions into a representation of the thematic content of text, but not the initial formation of a propositional representation of a sentence. Townsend (1983) has shown that readers and listeners use cues such as *if, because, after,* or *although* as signals to integrate propositions with context and expectations. For example, *if* is a signal to integrate the proposition immediately into a causal organization of text, but *though* is a signal to postpone integration. The fact that integrative processes operate on complete propositions is prima facie evidence that propositional perception is, in part, independent of processing for the thematic relations between propositions.

Although it has not been shown that skilled and less-skilled readers differ in their use of schemata for perceiving propositions, there is evidence that skilled readers' recall of both spoken and printed stories is more influenced by the thematic importance of propositions (Smiley, Oakley, Worthen, Campione, & Brown, 1977). Children who are skilled readers are better at recalling the propositional structure of text, even when equated with less-skilled readers in terms of reading miscues (Bridge & Tierney, 1981; Tierney, Bridge, & Cera, 1979). Skilled readers also differ from less-skilled readers in their knowledge of story structure (Stein, 1982). These studies suggest that deficits in reading comprehension may be associated with deficits in processing for the thematic relations between propositions.

Proposition and Schema Theories Compared

Proposition Theory proposes that comprehension involves the formation of "higher" levels of structure from "lower" levels of structure (Townsend & Bever, 1982). That is, letter (or phoneme) sequences are grouped into words, word sequences are grouped into phrases, and phrase sequences are grouped into clauses that correspond to propositions, which are semantically interpreted and integrated with the emerging representation of text. Most relevant to the present work is that (initial) decisions about propositional meaning are influenced only by representations of words and word groupings within the clause. Proposition Theory predicts that as reading becomes more proficient, the morphemic and sequential cues that signal the logical organization of word groupings have increasing effects on performance.

Schema Theory proposes that decisions at a lower level (e.g., the proposition) are influenced primarily by representations at a higher level (e.g., text organization, prior world knowledge). For example, Schank (1982) views skilled reading as a process of activating a schema from the early portions of a text and looking for information in the text that can fill "empty slots" in the activated schema. Understanding a sentence that states an event that is part of the schema is more a matter of confirming expectations than it is of performing a syntactic analysis of the sentence (Bower *et al.*, 1979). The skilled reader only draws on syntactic knowledge when activated discourse schemata do not uniquely determine the discourse relevance of the stimulus, for example, when the proposition expressed by a sentence does not occupy a central role in the schema (Riesbeck & Schank, 1978; Schank, 1982). Unskilled reading, on the other hand, occurs when the reader is either unfamiliar with the schemata that are needed to understand a passage or does not activate schemata that are available in memory (Pearson & Spiro, 1982; Schank, 1982). Improvement in reading comes about through the accumulation, activation, and use of relevant schemata during reading. Thus, Schema Theory predicts that the effects of structural cues on meaning while reading decline with increased reading skill.

As noted earlier, modality differences may be responsible for these different emphases on the nature of the comprehension process. Proposition Theory was derived from research on auditory comprehension, which might necessarily rely more on left-to-right processing because of the transitory nature of the stimulus and working memory; hence, the listener may rely more on morphemic, sequential, and intonational cues to meaning, and less on text organization. Schema Theory was derived primarily from research on the recall of printed text, which need not be processed in any particular order, and might allow for more strategic use of expectations and text structure.

In our research we have examined propositional processing and thematic processing during listening and reading among skilled and average readers at the college and middle-school levels. One series of experiments (Townsend, Carrithers, & Bever, in preparation) has focused on listening processes, and a second on reading.

LISTENING PROCESSES

In Townsend *et al.* (in preparation) we systematically examined listening processes in skilled and average readers. We administered a battery of listening tasks to a set of carefully selected subjects. We used 12 subjects in each of four groups: college-age skilled (mean verbal Scholastic Aptitude Test = 658, SD = 38.9), college-age average (mean VSAT = 490, SD = 40.2), school age skilled (mean verbal Standardized Achievement Test = 3.9 grades above level, SD = 1.04), and school-age average (mean VSAT = +0.2 grades, SD = 1.21); within age groups, subjects across levels of verbal skill were matched for quantitative achievement test scores. Table 7.1 summarizes the tasks that we used. We first compared overall reading and listening performance using texts consisting of a few paragraphs. We then examined how the subjects process propositions during listening: we examined how the structural and thematic roles of clauses affect processing at the levels of word order and meaning, and we examined the extent to which the subjects segment word sequences into independent units of meaning. Table 7.2 summarizes the major results of these tasks (see Townsend *et al.*, in preparation, for more details).

Using story-reading and listening tasks, we assessed overall reading and listening performance. Each subject received four texts: they heard and read 550-word texts (200 words for school-age subjects) under two levels of time pressure (approximately 3 words/sec versus 6 words/sec). After each text, the subjects received tests of comprehension of sentence meaning and recognition memory for specific words and sentences. Our results showed conclusively that skilled and average readers differ in

TABLE 7.1
Summary of Experiments[a]

Subjects: 24 college students and 24 sixth–eighth graders

Comparing reading and listening
    Story reading: comprehension and memory of printed text
    Story listening: comprehension and memory of spoken text

Listening Processes
    Meaning probe: on-line access to meaning in spoken sentences
      Though I liked calling up my aunt each night at . . . USING THE TELE-
      PHONE
    Word probe: on-line access to word order of spoken sentences
      Though I liked calling up my aunt each night at . . . UP
    Tone location: segmentation of speech into independent propositional units
      Because coffee spilled on her sky-blue dress she went home early.

---

[a] From Townsend, Carrithers, & Bever (in preparation).

both reading and listening performance, suggesting that reading and listening make use of similar strategies.

Less-skilled readers are also relatively less skilled in listening. Compared to skilled readers, average readers made 17% more errors on story reading and 25% more errors on story listening. On the story-listening tasks overall, average readers at the college level made 10% more errors than skilled readers, and at the school level they made 39% more errors. The differences on listening tasks were largest for comprehension (a 43% deficit for average college-age readers, a 78% deficit for average school-age readers), and smallest for recognition memory for sentences (a 10% advantage for average college-age readers, an 18% deficit for average school-age readers). The differences between skilled and average readers were similar across the two presentation rates. The story-reading and listening results strongly support the conclusions of Sticht (1972), Perfetti and Goldman (1976), and others, that differences in reading skills occur with differences in listening skills, and that listening and reading are instances of a single set of comprehension processes.

Using the same subjects, we examined the on-line effects of the structural and thematic roles of clauses on listening processes. We used a Meaning Probe task (Townsend & Bever, 1978) to assess the listener's accessibility to the meaning of a sentence as it was heard. The subject heard a sentence fragment that ended one word before the clause boundary, and then a short phrase, as in *Though I liked calling up my aunt each night at* . . . USING THE TELEPHONE. The subject's task was to say as quickly as possible whether the phrase was similar in meaning to the sentence fragment. We used a Word Probe task to assess the listener's on-line accessibility to the words and their order in a sentence. As in

TABLE 7.2
Overall Task Performance of Average
Readers Compared to Skilled Readers of
the Same Age[a,b]

	College-age	School-age
Reading/listening		
Story reading	18% more errors	15% more errors
Story listening	10% more errors	39% more errors
Listening		
Meaning probe	4% faster	18% slower
Word probe	12% faster	21% slower
Tone location	9% more errors	37% fewer errors

[a] From Townsend, Carrithers, & Bever (in preparation).
[b] Each percentage is based on ((score for average reader) − (score for skilled reader)) / (score for skilled reader).

the Meaning task, the subject heard a sentence fragment, but then a single word and said whether or not the word had occurred in the sentence. In order to assess sensitivity to the linear order of words, we compared response times for targets (e.g., . . . UP) that occurred in different positions (e.g., after *calling* or after *aunt*). We wanted to determine whether the structural and thematic roles of clauses affected access to representations of meaning and linear order in similar ways for skilled and average readers.

Reading skill was related to overall performance on the probe tasks in strikingly different ways at the two age levels (see Table 7.2). At the college level, average readers responded more quickly than skilled readers; at the school level, skilled readers responded more quickly. This shows that skilled reading involves very different processes at the two age levels: skilled reading emphasizes propositional processing only at the school level.

Skilled readers were more sensitive than average readers to the structural roles of clauses. Skilled readers accessed meaning faster in main clauses, but they accessed linear order more readily in *though* clauses, suggesting that they process main clauses as relatively independent units of meaning (see Table 7.3). The effects of clause structure on acces-

TABLE 7.3
Effects of Structural and Thematic Roles on
Access to Linear Order and Meaning[a]

| | Linear order[b] | | | |
| | College-age | | School-age | |
	Skilled	Average	Skilled	Average
Main clause	223	−66	−155	368
Though clause	340	−83	−7	115
If clause	119	90	−139	−189

| | Meaning[c] | | | |
| | College-age | | School-age | |
	Skilled	Average	Skilled	Average
Main clause	2.4	2.6	2.6	3.1
Though clause	2.7	2.5	2.7	3.2
If clause	2.6	2.3	2.6	3.0

[a] From Townsend, Carrithers, & Bever (in preparation).
[b] Entries are (response time for late target) − (response time for early target), in msec.
[c] Entries are response times in sec.

sibility to both meaning and form were smaller for school-age skilled readers than for college-age skilled readers, despite the fact that it was only at the school level that skilled readers responded more quickly overall than did average readers. These results indicate that increased skill at the college level entails increased sensitivity to structural relations between clauses, but at the school level it entails increased sensitivity to words and their organization into independent propositional units.

College-age skilled readers were more sensitive to the thematic roles of subordinate clauses in terms of their accessibility to representations of linear order (see Table 7.3). The skilled reader uses the causal organization of discourse to modify perceptual processes by focusing on meaning in causal events (*if*) and on form in denied causes (*though*) (Townsend, 1983). The distinction between *if* and *though* had greater effects for skilled readers at the college level than at the school level, and greater effects at the college level for skilled readers than for average readers. Both of these results are consistent with the view that increased comprehension skill involves increased sensitivity to morphemic cues. Surprisingly, average readers at the school level showed the largest differences of all four groups in processing *if* and *though*.

If the listener modifies perceptual processing depending on the thematic and structural relations between clauses, the clauses are not being processed as independent units. We also examined the extent to which subjects process clauses as independent units with a tone location task. Subjects heard an isolated sentence, such as *Because coffee spilled on her sky-blue dress she went home early*, with a tone superimposed on speech in or around the boundaries between clauses, for example, in *dress*, between *dress* and *she*, or in *she*. Their task was to indicate the location of the tone in a printed version of the sentence. (See Townsend *et al.*, in preparation, for specific procedural details; see also Bever, Lackner, & Kirk, 1969; Bever, Hurtig, & Handel, in preparation.) To the extent that the subject treats a clause as an independent unit of meaning, we expected that tone-location accuracy would be greater for tones between clauses than for tones in clauses. If increased comprehension skill involves increased segmentation into clausal units, skilled readers should show greater effects of clause structure; if it involves modifying propositional processing depending on the relation of the proposition to other propositions, as suggested by the probe tasks, skilled readers should show lesser effects of clause structure, at least at the college level.

The tone-location task showed that school-age skilled readers and college-age average readers have the strongest tendency to process clauses independently. For both school-age skilled and college-age average readers, the difference in location accuracy for tones between clauses and for tones within clauses was 40%; for school-age readers the corresponding difference was 31%, and for college-age skilled readers, 23%. A significant correlation between the relative advantage of *if* over *though* in the Meaning Probe task and a segmentation index suggests that these differences in tone location accuracy are due to differences in discourse-thematic processing: the greater a subject's advantage in response time to the meaning of *if* clauses, relative to *though* clauses, the smaller the effect of the clause boundary on the subject's tone-location judgments.

Our studies of listening processes clearly show that listening skill is related to reading skill. They also suggest that different abilities characterize skilled comprehension at the college- and school-age levels. At the school level, comprehension skill is defined by the extent to which the individual processes clauses internally; hence, skilled readers at this level show stronger sensitivity to the boundaries between clauses and less sensitivity to thematic relations between clauses. At the college level, comprehension skill is defined by the extent to which the individual integrates propositions; hence, the skilled reader shows less sensitivity to the boundaries between clauses and stronger sensitivity to thematic relations.

In the next sections we discuss some recent experiments on reading. In one series of experiments we have examined fluctuations of attention to print around clause boundaries. We have shown that sensitivity to morphemic cues to phrase structure is related to a shifting of attention away from print at the ends of propositional units. In a second series of experiments we have investigated the role of discourse thematic cues and expectations on reading time. Our results suggest that average readers rely heavily on expectations, but skilled readers modify reading processes depending on both morphemic cues and expectations.

SEGMENTATION IN READING

We have been developing techniques to examine fluctuations of attention during reading. In one technique, subjects crossed out instances of the letter *e* as they read. We compared detection accuracy for silent *e*s that occurred in the last word of a subordinate clause, for example, *natives* in *The teacher in charge of the Indian natives had to take hunting lessons,* or in the first content word of a main clause, for example, *natives* in *To learn some new ways the Indian natives had to take hunting lessons.*

Muncer and Bever (1984) showed that college students failed to detect silent *e*s more frequently at the ends of (subordinate) clauses than at the beginnings of (main) clauses. This effect, however, was significant only for subjects with relatively high verbal achievement (SAT) test scores. This result confirms that comprehension processes are similar for reading and listening: in both cases, the structural role of a clause has a greater effect on attention to form for skilled readers than for average readers (Townsend *et al.*, in preparation).

We wondered whether the skilled readers' structural effect is due to their use of morphemic cues for segmenting printed language into structural units. To determine the extent to which readers normally segment sequences of words into structural units, we administered a Find-the-Odd-Word Test. Subjects read paragraphs for the purpose of finding a word that did not fit in with the meaning of the paragraph. We presented paragraphs in either a phrase-chunked format:

> *Johnny came walking into the dining room*
> *with very dirty shoes after playing all day,*
> *and his angry mother sent him*
> *to clean his teeth*
> *and told him he was a bad boy.*

or a random format:

> *Johnny came walking into the dining room with*
> *very dirty shoes after*
> *playing all day, and*
> *his angry mother sent*
> *him to clean his teeth*
> *and told him he was a bad boy.*

In the chunked format the ends of lines coincided with phrase boundaries, but in the random format they did not. The ends of lines therefore provided cues to structural boundaries in the chunked format, but in the random format the only cues to boundaries were morphemic. If the structural effect for skilled readers is due to their reliance on morphemic cues to segment printed words into structural units, subjects whose reading is unaffected by formatting cues to phrase structure should show a larger effect of the structural boundary on *e* detection. This result would suggest that skilled readers normally rely on morphemic cues to phrase structure.

We tested 60 undergraduates from Nassau Community College and 35 sixth- and eighth-grade subjects from the Mt. Hebron School in Montclair, NJ. Each subject read 6 paragraphs of each type in the odd-word test, and 12 critical sentences in the *e*-detection test.

For school-age subjects overall, reading times for finding the odd word were 7% faster in chunked paragraphs than in randomly formatted paragraphs; for college-age subjects, the effect of chunking on reading time was less than 1%. The fact that phrase-chunked format had a smaller effect for older subjects implies that more-advanced readers normally use morphemic cues to determine phrase structure.

The *e*-detection task produced evidence for auditory recoding of the printing sentences during reading: silent *e*s overall were harder to detect than pronounced *e*s for both college and school-age students, confirming Corcoran (1966) and Muncer and Bever (1984). The fact that pronounced *e*s were easier to detect during reading indicates that the reader utilizes an auditory representation of the words, providing further evidence of a close correspondence between reading and listening.

Clause-final silent *e*s were harder to detect than were clause-initial silent *e*s. However, subjects whose reading time for the Odd-Word task was improved by formatting according to phrase structure showed a smaller boundary effect on *e*-detection (Table 7.4). There was a clause structure effect for format-insensitive readers, but not for format-sensitive readers. For those readers who use sequential and morphemic cues to sentence structure, attention to physical characteristics of the stimulus fluctuates around major structural boundaries. For those readers whose reading is improved by physical emphasis of phrase boundaries, attention to the visual form of words does not fluctuate as much around major structural boundaries.

These results show that visual attention fluctuates around major structural boundaries. Readers who normally rely on morphemic cues to structure, rather than physical cues such as the end of a line, are more

TABLE 7.4
Percentage of Silent *e*s Missed around Clause
Boundaries in Relation to Format-Sensitivity

	Clause final	Clause initial	Difference
College-Age			
Format-insensitive	26	20	6
Format-sensitive	25	22	3
Mean	26	21	5
School-Age			
Format-insensitive	15	5	10
Format-sensitive	19	17	2
Mean	17	11	6

sensitive to propositional structure while reading, just as skilled readers are more sensitive to propositional structure while listening.

DISCOURSE-THEMATIC PROCESSING IN READING

We have also been examining skilled and average readers' processing of thematically cued clauses. In one study, subjects read the clauses of stories one at a time on a computer screen at their own rate; we measured how long the subject spent reading each clause. Previous research has shown that the process of integrating the sentence with context has a large effect on sentence-reading time (see, e.g., Bower *et al.*, 1979; Haberlandt, 1980; Haviland & Clark, 1974; Townsend, 1983).

We specifically examined reading times for clauses that cued different thematic relations (*although* vs *because*). Since a *because* clause can be thematically integrated as its propositional meaning is obtained, whereas an *although* clause must await integration pending information in the following main clause, the reader should, in general, spend more time processing *because* clauses than *although* clauses (Townsend, 1983).

The contexts preceding the critical clauses were such that the critical clause was either schematically expected (high script relevance) or schematically unexpected (low script relevance), as determined by pretest ratings. The stories all described a routine sequence of activities, with the high relevance event being highly predictable, as in:

> *Johnny woke up very hungry for breakfast.*
> *He found a bowl and a spoon in the kitchen.*
> *He got a pitcher of milk from the refrigerator.*
> *Although he took down a box of cereal from the shelf, . . .*

and the low-relevance event being possible, but not typical, in the sequence of events, as in:

> *Johnny was watching his favorite programs on TV.*
> *He started to get hungry for a snack.*
> *He waited for a commercial to go into the kitchen.*
> *Although he took down a box of cereal from the shelf, . . .*

Since an event which is not predicted by the schema underlying a story is harder to integrate with the preceding context, schematically unexpected events should take longer to process than schematically expected events (Bower *et al.*, 1979).

If skilled reading relies more on the activation and confirmation of schemata and less on structural cues to meaning, the effects of schematic relevance will be greater for skilled readers than for average readers, and the effects of conjunction, particularly when introducing a schematically relevant event, will be smaller for skilled readers than for average readers. If skilled reading involves the use of morphemic cues to the construction of a representation of text, the effects of conjunction should be greater for skilled readers than for average readers.

We tested 48 undergraduates at Montclair State College and at Columbia University. The subjects were classified as skilled or average readers on the basis of verbal Scholastic Aptitude Test scores. Average readers had VSAT scores under 510, mean = 432; skilled readers had VSAT scores over 540, mean = 612. Each subject read eight stories for the purpose of constructing story titles, and then took either a sentence recognition test, measuring sensitivity to word order in the critical clause, or a recall test, measuring propositional recall of the critical clause.

We found that skilled readers were more "interactive processors" than were average readers. Whereas for average readers there were independent effects of schemata and conjunction on reading time, for skilled readers reading time reflected an interaction between local cues and the relationship between the sentence and the schema underlying the story.

Table 7.5 shows average reading times for the critical clauses. Overall, skilled readers read the critical clauses faster than did average readers. Overall, subjects read high relevance events faster than low relevance events and *although* clauses faster than *because* clauses. As in the Meaning and Word listening tasks (Townsend *et al.*, in preparation), both types of readers appear to be sensitive to the thematic relations that

TABLE 7.5
College Students' Clause
Reading Times (in Seconds) in
Script-Based Stories

	Script Relevance		
	High	Low	Average
Skilled readers			
because	3.1	3.0	3.1
although	2.8	2.9	2.9
Average	2.9	3.0	3.0
Average readers			
because	3.4	3.9	3.6
although	3.2	3.4	3.3
Average	3.3	3.7	3.5

conjunctions signal and modify their processing strategies accordingly. However, script relevance and conjunction interacted in different ways for subjects of different reading ability.

For skilled readers, there was no overall effect of script relevance. However, script relevance interacted with conjunction: the skilled reader showed differences in total processing time for *although* and *because* clauses only when they contained high relevance events. They read *although* clauses faster than *because* clauses when the clause stated a high-relevance event, but not when it stated a low-relevance event. Skilled readers process *because* and *although* propositions differently only when they are *more* contextually relevant. Thus, skilled reading does not involve decreased reliance on morphemic cues to meaning as schematic predictability increases.

For average readers, reading times were faster overall for high relevance events and for events introduced by *although*. In contrast to the skilled reader, the average reader's conjunction effect was much smaller in high-relevance contexts. The average reader relies less on morphemic cues to thematic relations as schematic predictability increases.

These results suggest that skilled and average readers use "expectation-based" processing for different purposes. Skilled readers use expectations for thematic integration, and morphemic cues as signals for how to integrate locally connected propositions. The skilled reader uses *although* as a signal to move on to the following main clause in order to discover what the storyteller had expected to follow from the event in the *although* clause (Townsend, 1983). *Because* signals that the expected event can be integrated into a cause–effect organization of the story; this integration requires effort, thereby increasing reading time for *because* clauses. Unskilled readers rely more on schemata, and less on morphemic cues, for thematic integration: when events are consistent with the schema underlying text, surface cues to propositional relations have little effect on processing time. The fact that schematic relevance has a much larger effect on processing time for *because* than for *although* suggests that average readers attempt to integrate propositions into a thematic organization when they are cued by *because* but not when they are cued by *although*.

The memory results showed that the effects of discourse schemata were greater for average readers than for skilled readers. Average readers showed 46% better recognition memory for word order changes in low relevance events than in high relevance events, but skilled readers showed no difference in recognition memory for low and high relevance events. Similarly, average readers showed 15% better rated recall of the meaning of high relevance events than of low relevance events, but skilled readers showed no difference. The memory results thus converge with the reading time results on the generalization that average readers rely relatively more on discourse schemata than do skilled readers. Skilled readers, on the other hand, modulate their processing and organization of propositions depending on both morphemic cues in text and discourse schemata.

CONCLUSION

Our research indicates that language-processing differences between skilled and average readers are much more extensive than had been considered previously. We have found differences in structural and thematic processing in several reading and listening tasks, despite controls for differences in general intelligence. Skilled and average readers differ in listening to isolated sentences, in listening to stories, in reading stories sentence-by-sentence, and in unconstrained reading of stories.

The differences that we have observed between skilled and average readers are not confined to reading, but in fact have often been greater in listening than in reading. In the Story Reading and Story Listening tasks (Townsend *et al.*, in preparation), in which we explicitly controlled for materials and tasks but varied modality, the differences in comprehension between skilled and average readers were greater in listening than in reading at both the school level and the college level.

Reading and listening comprehension share many of the same processes. In the wide range of tasks we have used, similar differences in task performance between skilled and average readers nearly always emerged in both reading and listening. We have found similar differences between skilled and average readers in their use of cues to thematic relations in the Probe tasks, which involved listening to isolated sentences, and the Sentence Reading task, which involved reading sentences in story contexts.

Our studies extend the conclusions of Sticht (1972), Perfetti and Goldman (1976), and others, that deficits in reading skills are accompanied by deficits in listening skills as well. Within the limits of our experimental tasks and the range of abilities we have examined, readers and listeners use similar perceptual strategies, regardless of (1) what modality the language appears in and (2) how effective their perceptual strategies are.

Our research allows a preliminary qualitative description of the comprehension processes of skilled and average readers at two age levels. The skilled college-age reader is an interactive processor, who modifies attention to propositional processing depending on morphemically cued structural and thematic relations. The average college-age reader is a "schema perceiver," who imposes discourse schematic knowledge on the meanings of sentences and texts, perhaps as a means of compensating for ineffective processing of morphemically cued propositional relations. The skilled school-age reader is a "proposition perceiver," who recodes a sequence of words corresponding to a proposition into its meaning, but engages in relatively little processing of the relations between propositions. The average school-age reader tends toward being a "word caller" not only in reading (Smith *et al.*, 1976), but in listening as well; this individual tends to process spoken and printed language as a series of words without structure.

For the college-age skilled reader, comprehension involves an interaction between propositional processing and thematic processing, rather than complete reliance on either proposition perception or schema perception. This type of reader uses morpheme/sequence cues to produce propositional representations, which are integrated with context in different ways depending on thematic and structural cues to the relations between propositions, and depending on how the propositions relate to schematic expectations. These integrative processes tend to occur toward the end of propositional units rather than near the beginning, but they depend on morphemic cues to relations with context. In any case, it is the product of propositional processing that is the unit on which integrative processes operate (Townsend, 1983; Townsend & Bever, 1982).

The college-age average reader does not show these interactions between propositional and thematic processing. The average college-age reader segments the linguistic stimulus into propositional units, but does not effectively modify integrative processing to take account of local relations between propositions. Integration of propositions with context for this type of reader is governed more by the extent to which the propositions agree with schematic expectations. Sentence processing out of context is, by and large, a matter of segmenting the sentence into propositional units without utilizing cues to propositional relations. In short, the average college-age reader organizes word sequences into propositional units, but tends not to form a representation of text from the morphemically cued relations between propositions relying instead on schematic expectations to develop an approximation of the meaning of text.

The school-age skilled reader is similar to the average college-age reader in segmenting the linguistic stimulus into propositional units, but differs from the average college-age reader in modifying to some degree propositional processing of structurally or thematically related clauses.

The skilled school-age reader tends to focus on internal analysis of sentence meaning at the end of a clause, but appears to be adopting the kinds of awareness of structural and thematic relations between propositions that the skilled college-age reader has.

The school-age average reader tends to process linguistic stimuli word by word. This individual shows relatively less segmentation of sentences into propositional units while listening and while reading. The average reader at the school level does not process main clauses as independent units of meaning, but does respond to thematic cues in the same way as the skilled college-age reader. The area of relative deficiency for the school-age average reader is in perception of the units (i.e., propositions) on which thematic processing operates, rather than in strategies for thematic processing. The major factor that differentiates younger and older average readers is that the older average reader has developed more effective processes for segmenting the linguistic stimulus into propositional units.

One factor emerges in the acquisition of effective reading skills: a shift from proposition-by-proposition processing of language to a modification of propositional processing strategies, depending on cues in the text and on expectations, for the purpose of structural and thematic integration of sentences. We have found three major differences between skilled readers at the college and school levels: (1) Structural and thematic cues to propositional relations have greater effects during listening at the college level than at the school level. (2) Segmentation into independent clauses during reading is weaker at the college level. (3) Segmentation into independent clauses during listening is weaker at the college level. These differences indicate that the skilled reader at the school level focuses on processing propositions independently of one another in both reading and listening.

Good reading skills at the school level are characterized by relatively simple propositional processing strategies: segmenting the word sequences into phrase and clause groupings and fixing propositional meaning at the ends of propositions. The structural and thematic relations between clauses interact very little with these propositional processes in school-age skilled readers. At the college level, however, the skilled reader modifies propositional processing strategies depending on structural and thematic cues to propositional relations and on the schematic context of the clause. Improvement in reading skill among skilled readers from the school level to the college level involves improvement in strategies for integrating propositions with context.

Increased comprehension skills, both within a given age level and across age levels, involves greater reliance on morphemic cues to propositional meanings and the relations between propositions. The specific kinds of cues that differentiate skilled and average readers, however, differ at the school and college levels. At the school level, skilled readers differ from average readers by showing greater use of morphemic cues to sentence structure. At the college level, skilled readers differ from average readers by showing greater use of morphemic cues for integrating propositions with context, but lesser used of schematic expectations for integrating propositions with context. This indicates that skilled comprehension is best viewed as an interaction of propositional perception and thematic integration: thematic processing, based on cues and expectations, operates on the products of sentence-level processing (i.e., propositions). The fact that we observed differences in performance between skilled and average readers even in unconstrained reading suggests that the use of morphemic cues overrides any differences in comprehension strategies that might arise from differences in the modality in which language occurs.

Our results may also be interpreted as an investigation of what standardized achievement tests measure. These tests do not measure similar abilities at different educational levels; that is, the standardized criteria for skilled reading emphasize different comprehension processes at different ages. At the school level, standardized tests define skilled reading as the extent to which the individual processes propositions independently of one another. Less-skilled reading at the school level involves relatively less segmentation of the linguistic stimulus into propositional units. At the college level, standardized tests define skilled reading as the extent to which the individual uses sentence structure cues to relate propositions. Less-skilled reading at the college level involves segmentation of the stimulus into propositional units, but ineffective use of sentence structure cues to relate propositions, and instead, the use of nonlinguistically based expectations to integrate propositions into a discourse representation. It is because the criteria for skilled reading are not isomorphic between these two age levels that skilled readers at the two levels showed different results on various tasks (e.g., tone location).

Accordingly, our research suggests some directions for instructional programs at different stages. Unskilled readers at the school level need to be more aware of phrase structure groupings of words and of sentences as units of meaning, and how within-sentence groupings of words relate to the meaning of a sentence. Attention to the intonation patterns of spoken language, practice in reading phrases rather than individual words, listening to skilled readers imposing intonation on printed language would all be helpful in increasing proposition perception processes at this level. Awareness of sentences as units of meaning, and of morpheme-sequence cues to meaning, might be increased by practice in expressing propositions in alternative sentence forms. Our research suggests that simply emphasizing word recognition skills would actually reinforce the ineffective processing strategies that average school-age readers already possess; similarly, simply emphasizing recognition of the discourse schemata that underlie texts would actually increase the acquisition of the ineffective processing strategies that average college readers utilize.

The average college-age reader needs instruction at two levels: how texts signal the relations between propositions, and how these signals relate to importance, expectations, presupposition, and thematic organization. Marzano (1978) suggests that writers can increase awareness of the various structural and thematic cues to sentence relations by highlighting different cues and thematic roles in different ways.

The fact that average readers also possess ineffective listening strategies suggests that reading instruction should be incorporated with instruction in general comprehension skills. The fact that skilled comprehension involves modifying propositional processing and integrating propositions with context suggests that instruction in perceiving propositions should occur in contexts which vary the relations between propositions as a function of morphemic cues and expectations.

To summarize, our research has two important theoretical implications. First, the fact that modality has little effect on comprehension processes suggests that abstract language structure exerts greater influence on processing than does modality-specific information or strategies. Second, we have no reason to believe that average readers differ from skilled readers in their basic knowledge of language: the average readers in our studies were not disabled readers, but were functioning adequately in normal educational settings. It seems likely that the two groups of readers possess similar rules for sentence acceptability. On that assumption, the fact that we observed differences in performance between the two groups suggests that "verbal ability" is a matter of how the individual deploys basic knowledge of language in comprehension situations.

ACKNOWLEDGMENTS

This research was supported by National Institute of Education grant #G-79-0040 to Columbia University, by National Science Foundation grant #BNS-8120463 to Montclair State College, and by Separately Budgeted Research grants from Montclair State College. Preparation of the manuscript was supported in part by a sabbatical leave to Dr. Townsend from Montclair State College.

We wish to acknowledge the assistance provided by Ms. Gertrude Goldstein at the Woodward School, Sister Pat Tavis at the Lacordaire School, and Dr. Mary Lee Fitzgerald, Mr. Frank Rennie, and Mrs. Agnes Bulmer of the Montclair Public Schools, as well as several teachers who gave up class time for these experiments.

We are most grateful to Steve Muncer for contributing in a major way to conducting the college-level portion of the reading segmentation experiment and analyzing data. B. De-Forest, M. Hoover, S. Jandreau, C. Moon, and J. Pesaniello assisted in preparing materials, testing subjects, and scoring results for other experiments.

REFERENCES

Aaronson, D. (1976). Performance theories for sentence coding: Some qualitative observations. *Journal of Experimental Psychology, 2,* 42–55.

Abelson, R. P. (1981). Psychological status of the script concept. *American Psychologist, 36,* 715–729.

Abrams, K., & Bever, T. G. (1969). Syntactic structure modifies attention during speech perception and recognition. *Quarterly Journal of Experimental Psychology, 21,* 280–290.

Adams, M. J., & Collins, A. (1979). A schema-theoretic view of reading. In R. O. Freedle (Ed.), *New directions in discourse processing* (Vol. 2). Norwood, NJ: Ablex.

Bartlett, F. C. (1932). *Remembering: An experimental and social study.* Cambridge: Cambridge University Press.

Bever, T. G., Garrett, M., & Hurtig, R. (1973). The interaction of perceptual processes and ambiguous sentences. *Memory & Cognition, 1,* 277–286.

Bever, T. G., Hurtig, R., & Handel, A. (in preparation). Response biases do not account for the effect of clause structure on the perception of nonlinguistic stimuli. In D. J. Townsend & T. G. Bever (Eds.), *Language comprehension: The case for the sentence.* Hillsdale, NJ: Erlbaum.

Bever, T. G., Lackner, J. R., & Kirk, R. (1969). The underlying structures of sentences are the primary units of immediate speech processing. *Perception & Psychophysics, 5,* 225–234.

Boomer, D. S. (1965). Hesitation and grammatical encoding. *Language and Speech, 8,* 148–158.

Bower, G. H., Black, J. B., & Turner, T. J. (1979). Scripts in memory for text. *Cognitive Psychology, 11,* 177–220.

Bransford, J. D., & Johnson, M. K. (1973). Consideration of some problems of comprehension. In W. G. Chase (Ed.), *Visual information processing.* New York: Academic Press.

Bridge, C. A., & Tierney, R. J. (1981). The inferential operations of children across texts with narrative and expository tendencies. *Journal of Reading Behavior, 13,* 201–214.

Caplan, D. (1972). Clause boundaries and recognition latencies for words in sentences. *Perception & Psychophysics, 12,* 73–76.

Clay, M., & Imlach, R. (1971). Juncture, pitch and stress as reading behavior variables. *Journal of Verbal Learning and Verbal Behavior, 10,* 133–139.

Cohen, G., & Freeman, R. (1978). Individual differences in reading strategies in relation to handedness and cerebral asymmetry. In J. Requin (Ed.), *Attention and performance, VII.* Hillsdale, NJ: Erlbaum.

Cooper, W., & Cooper, L. (1980). *Studies in speech production.* Cambridge, MA: Harvard University Press.

Corcoran, D. J. W. (1966). An acoustic factor in letter cancellation. *Nature (London), 210,* 658.

Cromer, W. (1970). The difference model: A new explanation for some reading difficulties. *Journal of Educational Psychology, 61,* 471–483.

Danley, M., & Cooper, W. E. (1979). Sentence production: Closure vs. initiation of constituents. *Journal of Linguistics, 17,* 1017–1038.

Denner, B. (1970). Representational and syntactic competence of problem readers. *Child Development, 41,* 881–887.

Duffy, S. (1983). *Predictive processing in story comprehension.* Paper presented at the meeting of the Eastern Psychological Association.

Durrell, D. D. (1969). Listening comprehension vs. reading comprehension. *Journal of Reading, 12,* 455–460.

Fodor, J. A., Bever, T. G., & Garrett, M. F. (1974). *The psychology of language.* New York: McGraw-Hill.

Fries, C. C. (1962). *Linguistics and reading.* New York: Holt.

Fry, M., Johnson, C., & Muehl, S. (1970). Oral language production in relation to reading achievement among select second graders. In D. Bakker & P. Satz (Eds.), *Specific reading disability: Advances in theory and method.* Amsterdam: Rotterdam University Press.

Gibbs, R. W., & Tenney, Y. J. (1980). The concept of scripts in understanding stories. *Journal of Psycholinguistic Research, 9,* 275–284.

Gibson, E. J., & Levin, H. (1975). *The psychology of reading.* Cambridge, MA: MIT Press.

Goldman, S. (1976). Reading skill and the minimum distance principle: A comparison of listening and reading comprehension. *Journal of Experimental Child Psychology, 22,* 123–142.

Goldman-Eisler, F. (1968). *Psycholinguistics: Experiments in spontaneous speech.* New York: Academic Press.

Goldman-Eisler, F. (1972). Pauses, clauses, and sentences. *Language and Speech, 15,* 103–113.

Green, T. R. (1979). The necessity of syntax markers: Two experiments with artificial languages. *Journal of Verbal Learning and Verbal Behavior, 18,* 481–496.

Guthrie, J. T. (1973). Reading comprehension and syntactic responses in good and poor readers. *Journal of Educational Psychology, 65,* 294–299.

Haberlandt, K. (1980). Story grammar and reading time of story constituents. *Poetics, 9,* 99–116.

Haviland, S., & Clark, H. H. (1974). What's new? Acquiring new information as a process in comprehension. *Journal of Verbal Learning and Verbal Behavior, 13,* 512–521.

Huggins, A. W. F. (1978). Timing and speech intelligibility. In J. Requin (Ed.), *Attention and performance, VII.* Hillsdale, NJ: Erlbaum.

Jarvella, R. J. (1971). Syntactic processing of connected speech. *Journal of Verbal Learning and Verbal Behavior, 10,* 409–416.

Kleiman, G. M. (1975). Speech recoding in reading. *Journal of Verbal Learning and Verbal Behavior, 14,* 323–339.

Mandler, J. M., & Johnson, N. S. (1977). Remembrance of things parsed: Story structure and recall. *Cognitive Psychology, 11,* 111–151.

Marslen-Wilson, W., & Tyler, L. (1975). The processing structure of sentence perception. *Nature (London), 257,* 784–786.

Marzano, R. J. (1978). Teaching psycholinguistically-based comprehension skills using a visual approach: A proposal. *Journal of Reading, 21,* 729–734.

Mitchell, D. C., & Green, D. W. (1978). The effects of control word content on immediate processing in reading. *Quarterly Journal of Experimental Psychology, 30,* 609–636.

Moeser, S. D., & Bregman, A. S. (1972). The role of reference in the acquisition of a miniature artificial language. *Journal of Verbal Learning and Verbal Behavior, 11,* 759–769.

Muncer, S. J., & Bever, T. G. (1984). Good readers distribute visual attention differentially to the beginnings of clauses. *Journal of Psycholinguistic Research, 13,* 275–279.

Oaken, R., Weiner, M., & Cromer, W. (1971). Identification, organization, and reading comprehension for good and poor readers. *Journal of Educational Psychology, 62,* 71–78.

Pearson, P. D., & Spiro, R. (1982). The new buzz word in reading is schema. *Instructor, 91,* 46–48.

Perfetti, C., & Goldman, S. (1976). Discourse memory and reading comprehension. *Journal of Verbal Learning and Verbal Behavior, 15,* 33–42.

Riesbeck, C. K., & Schank, R. C. (1978). Comprehension by computer: Expectation-based analysis of sentences in context. In W. J. M. Levelt & G. B. Flores d'Arcais (Eds.), *Studies in the perception of language.* New York: Wiley.

Rubin, A. (1980). A theoretical taxonomy of the differences between oral and written language. In R. J. Spiro, B. C. Bruce, & W. F. Brewer (Eds.), *Theoretical issues in reading comprehension.* Hillsdale, NJ: Erlbaum.

Rumelhart, D. E., & Ortony, A. (1977). The representation of knowledge in memory. In R. C. Anderson, R. J. Spiro, & W. E. Montague (Eds.), *Schooling and the acquisition of knowledge.* Hillsdale, NJ: Erlbaum.

Schank, R. C. (1982). *Reading and understanding: Teaching from the perspective of artificial intelligence.* Hillsdale, NJ: Erlbaum.

Schank, R. C., & Birnbaum, L. (1984). Memory, meaning, and syntax. In T. Bever, J. Carroll, & L. Miller (Eds.), *Cognitive, philosophical, and computational foundations of language.* Hillsdale, NJ: Erlbaum.

Smiley, S., Oakley, D., Worthen, D., Campione, J., & Brown, A. (1977). Recall of thematically relevant material by adolescent good and poor readers as a function of written vs. oral presentation. *Journal of Educational Psychology, 69,* 381–387.

Smith, E. B., Goodman, K. S., & Meredith, R. (1976). *Language and thinking in the school.* New York: Holt.

Sorenson, J. M., Cooper, W. E., & Paccia, J. M. (1978). Speech timing of grammatical categories. *Cognition, 6,* 135–153.

Stein, N. L. (1982). What's in a story: Interpreting the interpretations of story grammars. *Discourse Processes, 5,* 319–336.

Steiner, R., Weiner, M., & Cromer, W. (1971). Comprehension training and identification training for poor and good readers. *Journal of Educational Psychology, 62,* 506–513.

Sticht, T. G. (1972). Learning by listening. In J. B. Carroll & R. O. Freedle (Eds.), *Language comprehension and the acquisition of knowledge.* Washington, DC: Winston.

Tatham, S. M. (1970). Reading comprehension of materials written with select oral language patterns: A study at grades two and four. *Reading Research Quarterly, 5,* 402–426.

Tierney, R. J., Bridge, C., & Cera, M. J. (1979). The discourse processing operations of children. *Reading Research Quarterly, 14,* 539–573.

Townsend, D. J. (1983). Thematic processing in sentences and texts. *Cognition, 13,* 223–261.

Townsend, D. J., & Bever, T. G. (1978). Interclause relations and clausal processing. *Journal of Verbal Learning and Verbal Behavior, 17,* 509–521.

Townsend, D. J., & Bever, T. G. (1982). Natural units of representation interact during sentence comprehension. *Journal of Verbal Learning and Verbal Behavior, 21,* 688–703.

Townsend, D. J., Carrithers, C., & Bever, T. G. (in preparation). Spoken sentence processing strategies vary with reading skill.

Tyler, L. K., & Marslen-Wilson, W. D. (1977). The on-line effects of semantic context on syntactic processing. *Journal of Verbal Learning and Verbal Behavior, 16,* 683–692.

Vogel, L. (1974). Syntactic abilities in normal and dyslexic children. *Journal of Learning Disabilities, 7*, 103–109.

Weaver, P. A. (1978). Comprehension, recall, and dyslexia: A proposal for the application of schema theory. *Bulletin of the Orton Society, 28*, 92–123.

Weinstein, R., & Rabinovitch, M. (1971). Sentence structure and retention in good and poor readers. *Journal of Educational Psychology, 62*, 25–30.

Chapter 8

Prosody and Structure in Children's Syntactic Processing

Peter A. Schreiber

INTRODUCTION

Overview

The central claim we explore in this chapter is that prosody (the complex of suprasegmental phonological features which includes intonation, stress, and duration) plays an especially prominent perceptual role for children in their processing of the syntactic structure of speech. Specifically, I present evidence bearing on the suggestion that children are more sensitive to (and reliant on) prosodic signals of structure than adults are and that the prosodic cues may play a particularly important role demarcating the boundaries of syntactic constituents for children. This suggestion must still be regarded as tentative, though the evidence for it comes from two distinct experimental paradigms whose results converge; moreover, the claim is a priori plausible, for it is known that even during the babbling stage children produce prosodic contours remarkably like those of their target language. In view of this, it would be entirely natural for youngsters still in the process of acquiring full control of their native language to continue to use prosodic features as primary perceptual cues for segmentation, the (generally implicit) analysis of the speech signal into its appropriate constituent units and subunits.

COMPREHENDING ORAL AND WRITTEN LANGUAGE

If confirmed, the claim may be important not only because of its bearing on a central question about language development, however; it may also have important pedagogical implications in the area of reading instruction, as suggested at some length in Schreiber (1980), for if prosody plays a significant signaling role for children in their processing of spoken language, the absence of consistent print analogues to the prosodic cues may partially explain the difficulty many have in acquiring fluent reading skills. The explanation runs as follows.

To attain reading fluency, a reader must learn to chunk words into appropriate syntactic phrases; a substantial body of evidence, part of which is reviewed by Gibson and Levin (1975, chap. 10), supports this assertion. If, as Gibson and Levin (p. 39) suggest, part of what differentiates good and poor readers is the ability to segment written sentences into "syntactically critical units such as phrases" and if children use prosody as a primary cue for chunking speech, a part of the basis for the diversity in skills would be clear; graphic signals do not correspond systematically to the prosodic cues of spoken language. Hence, beginning readers must tacitly come to recognize the need to make better use of other cues. This explanation would suggest that the problem of "word calling" (halting, expressionless, word-by-word reading with concomitant lack of comprehension) is due to a failure to recognize this need and would also suggest a rationale for the reported success of certain proposed techniques of instruction that are intended to solve the word-calling problem.

Syntactic Parsing

An important contribution of modern linguistic study has been the emphasis placed on phrase structure (PS) as a crucial organizing principle of syntax; the view that sentences are hierarchically organized objects which can be represented in labeled tree (or similar) notations is common to virtually all present-day theories of syntactic structure. Disregarding notational variation and disagreement over specific details of analysis, syntacticians concur that there is a significant level of representation on which a sentence such as (1) below should be analyzed approximately as in (2):

(1)   *Your neighbors shovel the sidewalk carefully.*

(2)

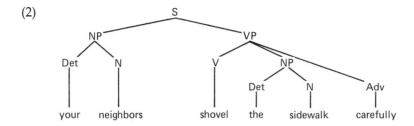

(In this representation, S stands for sentence, NP for noun phrase, VP for verb phrase, Det for determiner, N for noun, V for verb, and Adv for adverb.) The claim that PS embodies is that the linear string of words comprising a sentence falls into syntactically coherent units (constituents) such as the NP which themselves form, together with other constituents, higher-order units such as the VP. Such a conception has been motivated and justified on purely linguistic grounds by, among others, Wells (1947), Chomsky (1957), and Jackendoff (1977); moreover, a wide range of psycholinguistic experimentation supports the claim that PS plays an important role in language processing (e.g., Epstein, 1961; Johnson, 1965, 1966; Fodor & Bever, 1965; Rommetveit & Turner, 1967; Jarvella, 1971; Cooper & Paccia-Cooper, 1980).

This is not to say that the domain of syntax is exhaustively described by an account of the principles for assigning a surface structure analysis, that is, a representation of the PS for the observed sequence. Other levels of syntactic representation may also be required, including abstract levels of structure where the logical relations within the sentence are represented (see, e.g., Chomsky, 1965, 1981, 1986). However, the nature and status of other levels have been the subject of continuing debate, as illustrated, for example, by many of the papers in Jacobson and Pullum (1982), while the existence of labeled, hierarchical surface structure representations is by now virtually unchallenged, even if the appropriate form of such representations continues to be studied and discussed.

Assuming the reality of PS from both the linguistic and the psychological points of view, it can be argued that certain other formal features of language design play a teleological role with respect to PS. For example, in languages with rich morphological systems of concord, agreement phenomena function in part as a device to signal PS, Latin being a classic illustration of such a situation. Some linguistic analysis and experimental evidence suggest that certain acoustic properties of utterances, specifically prosodic features, have a similar function. These prosodic features are the several suprasegmental properties of utterances which, from the perceptual and linguistic points of view, include intonation, stress, and length; these linguistic constructs correlate in complex ways, and by no means perfectly, with the acoustic properties of fundamental frequency, intensity or amplitude, and duration. Other prosodic features are rhythm or timing, and pause or juncture; the acoustic basis of the former is presumably some regular interval defined over other prosodic elements such as stress.

Though many details concerning the nature of prosodic features remain obscure, there is ample evidence for the reality of certain types of prosodic marking and for the systematic character of prosody. Among these properties, some appear to correlate fairly consistently with certain structural boundaries; perhaps the most regular of these patterns is phrase-final lengthening, the increased duration of stressed syllables at the ends of multiword phrases. For example, the word *light* typically has a longer duration in a sentence like (3)a than in one like (3)b:

(3)   a. *The gentle light colors the sky pink.*
       b. *The gentle light colors pleased her mother.*

In (3)a, *light*, the head noun of the subject NP, terminates that phrase, while in (3)b *light* is a prenominal modifier of the head noun *colors*. Several studies have demonstrated the salience and consistency of such differences in duration (Martin, 1972; Klatt, 1975; Lehiste, Olive, & Streeter, 1976; Nooteboom, Brokx, & de Rooij, 1978; Cooper & Paccia-Cooper, 1980). While the etiology of the prosodic features may in part be physiological, they also appear to be associated with aspects of the production system, specifically, as suggested by Cooper and Paccia-Cooper, planning; their availability and regularity also make them fairly reliable cues for at least preliminary perceptual segmentation. Nooteboom *et al.* (p. 102) speculate that "prosody is constantly used in the ongoing perception of the sentences searching for the expected [major] syntactic boundary," though they also suggest that, once such a boundary has been found, "prosodic boundary markers are further discarded by listeners."

A good deal of psycholinguistic research, both theoretical and experimental, has been devoted to how a language processor determines the PS of linguistic input. Among the proposals put forth to account for the tacit ability of speakers to segment sentences into their constituent phrases and subphrases are those of, e.g., Bever (1970), Kimball (1973), Frazier and Fodor (1978), Wanner and Maratsos (1978), and Marcus (1980). While the proposals differ greatly in detail, they share certain basic assumptions; most importantly for our purposes, they all tend to be biased toward language abstracted away from surface phonetic detail. As Levelt (1978) notes in discussing studies of sentence perception generally, most of them treat acoustic properties of the speech signal as at best nuisance factors to be, if possible, controlled, but not explored as potential systematic signals of structure.

There is a sense in which this stance is appropriate, for it is undeniable that speakers, especially linguistic adults, can process language without relying on prosodic cues to structure, most notably when reading, but also under noisy conditions such as a bad phone connection or a cocktail party; in the former situation, the speech signal itself is degraded, while in the latter there is much interference in the surroundings. Also, prosody does not constitute a foolproof guide to structure; some PS boundaries are rarely marked prosodically, others are only optionally marked, and some occurrences of prosodic junctures do not mark syntactic boundaries. Nonetheless, the fact that speakers can process language in the absence of full acoustic information does not necessarily mean that they normally do so. Furthermore, even if linguistic adults are capable of abstracting away from acoustic cues, this does not entail that all speakers are equally able to do so; in particular, children still in the process of learning their language may be more reliant on overt signals of structure.

In any event, there is probably no one level of structural cues both necessary and sufficient to language processing. It is the conjoint effect of various cues (e.g., morphology, word order, lexical categorization and subcategorization, and prosody) which signals (often uniquely) the PS that should be assigned to a sentence; it is presumably on the basis of this structure that speakers go on to perform the higher-level computations that determine the meaning of the sentence.

PROSODY AND PROCESSING

Adults' Use of Prosody

Since the mid 1970s there have been several experimental studies of the role of prosody in adult language processing. Cooper and Paccia-Cooper (1980) and Cooper and Sorensen (1981) report extensive sets of experiments on the use of duration and fundamental frequency in speech production. They demonstrate that both these features correlate strikingly with surface syntactic structure and they in fact propose programmatic algorithms for predicting durational and fundamental frequency effects. As one example of the results obtained, Cooper and

Paccia-Cooper presented subjects (Ss) with ambiguous sentences like (4) in which the prepositional phrase can be construed as either an adverbal modifier of *hit* or a postnominal modifier of *the cop*.

(4)   *Jeffrey hit the cop with a stick.*

In the former case, a major constituent boundary occurs between the noun *cop* and the prepositional phrase, while in the latter *cop* and the prepositional phrase form a constituent. The sentences were presented to Ss with both the intended interpretations provided, and measurements were made of the duration of the segment /ka/ in the word *cop* in the Ss' reading of the sentences under both interpretations. A significant durational difference in the predicted direction was found; that is, the segment was longer before the major constituent break. Similar results were found in a wide variety of structurally different cases.

Of course, the fact that adults can make these distinctions does not mean that they normally do so. A study by Levelt, Zwanenburg, and Ouweneel (1970) provides some negative evidence. They found, as summarized by Levelt (1978, p. 23), that "disambiguating prosodic information is nearly absent if the ambiguous sentence is spoken in a disambiguating context." In contrast to these results, however, are those of Cooper and Paccia-Cooper, who also conducted an experiment with disambiguating (paragraph) context materials into which were embedded the same sentences which they had earlier found to produce prosodic effects in isolation. In this instance, even though subjects were unaware of the ambiguous nature of the stimulus sentence, durational effects comparable to those found in isolation did occur. On the basis of these (and other) studies, it seems fair to say that adults are able to signal structural differences by prosodic means; whether they do so in a consistent way in the course of normal language use, however, remains uncertain.

Results of experimentation on the role of prosodic cues in adult comprehension have also been somewhat mixed. Lehiste *et al.* (1976), Cooper, Paccia, and Lapointe (1978), and Streeter (1978) have shown that English-speaking adults can and do make use of these cues to parse ambiguous surface structures whose constructional homonymy arises from different possible bracketings, such as *the young men and women* which can be understood as meaning either that both the men and women are young or that only the men are. In the former, the bracketing may be represented as follows: ((the) (young (men and women))), while in the latter it is: ((the) ((young men) (and) (women))). Nooteboom *et al.* (1978) present similar results for Dutch. Other studies which demonstrate an effect of prosody on adult performance on various types of perceptual tasks include Wingfield and Klein (1971), Martin (1972, 1975), Dooling (1974), and Darwin (1975).

It should be noted that in all the studies cited here, prosodic effects show up only with surface PS; that is, where, for example, an ambiguity cannot be associated with a difference in surface bracketing but is attributable to lexical or deep structural differences, prosody does not reliably differentiate interpretations. For example, neither lexical ambiguities like *He stood by the bank* nor deep structural ambiguities like *The shooting of the hunters was dreadful* are consistently resolved by prosody. Indeed, the Lehiste *et al.* study, which was explicitly designed to compare the three types of ambiguities, shows reliable prosodic disambiguation only for the surface cases. A similar result emerges from experiments reported in Wales and Toner (1979) in which Ss were to interpret sentences with either lexical, deep structure, or surface structure ambiguities. To reduce the amount of bias that may be introduced by virtue of the sentences' having preferred interpretations, Wales and Toner evaluated their results in light of an independent estimate of bias for each reading of each sentence. Their outcome is that adult subjects can reliably disambiguate ambiguous sentences on the basis of prosody only with a restricted (but specifiable) subset of sentences, namely those with surface structure ambiguities which, moreover, have their preferred interpretation associated with a particular type of structural configuration.[1]

Children's Use of Prosody: Previous Work

Although the evidence for claims about children's syntactic processing is, if anything, smaller than for adults, there are both a priori and (slender) empirical grounds for supposing that prosody may significantly facilitate children's syntactic segmentation. With respect to the a priori considerations, it is well known that long before infants begin to speak their language, they string together sequences of sounds which are produced with the melodic contours of the target language of their linguistic community (Crystal, 1975). The prosodic melodies may arise as a result of imitation, though, possibly, they may have a deeper source, namely an innate rhythmic basis. The suggestion that rhythm provides an organizing principle which facilitates perception and memory can be traced back at least to Lashley (1951) in the modern period, and it has of course more ancient roots as well; the notion has been elaborated by Neisser (1967), who suggests that rhythm provides cues to syntactic structure, a view that draws on the insights of structural linguists such as Trager and Smith (1951/1957).

Whatever the virtue of my previous speculation regarding the innate basis of rhythm, however, it seems evident that prosodic and rhythmic signals of structure can play an important "bootstrap" function in the acquisition of syntactic segmentation. This claim rests on the observation that without prosodic cues the child often will not have sufficient information on which to base an analysis of the incoming speech signal. Hence, the hypothesis to be examined in the remainder of this chapter is that, for children, prosodic cues constitute a major set of signals to PS. Moreover, I suggest that children are more reliant on, as well as sensitive to, prosodic signals of structure than adults are.

The evidence supporting the hypothesis (first made in print, so far as I know, in Read, Schreiber, & Walia, 1978 and discussed in Schreiber and Read, 1980, in a somewhat more general context) comes from two types of experiments. The first of these involves a kind of conscious parsing of sentences and must therefore be viewed as relying on a certain level of metalinguistic awareness for the performance of the experimental task. In view of this, the results must be interpreted with considerable caution, for they clearly do not speak directly to the issue of normal on-line processing of language. Reports of experimental research using a parsing task in which prosodic features are manipulated can be found in Kleiman, Winograd, and Humphrey (1979) and Read and Schreiber (1982), the latter being a revised and considerably expanded version of Read, Schreiber, and Walia (1978). Cioffi (1980) reports a study in which children are asked to identify places in a set of stimulus sentences where they might pause while reading orally. Cioffi's results are consistent with the view that children rely on prosody to signal structure. Since all these studies are convergent, a brief summary of the Read and Schreiber results will suffice here.

The experimental task involved a game called Walrus and Alligator which was played with both adults and 7-year-old children. The S was to identify a certain grammatical constituent of sentences, such as the subject noun phrase (NP). Ss were told that they would hear some sentences and be expected to repeat a certain part of the sentence. The experimenters demonstrated the game, but did not give any grammatical (or other) characterization of the part to be repeated. For example, if the target was the subject NP, one experimenter (Walrus) would say *All of our basketball players are very tall,* and the other experimenter (Alligator) would say *all of our basketball players.* After several demonstrations, Ss were told it was their turn to play Alligator and would then receive several learning trials, upon the completion of which they then proceeded to play the game. There were several versions of the game in which the target was varied; in some of these, the part of Walrus was played "live" by one of the experimenters, and in others, the Walrus part was prerecorded and played back over headphones from a Uher 4000 series monophonic tape recorder. When the target constituent was the subject NP, 7 year olds correctly identified it approximately 70% of the time (and adults almost 100%) so long as the sentence was produced with normal prosody and contained a multiword subject NP. However, when the subject NP was a single word, especially a pronoun, the children were considerably less successful; they correctly identified nonpronominal single-word subjects only 48% of the time and correctly identified single-word pronominal subjects only about 11% of the time. Adult Ss had no such difficulty, correctly identifying the single-word subjects over 90% of the time. It is notable that single-word subjects, especially pronouns, are typically not prosodically marked as terminating a major phonological phrase, so one explanation for the children's diminished success in this condition may be that in these cases they lacked sufficient cues to identify the syntactic structural unit.

To test this explanation more directly, a new version was used (with different Ss) which contained sentences with misleading prosody constructed by tape slicing. There were several types of misleading stimuli; an illustration of one of these types follows. We first taped normal pronunciations of the following sentences:

(5)　　a. *Your neighbors shovel* their sidewalk carefully.
　　　　b. *Your neighbor's shovel* got lost in the snow.

The boldface portion of (5)b was then spliced in place of the boldface portion of (5)a, producing a sentence in which the prosodic contour misleadingly suggested that *shovel* was the last word of the subject NP whereas structurally this word must be the main verb. The overall results with the several misleading types were that our 7-year-old Ss were able to correctly identify the target constituent only 30% of the time in these cases, though they continued to perform successfully (83% correct) on the interspersed prosodically normal sentences. That the children were using the prosodic cues is indicated by the fact that 78% of the children's incorrect repetitions ended where the misleading prosodic phrase terminated in the stimulus. Interestingly, the children were more likely to follow the prosody when it misleadingly suggested a boundary which came before the head noun (83% incorrect) than when it suggested a boundary later in the sentence (56% incorrect). In other words, the children were less likely to be misled by the prosody when they had already encountered a syntactically plausible subject NP. These results are consistent with the speculation of Nooteboom *et al.* (1978) cited earlier. Adult Ss performing the same task as the children were clearly much less reliant on prosody as a cue to structure; they correctly identified the target constituent 82% of the time.

The results obtained in the Walrus and Alligator experiment, which are described in Read and Schreiber (1982), as well as the results of the Kleiman *et al.* study, support the hypothesis that children rely upon prosodic cues as signals of syntactic structure. It could be argued, however, that the task in these experiments requires a type of analysis by the Ss which may be sensitive to factors different from those operative in normal language processing. Therefore, we have attempted to examine the problem with a second, different experimental technique, one that does not involve either overt or covert grammatical analysis on the part of the Ss.

The technique we have been using is the next-word probe task described in Suci, Ammon, and Gamlin (1967) and Ammon (1968). The experimental procedure involves presenting subjects with a sentence, followed shortly thereafter by a single word from the sentence. The task is to recall and repeat the word that sequentially followed the stimulus (probe) word in the sentence. The dependent measure is latency to response. Both Suci *et al.* and Ammon found striking correlations between response time (RT) and structural syntactic continuity or discontinuity, for both adults and 9 year olds. The closer two words were in terms of constituent structure, the faster the RT, and conversely: RTs for pairs consisting of an adjective modifer as probe word with its following head as target were fastest, while those for pairs consisting of the last word of the subject NP as probe and the first word of predicate phrase as target were longest. In none of the several reported experiments was prosody considered as a possible experimental factor.

A small pilot study which I conducted replicated the next-word probe task with 7 year olds and adults; the stimulus materials consisted of 11 filler sentences with normal prosody and 4 target sentences with either normal or misleading prosody, the misleading examples having been constructed by tape splicing as described previously. The most interesting of these was a sentence created by splicing the boldface part of (6)b in place of the boldface part of (6)a:

(6)   a. *The large stone blocks the road.*
        b. *The large stone blocks are on the table.*

Hence, the prosody of the resultant sentence appeared to suggest that *the large stone blocks* was the subject NP, but the syntax of the sentence clearly required this word sequence to be analyzed as an NP *the large stone* followed by the main verb *blocks*. The overall results of the pilot were that on sentences with normal prosody, the children performed much like the adult control group and also much like adults and 9 year olds in previous next-word probe experiments. However, on sentences with misleading prosody, especially the sentence created by the splicing of the examples in (6), children and adults performed differently. Children followed the prosody while adults followed the structure. Specifically, the children that heard the normal version of (6) were processing a prosodically marked syntactic transition from subject NP to the main verb of the verb phrase (VP) and produced responses whose mean latency (1.54 sec) was consistent with such a transition and similar to other observed RTs for this transition (overall mean of 1.51 sec on the N/V transition for filler sentences). The children that heard the misleading version presumably perceived the transition between *stone* and *blocks* as the one suggested by the prosody, a modifier-to-head noun transition, and produced responses whose mean latency (1.16 sec) was similar to those for other instances of this type (overall mean of 1.11 sec on A/N transition for filler sentences).

Finally, the adult control group showed essentially no difference between the normal and misleading versions: the mean RT for the misleading version of this sentence was 30 msec shorter. This suggests that whatever role prosody may play in adult speech perception, its effects, if any, are overridden very rapidly by the assignment of the structurally necessary and appropriate constitutent analysis.

The results of the pilot are encouraging, but must be approached with caution, not only because this was a pilot study, but also because the results are open to an alternative interpretation, namely, that children are responding merely prosodically. On this interpretation, children's RTs are a function only of prosodic effects such as temporal (rhythmic) patterning, and not a function of constituent structure at all. The purpose of the study described in the next section was to examine the validity of our pilot and to test the alternative interpretations.

Children's Use of Prosody: Current Work

We have been testing the alternative interpretations of our data in two ways. In one, 10 stimulus sentences have been constructed from words recorded separately in random order and spliced together under computer control with fixed intervals of 25 msec between words. These sentences thus have a neutral prosody; each word carries a rising intonation and the resulting sentences sound like a list of words. I henceforth refer to this as the LI (for list intonation) condition. If subjects are responding only to prosody in performing the next-word task, any structural differences should disappear in the LI condition.

In the other test, which I refer to as the TJ condition, mnemonically referring to Tom and Jerry, 33 stimulus sentences are used; 21 of them have normal prosody and are presented to all subjects, while the remaining 12 are the target sentences which are recorded in two versions, prosodically normal and misleading. These target sentences are randomly assigned to two subject groups, both of which receive half the target sentences with normal prosody and half with misleading prosody, the difference between the groups being which version (normal or misleading) of each sentence is presented. To illustrate, the sentences (7) and (8) occur in both normal and misleading form:

(7)   *The rusty metal piles up in dumps.*

(8)   *The red plastic sticks to the wall.*

In the normal version of (7), there is a prosodic break at *metal,* while in the misleading version, the break is at *piles* (as if *the rusty metal piles* were an NP). Similarly, in (8) the break is at *plastic* in the normal version and at *sticks* in the misleading. One group is presented the normal version of (7) and the misleading version of (8), while the other group receives the misleading version of (7) and the normal version of (8).

To explore the meaning of our previous results, the interval between the end of the sentence and the probe word was varied: in one version it occurs 250 msec after the sentences, in another version 1 sec after, and in the last version 4 sec. These varying intervals were used because there is some evidence (Massaro, 1975) that the decay of a detailed acoustic image of stimuli occurs after about 250 msec, but that the gross acoustic signal is retained for about 1 sec. Moreover, within about 250 msec after reception of linguistic input, comprehension apparently begins, as suggested by the work of Marslen-Wilson and Tyler (see, e.g., Marslen-Wilson, Tyler, & Seidenberg, 1978; Marslen-Wilson & Tyler, 1980). Hence, it is to be expected that the largest phonetic effects in processing will be seen in the short (250 msec) condition, that smaller effects might persist in the 1 sec condition, and that no such effects will occur in the 4 sec condition.

Specifically, if Ss are using prosody as a signal of syntactic structure in performing the next-word probe task, the clearest evidence of this should be found in the short-interval condition where it is predicted that Ss' RTs on prosodically misleading sentences will follow the prosodically suggested structure rather than the syntactically required one. In the longer-interval conditions, there should be little or no effects of prosody, since the stimuli will have been fully processed and comprehended; RTs in this case will be a function of the correct syntactic (and semantic) structure of the stimulus sentences. The persistence of prosodic effects over long intervals would suggest that Ss are responding merely prosodically and that they are not fully processing the stimuli in terms of the PS required to comprehend the sentence. Thus, the hypothesis that children use prosody as an initial perceptual cue to syntactic structure but that they can correctly reanalyze a structure initially misparsed because of prosody predicts that no prosodic effects will be found in the long-interval conditions.

The series of experiments described below was conducted using essentially the same design, equipment, and procedures.[2] In LI, there were two interval conditions, 1 sec and 250 msec, and, as already noted, in TJ there were three; for TJ and LI, there were also sets of simple comprehension questions which some versions contained and some did not. Of the 24 potential versions of TJ (varying prosodic set, interval, question, and order), only the no-question versions of the 4-sec interval condition were not administered at all; in later presentations, the 4-sec interval condition was omitted entirely, since it was found to produce no effect substantively different from the 1-sec condition. Because all the stimulus tapes were created under computer control, the timing of the stimuli was identical throughout except for the manipulated variable of time to probe, which was varied as already indicated.

During the actual performance of the experiment, Ss were interviewed individually and were given instructions about the nature of the task. As is usual, children were told they would be playing a game, while adults were paid volunteer college students. The stimuli were presented over headphones from a Uher 4000 series monophonic tape recorder and the responses were recorded on a Uher 4000 series stereophonic recorder. The data collected were analyzed by a Data General MicroNova minicomputer; the digitally converted data were read by a program designed to measure oral RT with an accuracy of resolution of approximately 5 msec for the data described below. Our adult subjects were all undergraduates (mostly sophomores) from the University of Wisconsin and were all native speakers of English. Our first group of child Ss were all 7 year olds from the Huegel School in an upper-middle-class neighborhood in Madison, Wisconsin. Most of the children are white; neither SES nor reading-test data were available to us, but, within the normal range of a neighborhood school, these children appeared to be relatively homogeneous, given the information we acquired. Our second group of children were 6 through 8 year olds attending Camp Shalom, a summer day camp sponsored by the Madison Jewish Community Council but open on a nondenominational basis. Again, no background information regarding the children was available to us; however, this population is clearly a more socioeconomically and culturally diverse one than that of Huegel. Only children with normal speaking and hearing were used in any of these studies.

The List Intonation (LI) Condition

We consider first the LI condition because the results indicate whether, in the absence of normal prosodic cues, children use morphological and syntactic signals of structure when performing the next-word probe task. The null hypothesis here is that RTs will not differ as a function of syntactic structure, which amounts to the claim that, in responding to stimulus materials with both normal and misleading prosodies, children are performing exclusively in accord with the prosody.

Our first Ss, the Huegel children ($n = 35$), received the 1-sec interval version of the LI list with comprehension questions. Examples of the sentences presented include the following:

(9)　　a. *I never leave toys in the kitchen.*
　　　　b. *The angry farmer kicked over the bucket.*
　　　　c. *The flowers in our yard smell wonderful.*

These illustrate structural transition points like the following: V/N, *leave toys* in (9)a; A/N, *angry farmer* in (9)b; N/V, *farmer kicked* in (9)b; and PN/V, *yard smell* in (9)c. As these examples indicate, V/N is the transition between a main verb and the object noun, A/N between a prenominal adjective and the head noun it modifies, and N/V between the head noun of the subject and the main verb. PN/V represents the transition between an embedded prepositional object noun and the main verb. For the Huegel children, the mean RTs obtained on the first three of these transition types showed the same pattern as those obtained in previous research where prosodic factors were not specifically controlled, including, specifically, the results of Suci *et al.* The A/N transition is the fastest, the V/N is next, and the N/V is slowest. The actual means correspond fairly closely in fact to those reported in Suci *et al.*

The results from the embedded prepositional phrases were interesting and deserve more extensive discussion than would be appropriate here. Briefly, however, the RTs for these embedded constructions were longer than most and produced more errors or failures to respond than normal. The overall mean RT for the combined A/N, N/V, and V/N transitions was 1.29 sec; moreover, there were never fewer than 30 correct responses for any of these. The data for the embedded constructions have a different profile: the mean RT for the PN/V transition was 2.10 sec, with 28 correct responses. These data support the notion that in performing the next-word probe task, children are sensitive to syntactic structure independently of prosody; these effects would be predicted by a model of speech production and comprehension in which the branching depth of a constituent in a PS representation determines (in part) aspects of speech behavior (see, e.g., Cooper & Paccia-Cooper, 1980).

That is, if part of the definition of what constitutes perceptual complexity involves the hierarchical organization of syntactic structures as given in PS representations, the data fall into place. Overall, then, the results on the LI condition justify asserting that, in performing the next-word probe task, children are not responding merely to prosody.

The mean RTs for the 45 adult Ss who were presented with the 1-sec version of the LI condition were consistently faster than those of the children, but the pattern is generally the same as the children's. The adults' N/V transition was about one-third longer than the A/N transition, and adult RTs to the PN/V transition are substantially longer than those for other transitions, just as were the children's. Hence, while adults' performance in the LI condition reveals smaller structural differentiations for certain of the transitions, clear distinctions are nonetheless made.

A small number of Shalom Ss also performed the LI task. However, because of equipment failure, more than half the data were lost, including all cases where comprehension questions were used. The data that were obtained, however, were generally consistent with the Huegel data.

The Misleading Prosody Condition

Predictions. The LI condition demonstrates that children are not responding only to prosodic cues in performing the next-word probe task. The next question is whether they do, however, make use of such cues when they are available as potential signals of structure. To examine this, we employed the 33-sentence TJ list comprised of 21 filler sentences and 12 target sentences, the latter containing six N/V transitions and six A/N. As indicated above, each subject heard half these target sentences with normal prosody and half with misleading prosody created by computer tape splicing. Thus any given subject heard 27 sentences with normal prosody and 6 with subtly misleading prosody. The Huegel and adult Ss received the 1- or the 4-sec interval versions of TJ with comprehension questions. Thus, there were eight subject groups determined by task: two orders × two intervals × two sets of prosodically misleading (PM) sentences. The Shalom Ss were given the 1-sec or the 250-msec interval versions, again in two orders and with the same two sets of PM stimuli. Half the Shalom Ss were given comprehension questions and half were not.

If prosody functions as a signal of structure, the following effects would be expected in performance on TJ. First, of course, we would expect no significant effects on the filler sentences. On the prosodically normal (henceforth OK) versions of the target sentences, no effects are also predicted, though given the local ambiguity in the N/V targets, RTs might be somewhat longer than in simpler unambiguous structures. On the PM versions of the A/N targets, RTs longer than on the OK versions are predicted, while on the PM versions of the N/V targets, RTs shorter than on the OK versions are predicted. The reasons for these predictions on the PM targets are as follows. In the A/N targets, the prosody mis-leadingly suggests a structural break between the adjective and the following noun, a break like that between, say, an introductory adverbial phrase and a main clause. For example, the PM version of sentence (10)a below was created by splicing in the boldface segment of sentence (10)b in place of the boldface segment of (10)a:

(10)　a. *A drink of* **cold lemonade tastes good.**
　　　b. *When it is* **cold, lemonade tastes good.**

Hence, there is a prosodic break after the adjective *cold* in the PM version of (10)a misleadingly suggesting a major syntactic boundary. In the N/V targets, on the other hand, the prosody misleadingly suggests that the head noun of the subject phrase is a modifier of the following word, a verb which is homophonous with a plural noun. For example, the PM version of sentence (11)a below was created by splicing the boldface segment of sentence (11)b in place of the boldface segment of (11)a:

(11)　a. **The large stone blocks** *the main road.*
　　　b. **The large stone blocks** *are on the table.*

In the recorded PM version, there is thus no prosodic break between subject and predicate; in the OK version, the prosodic break does fall here. If Ss use prosodic cues to structure, then, the PM version should elicit faster RTs than the OK, since A/N transitions are generally faster than N/V.

We also expect, however, that the main effect of prosody will interact with other variables, especially time to probe and presence of comprehension question. As to the latter, Aaronson and Scarborough (1976) have demonstrated that differential effects of surface syntactic structure are most prominent when Ss are performing a simple recall task, and that when Ss perform a comprehension task, constituent structure effects are greatly diminished. Regarding the interval to the probe, as suggested earlier, there is considerable evidence that on-line processing is extremely rapid, and that normal sentences are generally comprehended within approximately 250 msec of completion of their presentation. As also noted earlier, there is evidence that the detailed acoustic image of a sentence is normally lost from memory after about 250 msec. As a consequence of these several factors, it is predicted that the largest effect of misleading prosody should appear in versions where the time to probe is 250 msec and where no comprehension question is presented.

Results. Turning now to the results obtained thus far, we observe that the mean RTs on the filler sentences have a profile similar to that of the LI condition for the Huegel and Shalom Ss (except for anomalously long RTs on transitions between V and immediately following direct object N: mean RT for all the child Ss across all conditions of 1.63 sec); the adult RTs have the same shape as the children's but are, as usual, faster. An additional pecularity of the adult data is that RTs for the N/V transition are virtually the same as those for the A/N transition. For all Ss, the PN/V (prepositional object noun to verb) transitions again elicit very long RTs. These are particularly interesting because the times cannot be accounted for by transitional probabilities between specific lexical items, since the same items also occur in another set of sentences containing what we called a N/VX transition. That is, Ss heard each of the following two PN/V and N/VX pairs, where the word in parentheses after each sentence is the probe word for that sentence:

(12)   a. *The string on my balloon started slipping. (balloon)*
        b. *My balloon started getting smaller and smaller. (balloon)*
(13)   a. *The book on that table looks interesting. (table)*
        b. *That table looks ugly in this room. (table)*

The PN/V transition in the first member of each pair elicits RTs much longer than those for the same lexical transitions in the second or N/VX member. The important point here is that the effect is apparently a structural one.

The data thus far generally support the view that the PS of the stimulus sentence determines RTs. We now turn to the target sentences and ask whether prosody is implicated in performance of the task and, by extension, in normal processing. The arrays in Table 8.1 represent the contrast between PM and OK versions of sentences with N/V and A/N transitions for all three subject groups. NV1 and NV2 refer to the two subgroups of target N/V sentences; each individual S was presented one of these subgroups in the PM version and the other subgroup in the OK version. The same pattern holds for AN1 and AN2. The Huegel and adult data are averaged across both orders of presentation, and across 1- and 4-sec intervals. Though there were some interactions among these factors, they did not bear on the OK versus PM comparison. (There were also no consistent sex or age differences within groups.) The Shalom data are averaged across 1-sec and 250-msec intervals, across orders of presentation, and across comprehension or no comprehension question. Inspection of the table shows no clear patterns revealed in these data.

It seems safe to conclude, based on the adult and Huegel results, that with time-to-probe intervals of 1 sec or greater, no consistent prosodic effects can be found with either children or adults performing this task.

Though the Shalom data in Table 8.1 seem equally unrevealing, interesting features begin to emerge when we conduct a more fine-grained examination of them. Specifically, if we compare results that take account of interval (250 msec versus 1 sec) and question or no question (Q versus NQ), prosodic effects surface.[3] Still averaging across orders, ages, and sexes, we find in the 250-msec NQ condition a clear difference in the predicted direction. The full set of Shalom data is presented in the two-way table of means given in Table 8.2. For the N/V and for the A/N sets, the results here are averaged across the two subgroups of target sentences. The difference between RTs in the 250 msec NQ cell all follow the predicted direction. One of the differences between mean RTs follows the predicted direction in both the 250-msec Q cell and the 1-sec NQ cell, though in the latter the difference is clearly very small. Finally, in the 1-sec Q cell, neither of the differences goes in the predicted direction.

Even with the small n, ANOVAs demonstrate that the difference of means between PM and OK in N/V is significant ($F = 17.28$; d.f. $= 1,4$; $p < .02$). The difference of means between PM and OK in A/N does not reach significance ($F = 2.09$; d.f. $= 1,5$; $p > .20$), presumably because of

TABLE 8.1
Mean RTs for Target N/V and A/N Transitions
across All Conditions for All Groups

	Adult ($n = 48$)		Huegel ($n = 51$)		Shalom ($n = 31$)	
	OK[a]	PM[b]	OK	PM	OK	PM
NV1	1.32	1.16	1.71	2.02	1.60	1.98
NV2	1.33	1.34	1.85	1.74	1.61	1.58
Total mean	1.32	1.25	1.78	1.89	1.61	1.81
AN1	1.21	1.31	1.46	1.75	1.30	1.35
AN2	1.00	0.92	1.55	1.36	1.52	1.55
Total mean	1.10	1.12	1.51	1.55	1.41	1.46

[a] Prosodically normal.
[b] Prosodically misleading.

the small n; transforming the data improves matters slightly, but the evidence remains weak. At this point, we can say only that the A/N result in the 250-msec NQ condition is consistent with the hypothesis; if the difference here persists with a larger n (say, 10 or more), the outcome will also be significant.

Finally, we tested adults on the 250-msec NQ condition. The results show only very marginal prosodic effects. Where the Shalom children overall showed a 263-msec difference of means in the predicted direction (that is, faster for PM than OK) in N/V, the adults ($n = 32$) showed only a 24-msec difference in the same direction: adult mean for OK = 1.187 sec and for PM = 1.163 sec. And where 75% of the children ($n = 8$) had faster mean RTs for PM than OK in N/V, only 56% of the adults ($n = 32$) did. The A/N comparison is less clear-cut. Where the children showed a group difference of 79 msec in the predicted direction (slower for PM than OK), the adults showed a 39-msec difference in the same direction.

TABLE 8.2

Two-Way Table of Means over PM and OK Stratified by Times to Probe and Comprehension Question for Shalom Ss ($N = 36$)

	No comprehension question	Comprehension question	Total	
	10	7	17	n
	1.535	2.073	1.727	mean NV (PM)
	.4979	.9673	.7154	SD
	1.798	1.456	1.676	mean NV (OK)
	.6575	.2313	.5579	SD
250 msec				
	1.671	1.419	1.593	mean AN (PM)
	.4437	.5792	.4793	SD
	1.592	1.262	1.468	mean AN (OK)
	.8281	.1754	.6699	SD
	13	6	19	n
	1.827	1.986	1.888	mean NV (PM)
	.5456	1.8386	1.1432	SD
	1.583	1.453	1.536	mean NV (OK)
	.3911	.5154	.4242	SD
1 sec				
	1.379	1.272	1.345	mean AN (PM)
	.6334	.4856	.5771	SD
	1.349	1.310	1.339	mean AN (OK)
	.4162	.3426	.3863	SD

And where 78% of the children ($n = 9$) had slower mean RTs for PM than OK in A/N, only 61% of the adults ($n = 31$) did. Not surprisingly, the adult data do not show any statistically significant effects; for the difference of means between PM and OK in N/V, the F value is 1.02 (d.f. = 1, 28), and for the difference in A/N, the F value is 1.32 (d.f. = 1, 27).

Interpretation. Given the outcome of these experiments, we now have some empirical evidence for the predictions made earlier regarding the expected pattern of results among the several conditions. While the following explanation is in part speculative, the profile of the data suggests that children use prosody as an initial primary perceptual cue for structural segmentation (hence the results on the 250-msec NQ condition), but that, beyond the level of the initial syntactic percept, they use other, more abstract structural signals and strategies for processing and comprehension.

In the 250-msec NQ condition, the children need mainly attend to the superficial organization of the sentence and so their RTs reflect a quite shallow level of processing. In the Q condition, since they are aware that they must comprehend the sentence and be able to answer a question about it, their level of processing is necessarily somewhat deeper, so that their RTs reflect surface features less sharply. Similarly, in the 1-sec condition, even with attention primarily focused on superficial details, they must fully encode the sentence in order to be able to identify the next word (recall that after about a quarter-second, the detailed acoustic image of the sentence decays and subsequent recall must be based on an encoded, i.e., fully processed, representation); thus again the RTs reflect the phonetic properties less directly. Finally, the convergence of the 1-sec and Q conditions produce the most unfavorable situation (within this fourfold set of conditions) for phonetic effects of the input signal to play a role. Note also that Kempen (1976) has argued that, over relatively long intervals, the syntactic boundary effect found in probe RTs should be viewed as a reflection of sentence production rather than as a storage (let alone a perception) effect. The outcome on the 1-sec Q condition is quite consistent with this claim, while the outcome on the 250-msec NQ condition is clearly not.

In light of the observations in the preceding paragraph, a further (partly methodological) question remains: if prosodic effects on the next-word probe task are manifested only under short time-to-probe intervals with no comprehension question, why did prosodic effects occur in the Walrus–Alligator game described earlier? Again, at this point one can only speculate; however, it is reasonable to suppose that the answer has to do with the metalinguistic character of the task in Walrus–Alligator.

Specifically, that task requires Ss to engage in a type of conscious analysis of the stimulus sentences; this may demand so much of children's capacity that they are (in part) unable to engage in full processing of the sentence and must rely more heavily on the primary acoustic cues. The outcomes may also be a function of task-specific factors; in the next-word probe, we measure RTs, while in Walrus–Alligator, we measure rate of success in (conscious) segmentation.

DISCUSSION

The results of our next-word probe experiments are encouraging; they support the general hypothesis, adopted on the basis of earlier experiments using the Walrus–Alligator paradigm, that children are especially sensitive to prosodic signals of syntactic structure. Moreover, these results, and the hypothesis they support, suggest a conclusion consistent with other research (e.g., Read, 1975), in which young language learners are found to be particularly attuned to the surface phonetic facts of language. Further, the results lend indirect evidence for the model of syntax acquisition outlined by Gleitman and Wanner (1982), who suggest that prosodic marking provides phrase boundary cues of great value in learning the syntactic rules of a language for "an infant who is innately biased to treat intonationally circumscribed utterance segments as potential syntactic constituents" (p. 26).

Our present results must be interpreted cautiously, however. For one thing, the children's n is small. Moreover, we cannot yet make definitive claims concerning the relative salience of prosody for adults performing this task; though the number of adult Ss was fairly large and the results nonsignificant for the 250-msec interval in both N/V and A/N, there was a small tendency for adult responses to follow the prosody. Perhaps at yet shorter intervals, the adult pattern would be more like that of the children. Therefore, it is still premature to suggest that our results confirm the previous finding that children are more sensitive to surface phonetic signals of structure than are adults. Perhaps adults' processing is simply much faster than children's. However, the data at present support the main hypothesis.

The research described above has been explicitly directed toward investigating oral language. However, it appears to have implications for written language as well, particularly with respect to the acquisition of reading fluency. Since these issues have been discussed at some length elsewhere (Schreiber, 1980; see also Snow & Coots, 1981, for similar observations) a summary here will suffice.

It is clear that, in order to attain reading fluency, a beginning reader who has (at least partially) mastered decoding skills must minimally learn to group words into appropriate syntactic phrases. This assertion is supported by a substantial body of evidence (Cromer, 1970; Golinkoff, 1975–1976; Levin, 1979; Coots & Snow, 1981). Research using the eye–voice span, for instance, points unequivocally to the syntactic phrase as a fundamental reading unit for skilled readers (Levin, 1979). Gibson and Levin (1975, p. 390) suggest that "children start taking advantage of grammatical structure sometime between the second and fourth grades." They also propose, as a plausible speculation, that part of the distinction between fluent and nonfluent readers derives from the ability to segment written sentences into "syntactically critical units such as phrases" (p. 379). Using the model of reading acquisition presented in LaBerge and Samuels (1974) and Samuels (1979), we can now view the issue as follows: How do students move from the second of Samuels's three stages in reading fluency acquisition to the third, where the former is the accuracy stage at which readers can accurately recognize printed words but must devote attention to the decoding process, while the latter is the automaticity stage at which readers can decode text automatically (i.e., without attention) thereby leaving attention free for comprehension?

If it is true that a primary cue to such chunking (for children) is the prosody of the sentence, it follows that the stage-two reader must learn to rely more heavily on morphological and abstract syntactic cues (and the strategies that are based on these cues) to assign a syntactically appropriate parsing to the written sentence. The reason is that graphic signals do not correspond systematically to the prosodic cues of spoken language; specifically, punctuation does not divide sentences into phrases as clearly and consistently in writing as prosody does in speech where a major sign of which words go together to form syntactically and semantically coherent phrases is the prosodic contour binding a series of words together. Hence, stage-two readers must tacitly come to recognize the need to compensate for the absence of graphic signals corresponding to the prosodic cues and must make better use of the morphological and syntactic cues that are preserved in order to move to automaticity.

If this account is correct, it would suggest that the problem of "word calling" is due to a failure to recognize this need. It also suggests a rationale for the success of certain proposed techniques of instruction that are intended to solve the word-calling problem, notably Samuels's (1979) method of repeated readings as well as the technique proposed by C. Chomsky (1978), both of which have the effect of forcing stage-two readers to begin to recognize the kinds of syntactic phrasing necessary to make sense of the reading materials. The recognition comes about as the readers become more aware of the syntactic, semantic, morphological, and contextual features which are found in the written form and which correspond to features that they do, to a greater or lesser extent, use in aural processing. Once this tacit recognition takes place, the step toward fluency is more than half complete.

While the claims of the preceding two paragraphs are difficult to test directly, there is now some interesting indirect evidence for them in a study by Dowhower (1986). The relevance of these results is discussed in detail in Schreiber (1986). Here, a few brief comments will have to suffice. Dowhower compares the effects of unassisted repeated reading and assisted (orally modelled) repeated reading treatments on normal children in transition from Samuels's stage two to stage three (fluency). A comparison of the two groups on measures such as reading rate, word accuracy, and comprehension shows that, while there are few individually statistically significant contrasts, there is a clear tendency overall for the assisted group to show faster or greater increases in fluency than the unassisted. Further, Dowhower also examines a variety of indicators of so-called prosodic reading, including absence of inappropriate pausal intrusions, appropriate use of phrase-final lengthening, and variations in terminal pitch rise–fall patterns. As is the case with measures of fluency, though there are not many statistically significant differences between the groups, there is a strong tendency overall for the assisted group to give prosodically more appropriate oral readings than the unassisted group. The full array of results indirectly supports the very general model of fluency acquisition suggested above.

One final point deserves some mention, though it cannot be adequately addressed. Throughout we have assumed that a reliance on prosody is characteristic of children, whereas adults typically are less dependent on superficial phonetic cues. Hence, there is an implicit developmental assumption underlying this account. It would be interesting to test the assumption that reliance on prosody is indeed developmental; it is by no means inconceivable that the adults' use of more abstract syntactic strategies is in part a function or perhaps a consequence of literacy itself. One way to test this issue would be to examine the performance of adult illiterates on tasks that are sensitive to prosody. Should it turn out that their performance is like that of children on these tasks, that would present prima facie evidence for a striking effect of literacy on language-processing strategies. Alternatively, the developmental story might be confirmed. In either case, we would have a significant insight into the workings of the human language faculty. (This way of examining the developmental question is suggested by the approach of Read (1985, 1986) in studies of phonological segmentation skills among children, literate adults, and illiterate adults.)

Having raised the developmental issue, we may briefly note here that it stimulates a further question: By what process do adults lose their reliance on prosodic (and other concrete phonetic) features? Though the question is still premature (and is also tangential to the concerns of this chapter), a speculation may not be out of order. Children acquiring the vast and complex system that is their language need all the help they can get; as Read and Schreiber (1982) and Gleitman and Wanner (1982) suggest, the kinds of overt cues that prosody provides may constitute a "bootstrap" device that allows children to get into the system, offering crucial signals for phrasal segmentation, for instance. But once the full system has been acquired, the need for reliance on these surface cues diminishes; adult linguistic competence is knowledge of a highly abstract symbolic system, and the linguistic performance (speech behavior such as processing) that relies on this competence appears to be implemented via a set of abstract processing strategies whose rapidity and flexibility are in part the consequence of not being dependent on detailed analysis of concrete features of the speech signal. Hence, once the full system of linguistic knowledge is acquired, the dependence on surface cues declines in language processing.

CONCLUSION

The experimental results reviewed in this chapter have been interpreted as evidence supporting the hypothesis that children use prosodic cues as a primary set of devices for initial perceptual processing of the syntactic structure of speech. We have suggested that children's reliance on these cues, moreover, accounts for an important difficulty that many students have in acquiring reading fluency, and we have offered a partial rationale for the success of certain remediation techniques. Finally, we have noted some developmental issues that go well beyond the specific concerns of this chapter, touching at least on the fundamental character of language acquisition.

Many important questions, of course, remain: For example, which specific prosodic features are particularly salient to children? Is the effect of prosody equally robust in complex structures of a sort we have not yet investigated? Can exaggerated prosody facilitate—and inadequate prosody retard—the acquisition of structures? Moreover, none of our research has explored the role of prosodic cues in discourse level processing; as one obvious example, it would be most interesting to examine whether there are characteristic and systematic prosodic signals of "paragraph structure." That is, do speakers distinguish prosodically in some reliable fashion between otherwise identical sentences depending on whether they occur paragraph-finally or not? But though these and many other questions are still open, the outcome of the research so far is clearly relevant not only to theoreticians but also to those in the educational frontlines, because children in just the age range we have been studying are beginning the crucially important early stages of school instruction in a skill of paramount importance, reading.

NOTES

[1] It should be noted that Wales and Toner's own initial hypothesis is that "in general, intonation cannot be used to reliably select both readings of ambiguous sentences" (p. 137). They take their overall results as supporting the conclusion that "there is no direct interaction between syntax and intonation" (p. 153). While this claim is confirmed for deep structure syntax, I believe it is, on the basis of their own evidence, disconfirmed at least for certain types of surface structure configuration. It would, however, take us too far afield to describe the reasons for my contention.

[2] Persons interested in receiving an appendix with a more detailed description of the research materials and methods for the next-word probe experiments discussed in this chapter should write to Peter A. Schreiber, English Department, University of Wisconsin, Madison, Madison, WI 53706.

[3] Recall here, and in the discussion that follows, the distinction Aaronson and Scarborough make between coding strategies used in performing recall tasks and comprehension tasks. In the experiment they conducted, the effects of surface structure were substantial in the former but minimal in the latter. Their experimental results were based on written language stimuli, but since prosody is a cue to surface structure, one would predict that the effects of misleading prosody would also be reduced in a comprehension task with oral stimuli, if their finding has cross-modal applicability. Our results suggest clearly that it does. At the same time, however, there is now evidence that calls into question Aaronson and Scarborough's interpretation of their results: See Schreiber, Stowe, & Williams, 1986.

ACKNOWLEDGMENTS

The research reported in this chapter was funded by the Wisconsin Center for Education Research through a grant from the National Institute of Education (Grant No. NIE-G-81-0009). The opinions expressed in this paper do not necessarily reflect the position, policy, or endorsement of NIE. I wish to thank my research assistants, Carol Graham, Laurie Stowe, Ann Albuyeh, and Richard Williams, for their important contributions to the work. I am also grateful to Clifford Gillman from the Waisman Center on Mental Retardation and Human Development and to Charles Read from the Linguistics Department for help in preparing the stimulus recordings and analyzing the response recordings. I also wish to acknowledge the help of Jacob Evanson from the Wisconsin Center for

Education Research in performing statistical analysis. Finally, thanks to the principals, teachers, and students of the Crestwood and Huegel Elementary Schools in Madison, Wisconsin, and to the directors, counselors, and campers of Camp Shalom in Madison for helping us to conduct the experiments.

REFERENCES

Aaronson, D., & Scarborough, H. S. (1976). Performance theories for sentence coding: Some quantitative evidence. *Journal of Experimental Psychology: Human Perception and Performance, 2,* 56–70.

Ammon, P. R. (1968). The perception of grammatical relations in sentences: A methodological exploration. *Journal of Verbal Learning and Verbal Behavior, 7,* 869–875.

Bever, T. G. (1970). The cognitive basis for linguistic structures. In J. R. Hayes (Ed.), *Cognition and the development of language.* New York: Wiley.

Chomsky, C. (1978). When you still can't read in third grade: After decoding, what? In S. J. Samuels (Ed.), *What research has to say about reading instruction.* Newark, DE: International Reading Association.

Chomsky, N. (1957). *Syntactic structures.* The Hague: Mouton.

Chomsky, N. (1965). *Aspects of the theory of syntax.* Cambridge, MA: MIT Press.

Chomsky, N. (1981). *Lectures on government and binding.* Dordrecht, The Netherlands: Foris.

Chomsky, N. (1986). *Barriers.* Cambridge, MA: MIT Press.

Cioffi, G. (1980, October). *The perception of sentence structure by good comprehenders and skilled decoders in contextually limited environments.* Paper presented at the Boston University Fifth Annual Conference on Language Development, Boston.

Cooper, W. E., & Paccia-Cooper, J. (1980). *Syntax and speech.* Cambridge, MA: Harvard University Press.

Cooper, W. E., Paccia, J. M., & Lapointe, S. G. (1978). Hierarchical coding in speech timing. *Cognitive Psychology, 10,* 154–177.

Cooper, W. E., & Sorensen, J. M. (1981). *Fundamental frequency in speech production.* New York: Springer-Verlag.

Coots, J. H., & Snow, D. P. (1981). *Comprehension skills and text organization ability in reading* (Tech. Note 2-81/11). Los Alamitos, CA: Southwest Regional Laboratory.

Cromer, W. (1970). The difference model: A new explanation for some reading difficulties. *Journal of Educational Psychology, 61,* 471–483.

Crystal, D. (1975). *The English tone of voice.* London: Arnold and New York: Springer-Verlag.

Darwin, C. J. (1975). On the dynamic use of prosody in speech perception. In A. Cohen and S. G. Nooteboom (Eds.), *Structure and process in speech perception.* Berlin/Heidelberg/New York: Springer-Verlag.

Dooling, D. J. (1974). Rhythm and syntax in sentence perception. *Journal of Verbal Learning and Verbal Behavior, 13,* 255–264.

Dowhower, S. L. (1986). *Effect of repeated reading on selected second graders' oral reading and comprehension.* Unpublished doctoral dissertation, University of Wisconsin, Madison.

Epstein, W. (1961). The influence of syntactical structure on learning. *American Journal of Psychology, 74,* 80–85.

Fodor, J. A., & Bever, T. G. (1965). The psychological reality of linguistic segments. *Journal of Verbal Learning and Verbal Behavior, 4,* 414–420.

Frazier, L., & Fodor, J. D. (1978). The sausage machine: A new two-stage parsing model. *Cognition, 6,* 291–325.

Gibson, E. J., & Levin, H. (1975). *The psychology of reading.* Cambridge, MA: MIT Press.

Gleitman, L., & Wanner, E. (1982). Language acquisition: The state of the state of art. In E. Wanner & L. Gleitman (Eds.), *Language acquisition: The state of the art.* London: Cambridge University Press, 1982.

Golinkoff, R. (1975–1976). A comparison of reading comprehension processes in good and poor comprehenders. *Reading Research Quarterly, 11,* 623–659.

Jackendoff, R. (1977). X̄-syntax: A study of phrase structure. *Linguistic Inquiry Monograph, 2.*

Jacobson, P., & Pullum, G. (Eds.). (1982). *The nature of syntactic representation.* Dordrecht, The Netherlands: Reidel.

Jarvella, R. (1971). Syntactic processing of connected speech. *Journal of Verbal Learning and Verbal Behavior, 4,* 469–475.

Johnson, N. F. (1965). The psychological reality of phrase structure rules. *Journal of Verbal Learning and Verbal Behavior, 4,* 469–475.

Johnson, N. F. (1966). On the relationship between sentence structure and the latency in generating the sentence. *Journal of Verbal Learning and Verbal Behavior, 5,* 375–380.

Kempen, G. (1976). Syntactic constructions as retrieval plans. *British Journal of Psychology, 67,* 149–160.

Kimball, J. P. (1973). Seven principles of surface structure parsing. *Cognition, 2,* 15–47.

Klatt, D. H. (1975). Vowel lengthening is syntactically determined in a connected discourse. *Journal of Phonetics, 3,* 129–140.

Kleiman, G. M., Winograd, P. N., & Humphrey, M. N. (1979). *Prosody and children's parsing of sentences* (Tech. Rep. No. 123). Urbana- Champaign, IL: University of Illinois, Center for the Study of Reading.

LaBerge, D., & Samuels, S. J. (1974). Toward a theory of automatic information processing in reading. *Cognitive Psychology, 6,* 293–323.

Lashley, J. S. (1951). The problem of serial order in behavior. In L. A. Jeffress (Ed.), *Cerebral mechanisms in behavior.* New York: Wiley.

Lehiste, I., Olive, J. P., & Streeter, L. A. (1976). Role of duration in disambiguating syntactically ambiguous sentences. *Journal of the Acoustical Society of America, 60,* 1199–1202.

Levelt, W. J. M. (1978). A survey of studies in sentence perception: 1970–1976. In W. J. M. Levelt & G. B. Flores d'Arcais (Eds.), *Studies in the perception of language.* New York: Wiley.

Levelt, W. J. M., Zwanenburg, W., & Ouweneel, G. R. (1970). Ambiguous surface structure and phonetic form in French. *Foundations of Language, 6,* 260–273.

Levin, H. (1979). *The eye–voice span.* Cambridge, MA: MIT Press.

Marcus, M. P. (1980). *A theory of syntactic recognition for natural languages.* Cambridge, MA: MIT Press.

Marslen-Wilson, W., & Tyler, L. K. (1980). The temporal structure of spoken language understanding. *Cognition, 8,* 1–71.

Marslen-Wilson, W., Tyler, L. K., & Seidenberg, M. (1978). Sentence processing and the clause boundary. In W. J. M. Levelt & G. B. Flores d'Arcais (Eds.), *Studies in the perception of language.* New York: Wiley.

Martin, J. G. (1972). Rhythmic (hierarchical) versus serial structure in speech and other behavior. *Psychological Review, 79,* 487–509.

Martin, J. G. (1975). Rhythmic expectancy in continuous speech perception. In A. Cohen & S. G. Nooteboom (Eds.), *Structure and process in speech perception.* New York: Springer-Verlag.

Massaro, D. W. (1975). Perceptual images, processing time, and perceptual units in speech perception. In D. W. Massaro (Ed.), *Understanding language: An information-processing analysis of speech perception, reading, and psycholinguistics*. New York: Academic Press.

Neisser, U. (1967). *Cognitive psychology*. New York: Appleton.

Nooteboom, S. G., Brokx, J. P. L., & de Rooij, J. J. (1978). Contributions of prosody to speech perception. In W. J. M. Levelt & G. B. Flores d'Arcais (Eds.), *Studies in the perception of language*. New York: Wiley.

Read, C. (1975). *Children's categorization of speech sounds in English*. Urbana, IL: National Council of Teachers of English.

Read, C. (1985). Reading and spelling skills in adults of low literacy. *Remedial and Special Education, 6*, 43–52.

Read, C. (1986). *Children's creative spelling*. London: Routledge and Kegan Paul.

Read, C., & Schreiber, P. (1982). Why short subjects are harder to find than long ones. In E. Wanner & L. Gleitman (Eds.), *Language acquisition: The state of the art*. London: Cambridge University Press.

Read, C., Schreiber, P., & Walia, J. (1978). *Why short subjects are harder to find than long ones* (Tech. Rep. No. 466). Madison, WI: University of Wisconsin, Wisconsin Research and Development Center for Individualized Schooling (now Wisconsin Center for Education Research).

Rommetveit, R., & Turner, E. (1967). A study of "chunking" in transmission of sentences. *Lingua, 18*, 337–351.

Samuels, S. J. (1979). The method of repeated readings. *Reading Teacher, 32*, 403–408.

Schreiber, P. A. (1980). On the acquisition of reading fluency. *Journal of Reading Behavior, 12*, 177–186.

Schreiber, P. A. (1986). *On the role of prosody in children's syntactic processing* (Program Report 86–11). Madison, WI: Wisconsin Center for Education Research.

Schreiber, P. A., & Read, C. (1980). Children's use of phonetic cues in spelling, parsing, and—maybe—reading. *Bulletin of the Orton Society, 30*, 209–224.

Schreiber, P. A., Stowe, L., & Williams, R. (1986). *Syntactic processing: Comprehension and recall*. Madison, WI: Wisconsin Center for Education Research.

Snow, D. P., & Coots, J. H. (1981). *Sentence perception in listening and reading* (Tech. Note 2-81/15). Los Alamitos, CA: Southwest Regional Laboratory.

Streeter, L. A. (1978). Acoustic determinants of phrase boundary perception. *Journal of the Acoustical Society of America, 64*, 1582–1592.

Suci, G. J., Ammon, P., & Gamlin, P. (1967). The validity of the probe-latency technique for assessing structure in language. *Language and Speech, 10*, 69–80.

Trager, G. L., & Smith, H. L., Jr. (1951). *An outline of English structure, Studies in Linguistics, Occasional Papers 3*. (Reprinted Washington, DC: American Council of Learned Societies, 1957).

Wales, R., & Toner, H. (1979). Intonation and ambiguity. In W. E. Cooper & E. C. T. Walker (Eds.), *Sentence processing: Psycholinguistic studies presented to Merrill F. Garrett*. Hillsdale, NJ: Erlbaum.

Wanner, E., & Maratsos, M. (1978). An ATN approach to comprehension. In M. Halle, J. Bresnan, & G. A. Miller (Eds.), *Linguistic theory and psychological reality*. Cambridge, MA: MIT Press.

Wells, R. S. (1947). Immediate constituents. *Language, 23*, 81–117.

Wingfield, A., & Klein, J. F. (1971). Syntactic structure and acoustic pattern in speech perception. *Perception & Psychophysics, 9*, 23–25.

Chapter 9

Processing Strategies for Reading and Listening

Joseph H. Danks
Laurel J. End

INTRODUCTION

Historically, linguists have considered speech as the primary form of language and writing as secondary. Reading and writing are parasitic on listening and speaking. For example, Fries claimed that

> learning to read . . . is *not* a process of learning new or other language signals than those the child has already learned. . . . The process of learning to read is the process of transfer from the auditory signs for language signals which the child has already learned, to the new visual signs for the same signals. (Fries, 1963, p. xv).

This view assumes that the reader converts print to a form compatible with listening processes. The previously acquired listening processes then take over for comprehension. If this view is accurate, then all reading teachers need to be concerned about is teaching the child how to convert print to an auditory form.

This view has been challenged as research on reading processes has gained parity with research on listening. Differences between listening and reading processes may extend beyond the initial processing stages of speech and print. The comprehension processes by which meaning is constructed, although closely related, may differ because of fundamental differences in printed texts and oral discourse. If this view holds true, then reading instruction has an additional task of teaching children new comprehension strategies as well. Thus, comparison of listening and reading bears on psycholinguistic conceptions of language processing as well as on reading instruction.

When comparing listening and reading, what exactly should we compare? There are a variety of answers to this question depending on one's interests: Researchers who are interested in whether the final comprehension product is the same in both cases compare some sort of comprehension behavior following listening and reading. Those researchers who are concerned with the comparative advantages of the two modalities examine whether information transmission is more efficient, easier, or more precise in one modality than the other. Our approach is different from either of these. Our interest in comparing listening and reading is to determine whether the cognitive processes triggered by listening and reading tasks are the same, similar, or different, and how these processes are related to one another. Implications both for theory and for instruction can be drawn most accurately when we understand the underlying processes.

The thesis of this chapter is that listening and reading can be both similar and different processes. They are different to the extent that the two modalities impose different demands on the cognitive processing system. So, for example, the fact that readers in general have the opportunity to reread portions of the text and listeners cannot "relisten" means that listeners have to make decisions about meaning based on different information than do readers. Listening and reading processes are similar to the extent that listening and reading tasks make similar cognitive demands. For example, both listeners and readers use their knowledge of syntactic structure to aid in constructing meanings for sentences because both speech and print use the same core grammar. However, other factors may impose cognitive demands that result in greater variation in the comprehension processes than does input modality, in which case, the similarities and differences in listening and reading may be masked.

Our approach here is based on several assumptions about cognitive processes in general, and language processes in particular. A principal assumption is that both listening and reading are composed of several component processes; that is, there is not a single, holistic process that underlies listening and reading either separately or jointly. Rather, processing components are organized in a more-or-less efficient way to accomplish the task facing the comprehender. How these processing components are organized is a matter of considerable concern among many theorists. The emerging opinion is that these components operate interactively, but the precise nature of this interaction is not entirely clear (see the papers in Lesgold & Perfetti, 1981; Flores d'Arcais & Jarvella, 1983).

A second assumption of our analysis is that listening and reading comprehension processes are flexible and adaptable. The overall process can be altered, for example, by emphasizing different processing components, by modifying the internal operation of a specific component, or by reordering or restructuring the components within the whole. What sorts of factors initiate these changes and determine the type of change? The most prominent are differences in the specific task, differences in the form and the content of the text, and differences between individual comprehenders. These factors can be grouped into two classes—cognitive demands and cognitive skills.

Cognitive demands are the requirements imposed on the comprehender by the task, the text materials, and, we would argue, by the input modality, speech or print. The task requirements result in specific demands on the cognitive system to produce certain types of information that will satisfy the task requirements, for example, the purpose comprehenders have in processing text. If readers are looking for an answer to a specific question, they may sample some portions of the text superficially. If they are studying for an exam, they will read more slowly and carefully. The nature of the text also influences the kind of processing by constraining the information available in the speech or print or by making available certain information that would help satisfy the task demands (Rubin, 1980). Text difficulty can influence the level at which text is processed; for instance, James Michener's *Hawaii* is read at a different level than is James Joyce's *Ulysses*. Text structure can lead to different processing strategies. For example, novels are read differently from poetry and poetry differently from newspapers. Conversations are listened to differently from lectures and lectures differently from dramas.

Likewise, each input modality, speech or print, imposes its own demands on cognitive processing. The auditory system is temporally based. The listener has limited control over speech rate and has no continuing access to it. In listening situations, however, the speaker and listener typically interact face-to-face so that the listener has some immediate control. In contrast, the visual system is spatially oriented. The reader has continuous access to the complete text, at least in naturalistic situations, and also has more-or-less complete control over the rate and order of input. There typically is no feedback to and from the writer, however, because the reader and writer usually are separated in time and space. In addition, the structure of the text varies because of differences between speaking and writing styles. The linguistic patterns used in speaking and writing are demonstrably different (Schallert, Kleiman,

& Rubin, 1977; see also Chafe & Danielewicz, this volume). At least some of these stylistic differences result from the constraints imposed by speech and print media and from the cognitive demands made by listeners and readers.

A second set of factors that result in variation in the comprehension processes are those associated with individual differences in cognitive skills. What cognitive skills does a listener or reader have available to meet the cognitive demands? Differences in reading skill influence the ability of the reading process to meet the task demands. For example, inadequate decoding skill constrains the resulting comprehension representation (Perfetti & Lesgold, 1979). Differences in vocabulary and the ability to comprehend complex syntactic structures affect how the comprehender obtains the information required for the task (Perfetti, 1983). An insufficient knowledge base may limit construction of an appropriate representation (Britton & Tesser, 1982; Spilich, Vesonder, Chiesi, & Voss, 1979). Familiarity with the genre, with the discourse style, or with a specific speaker's or writer's style may facilitate the processing strategies adopted by the comprehender. For example, experienced scientists approach technical articles more efficiently than do students because they are familiar with the structure and style of such texts. In general, comprehenders use whatever knowledge, strategies, and skills they have available to solve the problem of obtaining the information needed to complete a task (Stanovich, 1980).

The difference between listening and reading can be considered a task factor, that is, readers receive visual input and listeners auditory input. Both must determine an abstract meaning for it. Listening and reading tasks are obviously different at a peripheral level because they use different sensory modalities. Beyond that level, what processing components differ, if any? Since the components' operation is dependent on other factors besides modality (i.e., comprehender, text, and task factors) or cognitive demands and cognitive skills, experimental rationales must focus on how processing components function across a variety of situations rather than in only one pure case.

How can the operation of processing components be compared in listening and reading? Since the components cannot be observed directly, their processing structure must be inferred from different patterns of results, i.e., functional relations between independent and dependent variables. An independent variable, such as signal degradation, vocabulary difficulty, syntactic complexity, or script schema, may produce an effect on a dependent variable, such as word-recognition accuracy, comprehension speed, or text recall. These functional relations, or patterns of results, indicate how the processes of the underlying components operate. So, in order to compare the processes involved in listening and reading, the patterns of results obtained from similar paradigms using listening and reading tasks must be compared. If the patterns are the same, then we reasonably can conclude that the processing components operate in similar fashions for listening and reading. This comparison is complicated by the fact that other factors in addition to modality alter the processes in systematic ways. So we have the additional task of determining whether the operation of the components changes in systematic ways across several listening–reading situations, such as variation in the skill levels of the comprehenders, the linguistic properties of the text, and the information the comprehenders are required to produce.

In this chapter we compare listening and reading processes by comparing whether five processing components operate in similar or different ways when the input modality is speech or print. The five components we consider are speech perception/print decoding, lexical access, clause/sentence integration, discourse understanding, and comprehension monitoring (Danks & Hill, 1981; Just & Carpenter, 1980). Although discussed separately, these components are not serially ordered components that operate autonomously, but are mutually interacting processes. The operation of each component is examined over a range of comprehender, text, and task variables, focusing on variation in listening and reading modalities. The comparisons are not based on "main effect" differences in listening and reading. As has been noted, these usually are not informative because they can be attributed to many factors (Danks, 1980). We compare instead patterns of results for listening and reading and interactions involving listening and reading as indicative of whether the same processing principles operate in both modalities. Research on each processing component is discussed below with the primary focus being on how cognitive demands and cognitive skills affect the operation of the components. The studies considered in each section are not exhaustive reviews, but serve to illustrate the kinds of investigations needed to effectively compare listening and reading processes.

SPEECH PERCEPTION AND PRINT DECODING

Since we are dealing with inputs from two different sensory channels, some differences in processing result from the physical differences between print and speech signals and from the anatomical and neurophysiological differences between the visual and auditory sensory systems.

Acoustically, the information in speech is distributed temporally in a fading signal. Visually, print is spatially distributed in a relatively permanent record. Print is basically a two-dimensional pattern whereas speech is multidimensional. Although speech is commonly represented in three dimensions by a speech spectrograph—time, frequency, and amplitude—it is not clear that these dimensions are sufficient to specify the linguistically relevant information in speech (Pisoni, 1977).

Segmentation of primary constituents, i.e., phones and letters, is a major problem for speech perception, but not for print decoding. Print has well-specified, discrete characters, at least at the letter level. The phonetic units of speech are represented in continuous, overlapping segments of the signal and there is no agreed-upon mapping from acoustic information to identification of phones or phonemes (Pisoni, 1977). At more abstract levels of constituent structure, the segmentation question becomes more complex. Speech contains prosodic cues that provide valuable information to listeners about how to segment syntactic constituents such as phrases and clauses (Schallert *et al.*, 1977; Schreiber, this volume). Print has fewer cues for syntactic constituents but punctuation provides some information. The more formal style used in writing also may make syntactic structure more evident to readers.

The mechanics of perception are somewhat different for audition and vision. Listeners receive a continuous signal over which they have very little control. They are forced to process the signal immediately regardless of whether they are prepared to receive new information or whether they are still processing the immediately preceding signal. Readers, in contrast, receive successive "snapshots" from eye fixations that are under their control. This difference in control has important ramifications for more abstract processing components. For example, readers can regress to identify the antecedent for a pronoun (Carpenter & Just, 1977), but listeners cannot.

Simply because different sensory channels are used in listening and reading, the same process cannot be used for speech perception and print decoding. But it may be that speech perception and print decoding processes obey some of the same principles. Some speech perception phenomena may be found in print decoding, although perhaps only in analogous forms. For example, is there selective adaptation of visual features of letters? Is there categorical perception of letters? Is there a right (or left) visual-field advantage for print decoding? Is there a letter restoration effect for distorted letters? Does linguistic context facilitate identification of letters in words and sentences?

Some evidence is available to answer some of these questions. For example, linguistic context does appear to facilitate the identification of letters in words and sentences and there appears to be a letter restoration effect (McClelland & Rumelhart, 1981; Rumelhart, 1977). However, most of the research has not been designed to permit comparison of speech perception and print decoding phenomena. If appropriate comparisons can be designed, the results might illuminate both components (Perfetti & McCutchen, 1982). In any case, the proper comparison between speech perception and print decoding is at the level of phenomena. If analogous phenomena were obtained in both modalities and if similar principles were demonstrated to be at work in both components, then the initial processing in listening and reading would be similar. Of course, any functional similarities that are discovered may be general properties of perceptual processing rather than being specific to listening and reading. If so, the processing of linguistic input should not be accorded special status.

In sum, although the auditory and visual channels have very different properties, the initial processing of speech and print still may operate under similar principles. Some comparable phenomena, such as contextual facilitation of identification, suggest similarities, but more extensive comparisons are needed. Regardless of similarities or differences, both speech perception and print decoding provide the raw data for another processing component, lexical access.

LEXICAL ACCESS

The lexical access component locates the word in the reader's mental dictionary so that semantic, syntactic, and pragmatic information becomes available to other processing components. One continuing controversy has been whether lexical access in reading is mediated by some sort of phonological representation or whether there is direct visual access to the mental lexicon. Many experimenters have attempted to decide whether phonological mediation is necessary, sufficient, or simply a possibility (Baron, 1973; Barron & Baron, 1977; Frederiksen & Kroll, 1976). Likewise, others have attempted to show that direct visual access is a possible route or the only route to lexical access (Massaro, 1975; Glushko, 1981). Perfetti and McCutchen (1982) provide an excellent review and discussion of this literature and pose the possibility that phonological activation may be a postlexical access effect.

A second issue concerning lexical access is whether top-down contextual information is used to locate the lexical item or whether it comes into play only during post-access selection of an appropriate meaning, syntactic form, etc. We discuss this question in terms of whether similar sorts of processes are involved in lexical access in listening and reading.

Marslen-Wilson (1975; Marslen-Wilson & Welsh, 1978) has conducted a number of experiments on lexical access in listening. He has used a speech-shadowing task in which listeners hear and repeat speech concurrently. Listeners repeat what they have just heard at the same time that they are hearing new text. Marslen-Wilson distorted three-syllable words by altering one of the syllables, e.g., *tragedy* became *travedy*. Although the distortion produced a nonsensical word, there were sufficient phonological and contextual cues for listeners to recognize the intended word. When listeners shadowed discourse containing these sorts of violations, they frequently restored the original form of the word rather than repeating the nonsense form (49% restorations; Marslen-Wilson & Welsh, 1978), especially when the change occurred in the second or third syllable. Top-down contextual information permitted listeners to identify the original word before they realized that the second or third syllable had been altered.

We have used oral reading to study reading processes, and one condition yielded results comparable to those Marslen-Wilson obtained with speech shadowing (Danks, 1982; Danks, Bohn, & Fears, 1983; Danks & Hill, 1981). Oral reading is directly analogous to speech shadowing (Danks & Fears, 1979). Readers are presented with print input and must produce an oral rendition of the print immediately after seeing it. The ear–voice span in speech shadowing is typically shorter than is the eye–voice span in oral reading, but in both cases the oral response is produced while additional text is being received.

We altered the text of stories so as to violate different types of information. In one condition, syntactic information was violated by altering the endings of critical words. For example, in the sentence *She imagined her daughter being injured by the other children,* the critical word *injured* was changed to *injury,* which changed the part of speech, or to *injures,* which produced a syntactic violation without changing the part of speech. During oral reading by college students, 25% of disruptions in the oral rendition were restorations of the original critical word. Of these restorations, 52% were fluent, that is, there were no pauses or other disruptions immediately before or during the restoration. Comparable results have been obtained with average second (32% restorations), fourth (44%), and sixth (38%) graders as well. The prior linguistic context provided sufficient information for readers to access the original critical word using only the initial portion of the word, or word stem, without fully processing it. The change that produced the syntactic violation occurred at the end of the critical word and apparently was not noticed. So oral readers restored the critical word just as speech shadowers restored words when there was a change in the second or third syllable (Marslen-Wilson, 1975).

Both in speech shadowing and in oral reading, top-down contextual information facilitated lexical access so that subjects accessed the words in their mental lexicons before they completed processing the input. Thus, distortions in the later parts of the words were restored. Based on the speech-shadowing and oral reading results, Marslen-Wilson and Welsh (1978) and Danks and Hill (1981) have proposed similar interactive models of lexical access. The phonological and graphic information in the initial word segment activates a cohort of words in the mental lexicon that are consistent with that information. Then cohort members that are inconsistent with contextual and additional phonological/ graphic information are eliminated until only one candidate remains. In both the listening and reading experiments, the contextual constraint was sufficiently strong to identify the critical word before phonological/ graphic processing of the later segments was complete, leading to restoration of the original critical word.

Although the demand characteristics of listening and reading modalities do not appear to have altered the lexical access strategies, other factors may. For example, comparison of listening and reading may be influenced by the linguistic structure of the language being studied. When we repeated the oral reading experiments in Polish (Danks & Kurcz, 1984; Kurkiewicz, Kurcz, & Danks, 1981), there were few restorations (less than 12%), and no fluent ones, of syntactic violations. Why? Polish marks syntactic structure primarily with inflectional endings, whereas English syntactic structure is encoded primarily in word order. Because the word endings contain more important information for Polish readers than for English readers, distorting the suffix was more salient to Polish than English readers. Evidently Polish readers attended more to the word endings, and thus were more disrupted by a violation there. Whether there would be fewer fluent restorations in speech shadowing in Marslen-Wilson's experiments were repeated in Polish we do not know. But the Polish oral reading results serve as a reminder that the entire complex of cognitive demands placed on comprehenders must be examined.

CLAUSE AND SENTENCE INTEGRATION

Simply accessing words in the mental dictionary is not all there is to reading (although some investigators seem to think so). The word meanings must be integrated to form representations of clauses and sentences; syntactic information is used as a guide to structure the integration. Another processing component effects the construction of clause and sentence meanings from the information found in the mental dictionary. Is this integration accomplished by the same process in listening and reading? During lexical access the same entry of a given word is accessed regardless of whether the instigating input is speech or print (Hanson, 1981). Yet how those meanings are integrated may differ in listening and reading because of different demands imposed by the peripheral channels or because of the different structure of printed and spoken discourse. There are several plausible reasons for such a difference, for instance the differential control that the comprehender has over the order and rate of input and the differential distribution of information in the text.

Several investigators have tested for the presence of processing strategies in reading and listening that have been identified previously in the other modality alone. If the same strategies are operative in both modalities, then it is reasonable to conclude that listening and reading are using a clause/sentence integration component in common. If different strategies emerge, then separate components need to be postulated. The studies described here exemplify this research strategy, but only for a narrow range of properties for the clause/sentence integration component.

In an especially good example of this process-analytic rationale, Mosenthal (1976–1977) compared sentence comprehension in listening and in oral and silent reading by testing Clark's theory of linguistic comprehension in all three tasks. Clark (1969b) established three principles that operate in sentence verification tasks. Although these principles may be more relevant to sentence utilization than to sentence comprehension (Clark & Clark, 1977), they still provide a firm basis for comparing listening and reading comprehension. Mosenthal tested whether or not they operated identically in listening and in oral and silent reading. If they did, then one could conclude that listening and reading sentence-integration processes were identical. If a principle did not operate in both tasks, or operated differently, then listening and reading processes would differ, at least with regard to that principle.

Using Clark's basic syllogistic reasoning task (Clark, 1969a), Mosenthal tested second- and sixth-grade children. In one experiment he compared oral reading with listening and in two additional experiments he compared silent reading with listening. In the first experiment, there was a significant decrement in the overall level of performance from listening to oral reading, but the pattern of results was the same for both modalities. In the last two experiments, not only was the pattern of results the same, but there was no difference in the level of performance between listening and silent reading. Mosenthal concluded that silent reading and listening involved the same comprehension processes but that oral reading comprehension was different. However, since Clark's principles operated in the oral reading task in the same way as they did in the listening task, that is, the pattern of results was the same, the proper conclusion is that the sentence verification process was the same for oral reading as well.

Another principle that describes how comprehenders integrate word meanings in sentences is the minimum distance principle. For example, the sentence *John told Bill to leave* satisfies the minimum distance principle because the subject of the infinitive phrase is the nearest noun, *Bill*. But the sentence, *Jane promised Mary to leave* is an exception to the minimum distance principle because the subject of the infinitive phrase is the farther noun, *Jane*. Chomsky (1969) has described the child's acquisition of the minimum distance principle in four stages. Goldman (1976) tested for the emergence of the minimum distance principle in listening and reading tasks. She found that use of the principle emerged in a regular sequence with the listening task, replicating Chomsky, but not in the reading task. In reading, the stages seemed to emerge all at once. She interpreted these results as indicating that reading comprehension is dependent on listening: once a comprehension strategy has been acquired in listening, it is transferred directly to reading as a unit. Although acquisition of the minimum distance principle differed in listening and reading, its utilization, once acquired, apparently was the same.

As people comprehend sentences they use information from the preceding text to anticipate what words will follow. Exactly how the contextual information is used is not clear, but the influence of context on comprehension has been widely demonstrated (Danks & Glucksberg, 1980). Neville and Pugh (1976–1977) evaluated the influence of context in the listening and reading of 9-year-old children using a cloze test in which subjects had to fill in missing words. The listening cloze scores were significantly lower than unrestricted reading cloze scores. However, when access to the text was restricted, that is, when readers could see only a small portion of it, the reading and listening cloze scores were essentially the same. So the original listening–reading difference was due to the unrestricted access that readers had to review past text and to read ahead. Poor readers performed similarly on reading and listening, regardless of whether the reading task was restricted or unrestricted. However, good readers performed better on the unrestricted reading task, making better use of the additional contextual information. In terms of information availability, the restricted reading task was more similar to listening than was the unrestricted reading task. Thus, the apparent difference between listening and reading was not due to differences in the listening and reading sentence integration processes per se, but in the differential availability of information in typical listening and reading conditions.

As demonstrated by Neville and Pugh's experiment, differences found in a simple comparison of listening and reading tasks cannot be taken as prima facie evidence of a processing difference. The specific demands placed on the cognitive processing system by each task must be analyzed for equivalence. In another example of this same point, Flagg and Reynolds (1977) tested sentence integration in listening and reading using Bransford and Franks's (1971) recognition memory paradigm. In listening, they replicated Bransford and Franks's finding that listeners could not discriminate between sentences they had actually heard before and those they had not as long as the sentences were consistent with a single, holistic representation. However, in reading, they found that readers could discriminate between old and new sentences. Evidently, sentence-specific surface information was retained from a visual presentation, but not from an auditory one. There was no need to postulate differences in sentence integration processes. The differential availability and memorability of auditory and visual information provided a sufficient explanation.

The listening–reading modality difference was turned into an analytic tool by Eddy and Glass (1981) to study imagery in sentence comprehension. They found that when high-imagery sentences were read they were comprehended and verified more slowly than low-imagery sentences, but there were no differences when the sentences were heard. In contrast, when subjects judged grammaticality there were no differences between high- and low-imagery sentences in either reading or listening. These results might be viewed as indicating different comprehension processes in listening and reading, namely, that sentences are imaged in reading, but not in listening. However, the simpler explanation is that using the visual channel in reading interfered with the use of imagery in sentence comprehension, but the use of the auditory channel in listening did not.

These studies demonstrated some similarities in how clauses and sentences are integrated in listening and reading. They are similar in sentence verification strategies, in the use of the minimum distance principle, in cloze anticipations, and in forming an integrated memory representation. Different results from listening and reading tasks could be attributed to the differential demands imposed by the modalities, for example, differential access to the preceding text and auditory–visual memory differences, and not to intrinsic processing differences. The specific aspects of the clause/sentence integration component tested in these experiments fail by some measure to represent a complete description of clause/sentence integration. However, these experiments do illustrate how to attack the problem of comparing listening and reading in clause/sentence integration and the research rationales can be used as a guide to expand investigation of this component.

DISCOURSE UNDERSTANDING

In another processing component, the clausal representations of sentences, propositions, are organized systematically to form an encompassing representation of the entire discourse, whether that discourse be a story, a nonfiction narrative, a conversation, a lecture, or whatever. There are two aspects to discourse understanding—establishing internal and external coherence and constructing a macrostructure (Halliday & Hasan, 1976; Kintsch & van Dijk, 1978). To establish internal coherence, or cohesion, the comprehender identifies referential commonalities so that a microstructure representation can be constructed. Aiding this process is external coherence, that is, connections between the text and prior knowledge and the immediate context. Once coherence has been established in a microstructure, the gist of the text is extracted to construct a macrostructure representing the main ideas of the text. The comprehender depends on prior knowledge as well as on linguistic cues to identify which information is important and which is detail.

Studies investigating the discourse understanding component necessarily use extended texts ranging from a few sentences to lengthy stories, articles, and lectures. Virtually all of the studies mentioned in the preceding sections used single words or sentences. Given that we are dealing with the understanding of extended texts, how can we best assess discourse understanding? Most of the studies that have compared listening and reading at the level of discourse understanding have relied on a global measure of comprehension using a memory task. This procedure presents two problems. First, measures such as amount recalled and the number of questions answered correctly do not differentiate among the types of discourse information that might be retained. Although the same amount of information may be retained in listening and reading, it might be distributed among different types, such as literal facts and inferences. Second, most studies do not measure processing "on-line," that is, they do not measure comprehension when it is occurring. The inferential leap from memory representations to processes is tenuous because the same representation could result from different processes.

A prime example of these problems is a study reported by Elgart

(1978). She compared listening with oral and silent reading in third graders using selections from the Gates-MacGinitie Reading Comprehension Test. First, oral reading comprehension scores were significantly better than silent reading scores. Listening scores were intermediate and did not differ significantly from either of the reading conditions. Illustrative of the above-mentioned problems, there was no diferentiation of "comprehension" (memory) scores as to what kinds of information were remembered. Second, although listening scores did not differ from either reading condition, different processes may have yielded comparable total memory scores. In addition to these measurement problems, a third problem was present: the amount of time the comprehenders had access to the text was uncontrolled. The oral readers probably had the text available longer than either the silent readers or listeners, and the listeners longer than the silent readers. These estimates of the time available to study the material correlated perfectly with the recall scores. Thus, one cannot determine whether discourse understanding processes were similar in listening and reading because the conditions were not comparable (Danks, 1980).

The first problem has been eliminated in two other studies. In one by Kintsch and Kozminsky (1977), college students either read (presumably silently) or listened to stories. They then produced summaries that were analyzed according to Kintsch's (1974) propositional analysis. The listening and reading summaries differed very little in their content. For example, the percentages recalled in the categories of narrative responses, exposition, complications, and resolutions were quite similar for listening and reading.

In another study, Smiley, Oakley, Worthen, Campione, and Brown (1977) had good and poor seventh-grade readers listen to one prose passage and read another. The recall protocols were evaluated at four levels of importance to the passage. Poor readers did not recall as much as good readers and their recalls were not as closely related to the levels of importance. However, reading recall performance was highly correlated with listening recall performance, indicating that "poor readers suffer from a general comprehension deficit and that similar processes are involved in reading and listening comprehension" (Smiley *et al.*, 1977, p. 381).

The problem with the Kintsch and Kozminsky and the Smiley *et al.* studies is that the analysis of memory protocols does not give much insight into the process by which listeners and readers constructed the discourse representations. Some sort of on-line, concurrent measure is needed to obtain information about underlying processes. Reading time, a measure used in some studies (e.g., Cirilo, 1981; Cirilo & Foss,

1980), holds promise if an analogous procedure can be devised for listening.

Another way of analyzing discourse structure to avoid depending on a global measure of comprehension is to identify the inferences needed to establish coherence. One type of glue that holds stories together is inferences from literal statements. Listeners must focus more intently on understanding the central themes of discourse because the input fades quickly and is not available for review as new information continues to stream in. In contrast, readers can afford to delay formation of discourse meaning a bit longer and can attend more to lower-level details, especially if they know that their memory for the text will be tested.

Hildyard and Olson (1978) tested recognition memory for two kinds of inferences as well as for factual details. Central inferences were inferences that were necessary for the comprehender to make in order to understand the story, that is, to make it coherent; peripheral inferences were not necessary for coherence, but were invited by the text and were obviously true; and factual details were facts that were literally present in the story but which were relatively unimportant to understanding the gist of the story. Listeners showed greater recognition of the central inferences than readers did, but readers recognized peripheral inferences and factual details better than listeners. Although listening and reading conditions produced different results, they can be attributed to the different cognitive demands imposed by the presentation modalities rather than to intrinsic differences in listening and reading processes.

Listening and reading tasks make different demands on working memory. Speech proceeds at a rate not under the control of the listener and without leaving a permanent record to be reexamined by the listener in case of processing difficulty. The only record that remains for the listener is what has been encoded in memory. Reading places fewer demands on memory because the printed text can be referred to as necessary. Daneman and Carpenter (1980) determined a working-memory span for college students by having them recall the last words of sentences from sets that gradually increased in size. The working-memory span was measured for oral and silent reading and for listening. The students then read or listened to stories and answered questions about simple facts or questions about pronominal reference that made demands on memory. All three measures of working-memory span correlated significantly with both types of questions, regardless of modality. However, the listening working-memory span correlated more highly with listening comprehension questions and the reading working-memory spans correlated more highly with the reading comprehension questions. Although there was substantial commonality in the use of working memory by listening and reading, there was some modality specificity as well. Since the working-memory spans measured both the structural capacity of working memory and how efficiently it is used in processing, perhaps listening and reading have equal access to the structural capacity, but they use it differently.

Most studies that have compared listening and reading have employed texts that were originally composed for reading rather than for listening (Danks, 1980). In an exception, Walker (1975–1976) compared reading and listening comprehension of text derived from spontaneously produced speech, rather than planned writing. Discussions among eleventh graders were videotaped and transcribed. Although there was no difference in the overall amount recalled, recall following listening to(and viewing) the videotape was less precise than after reading. Readers recalled a greater proportion of ideas than did listeners. The reading group also recalled more original ideas, whereas the listening group produced more importations. So the recalls of the two groups differed qualitatively, but not quantitatively. Unfortunately, a sample of planned writing was not tested in addition to the discussions. The linguistic variation among written samples and among spoken samples is probably as great as is the difference between written and spoken texts.

A study that used a completely crossed design was conducted by Hildyard and Hidi (1982), in which they included the especially interesting twist of having children construct their own text. Sixth-grade children produced stories either orally or in writing in response to a brief introduction. Four days later, the children recalled their stories; half of each initial group recalled orally and half in writing. There were no differences in gist (paraphrase) recall, but children who both produced and recalled their stories in writing remembered more verbatim propositions (idea units) than did any other group. Writing in production or in recall alone was not sufficient to make a difference. Apparently there is something about the written mode that aids verbatim memory. This finding was buttressed by the additional result that oral recall, especially when combined with oral production, contained many more intrusions of new information that was not contained in the original story. Part of the recall difference was due to the fact that the written stories were much more complete and coherent. When better-structured stories are combined with the possibility of planning and rereading written recalls, it should not be surprising that the written recall of written stories was better. Writing and speech placed different demands on memory, and thus influenced in a rather direct way the results obtained from listening and reading tasks.

Solutions to the problems created by making listening and reading tasks procedurally equivalent are not simple because the process of making them equivalent also eliminates their respective virtues. For example, listeners have much less control over the time course of input than readers, but taking that control away from readers drastically alters the task. Wilkinson (1980) avoided some of the problems through the use of a complex methodology. He tested second through sixth graders on oral reading and listening–looking (that is, the children followed a text visually while they heard it read). He also compared silent reading with plain listening in another study with fifth-grade children. Reading rates and listening presentation rates were on-line measures of the difficulty the children may have been having with different portions of the text. There were two qualitatively different types of recall questions: one type that was affected primarily by comprehension differences but not memory differences, and a second type that was affected more by memory than by comprehension.

The results indicated a complex interaction between cognitive task demands, specified in part by the differences in listening and reading tasks, the skill level of the children, and the content of the texts. Younger readers (second and third graders) suffered losses in comprehension and memory when they were faced with a secondary task as in oral reading. Producing an oral rendition absorbed some attention that might have been devoted to comprehension. The lack of oral reading errors, indicating careful attention to decoding, confirmed this reasoning. Whenever more skilled readers (fifth and sixth graders) were given the opportunity to both read and listen as in the listening–looking condition, their comprehension and memory scores increased because they were able to divide their cognitive resources in an efficient manner. In oral reading, more skilled readers showed a trade off between their reading rates and comprehension scores. A general, all-encompassing conclusion about listening and reading processes was not possible because the specific cognitive demands produced by the listening and reading tasks, the skill level of the comprehender, and the type of text interacted. The results were consistent with an interactive-compensatory model of reading (Stanovich, 1980) and with the task dependent model we are advocating here.

Instead of striving for strict control and comparability, which is not possible in any case, task, text, and reader variables can be manipulated orthogonally. Relative comprehension performance then indicates how processes tied to the specific manipulations interact. For example, Horowitz and Samuels (1985) had good and poor sixth graders listen to and read aloud easy and difficult texts. In the listening task, good and poor readers did not differ in comprehension (although easy texts were comprehended better than difficult ones). However, in oral reading, good readers comprehended both types of text better than did poor readers. Good and poor readers apparently differed in decoding, an oral reading skill, rather than in general language comprehension. Thus, listening served as a standard task for comparing good and poor readers.

Studies of discourse understanding have risen in number since the mid-1970s, and models of discourse processing have followed (Danks & Glucksberg, 1980). A prime example of such models is that proposed by Kintsch and van Dijk (1978) in which the cognitive limitations of the comprehender interact with the linguistic properties of the text to determine how it is represented. The studies reviewed here have demonstrated that most of the differences between listening and reading in discourse understanding involve interactions between the cognitive demands imposed by listening and reading tasks, the properties of the texts, and the skills and abilities of the comprehenders. These interactions are especially salient when they involve linguistic structure and memory capacities. As models of discourse understanding, such as Kintsch and van Dijk's, become more completely specified, it will be easier to compare listening and reading processes by comparing the values of the models' parameters which account for the various results.

COMPREHENSION MONITORING

A fifth processing component appears to be qualitatively different from the other components because it takes the other processes themselves as data. During the course of discourse processing, listeners and readers monitor their comprehension processes to determine whether they are proceeding in a reasonable way that will meet the comprehenders' needs, or whether there are errors, breakdowns, or disruptions. If the task at hand requires a particular level of information, such as word recognition in a laboratory task or low-level understanding in conversational small talk, then the normal comprehension process may be truncated once the requisite information has been extracted. If the discourse contains ambiguities, inconsistencies, or complexities that are necessary to resolve for complete understanding, the comprehender needs to be alerted so that appropriate remedies can be initiated. It is unclear whether such comprehension monitoring is performed by a specialized executive routine or whether the monitoring is implicit in checks and balances internal to the comprehension process itself. Whichever is the case, does comprehension monitoring function similarly or differently in listening and reading?

The notion of metacognitive functions is a relatively recent theoretical concept, and comprehension monitoring (Brown, 1980; Markman, 1979) has emerged as one of the more interesting metacognitive functions. Given the newness of the concept of comprehension monitoring, it is not surprising that there have been no published studies comparing comprehension monitoring in listening and reading. In an unpublished study, we compared comprehension monitoring in oral and silent reading and in listening with third and sixth graders and college students. Factual inconsistencies were written into two brief stories. One was a physical inconsistency, for example, a child was building a snowman on a hot sunny beach. The other inconsistency was between a psychological trait and the actual behavior of the protagonist (adapted from stories used by Stein & Trabasso, 1982). For example, a kind boy kicked a girl who had just fallen off a bicycle. Two other stories were control stories that did not contain any factual inconsistencies. Children read the stories orally or silently or listened to an experimenter read them.

In order to assess comprehension monitoring, we asked a series of 13 questions after the story had been presented, a procedure adapted from Markman (1979). The questions became successively more specific in probing for recognition of the inconsistencies. The point in the question series at which the comprehender explicitly recognized the existence of the inconsistency was the primary dependent variable. The older subjects recognized the inconsistencies earlier than younger subjects and the physical inconsistencies were recognized sooner than were the psychological–behavioral ones. However, task modality—oral or silent reading or listening—had no effect on the point of recognition. So comprehension monitoring was the same in listening and reading, at least given these stories, subjects, and task.

This conclusion must be considered quite tentative for several reasons. The questioning procedure may be a relatively insensitive measure of comprehension monitoring during processing. An on-line measure of comprehension monitoring such as inconsistency detection latency might be more sensitive than post-comprehension questioning. Also, the inconsistencies did not cause reading times to increase, and this result conflicts with earlier studies (Danks & Miller, 1979; Danks, Bohn, & Fears, 1983). However, results supporting the conclusion can be found in a study by Baker (in press). She presented children with stories containing nonsense words, internal inconsistencies, and knowledge violations. Children 5, 7, and 9 years old listened as the stories were read to them and a group of 11 year olds read the stories. In general, the children detected the nonsense words and knowledge violations better than the internal inconsistencies. Although listening and reading tasks were confounded with age, the few group differences that were obtained were better attributed to developmental changes than to modality of presentation. In any case, whether comprehension monitoring differs in listening and reading will not be determined by simple comparative studies. Other factors, for example, text difficulty and reading skill, may interact with listening and reading tasks to determine the extent to which comprehenders are able to keep track of how well they are comprehending.

SUMMARY AND CONCLUSIONS

In our review of the research comparing listening and reading processes over the five processing components, both similarities and differences in processing have appeared. However, there are two problems with drawing any firm conclusions. One is that in some components no or very few comparisons have been conducted and often those that have contain methodological faults that make interpretation difficult or impossible. The second problem is that in those components where several good comparisons are available, either the operation of the underlying processing component is still theoretically unclear or only a narrow aspect of the component has been examined. However, some tentative conclusions can be summarized.

Comparisons of speech perception and print decoding are virtually nonexistent, probably because the two modalities are so obviously different at this level of processing. However, comparisons at a more abstract level of conceptual analysis, for example, the level of phenomena and operating principles, are possible. Lexical access has been studied heavily in both listening and reading research, but the issues that have been examined in each modality have been quite different so that comparisons are not evident. The evidence that is comparable indicates that the processes operate according to similar principles, but on different data representations. Direct comparisons of listening and reading processes in clause/sentence integration and discourse understanding components have been relatively more numerous, but often severe methodological problems are present. Both components appear to operate in similar ways in listening and reading when the cognitive demands are made equivalent, as they can be in the laboratory. However, in most everyday situations, the cognitive demands, say on memory, are different as the nature of oral and printed texts. Thus, under these conditions differences in listening and reading processes emerge. These are not due to inherent differences in listening and reading processes, but result from the comprehenders' efforts to comprehend the text in an efficient way. There has been too little research to conclude anything about a comprehension monitoring component, but it would seem plausible for listening and reading to tap a common resource for comprehension monitoring.

The critical consideration for the comparison of listening and reading comprehension processes is to determine the cognitive demands imposed by the various listening and reading tasks. Neither listening nor reading is a homogeneous process that functions the same way in all situations. Rather, they are amalgamations of subprocesses that are adapted by the comprehender to accomplish a specific task. The strategies and skills that the comprehender has available constrain what form the listening or reading process assumes. What information is available in the text and how it is represented limits which strategies and skills are productive for comprehension. If listening and reading tasks are made equivalent through strict experimental control over texts, skill levels, and procedural demands, then the experimental results are the same. The research reviewed here has shown that to be the case. When listening and reading tasks were constrained in similar ways, the patterns of results were similar. However, such restrictive controls vitiate the virtues that the differences between listening and reading have in everyday situations. Outside the laboratory, the situations in which listening and reading occur force different values on the variables that were so carefully controlled in the laboratory. In those experiments where the texts, skills, and procedural demands differed between listening and reading presentation modes, different results emerged.

So, to the question, "Are listening and reading processes the same or different?," the answer is, "Both." Listening and reading are the same in that both are language comprehension processes that have available to them the same set of strategies to accomplish the task of comprehension. They differ to the extent that the cognitive demands imposed by text characteristics, situational factors, and cognitive skills available to the comprehender result in different processing strategies being heuristic. Either similarities or differences in listening and reading tasks can be demonstrated through the appropriate manipulation of these factors. The important consideration is not to compare listening and reading tasks directly, but to investigate how the subprocesses interact to form specific processing strategies that comprehenders adopt in specific situations.

ACKNOWLEDGMENTS

Portions of this chapter were presented at the meetings of the 26th International Reading Association Conference held in New Orleans. Preparation of this paper was supported by grants NIE-G-78-0223 and NIE-G-82-0028 from the National Institute of Education.

REFERENCES

Baker, L. (in press). Children's effective use of multiple standards for evaluating their comprehension.

Baron, J. (1973). Phonemic stage not necessary for reading. *Quarterly Journal of Experimental Psychology, 25,* 241–246.

Barron, R. W., & Baron, J. (1977). How children get meaning from printed words. *Child Development, 48,* 587–594.

Bransford, J. D., & Franks, J. J. (1971). The abstraction of linguistic ideas. *Cognitive Psychology, 2,* 331–350.

Britton, B., & Tesser, A. (1982). Effects of prior knowledge on use of cognitive capacity in three complex cognitive tasks. *Journal of Verbal Learning and Verbal Behavior, 21,* 421–437.

Brown, A. L. (1980). Metacognitive development and reading. In R. J. Spiro, B. C. Bruce, & W. F. Brewer (Eds.), *Theoretical issues in reading comprehension.* Hillsdale, NJ: Erlbaum.

Carpenter, P. A., & Just, M. A. (1977). Reading comprehension as eyes see it. In M. A. Just & P. A. Carpenter (Eds.), *Cognitive processes in comprehension.* Hillsdale, NJ: Erlbaum.

Chomsky, C. (1969). *The acquisition of syntax in children from 5 to 10.* Cambridge, MA: MIT Press.

Cirilo, R. K. (1981). Referential coherence and text structure in story comprehension. *Journal of Verbal Learning and Verbal Behavior, 20,* 358–367.

Cirilo, R. K., & Foss, D. J. (1980). Text structure and reading times for sentences. *Journal of Verbal Learning and Verbal Behavior, 19,* 96–109.

Clark, H. H. (1969a). Influence of language on solving three-term series problems. *Journal of Experimental Psychology, 82,* 205–215.

Clark, H. H. (1969b). Linguistic processes in deductive reasoning. *Psychological Review, 76,* 387–404.

Clark, H. H., & Clark, E. V. (1977). *Psychology and language.* New York: Harcourt.

Daneman, M., & Carpenter, P. A. (1980). Individual differences in working memory and reading. *Journal of Verbal Learning and Verbal Behavior, 19,* 450–466.

Danks, J. H. (1980). Comprehension in listening and reading: Same or different? In J. Danks & K. Pezdek, *Reading and understanding.* Newark, DE: International Reading Association.

Danks, J. H. (1982). *Letters, words, sentences, and text: Some studies of reading comprehension.* Paper presented at the meeting of the Midwestern Psychological Association, Minneapolis.

Danks, J. H., Bohn, L., & Fears, R. (1983). Comprehension processes in oral reading. In G. B. Flores d'Arcais & R. J. Jarvella (Eds.), *The process of language understanding.* Chichester, England: Wiley.

Danks, J. H., & Fears, R. (1979). Oral reading: Does it reflect decoding or comprehension? In L. B. Resnick & P. A. Weaver (Eds.), *Theory and practice of early reading* (Vol. 3). Hillsdale, N: Erlbaum.

Danks, J. H., & Glucksberg, S. (1980). Experimental psycholinguistics. *Annual Review of Psychology, 31,* 391–417.

Danks, J. H., & Hill, G. O. (1981). An interactive analysis of oral reading. In A. M. Lesgold & C. A. Perfetti (Eds.), *Interactive processes in reading.* Hillsdale, NJ: Erlbaum.

Danks, J. H., & Kurcz, I. (1984). A comparison of reading comprehension processes in Polish and English. *International Journal of Psychology.*

Danks, J. H., & Miller, R. (1979). *Comprehension processes in children's oral reading.* Paper presented at the meeting of the Psychonomic Society, Phoenix.

Eddy, J. K., & Glass, A. L. (1981). Reading and listening to high and low imagery sentences. *Journal of Verbal Learning and Verbal Behavior, 20,* 333–346.

Elgart, D. (1978). Oral reading, silent reading, and listening comprehension: A comparative study. *Journal of Reading Behavior, 10,* 203–207.

Flagg, P. W., & Reynolds, A. G. (1977). Modality of presentation and blocking in sentence recognition memory. *Memory & Cognition, 5,* 111–115.

Flores d'Arcais, G. B., & Jarvella, R. J. (Eds.). (1983). *The process of language understanding.* Chichester, England: Wiley.

Frederiksen, J. R., & Kroll, J. F. (1976). Spelling and sound: Approaches to the internal lexicon. *Journal of Experimental Psychology: Human Perception and Performance, 2,* 361–379.

Fries, C. C. (1963). *Linguistics and reading.* New York: Holt.

Glushko, R. J. (1981). Principles for pronouncing print: The psychology of phonography. In A. M. Lesgold & C. A. Perfetti (Eds., *Interactive processes in reading.* Hillsdale, NJ: Erlbaum.

Goldman, S. B. (1976). Reading skill and the minimum distance principle: A comparison of listening and reading comprehension. *Journal of Experimental Child Psychology, 22,* 123–142.

Halliday, M. A. K., & Hasan, R. (1976). *Cohesion in English.* Londo: Longman.

Hanson, V. L. (1981). Processing of written and spoken words: Evidence for common coding. *Memory & Cognition, 9,* 93–101.

Hildyard, A., & Hidi, S. (1982). Remembering what you said versus remembering what you wrote: Children's recall of their own oral and written narratives. In A. Flammer & W. Kintsch (Eds.), *Discourse processing.* Amsterdam: North-Holland.

Hildyard, A., & Olson, D. R. (1978). Memory and inference in the comprehension of oral and written discourse. *Discourse Processes, 1,* 91–119.

Horowitz, R., & Samuels, S. J. (1985). Reading and listening to expository text. *Journal of Reading Behavior, 17,* 185–198.

Just, M. A., & Carpenter, P. A. (1980). A theory of reading: From eye fixations to comprehension. *Psychological Review, 87,* 329–354.

Kintsch, W. (1974). *The representation of meaning in memory.* Hillsdale: NJ: Erlbaum.

Kintsch, W., & Kozminsky, E. (1977). Summarizing stories after reading and listening. *Journal of Educational Psychology, 69,* 491–499.

Kintsch, W., & van Dijk, T. A. (1978). Toward a model of text comprehension and production. *Psychological Review, 85,* 363–394.

Kurkiewicz, D., Kurcz, I., & Danks, J. H. (1981). Reading comprehension processes in Polish and English. *Polish Psychological Bulletin, 12,* 25–31.

Lesgold, A. M., & Perfetti, C. A. (Eds.). (1981). *Interactive processes in reading.* Hillsdale, NJ: Erlbaum.

Markman, E. M. (1979). Realizing that you don't understand. Elementary school children's awareness of inconsistencies. *Child Development, 50,* 643–655.

Marslen-Wilson, W. D. (1975). Sentence perception as an interactive parallel process. *Science, 189,* 226–228.

Marslen-Wilson, W. D., & Welsh, A. (1978). Processing interactions and lexical access during word recognition in continuous speech. *Cognitive Psychology, 10,* 29–63.

Massaro, D. W. (1975). *Understanding language.* New York: Academic Press.

McClelland, J. L., & Rumelhart, D. E. (1981). An interactive activation model of context effects in letter perception: Part 1. An account of basic findings. *Psychological Review, 88,* 375–408.

Mosenthal, P. (1976–1977). Psycholinguistic properties of aural and visual comprehension as determined by children's abilities to comprehend syllogisms. *Reading Research Quarterly, 12,* 55–92.

Neville, M. H., & Pugh, A. K. (1976–1977). Context in reading and listening: Variations in approach to cloze tasks. *Reading Research Quarterly, 12,* 13–52.

Perfetti, C. A. (1983). Individual differences in verbal processes. In R. F. Dillon & R. R. Schmeck (Eds.), *Individual differences in cognition* (Vol. 1). New York: Academic Press.

Perfetti, C. A., & Lesgold, A. M. (1979). Coding and comprehension in skilled reading and implications for reading instruction. In L. B. Resnick & P. Weaver (Eds.), *Theory and practice of early reading* (Vol. 1). Hillsdale, NJ: Erlbaum.

Perfetti, C. A., & McCutchen, D. (1982). Speech processes in reading. In N. J. Lass (Ed.), *Speech and language: Advances in basic research and practice* (Vol. 7). New York: Academic Press.

Pisoni, D. B. (1977). Speech perception. In W. K. Estes (Ed.), *Handbook of learning and cognitive processes* (Vol. 5). Hillsdale: NJ: Erlbaum.

Rubin, A. D. (1980). A theoretical taxonomy of the differences between oral and written language. In R. J. Spiro, B. C. Bruce, & W. F. Brewer (Eds.), *Theoretical issues in reading comprehension.* Hillsdale, NJ: Erlbaum.

Rumelhart, D. E. (1977). Toward an interactive model of reading. In S. Dornic (Ed.), *Attention and performance VI.* Hillsdale. NJ: Erlbaum.

Schallert, D., Kleiman, G., & Rubin, A. (1977). *Analysis of differences between written and oral language* (Tech. Rep. No. 29). Urbana: University of Illinois, Center for the Study of Reading.

Smiley, S., Oakley, D., Worthen, D., Campione, J. C., & Brown, A. L. (1977). Recall of thematically relevant material by adolescent good and poor readers as a function of written versus oral production. *Journal of Educational Psychology, 69,* 381–387.

Spilich, G. J., Vesonder, G. T., Chiesi, H. L., & Voss, J. F. (1979). Text processing of domain-related information for individuals with high and low domain knowledge. *Journal of Verbal Learning and Verbal Behavior, 18,* 275–291.

Stanovich, K. E. (1980). Toward an interactive-compensatory model of individual differences in the development of reading fluency. *Reading Research Quarterly, 16,* 32–71.

Stein, N. L., & Trabasso, T. (1982). What's in a story: Critical issues in comprehension and instruction. In R. Glaser (Ed.), *Advances in the psychology of instruction* (Vol. 2). Hillsdale, NJ: Erlbaum.

Walker, L. (1975–1976). Comprehending writing and spontaneous speech. *Reading Research Quarterly, 11,* 144–167.

Wilkinson, A. C. (1980). Children's understanding in reading and listening. *Journal of Educational Psychology, 72,* 561–574.

Chapter **10**

Factors That Influence Listening and Reading Comprehension

INTRODUCTION

At no time has there been disagreement between researchers and educators about the fact that listening and reading skills are interrelated. In fact, the tie which binds these skills is so strong that reading has usually been viewed as being parasitic on listening. According to this view, in order to read with understanding, all that one must do is recode the printed words to subvocalized speech and then the same mechanisms used for listening comprehension will allow the reader to understand the text. While this compact explanation of how readers understand text is probably wrong (Gough, 1984), or at best, only partially correct, it does underscore the link between reading and listening.

This chapter has as its major objective the description of those inside-the-head and outside-the-head factors which influence listening and reading comprehension. Knowledge of what these factors are is important for several reasons. First, from a pedagogical viewpoint, it is important because it suggests what skills must be taught in the classroom. Failure on the part of the school to teach certain component skills may lead to student failure. In reading, for example, one of the goals of instruction is to enble the students to recognize words they have never seen in print before. If beginning readers are given instruction in letter–

COMPREHENDING ORAL AND WRITTEN LANGUAGE

Copyright © 1987 by Academic Press, Inc.
All rights of reproduction in any form reserved.

295

sound correspondences but not sound blending, many of the students will fail to recognize new words because an essential skill has been omitted. Second, knowledge of the factors which influence comprehension can lead to more effective speaking and writing. For example, if the speaker or writer is unaware of how important it is to gauge the level of knowledge of the audience, the speaker's or writer's message may be inappropriately geared for the audience. Third, if there is a failure on the part of a student to master listening and reading, it is essential that one know what the component skills are in order to make an accurate diagnosis regarding the cause of the failure.

Unfortunately, educators often seem to be less logical and knowledgeable about the causes of listening and reading failure than mechanics are in determining causes of automobile failure. Many reading clinicians and communication disorder specialists believe that listening and reading problems originate from single causes such as poor visual or auditory discrimination or attentional deficits. Their solution is often based on preconceived notions of the problem and may not be an appropriate remediation for the student's problem. Instead of starting with narrow, preconceived notions of what may be causing a reading or listening problem, educators should have an interactive model of inside-the-head and outside-the-head factors which influence comprehension. By using complex models similar to the one presented in this chapter, it will be possible to diagnose the cause of the communication problems more accurately.

The focus of this chapter is on diagnosis. The reason for this emphasis is that diagnosis of communication problems is so difficult that even expert diagnosticians have difficulty. A recent study of the accuracy of diagnostic decision-making by reading experts (Vinsonhaler, Weinshank, Wagner, & Polin, 1983) revealed a shocking lack of interrater and intrarater reliability. When, however, undergraduate students were trained to use a framework similar to one in Tables 10.1 and 10.2 as a guide to their diagnostic probes, the undergraduates were superior to the experts in the reliability of their diagnostic decisions.

LISTENING

Although there is considerable overlap among the component skills of reading and listening, these two skills are treated separately in this chapter; this section addresses the components of listening. Table 10.1, which outlines factors influencing listening comprehension, suggests a useful framework to assist diagnostic decision-making.

The framework is useful because it forces one to consider the numerous interacting factors which influence comprehension of language. Comprehending either spoken or written language is a complex process in which the receiver of the message must construct a meaning out of the information provided by the sender. Constructing a meaning out of the message depends on factors which are inside the head of the receiver as well as on environmental factors which are external to the receiver. Failure to comprehend may result from two interacting forces: lack of inside-the-head knowledge or outside-the-head factors such as poor communication skills on the part of the person who sends the message.

Listening comprehension is interactive in that it involves reconstructing the intended spoken message by translating its lexical and grammatical information into meaning units that can be combined with the listener's knowledge and cognitive structures. To the extent that there is a good match between the knowledge structures of the listener and the speaker, the message may be accurately reconstructed; to the extent that the match is poor, there will be inaccuracy in the reconstruction. On practical grounds, knowing the range of factors influencing listening can guide the search for potential trouble spots when there is a breakdown in comprehension. Table 10.1 shows the inside- and outside-the-head factors which influence comprehension.

Inside-the-Head Factors

Intelligence

If a student is having trouble with listening comprehension, one of the first questions generally asked is whether the student's level of intellectual functioning is sufficient for the task. Except for a small percentage of the population, most students have the necessary level of functioning to make sense of what the speaker is saying, providing the topic is one which is familiar to them. In *Biological Foundations of Language,* Lenneberg (1967, p. 311) states, "If we take a population whose IQ is at or just above threshold . . . intelligence figures correlate quite poorly with language development. Only if we confine our observations to the low grades of feeblemindedness can a relationship between intelligence and language learning be established." Below an IQ level of 20, it is doubtful that meaningful speech or comprehension will take place, and above an IQ level of 50, fully established language has been observed. Thus, for students with IQ levels above 50, meaningful comprehension of spoken laguage should occur, providing the topic is familiar.

TABLE 10.1
Factors Influencing Listening Comprehension

Inside-the-head	Outside-the-head
1. Intelligence: Does the listener have the intelligence to comprehend language?	1. Discussion Topic: Is the topic one which the listener has sufficient background to understand?
2. Language facility	2. Speaker awareness of audience need

1. Intelligence: Does the listener have the intelligence to comprehend language?
2. Language facility
   Is the listener accurate and automatic in the recognition of words and in the ability to segment and parse the speech stream into morpheme and syntactic units?
   Vocabulary: Does the listener have an extensive vocabulary? Does the listener know the variety of ways in which a word can be used?
   Syntax: Can the listener take embedded sentences and parse them into understandable units? Is the listener able to make the inferences necessary to comprehend the eliptical sentences commonly used in casual conversation?
   Dialect and idiolect: If a dialect different from the listener's is spoken, can the listener understand it?
   Anaphoric terms: Can the listener identify the referent for the anaphoric terms used?
3. Background knowledge and schema
   Does the listener have the necessary background knowledge to understand the topic?
   Can the listener make appropriate inferences?
4. Speech registers and awareness of contextual influences
   Is the listener aware of the different styles of speech used for different contexts?
   Can the listener identify the status of the speaker in order to interact appropriately?
5. Metacognitive strategies
   Is the listener aware of when there is a break in comprehension?
   Is the listener aware of how and when it is appropriate to request additional information or clarification from a speaker?

1. Discussion Topic: Is the topic one which the listener has sufficient background to understand?
2. Speaker awareness of audience need
   Has the speaker correctly judged the level of background knowledge of the listener? Is there an appropriate match between information presented by the speaker and the listener's background knowledge. Does the speaker make appropriate adjustments for the listener's background in terms of examples given, rate and pacing of information presented? Does the speaker present too much information?
   Is the speaker aware of the need to modulate the loudness of the voice according to the distance between the speaker, the listener and acoustic properties of the room?
   Is the vocabulary appropriate?
   Is the sentence structure too complex for the listener?
3. Clarity and Speaker Effectiveness
   Does the speaker use too many anaphoric terms? Is the referent clearly indicated for these terms?
   Does the speaker shift topic without indicating there has been a shift?
   Does the message lack cohesive ties and causal links?
   Does the speaker indicate in formal presentations the goals and objectives of presentation, the major thesis, the supporting ideas? Is the presentation well structured? Are there summaries, reviews, questions from the speaker to the listeners?
   Does the speaker use pitch, stress, and pauses appropriately?
4. Context
   Are there contextual cues present which support what the speaker is saying?

TABLE 10.1 (*Continued*)

Inside-the-head	Outside-the-head
Can the listener summarize the major points made during a conversation or lecture?	
6. Kinesics Can the listener understand the nonverbal signals used in spoken communication?	
7. Motivation Is the listener sufficiently interested to focus attention and to interact appropriately on what the speaker is saying?	

When instructing slow learners, one consideration which should be kept in mind pertains to the pacing of instruction. If the pacing is too fast, slow learners often become discouraged and stop paying attention. In order to maintain motivation and time-on-task, the pacing should be slower and there is greater need for review. Although the slow learner may take longer to acquire mastery, once the material has been mastered, there is often little difference between the faster learner and the slower learner in memory for the information or the skill (Shuell, 1972). The important implication from Shuell's study is that, given enough time, the slow learner is able to comprehend and recall the information taught in school, especially if the content is interesting and the student considers it important.

Language Facility

Accuracy and Automaticity. The ability to segment and analyze speech accurately and automatically into appropriate morpheme and syntactic units is essential when listening to spoken language. To illustrate the importance of accurate and automatic segmentation of what we hear into appropriate units, one need only recall how difficult it is to understand a spoken foreign language. So much attention is used trying to identify the words and phrases that the message and meaning get lost. The reason for the loss of the message when we can not segment automatically is that the amount of attention each individual has for information processing at any moment is limited. For listening comprehension to occur, numerous cognitive tasks must take place in a brief period of time, and they all require attention. When listening, the activities which require attention include segmenting the speech stream into morpheme and syntactic units, holding idea units in memory, identifying anaphoric terms, finding the referent for these terms, and integrating information from the speaker with knowledge stored in the memory of the listener.

Since the amount of attention the listener has is limited, it is essential for the sake of efficiency to have as many of the subtasks listed above performed with as little attention as possible. In fact, automaticity can be conceptualized as the ease with which a task can be performed. When a task can be performed with ease, little attention is required. Thus, the reason we want the segmenting to be done accurately and automatically is that it does not draw too heavily upon the limited attention capacity of the individual. Whatever attention capacity remains after the segmenting tasks have been completed can be used for the other tasks necessary for understanding the message.

Vocabulary. Another requirement for good listening comprehension is knowledge of the vocabulary used by the speaker. A problem many young students have, of which adults seem to be unaware, relates to the multiple meanings of words and the fact that many students know only the most common meaning of a word. When a word is encountered in one of its less common uses, students are confused. This can be illustrated with the following sentence in which the word *bank* appears several times, each time with a different meaning. Although unusual, the sentence does make sense, providing all the uses of *bank* are known:

(1)   *You can bank on me to meet you at the river bank after I put the money in the bank.*

In a second example of how the multiple meanings of words can cause confusion, imagine the problem for a student who knows only one meaning for the word *bore*, as in *The drill bored a hole in the wall*, when the student encounters

(2)   *The talk bored the audience.*

The student must imagine that the speaker is using pointed remarks. About this problem, Mason, Kniseley, and Kendall (1979) state: "Knowledge of words . . . has at least three instructional aspects: learning a meaning of a word, learning more than one meaning, and learning how to choose the contextually supported meaning." The latter two categories create the most difficulty for children.

One can argue, in fact, that it is context which determines the nuances and subtleties surrounding word meaning, whereas the dictionary definitions tend to offer only the minimal clues as to the meaning of a word. To illustrate this point, one may think of the dictionary meaning of the word *eat* as the act of taking nutrients into the body. Notice how different the behaviors are in each of the following contexts for eat.

(3)   *The baby ate the steak.*

(4)   *The executive ate the steak.*

(5)   *The dog ate the steak.*

In each case, how the act of eating is performed is determined by knowledge about the subject of the sentence. When there is confusion about the meaning of a sentence, a possible source of difficulty, especially for young children, is lack of knowledge of the multiple meanings of words which are context sensitive.

Syntax: Embedding and Ellipses.   Good listening comprehension requires the ability to segment complex embedded sentences into more basic syntactic units. In order to be understood, the complex sentence (6)a, must be segmented into (6)b and (6)c.

(6)   a. *The police officer found the money that belonged to Smith.*
        b. *The police officer found the money.*
        c. *The money belonged to Smith.*

Another example involves the farmer in the children's story who, in an effort to get the cow to jump over the fence, starts a chain of events which ends with *So the farmer yelled at the dog who bit the donkey who kicked the cow who then jumped over the fence.* In order to understand this embedded chain, the listener must segment the chain into: The farmer yelled at the dog; the dog then bit the donkey; the donkey then kicked the cow; the cow then jumped over the fence. If the listener cannot parse the complex sentence into its constituent parts, comprehension will suffer. What is not clear is how much difficulty poor comprehenders have with this type of task.

While the cognitive task of making sense of embedded sentences requires analysis of the complex utterances into more basic units, the listener must also know how to add the missing elements in incomplete elliptical sentences. For example, normal conversation is characterized by the frequent use of elliptical sentences such as the following dialogue: Teacher: *What time will you arrive tomorrow?* Student: *Seven o'clock.* In another example, a child is looking for a lost toy. The mother points under the couch and says, *Here!* The child looks, finds the toy, and says, *Thanks.* In order to make sense of the elliptical statements, one must use the entire context of the situation as well as the previous utterances.

Dialect and Idiolect.   Sometimes, the language of a speech community differs enough from the listener's language in pronunciation, grammar, and vocabulary to be considered a distinct type but not a different language. These language differences can reflect geographical regions such as Northeastern as opposed to Southern dialect, or the differences may exist within the same region but reflect social class differences. Dialect differs from idiolect in that dialect refers to an entire community, whereas idiolect refers to the peculiar speech of an individual within a community. The existence of either type of speech difference can severely interfere with listening comprehension.

Anaphoric Terms. An anaphoric term is a word used as a substitute for a preceding word or group of words, such as *it* in *I know it and he does, too* or *them* in *John and May need help. Please help them.* A common source of difficulty for many students is identifying the referent for an anaphoric term (Pearson & Johnson, 1978, p. 22). Sentences such as the following are confusing to many students:

(7)   *Mary gave Sue a T-shirt. She thanked her for it.*

(8)   *She dunked John's cards in the water. Because it made him cry, she apologized to him for doing it.*

(9)   *Because Fred did not bake a cake for Mary's birthday, John did O. She could not eat it because it was chocolate.*

(O indicates there is an implied anaphoric term that refers to the fact that John baked a cake.)

Background Knowledge

Background knowledge about a topic is one of the more important variables that can influence listening. If, for example, the student is automatic at the listening subtasks which have been discussed and comprehension is poor, lack of knowledge is a possible cause. In order to test if poor comprehension is due, in part, to lack of necessary background, one simply has to have the student listen to a message on a familiar topic. If comprehension is good on the familiar topic, one may assume that lack of necessary background information accounted for the poor comprehension on the other topic.

Another way to test if the student lacks background knowledge is to ask inferential questions requiring inferential response. Inability to answer these may indicate poor background knowledge. An analysis of where the breakdown in comprehension occurs may reveal that there is adequate literal comprehension but inadequate inferential comprehension. To determine a student's comprehension of a sentence such as *Mother cooked breakfast for John,* an educator may ask literal comprehension questions such as *Who cooked breakfast? For whom was breakfast cooked?*

What did mother cook? Or the educator may ask inferential questions such as *What foods did mother cook? Where did mother do the cooking? What utensils did mother use?* In order to answer the inferential questions, the student must rely on prior knowledge about what foods are traditionally served for breakfast, how foods are prepared, and where food preparation takes place. Responses to such inferential questions will indicate the state of the student's knowledge relative to that subject matter.

Speech Registers

A speech register is the style of language used in a particular social context. For example, in the classroom we may use a formal register to communicate, while on the school playground we may use an informal register. The style of speech used may vary depending on the perceptions of the participants—whether they view the situation as being serious or casual, formal or informal, high personal risk or low personal risk, and their notions of the status and power of the other people in the social context relative to their own power. Recent research indicates that what one comprehends and how much one comprehends is context bound and related to the registers used by the speakers(Mosenthal & Jin Na, 1980; Spiro, 1977). For example, information presented in a graduate class by a well-known scholar using a formal speech register will be retained for a longer period of time than the same information presented in a school cafeteria by a stranger using an informal register. The reason for the difference in recall is that the listener perceives the first situation as one in which the information is important and must be remembered for recall on future tests, whereas the second situation is perceived as one in which the information will be of no future use, and no attempt is made to retain the information. Mosenthal and Jin Na (1980) have demonstrated that in formal settings recall is related more to intellectual ability, but in informal settings recall is related more to the verbal style, register, and pattern of interaction with the speaker. Thus, what and how much we comprehend is determined in part by the registers we use in communicating with each other.

Metacognitive Strategies

These strategies refer to self-monitoring and self-regulatory mechanisms used by an active problem solver who wishes to achieve a goal. The problem solver can be a speaker (or writer) who wishes to communicate an idea or a listener (or reader who wishes to understand a message. Highly complex operations such as communication require an overall awareness of the success of the communication and knowledge of strategies one can use to insure that one's communication goals are being met. If one is a listener, it is as if one asks: Why am I engaged in this interaction? Is this information important? What are the major and minor points being made? When the speaker is unclear, do I know appropriate ways to request clarification? When the information is important, do I know techniques for improving recall? Do I know how to negotiate meaning, alternating the role of listener and speaker in a manner appropriate for the status of the speaker? Finally, can I identify the structure of the message (if there is one) as an aid to comprehension and recall?

The Garner (1983) study of the student's knowledge of metacognitive strategies and the Taylor and Samuels (1983) study of student's awareness of discourse structure identifies these two factors as cognitive skills which distingish good from poor comprehenders. Both studies found that good comprehenders were superior with regard to the two factors. In the Taylor and Samuels study, elementary school students were placed in two categories, those who were aware of expository text structure and those who were unaware. These two groups then read texts which were well structured and texts which were unstructured. After reading the structured and the unstructured texts both groups were asked to recall as much of the texts as possible. On the well-structured text, as one might predict, the aware group did significantly better than the unaware group. On the unstructured text, there was no difference between good and poor comprehenders in recall, indicating that the difference in comprehension between the two groups is not due to one group having superior memory (since both have the same level of recall on unstructured text) but to knowledge of text structure. The third finding of importance is that for the poor comprehenders, recall of the well-structured text was no better than for the poorly structured text. Thus, for the students who were unaware of structure, giving them well-structured or badly structured text makes no difference on their comprehension and recall. They do equally poorly on both types of texts. From the viewpoint of instruction, with diagnosis and remediation considered as part of the instructional process, both metacognitive strategies and text-structure awareness are teachable skills, and once the skills are mastered, comprehension improves.

Kinesics

The nonverbal signals sent by a speaker, the facial expressions, eye contact, direction of gaze, hand gestures, and body motions, all convey meaning and are part of the context in which communication occurs. These forms of nonverbal communication are part of the message and may provide important information about how the speaker is feeling. For example, a speaker may say he has great confidence in himself while the slumped posture, avoidance of eye contact, and clasping and un-clasping of hands may suggest a discrepancy between what the speaker says and the way he actually feels.

In classrooms as well as social situations such as cocktail parties, the nonverbal forms of communication serve a function which is at least as important as the verbal forms. For example, when the duration of eye contact extends beyond some norm, it is a powerful signal that an ap-proach would meet with approval. Similarly, one's posture and pro-longed direction of gaze away from the speaker may indicate the listener is bored with the speaker. While these nonverbal signals vary so much from individual to individual that they are often hard to interpret, those who are sensitive to them have an advantage.

Motivation

Principles of learning and cognition state that without motivation and attention to a task, learning does not occur and comprehension is im-peded. Motivation has several functions. As noted earlier, skilled listen-ing comprehension is a complex activity requiring the simultaneous co-ordination of numerous subskills. Low-level subskills become automatic through practice and require less attention for their execution. However, during the early learning stages before automaticity is reached, these skills require considerable amounts of attention and effort, and it is during this early stage of learning that the task is difficult and motiva-tion is required. Thus, one important function of motivation is that during the difficult stage of learning it provides the energy for directing attention to the task to be learned. The basic reason for wanting the low-level tasks to become automatic is that attention is required by the high-level tasks, such as integrating information the speaker is presenting with information in memory and evaluating the information. High-level tasks like understanding a lecture do not become automatic; conse-quently, motivation and attention are always required for comprehen-sion. This use of attention in higher-level processing brings us to the second function of motivation: it is the driving force which directs the listener's attention in the direction of the speaker and aids in the infor-mation processing.

Outside-the-Head Factors

Discussion Topic

Listening comprehension may be thought of as an interactive process in which the listener's knowledge is used to make sense of information provided by the speaker. The ability to understand and to construct meaning out of what a speaker is saying is determined, in part, by the listener's prior knowledge of the message. Unfortunately, there are a number of reasons why comprehension may be poor even when the listener has the necessary knowledge to understand the speaker. Barriers to comprehension include lack of awareness that one's knowledge is applicable to the discussion topic, lack of motivation to attend to the message, and failure to use appropriate metacognitive listening strategies.

Speakers who are aware of these comprehension barriers can do much to help the listener. For example, to help the transfer of knowledge from one context to another (Pearson & Johnson, 1978), analogies, examples, illustrations, and prior discussion, in which one draws out what the listener knows about a topic before a lecture is given, can be used. To encourage listeners to pay attention, a number of rhetorical devices have been used by teachers and public speakers. One technique which has been used by teachers to encourage students to pay attention during lectures has been the alternation of lecture and questioning of students. If the lecturer only calls on students who raise hands, this technique does not work as well as when the instructor calls on students at random. Since with the random method the student cannot predict when a question will be asked, all students are encouraged to pay attention. Another motivating device long used by teachers to encourage students to come to lecture and pay attention is to include on all tests questions which come only from the lecture material and not from the text used for the course.

Finally, when a message contains more material than can be stored easily in memory or when the message is poorly organized and presented, special listening skills are required to understand and recall the message. The barriers to comprehension and recall are that the listener may not possess the necessary skills for handling the information overload or may lack the motivation to use the skills. Thus, even when the listener has the necessary background knowledge to understand the topic, presenting too much information or presenting information in a disorganized manner may interfere with listener comprehension.

Speaker Awareness of Listener Needs

To communicate effectively, it is helpful if the speaker is aware of listener needs and the factors which influence comprehension such as the amount of information a listener has about a topic, the educational and intellectual level of the listener, the listener's interest in the discussion topic, and momentary fluctuations in attention. For example, it is useful for the speaker to know the extent of the listener's background information on a topic. If the level of knowledge is inadequate, it may be necessary to provide the missing information. On the other hand, if the listener is familiar with a topic, the speaker need not cover all the basic points because any gaps can be filled in by inferences derived from the listener's knowledge.

Being aware of the listener's educational and intellectual level helps the speaker decide on the type of vocabulary and syntax to use, as well as the rate of information presentation. If these are inappropriate for the needs of the listener, comprehension will suffer. As mentioned previously, the low IQ individual can master complex tasks providing the rate of information presentation is slow and there are opportunities for review and rehearsal.

By knowing if a listener is motivated and interested in a topic, the speaker is able to make various types of adjustments in a presentation. For example, when the listener is not interested in a topic, the speaker may have to devote a considerable portion of time to convincing the listener that the topic is important and worthy of attention. If, on the other hand, the listener is already interested, the time may be spent in other ways. By being sensitive to the nonverbal signals of the listener, the speaker can estimate when there are lapses in listener attention and the speaker can make the necessary adjustments to recapture the attention of the listener.

Finally, the speaker's sensitivity to the acoustic characteristics of the physical space where the talk or discussion is taking place also influences comprehension. Depending on the characteristics of the space, as well as the distance between the speaker and listener, the speaker may have to adjust voice loudness to accommodate the listener's needs. Recent findings about the ability to adjust voice loudness to compensate for the distance between the listener and speaker indicate that the ability seems to be age related. While young children in the primary grades seem to be able to raise their voices appropriately when the listener is at a distance, they seem to have more difficulty reducing their voice level when the listener is near. This finding may help to explain why many children in the primary grades get into trouble in the classroom because they speak too loudly instead of speaking in a whisper (G. Siegel, personal communication, 1983).

Message Clarity

The speaker controls numerous factors which influence the clarity and recall of a message. In formal and often in informal talks, it is helpful to the audience if the speaker clearly indicates the underlying purpose or goal as well as the major supporting arguments and evidence. If these devices are omitted, the listener is left to infer what these elements may be and may be incorrect in making the required inferences. When the talk is in a classroom setting, devices such as summaries, reviews, and questions by the speaker can help the listener understand the major points and facilitate comprehension and recall.

According to Pearson and Johnson (1978), the use of anaphoric terms poses one of the most difficult problems for comprehending a message, because to understand the anaphoric term, one must locate the referent. While this task is difficult enough in reading, it is far more difficult in a listening situation. When reading, if one cannot recall the referent to an anaphoric term, the reader can go back in the text to locate it. When listening, however, what does one go back to? In some situations the speaker can be asked to repeat the referent for the anaphoric term, but in many situations this strategy may be inappropriate.

There are still other reasons why comprehending a text under certain conditions is easier than comprehending spontaneous spoken language. Except for some formal presentations, a spoken language event usually has had less planning and revision than a written text. A well-written text has a structure and cohesive ties which bind the various parts together, features often lacking in the ebb and flow of conversation or in a lecture given in class, unless the lecture has been carefully prepared.

On the other hand, a number of factors work in favor of spoken over written language. Those factors which may enable spoken language to be more comprehensible than written are the degree of interaction possible between the message receiver and sender and the extent to which the message sender can add subtle degrees of emphasis and emotional modulation to the message. Regarding the first factor, the face-to-face interactive nature of conversation makes it possible for speakers and listeners to actively negotiate meaning. In informal situations, when the listener has difficulty understanding, the speaker may be asked to clarify. Listeners and speakers take turns, build on each others' statements and ideas, and create their own set of meanings as they converse.

The second factor which may make spoken language easier to understand than written language has to do with the fact that with speech the speaker can modulate what is being said by varying pitch, stress, and pauses between words and phrases. This type of vocal modulation can add richness, emphasis, and interest to what the speaker is saying. Unfortunately, however, there are speakers who do not modulate their voice, speaking instead in a dull monotone. While vocal modulation is easily expressed in speech, it is poorly represented in texts (Schreiber, 1980), a factor which adds to the difficulty of learning to read. In fact, Schreiber believes that one of the important tasks in beginning reading is learning how to construct meaning when pitch, stress, and pauses are missing from the written code.

Context

In general, when the environment contains the objects to which the speaker is referring, comprehension is facilitated. For example, the speaker can help the listener understand the sentence *Give it to him* by pointing to the individual referred to as *him*. Similarly, as G. Siegel (personal communication, 1983) has stated, when working with children who have speech and communication difficulties, the examiner should work with the child in two environments, one in which there are environmental supports for the message and the other decontextualized, in order to find out the extent to which the child needs contextual supports for understanding what is said. Finally, Spiro (1980) has found that the context in which an event occurs may indicate if what is learned is important and to be remembered or whether it should be expunged from memory as soon as possible.

Summary

A range of interactive inside- and outside-the-head factors which influence listening comprehension has been presented. Awareness of these factors is a first step in analyzing the listening communication problems which students may experience. Knowledge of what these factors are should help educators and specialists in the area of communication disorders to look broadly at the range of factors which are related to causes of poor listening comprehension.

READING

As mentioned previously, there is considerable overlap between the factors which influence comprehension and those which influence reading comprehension. In this section of the chapter, those factors which influence reading comprehension are addressed. Table 10.2 shows those inside-the-head and outside-the-head factors which influence learning to read and reading comprehension.

Inside-the-Head Factors

Intelligence

Unlike listening and speaking, which are universal skills and which seem to be genetically determined behaviors, reading is not a universal behavior and is found only in literate societies. Thus, while the ability to

TABLE 10.2
Factors That Influence Learning to Read and Text
Comprehension

Inside-the-head	Outside-the-head

1. Intelligence: Does the student have the intelligence to learn to read?
2. Language of instruction: Does the student understand technical terms used during instruction, such as "word," "sentence," "paragraph"?
3. Decoding ability
    Is the student accurate at word recognition?
    Is the student automatic at word recognition?
    Can the student read orally with expression?
4. Background knowledge and schema
    Does the student have the necessary background knowledge to understand the text topic?
    Can the student make appropriate inferences?
5. Text structure: Is the student aware of text structure used in scientific articles, expository text, narratives, fairy tales, etc.?
6. Anaphoric terms: Can the student find the referent for anaphoric terms?
7. Metacognitive strategies
    Is the student aware of when there is a breakdown in understanding the text?
    Can the student identify the major points and details in a text?
    Can the student synthesize, summarize, and construct a conceptual map of a text?
8. Language facility
    Vocabulary: Does the student have an extensive vocabulary? Does the student know the variety of ways in which a word can be used?
    Syntax: Is the student aware of how various propositions may be embedded in a sentence to make it complex?
	1. Quality of instruction
	    Is the teaching style task and human relations oriented?
	    Is there direct teaching of decoding and comprehension skills?
	    Is sufficient practice time given so that skills can develop beyond accuracy to automaticity stage?
	    Is there quality control over the progress of each student?
	    Is the classroom program carefully structured?
	    Is the teacher explicit about the goals for each lesson, and does the teacher explain why the goals are important?
	    Does the teacher clarify how to do the task?
	    If a student cannot answer a question, does the teacher help the student arrive at the correct answer?
	2. Text topic: Is the topic one that the student has sufficient background to understand?
	3. Conventions of print: Does the student understand the meaning of print conventions, such as quotation marks, exclamation marks, question marks, side heads, capital letters, etc.?
	4. Clarity of writing style
	    Has the writer correctly judged the audience?
	    Is there an appropriate match between information in the text and the reader's background knowledge?
	    Do the sentences contain too much information?
	    Are there too many anaphoric terms?
	    Does the text lack cohesive ties and causal links?
	5. Text readability
	    Is the vocabulary appropriate for the student?
	    Is the sentence structure too complex for the student?

TABLE 10.2 (*Continued*)

Inside-the-head	Outside-the-head

9. Graphic literacy: Can the student interpret a variety of graphs and figures?
10. Motivation, attention: Is the student sufficiently interested to focus attention on learning and on the text topic?
	6. Format design and structural text elements
	   Does the text have titles, chapter heads, and side heads?
	   Does the text use abstracts, statements of objectives, questions at the beginning, middle and end of text, marginal gloss?
	   Is the text easy on the eyes?
	7. Time: Is enough time given for the student to read and comprehend the text?

express thoughts and emotions through speech and the ability to understand speech may be found in all societies, the ability to express ideas through writing and the ability to read is found only in the literate societies, and the development of these reading and writing skills requires formal instruction of some kind.

As Lenneberg (1967) has stated, intelligence quotients correlate quite poorly with the production and comprehension of speech. Unlike speech, however, intelligence quotients correlate reasonably well with reading achievement, ranging from the .40s and .50s in Grade One and to the .70s in Grade Four, where the correlation remains until college (Harris & Sipay, 1975). Although it is not a well-known fact, educable retardates, with IQ scores in the 50–80 range, can learn to process text for meaning, especially if the topic is one with which they are familiar. However, because the retardates' rate of learning is slower, greater time must be allowed for them to master the reading skills.

One problem slow learners have is that the pacing of instruction is often too fast for them to become automatic at decoding. Because of this, slow learners can easily become discouraged and stop paying attention to the learning tasks. In order to maintain motivation and time-on-task, the materials should be simple, meaningful, and interesting. With slow learners, and with students who have not become automatic at decoding, the method of repeated reading has been used successfully to build accuracy and automaticity as well as the skills required for reading orally with expression.

Language of Instruction and the Conventions of Print

When teachers communicate with students, numerous technical words specific to instruction are used. For example, in a simple instructional command which might be given at the first grade level, *Read the second word in the sentence,* one finds four technical words which first graders will not understand unless they have been taught the meanings of these words: *word, sentence, second,* and *read.* If the child fails to read the designated word, it is not clear whether the problem was inability to read the word, failure to understand the directions, or both. In order to locate the designated word, the student has to know that a printed word is a letter or group of letters surrounded by space, while a sentence is a group of words which begin with a capital letter and end with a period, question mark, or exclamation mark.

A common misconception which many teachers have is their assumption that because the explanation or instruction seems simple to the teacher, it is equally simple and understandable for the student. I have been in remedial reading classes at the junior high level and found students who, unknown to their remedial reading teachers, still had difficulty with concepts such as word, sentence, and paragraph. While it is true that many students come to school with knowledge of these terms because of instruction which they have acquired at home, it is equally true that numerous students come to school without mastery of these important concepts, and it the responsibility of the school to teach these concepts.

Another problem area for students is what may be thought of as the conventions of print. Many poor readers are unaware of the meanings of print symbols such as quotation marks, exclamation marks, colons, and capital letters. Students need to be taught the significance of these and numerous other symbols. Part of the kindergarten and first grade curriculum should include instruction in the language of instruction and the conventions of print. When students are experiencing difficulty learning to read, one of the first questions the teacher should ask as a routine matter, is whether the student understands the technical terms used in instruction and the conventions of print. The diagnosis is simple to make. One simply asks the student to count how many words are in a particular sentence or how many sentences are in a paragraph, or how many paragraphs are on a page. It is surprising how many poor readers have difficulty with these concepts.

Decoding Ability

Decoding here means what is thought of as word recognition. If a student is having trouble with reading comprehension, one can logically ask whether the student has mastered the decoding skills. At the broadest level, decoding can be divided into two components. The first part, which has to do with word-recognition accuracy, can be tested by having the student read aloud and recording the recognition errors. The second part, which has to do with automaticity, can also be tested rather simply.

Automaticity can be thought of as the ease and speed with which a word can be recognized. When a person is automatic at word recognition, little attention is required, and the available attention can be used for comprehension (LaBerge & Samuels, 1974). If too much attention is used for word recognition, there will not be enough to meet the demands of the comprehension process. Thus, accuracy and automaticity are necessary conditions for comprehension. However, it should be pointed out that although automaticity is necessary, it will not guarantee good comprehension, since comprehension is a complex process requiring other skills in addition to automatic decoding.

Perhaps the easiest way to determine if a student is automatic at decoding is to have the student orally read a passage which has not been previewed. The student should be told that immediately after the oral reading, recall of the passage will be required. One indicator of automaticity is the accuracy of the recall. In order to be able to comprehend while reading orally, the student has to decode the passage with little attention, and this, in essence, is what is meant by automaticity.

Another indicator of automaticity is the ability to read orally with expression. Teachers often make the mistake of telling their students to read with expression. The error is the belief that the student has the ability to read with expression but is voluntarily withholding this ability. Dull, word-by-word reading in a monotone usually means that the student is at the accurate but not the automatic level of reading. When a student orally reads the same short passage a number of times, as with the method of repeated reading (Samuels, 1979), one may observe with each rereading of the passage how rapidly the student advances from reading in a monotone to reading with expression.

Another way to determine if decoding problems are contributing to poor comprehension is to compare comprehension on a listening task with comprehension on an oral reading task, assuming that the level of difficulty for both passages is the same. If listening comprehension is superior to reading comprehension, a decoding problem may be suspected. This comparison was studied by Samuels and Horowitz (1982; Horowitz and Samuels, 1985). In this investigation, good and poor sixth grade readers were asked to listen to and to read orally expository texts which were comparable in difficulty. After listening and after reading orally, the students recalled the texts. The good readers were reading at a ninth-grade level and the poor readers were reading at a fourth-grade

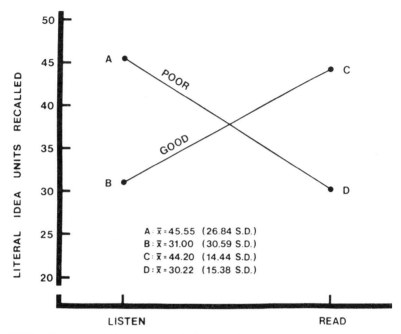

FIGURE 10.1. Literal idea units recalled by good and poor readers for listening and reading easy texts.

level. The easy texts were written at a fourth–fifth grade readability level and the hard texts were at the seventh–eighth grade readability level. The easy texts were 300 words long while the hard texts were 367 words long.

Figure 10.1 shows the recall for good and poor readers on the easy text. The good readers (B–C) were significantly better on reading than on listening ($p < .05$, two-tail), but just the opposite (A–D) is found with the poor readers ($p < .05$, two-tail). When one compares good versus poor readers on the listening task (A–B), because of the large standard deviations, there was no difference between the groups in recall on the listening task. There was a significant difference between good and poor readers in recall on the reading task (C–D), favoring the good readers ($p < .02$, two-tail). The fact that the poor readers were significantly better on listening than reading indicates that even on the easy texts which were written at their reading level, they were experiencing decoding difficulties. Good readers, on the other hand, were not having decoding problems with texts written at this level of difficulty.

With the more difficult texts, as seen in Figure 10.2, a somewhat

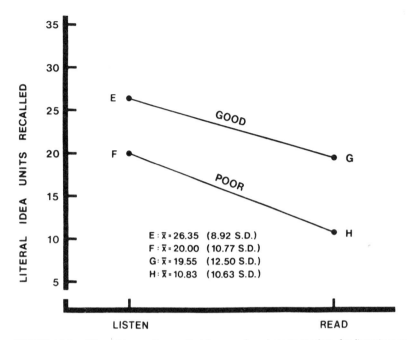

FIGURE 10.2. Literal idea units recalled by good and poor readers for listening and reading difficult texts.

different picture emerges. For the good readers there was no significant difference between listening and reading (E–G) and for the poor readers there is no significant difference between listening and reading (F–H). When good and poor readers are compared on listening recall (E–F), there is no significant difference. However, when they are compared on recall for the reading task (G–H), the good readers are significantly superior.

Thus, on both the easy and the hard texts, when good and poor readers are compared, a pattern emerges. The pattern is one in which there is no significant difference between good and poor readers on listening comprehension but there is a significant difference between them on reading comprehension. It appears, then, that the difference between good and poor readers, at least with this sample, is with decoding skill rather than with listening comprehension.

This study also illustrates how important it is to consider text difficulty when trying to diagnose a student's reading problems. If only difficult texts had been used to compare listening and reading comprehension, it would appear that the poor readers did not have a decoding problem since comprehension under listening and reading was not significantly different. But for the poor readers, when easy texts were used for listening and reading, listening comprehension was significantly better than reading comprehension, indicating a decoding problem. It appears, then, that if only one level of text difficulty is to be used in trying to diagnose whether a student has a decoding problem, it should be an easy text.

Background Knowledge

This factor, as discussed under listening comprehension, is equally applicable to reading comprehension.

Text Structure

Just as different buildings have different structures, different text types, such as fairy tales, narratives, and exposition, have different structures. Students who are aware of text structure have better recall than students who are unaware of it. In fact, lack of awareness of text structure seems to impede comprehension and recall.

To determine if the student is aware of text structure, the person doing the diagnosis should have the student read texts with different kinds of structures and then test the student's recall in writing, if possible. What one looks for is the extent to which the sequences of ideas and categories of information in the recall match those presented in the text. With certain text types, such as narratives, in which one event causes another to happen, as, for example, when Little Red Riding Hood's mother tells her to visit her grandmother and these instructions lead to a series of causally linked events, and with instructions on how to construct an object, sequence of information is important. With other text types, such as an expository text describing the agricultural products of different countries, what is important is the clustering of information in categories around specific countries. Generally, when a student who is aware of text structure is asked to recall a well-structured text, the order of recalled information is similar to the text and there is a clustering of information that should be kept together. When students who are unaware of text structure are asked to recall a text, the ideas and concepts recalled seem to resemble a random jumble of information with little resemblance to the text structure.

Anaphoric Terms

Anaphoric terms are found in written texts just as they are found in spoken texts. The previous section on listening has a discussion of these terms.

Metacognitive Strategies

Metacognitive strategies are important in reading comprehension just as they are in listening comprehension. Highly complex operational systems, such as factories and school systems, require an administrator or executive whose job it is to oversee and control the entire operation in order to ensure that the goals of the organization are being met. Metacognition refers to the administrative and executive functions that operate during text processing to ensure that the goals of reading are being fulfilled.

During reading, the executive asks such questions as Why am I reading this? Do I want to read this for superficial overview or for detail? Am I aware of when there is a breakdown in comprehension? When there is a breakdown in comprehension, do I know how to get back on the track again? What are the major and minor points of this text? Can I summarize or synthesize the major points in this text?

Differences in use of metacognitive strategies seems to be one of the factors that differentiate the sophisticated from the less-sophisticated reader. To assess these strategies, several different techniques are available. One technique entails asking the student questions such as What are the reasons why people read? Describe how you would read a morning newspaper when you only have 20 minutes? How should one study for an important test when the examination is three months away? . . . a week away?

To test self-awareness or monitoring of one's reading to determine when there is a breakdown in comprehension, a simple technique can be used: At various points in a well-written text a word or sentence that either does not make sense or violates a point made earlier in the text is inserted. The student is asked to read and to indicate whenever something does not make sense. If the student fails to do this each time the nonsense element occurs, it indicates that the student has difficulty with this strategy.

The ability to identify and summarize major points and separate them from minor points can be tested directly by asking the student to read an article and to summarize it or by asking the student to list the major and the minor points. The student can also be asked to construct a conceptual map or network and, by listing the major points and drawing interconnecting lines, to show how the ideas interrelate.

Language Facility

The two aspects of language that are important for text comprehension are vocabulary and syntax. Poor comprehension may be the result of vocabulary or syntax which is too difficult and complex for the reader.

To determine if the vocabulary is a potential source of difficulty, the student can be asked to give the meanings of potentially troublesome words. A simple, useful, but frequently ignored, technique for helping students comprehend the texts used in school is to introduce new and difficult vocabulary in the same context as found in the text. Similarly, in order to find out if students are having difficulty with sentence structure, the student can be asked to paraphrase potentially troublesome sentences. Some students seem to be unaware that complex embedded sentences are in reality several separate sentences that have been combined into one. A useful method for helping students understand complex sentences is to provide writing instruction in sentence combining. With this method, short simple sentences are given and the student's task is to synthesize the sentences into a single, more complex sentence. This experience with combining sentences will help the student understand how to analyze meaning.

Writers of school materials who use readability formulas to determine if the text is suitable for students often try to alter the text if the formulas indicate that the text is too difficult for the intended audience. The two major variables in readability formulas are word frequency and sentence length. In the attempt to improve the readability of the text as indicated by the formula, the writers try to find high-frequency synonyms which can substitute for the low frequency words and they reduce sentence length by breaking long sentences into shorter sentences. Unfortunately, this is not a recommended procedure since in the attempt to find simpler words and less complex sentences, important nuances of meaning may be lost or altered. In fact, an altered text with shorter sentences may be more difficult to understand because in order to reduce sentence length, important connecting words indicating causality may have to be eliminated. For example, the longer sentence *Because of his concern that the woman who was having a seizure would injure herself, the physician put a stick between her teeth* can be split into two shorter sentences: *The woman was having a seizure. The physician put a stick between her teeth.* While according to the formulas the shorter sentences would indicate an increase in comprehensibility, in reality they are more difficult to understand. The proper use of readability formulas is on an already-existing text to estimate its comprehensibility. The improper use of the formulas is as a guide to altering and revising text.

Graphic Literacy

Reading technical material often involves the interpretation of figures and graphs. To determine if the student has the skills necessary for interpreting these materials, it is necessary to provide a variety of typical figures and graphs and ask the student to answer questions about them.

Motivation and Attention

The same general principles of motivation and attention as discussed in the section on listening apply to reading as well. A technique which can be used during the reading situation to determine if the student is paying attention and on-task is to observe the student over periods of time in different settings such as reading or art, using a technique called "the 6-sec observation schedule." To use this technique, first the observer must know what the instructional task is for the students. The observer looks at the student for 6 seconds; if the student is engaged in what the teacher had instructed the student to do, the observer puts a plus on the recording sheet. If the student is not engaged in the appropriate task, a minus is indicated. By dividing the engaged time by the total number of observations, the observer can determine the percentage of time the student attended to the task.

Outside-the-Head Factors

There are a number of outside-the-head factors which can influence learning to read and reading comprehension. Difficulty in learning to read may result from what may be thought of as iatrogenic sources, that is, school-produced failure. When the quality of instruction is inadequate, we can anticipate that numerous students will have difficulty learning to read with good comprehension.

Quality of Instruction

There are a number of components to consider under instructional quality.

Teaching Style. Productivity in educational and business settings is related to managerial style. Studies in these settings have revealed that in order to maximize learning and performance, the most effective managerial style is a blend of task and human relations orientation. There is reason to believe that a critical factor relating to the greater productivity of the Japanese worker in comparison to the American worker is the way the workers are treated by management. In the large Japanese factories, where the workers are treated with great concern for their psychological welfare and where they enjoy virtually lifetime job security and benefits, there seems to be greater esprit de corps, a greater feeling of shared goals and responsibility for the success of the organization, and less conflict between labor and management. In the Japanese factory there is more of what can be thought of as cooperative grouping and effort, where the goals of the groups are in harmony and the groups coordinate efforts to maximize productivity.

Studies of outstanding reading programs have found aspects of these programs which are similar to what one finds in the Japanese factory. For example, schools with outstanding reading programs have a managerial style described as task and human relations oriented. There is excellent rapport between teachers and students and warm, emotionally supportive classroom climates. In evaluating the instructional component, educators should be sensitive and aware of the importance of classroom climate and style of interaction between teacher and student. Based upon these studies, we may anticipate that in classroom settings where the teacher is able to maintain task orientation and warm, emotionally supportive interactions with the students, academic achievement should be maximized.

Direct and Explicit Instruction.   Too often what passes for reading instruction is actually nothing more than skill testing. Asking word-recognition and comprehension questions, while of some value in that it provides feedback to student and to teacher, should not be mistaken for direct and explicit instruction in the skill. There are components of good instruction which, though adequate for many students, prove to be inadequate for numerous others. For example, providing an educational setting in which the student is motivated to read, reading materials which are easy and interesting, and a teacher who guides the student through the material by asking meaning-oriented questions and who answers student questions, as needed, is an appropriate method for many children. However, many students fail to learn unless there is direct and explicit instruction (Duffy, Roehler, & Mason 1984). In addition to the components of good reading instruction just listed, the teacher should explain the strategies and demonstrate the processes necessary for decoding and comprehending text. Explicit instruction has the following characteristics: (1) It provides the cognitive strategies necessary to perform a task. (2) The hidden processes of the mind are made public. (3) The instructor models or explains the steps one must go through to perform the task.

Practice.   Everyone agrees that practice makes perfect. It is unfortunate, however, that despite this agreement, some students (usually the slower learners) are moved through their skills and basal readers too quickly and never master what has been presented. Practice time should be balanced between reinforcing skills that have been presented previously by the teacher and reading for pleasure. The slower learners seem to be the ones who spend the least amount of time reading easy, meaningful texts for pleasure, and ways should be found, such as home-based reading, to increase the amount of practice time so that they can improve beyond accuracy to automaticity.

The Reverend Jesse Jackson, speaking to Chicago-area educators, had this to say about the importance of practice:

> We say that Johnny can't read because he is deprived, because he's hungry, because he's discriminated against. We say that Johnny can't read because his Daddy's not at home. Well, Johnny learns to play basketball without Daddy. We do best what we do most, and for many children that is playing ball. One reason Johnny doesn't do well in reading is that Johnny doesn't practice reading.

Quality Control. Models of the teaching process contain a component on evaluation. Student evaluation can be accomplished in two ways, either by assessing on an ongoing basis the student's progress on the subskills considered important for reading (formative evaluation) or by deciding on an overall global assessment of student progress which is usually instituted at predesignated time periods (summative evaluation). At some risk of overgeneralizing, there are several important differences between formative and summative evaluation. With formative evaluation, assessment is done on an ongoing basis for each of the important subskills, while with summative evaluation the assessment is done less frequently, often just once for a report card, and the assessment is over a large body of material.

For purposes of instructional decision-making, the advantage of formative evaluation is that if a student is having a problem learning the subject matter, the instructor can discover the problem as soon as possible and take the necessary means to correct it. One of the characteristics of outstanding reading programs is their use of formative evaluation, which can provide important feedback to the student and to the teacher. Unfortunately, many teachers see themselves as dispensers of information, and they view the fine-grained formative assessment of each student as an imposition and barrier to their teaching. Since formative skills assessment is an ongoing process which is engaged in frequently, it functions as a quality control measure to prevent a student from falling behind in reading.

Structure. Another characteristic of outstanding reading programs is that they are carefully structured. There are several aspects to classroom structure. First, there are established routines so that there is little wasted time. The time saved is used by the students for time-on-task activities and by the teacher for high-level decision-making, such as diagnosing and remediating student achievement problems. Second, the teacher has a clear concept of the goals of instruction as well as the means to be used to achieve them. Thus, in deciding if there is structure in the class, one looks for well-established routines and knowledge of the goals and methods of instruction.

Importance of and Interrelationship among Goals.   Although the importance of each day's lesson and the interrelationships among the lessons may be clear to the teacher, they may not be clear to the student. Without clear and precise explanation of the importance of a lesson and how it relates to other skills, the lesson lacks importance for many students. The student who cooperates without knowing why the task is important is doing so out of a sense of obedience, as described in the lines of the poem, "The Charge of the Light Brigade": "Theirs not to reason why, theirs but to do and die."

Clarity of Writing

Poor comprehension may result from lack of clarity of writing rather than shortcomings on the part of the reader. Text characteristics associated with poor writing are overuse of anaphoric terms (which was discussed in the previous section), misjudging the audience, information overload, and lack of cohesive ties and causal links.

Misjudging the Audience.   The writer must estimate the degree of background knowledge of the audience regarding the text topic. At times the writer overestimates this knowledge, and the text fails to provide enough necessary information. Another way to misjudge the audience is to use vocabulary which is too difficult. On the other hand, the writer may underestimate the knowledge of the audience and provide more information than the audience needs. If the text provides too little information, the text is too difficult, but if it provides too much information, the text becomes boring and uninteresting.

Information Overload.   Sentences that contain too much information can lead to poor comprehension. For example, two texts may contain the same number of words, but one of the texts may contain more concepts. The text with the greater density of concepts will be more difficult to comprehend.

Lack of Cohesive Ties and Causal Links.   As discussed previously, readability formulas are useful when they are used to estimate the comprehensibility of naturally occurring texts. However, when one uses these formulas to artificially create a text that meets some grade level for readability, one often creates comprehension problems by omitting words which show relationships and causality.

Text Comprehensibility

Among the many variables which influence text comprehension are word familiarity and sentence complexity. Often poor comprehension results when the reader does not know the meanings of a large percentage of the words used in a text. One way to overcome this problem in a classroom setting is to introduce potentially difficult words in the same context as contained in the text. Another problem relates to sentence complexity. If a sentence contains too much information, it is difficult to understand. Text revision is a long and respected tradition in the field of writing. Long and needlessly complex sentences can be revised so that the same concepts are expressed in a simpler way; however, in revising, one must be careful to preserve the cohesive ties and links.

Format Design and Structural Text Elements. A variety of aids can be added to a text to facilitate text comprehension. If a student is having difficulty, one can determine if the text contains these aids and if the student is using them. If titles, chapter heads, and side heads are present in a text, they can be used to activate relevant schemata for text comprehension. In addition, these text elements can be used as memory pegs to aid recall of text information.

A number of adjunct aids can be used to aid text comprehension. These aids include abstracts, advance organizers, statements of objectives, study questions interspersed in the text to maintain attention, glossaries, conceptual maps which show the major ideas and their structural relationships to each other, and marginal glosses to help explain particularly difficult concepts.

Eye Strain. With the increasing popularity of the computer, the need for minotors that can be read easily is increasing in importance. However, even the printed page can be of such poor quality that it poses problems.

Time. In testing situations, where less time is given to the student than the student needs, the test score may indicate that the student has a comprehension problem. If additional reading time were allowed, the student's comprehension score might improve significantly. With enough time and motivation to reread, even inconsiderate texts can be comprehended.

SUMMARY AND CONCLUSION

This chapter presents a cognitive approach to diagnosing listening and reading problems. The approach assumes an interaction among factors which are external and internal to the student. Examples of external factors include the topic of the message, word frequency, sentence complexity, and the degree of structure contained in the message. Internal factors include one's language skills, prior knowledge of the topic, and awareness of the structure of a message. If there is a comprehension problem, it is useful to have a model of inside-the-head and outside-the-head factors which influence comprehension, such as the one presented in this chapter, in order to diagnose the difficulty.

REFERENCES

Duffy, G., Roehler, L., & Mason, J. (1984). *Comprehension instruction.* New York: Longman.

Garner, R. (1983). Correcting the imbalance: Diagnosis of strategic behaviors in reading. In S. J. Samuels (Ed.), *Issues in reading diagnosis.* Montgomery, MD: Aspen Systems.

Gough, P. B. (1984). Word recognition. In P. D. Pearson (Ed.), *Handbook of reading research.* New York: Longman.

Harris, A. J., & Sipay, E. R. (1975). *How to increase reading ability.* New York: McKay.

Horowitz, R., & Samuels, S. J. (1985). Reading and listening to expository text. *Journal of Reading Behavior, 17,* 185–198.

LaBerge, D., & Samuels, S. J. (1974). *Basic processes in reading: Perception and comprehension.* Hillsdale, NJ: Erlbaum.

Lenneberg, E. H. (1967). *Biological foundations of language.* New York: Wiley.

Mason, J. M., Kniseley, E., & Kendall, J. (1979). Effects of polysemous words on sentence comprehension. *Reading Research Quarterly, 15,* 49–65.

Mosenthal, P., & Jin Na, T. (1980). Quality of children's recall under two classroom testing tasks: Towards a socio-linguistic model of reading comprehension. *Reading Research Quarterly, 15,* 504–528.

Pearson, P. D., & Johnson, D. D. (1978). *Teaching reading comprehension.* New York: Holt.

Pisoni, D. (1981). Some current theoretical issues in speech perception. *Cognition, 10,* 249–259.

Samuels, S. J. (1979). The method of repeated reading. *The Reading Teacher, 32,* 403–408.

Samuels, S. J., & Horowitz, R. (1982). Reading and listening comprehension. *Australian Journal of Remedial Education, 14*(1 & 2), 60–62.

Schreiber, P. (1980). On the acquisition of reading fluency. *Journal of Reading Behavior, 12,* 177–186.

Shuell, T. (1972). *Individual differences in learning and retention* (Final Report, Project No. 0-0341). Washington, DC: U.S. Department of Health, Education and Welfare, Office of Education.

Spiro, R. (1977). Remembering information from text: The state of schema approach. In R. C. Anderson, R. Spiro, & W. Montague (Eds.), *Schooling and the acquisition of knowledge.* Hillsdale, NJ: Erlbaum.

Spiro, R. (1980). Constructive processes in prose comprehension and recall. In R. Spiro, B. Bruce, & B. Brewer (Eds.), *Theoretical issues in reading comprehension*. Hillsdale, NJ: Erlbaum.

Taylor, B., & Samuels, S. J. (1983). Children's use of text structure in the recall of expository material. *American Educational Research Journal, 20*, 517–528.

Vinsonhaler, J. S., Weinshank, A. B., Wagner, C., & Polin, R. (1983). Diagnosing children with educational problems: characteristics of reading and learning disabilities specialists, and classroom teachers. *Reading Research Quarterly, 8*(2), 134–164.

PART IV

THE ACQUISITION
OF LITERACY
AND SCHOOLING

Chapter **11**

From Meaning to Definition: A Literate Bias on the Structure of Word Meaning

Rita Watson
David R. Olson

INTRODUCTION

The meaning of the spoken word is largely bound up with its use on given utterance occasions, as Wittgenstein (1953) and many since have argued. The comprehension of expressions in oral discourse, where speaker and hearer share the same "real-world" context, is usually accomplished by appeal to context and to the shared expectancies established prior to and during the conversation by the participants (Garfinkel, 1964). In contrast, the meaning of written expressions must be recoverable from text: writer and reader must construct and reconstruct interpretations largely on the basis of the words alone (Olson, 1977; 1986). Oral and written language can thus be differentially associated with two aspects of meaning. Speaker's meaning or situationally constructed meaning is more central to the listener's interpretation of meaning in oral discourse, and word or sentence meaning is more central to the reader's interpretation of meaning in a written text. Texts require the explicit, linguistic expression of meaning, since appeal to speakers' shared expectancies or situationally constructed meanings common in oral discourse is minimized by the distance between writer and reader. In this way, the use of texts could be said to bias the structure of mean-

COMPREHENDING ORAL AND WRITTEN LANGUAGE

ing away from the inchoate structures of oral discourse toward linguistically expressible meanings that can be represented in the text itself.

The notion of meaning as a property of language, rather than one of speaker's intentions, has been linked to literacy (Olson, 1977, in preparation; Stock, 1983). Stock suggests that, historically, the rise of literacy led to massive changes in the assumptions, shared by those who could read and write, about the properties and uses of language. Meaning was preserved in texts that survived their authors. Reflection upon the constituents and properties of language, and their role in determining meaning, became possible. Indeed, it has been argued elsewhere that the consequences of both literacy and print have permeated our view not only of language, but of the world (McLuhan, 1962; Olson, 1986, in preparation). With respect to word meaning, it was the preservation of the word in written form that led to its identification as a meaning-bearing constituent in the language.

From an ontogenetic perspective, the child's acquisition of literacy demonstrates some parallels with the historical case. Literate children are more capable than preliterate children of differentiating speaker's meaning from sentence meaning, perception from inference (Olson, 1986), and words from things (Papandropoulou, 1978). Yet they acquire literacy skills within a complex matrix of literate cultural practices, such as schooling, which could also be expected to engender cognitive and linguistic change. However, whether these capabilities are attributed to the acquisition of print-related skills or to participation in the practices of a literate culture, such as schooling, it still suggests that written language, and the uses and cultural practices it supports, biases our view of meaning as a property of words, sentences, and inferences rather than of things, speakers, and perceptions.

In what follows, we argue that the differentiation of word or sentence meaning from speaker's meaning is to a large extent a consequence of the uses of text. Further, we argue that views of word meaning as opaque, autonomous, generalizable, conceptual, and linguistically expressible, are to a large extent engendered by text and its uses. Finally, we argue that explicit linguistic expressions of word meaning, or definitions, have emerged as both conventional and authoritative in our culture, and reflect a literate bias on the structure of word meaning.

MEANING

The dictionary tells us that the verb *to mean* derives from the Old English word *maenen*, which seems to have meant 'purpose,' and connects *to mean* with the root *men-*, which means 'to think.' When the word is predicated of a person, it means 'to intend,' when it is predicated of a thing, it means 'to signify.' In a remarkable book, *Thought and Language,* Ballard (1934) related these two sides of meaning in this way:

> The change from purpose to significance took place through our habit of transferring verbs from human subjects to neuter subjects. Meaning could at first be properly ascribed to human beings only; they alone could mean, or intend, or give significance. Dead things, such as signs or symbols, could of themselves mean nothing. But by an unconscious sort of personification the capacity to mean has been conferred on these inanimate things, and they too are now said to have meaning. (p. 43)

This distinction between purpose or intention and significance is just the one we require for analyzing development from meaning to definition. The former may be described as speaker's meaning, or simply intended meaning—what the speaker meant by saying something. The latter may be described as word (or sentence) meaning—what the word (or sentence) per se means independently of what the speaker may have intended by it. The following example illustrates these two senses of meaning in a conversation between two children:

Child 1: *You know what? My dad's tall and puny.*
Child 2: *Well, what does puny mean?*
Child 1: *Like . . . skinny, it means skinny.* (a)
Child 2: *Well, like how d'ya mean?*
Child 1: *Like how do I mean what?* (b)

The sense of (a) is signification: what the word *puny* means. The sense of (b) is intention: what the child means by the use of that word in that utterance context. It is only in the former sense, signification, that we can talk about word meaning and sentence meaning at all. The problem of word meaning, then, is one of signification; the problem of ordinary oral discourse is one of intention.

The study of developmental pragmatics suggests that a sense of speaker's meaning develops prior to a sense of word meaning. Context is crucial to the child's early comprehension and production of language, and to the adult's disambiguation of the child's early prelinguistic and protolinguistic communication (Barrett, 1985; Bruner, 1983; Bates, 1976; Dore, 1985; Greenfeld & Smith, 1976; Nelson, 1985; Ochs & Schieffelin, 1979). There is also evidence that in discourse preliterate children attend primarily to what they take to be the speaker's intention while older children can differentiate speaker's intentions from the meaning of the linguistic expression per se (Olson, 1986). This is evident when preliterate (4.0 years of age) and literate (7.0 years of age) children are asked to recall sentences embedded in meaningful social situations, where the speaker's intended meaning is not identical with the literal meaning of the linguistic expression used by the speaker. After being read a story in which two children go to the movies and get popcorn, one child says to the other, *You have more than me.* When the younger children were asked *What did she say?*, they more often responded with the speaker's intended meaning: *She said give me some.* Older children were more likely to report the actual linguistic expression, as well as the speaker's intended meaning.

Similarly, Robinson (1980) and Robinson, Goelman, and Olson (1982) found that children of 5 years of age and younger have difficulty in determining the adequacy of linguistic expressions. In these studies, a request is made using an expression that does not contain enough information for the listener to fulfill the request. The listener is asked to *Pick up the balloon,* for example, when both a red balloon and a blue balloon are present. If the listener is then told he or she has picked up the wrong balloon, the young child tends to blame the listener for making a mistake rather than blaming the inadequate message. Further, if asked what the speaker said, the listener incorrectly reports an assumption of what the speaker intended (*He said pick up the red balloon*) rather than reporting the literal expression (*He said pick up the balloon*). The listener doesn't identify the linguistic form of the expression as informationally inadequate. Older children are much more likely to correctly identify the ambiguous expression as the source of error.

It has long been argued that between the ages of 5 and 10, children begin to acquire a greater awareness of the rules of language implicit in oral language use (Chomsky, 1969). Children begin to develop metalinguistic knowledge about words and procedures for reflecting upon the structure of language in accomplishing linguistic tasks (Karmiloff-Smith, 1979; Papandropoulou & Sinclair, 1974). The ability to reflect upon and describe cognitive processes in general and language processes in particular has been found to bear a relationship to formal schooling and literacy (Scribner & Cole, 1981; Luria, 1976; Sharp, Cole, & Lave, 1979); and not surprisingly, the above developments in children begin to emerge as children acquire literacy skills in the context of formal schooling, typically after 5 or 6 years of age in our culture.

LITERACY, DEFINITION, AND THE WORD

Historically, our sense of *word* and word meaning appears uniquely associated with literacy. According to Putnam (1975),

> I would suggest that the question: How do we understand a new *word* has to do with the whole phenomenon of giving definitions and writing dictionaries. . . . And it is this phenomenon . . . of writing and needing dictionaries that gives rise to the whole idea of semantic theory. (p. 149)

Putnam implies here that defining words is an aspect of literacy, rather than of ordinary conversational discourse. There does appear to be an historical association of the sense of *word* as a linguistic constituent, and the process of defining words, with literacy. Havelock (1963, 1978) has shown that the Homeric epics, an embodiment of the oral tradition, set out to define abstract concepts such as courage and justice not through definitions and principles, but through descriptions of the exemplary deeds and experiences of gods and heroes. He points out that it was an early literate, Hesiod, who made the earliest known attempts at defining words. Hesiod spent much of his efforts in collecting, examining, and comparing the various uses of words throughout written texts of the Homeric epics in order to formulate general definitions: "A sort of architecture of the eye imposing itself upon echo patterns of the ear" (Havelock, 1978, p. 328). Fixing oral "literature" in written form thus led to both a sense of the word as a linguistic element that had some identity across different contexts of use and a sense that the meaning of a given word had some constancy across occasions of use, a meaning that could be explicitly stated and formally recorded.

Plato, Havelock further suggests, was subsequently the master of the definition, which he viewed as an attempt to fully express the abstract, formal features of the meaning of a given word: Courage is the willingness to pursue important goals in the face of danger, and so on. For Aristotle, to have a "true" definition was to have the most important possible knowledge (Robinson, 1950). The attempt to formulate explicit definitions for words, the meanings of which were largely implicit in oral language, became an important and general form of classical Greek thought:

> When a Greek said "a circle is the locus of points equidistant from a given point," he was not introducing the word 'circle' for the first time, he was specifying it in a new way and giving it new connections; to himself he seemed to be expounding a truth of great importance about circles. (Kneale & Kneale, 1962, p. 6)

Is this "truth of great importance" predicated of all objects occurring naturally in the world to which the word *circle* could be applied? This seems unlikely, not only because objects are rarely described in terms of points and distances between points in their configuration, but simply because by these criteria few objects could be considered circular, and the procedure for verifying circularity requires a precision atypical of ordinary real-world contexts. It seems more likely that this "truth" is being predicated of the word *circle* in a formal, abstract sense. Historically, then, it appears that it was not the existence of "*things*" that prompted systematic attempts at definition. Rather, it was the existence and reflection upon the written word that led to the formal expression of meaning in the form of definition.

While the idea of the word as a linguistic entity, and that of the definition as an expression of its meaning emerged with literacy, the formal authority we now associate with the dictionary definition came largely with print and the wide impersonal distribution of language it permitted (McLuhan, 1962; Starnes & Noyes, 1946). In manuscript cultures, where it was not uncommon for writer and reader to be personally acquainted, or at least to share the same world view and presuppositional knowledge base, it was not necessary to systematically define all the terms that one used. However, when printed texts became widely distributed, a consistent, authoritative system for identifying what words meant across diverse contexts by many different writers became necessary. Indeed, the first English–English dictionary appeared only after the growth in popular literacy sparked by the invention of print (Starnes & Noyes, 1946). In establishing the method of definition that survived for centuries, Johnson (1755) appealed to words as they had been used in texts to establish his "complete" and authoritative archive of word meaning.

There is also cross-cultural evidence that the sense of "word" is associated with written language, rather than ordinary oral discourse. Lord (1960), in his study of contemporary oral poets in Yugoslavia, found that they had no word corresponding to our concept of "word." They did, however, have a word which referred to units of speech of any size from syllable, word, or utterance to a complete poem. Goody (1977) reported that there was no word for "word" in either of the two West African languages with which he worked. It is of interest to note that common oral language expressions in our own culture suggest that our common-sense use of "word" differs from what could strictly be regarded as a word. The expressions *I must have a word with him* and *A word to the wise is sufficient* both imply complete utterances rather than what could strictly be referred to as a word. Goody (1977) concludes,

> In the beginning, then, was not the word but speech. When necessary its flow could be broken into parts by the use of a single term applied relatively. Writing changes this situation; at the cultural level, it enables people to analyze, break down, dissect, and build up speech into parts and wholes, into types and categories, which already existed but which, when brought into the area of consciousness, have a feedback effect on speech itself. People now speak words (though early writing systems did not insist on separation in the sentence, only in the list), are aware of ordering such as subject, verb, object (SVO), of categories such as verb and adverb. (p. 115)

The effects to which Goody refers may be restricted to literacy in word-segmented scripts. Scribner and Cole (1981) for example, studied literate and illiterate Vai, whose script is syllabic. They found a lacuna in the Vai language corresponding to the word *word*. The Vai have rather an expression that refers to a "piece of speech" or utterance, which can refer variously to words, phrases, or sentences. When Vai literates were requested to divide a written text into "speech" units, they divided it predominantly into meaning-carrying phrases, such as *my big brother*. Syllabic writing systems, then, do not appear to create a distinctive notion of the word as a basic linguistic element.

Is it possible that words are simply literate artifacts that have no relation to the structure of oral language whatsoever? This view has occasionally been expressed by some linguists, such as Sweet (1890), who argued that oral language should be analyzed by "stress groups" rather than words, and Mikus (cited in Vachek, 1976), who argued that the concept of word was "pre-scientific." Linguists have traditionally analyzed morphemes as the minimal meaning-bearing units of language, and these may not always coincide with words (the word *disbelief* for example, is composed of two morphemes). However, most linguists have assumed a fairly direct relation between words and the structure of the linguistic system underlying speech. All speakers of a language must have some implicit knowledge of the constituents of language, at least to the extent of being able to use them productively in their own speech. But speech consists of a continuous stream of sounds, while the concept of "word" requires the segmentation of the stream of speech into meaningful units of a particular configuration. It seems that alphabetic, word-segmented scripts engender the notion that utterances are decomposable into lexical constituents called words.

On reflection, it is not surprising that young children and members of preliterate societies have some difficulty in segregating and defining words. For them the task is rather like asking a literate adult to define the meaning of such suffixes as *-ly, -ness* or *-er*. It requires a particular and unusual form of analysis (J. S. Bruner, personal communication, 1981).

In the preceding discussion, it was suggested that the notion of "word" appears to be associated with literacy. With respect to the structure of word meaning, we have suggested that the implications of literacy are twofold. First, the acquisition of literacy effects a sense of the word as a constituent of language, with a meaning that can be differentiated from a speaker's intended meaning on a particular utterance occasion. This differentiation leads to the notion that words have meaning in and of themselves. Second, literate language use necessitates some conventionalization of word meaning, to enable consistency in use and comprehension across the diverse uses of the language engendered by a literate culture. Historically, these considerations led to a particular archival form—the definition.

SOME FORMS AND FUNCTIONS OF DEFINITIONS

The definitional form reflects an explicit rendering of the tacit word meanings of ordinary discourse. The function of such explicit expression is uniquely suited to the requirements of literate language use. An examination of the linguistic form of definitions suggests that they comprise a particular class of linguistic expressions that can be differentiated from the more general forms of expression common to oral discourse.

As Bierwisch and Kiefer (1969) have pointed out, definitional sentences cannot be strictly identified by their form alone since the syntactic structures may vary. Similarly, Robinson (1950) has noted 18 different types of definition. They range from the ostensive *That is an X*, where X is a lexical term, in which the linguistic expression is simply a frame for a gestural indication of the referent of the term; to the stipulative *A circle is the locus of points equidistant from a given point,* in which the specification of the meaning of the term is entirely contained in the linguistic form.

The most familiar form of definitional statement, however, and the object of most formal and empirical inquiry, is the definitional statement of equivalence. It employs the existential copula *is* and takes the form *NP1 is NP2,* where NP1 is equivalent to or an abbreviation for NP2 (Bierwisch & Kiefer, 1969). Of course, strict linguistic equivalence can only be achieved in stipulative definitions, since definitions of natural-kind terms such as *tiger,* for example, cannot fully specify the meaning of the term (Kripke, 1972; Putnam, 1975). It can, however, be said that all definitions of the form *NP1 is NP2* are statements of semantic relations that hold between a given word (the definiendum, or head noun of NP1) and other words in the user's lexicon or dictionary (the definiens, or words forming the expression NP2).

Sentences of this definitional form appear to be distinctive from other sentences employing the copula *is,* as can be seen by comparing the ordinary descriptive sentences of Type A:

A. *John is in the bathroom.*
The circle is over the square.
There is a unicorn in the garden.

with the definitional sentences of Type B:

B. *A boy is a young, human male.*
Melancholia is a form of mental illness marked by depression.
The Prime Minister is the principal minister or sovereign of a state.

A third type of sentence, lying halfway between these two, is interesting because examples of this type are frequently encountered in school texts:

C. *Gaul **is** divided into three parts.*
*Most species of birds **are** migratory.*
*Canada's primary exports **are** pulp and paper products.*

For sentences of Type A and Type C there is no semantic relation between the noun phrases related by the copula *is*—there is no intrinsic relation between the words *John* and *bathroom* or between *Gaul* and *three parts*. There is only a relation between the referents (the objects, actions, locations, etc.) represented by those words. In Type B there is such an intrinsic conceptual relation between the words themselves. Sentences of Type C differ from those of Type A in that the former indicate a somewhat general and timeless meaning; they hold across speech episodes not because they are so defined as in B, but because they are general, objective, and socially significant. We could roughly paraphrase this point by saying that Type B sentences are intended to hold in all possible worlds, Type C sentences to hold on all occasions of this world, and Type A sentences only on particular occasions of this world. Further, we could say that sentences of Type B are analytic—they are true by virtue of their form—while those of Types A and C are synthetic (Lyons, 1977).

These classes of sentences are interesting not only in that they differentiate sentences which are contextually specifiable and empirically falsifiable (Type A) from those which are definitional and analytic (Type B), but also because they correspond to alternative ways in which new words may be introduced into the lexicon. Sentences of Type A are context dependent—they require the co-presence of word and referent. Hence, sentences of Type A are suitable for indicating word meaning in the shared contexts of oral language.

This way of incorporating word meanings into the lexicon, that is, by experiencing words in the contexts of their use, can be referred to as the **implicit** introduction of word meanings (Bierwisch & Kiefer, 1969).

Sentences of Type B require neither the co-presence of speaker and hearer nor of word and referent (although it does not necessarily exclude them). The introduction of word meanings into the lexicon by way of definitional sentences of Type B could be called **explicit** (Bierwisch & Kiefer, 1969). To the extent that written language is independent of particular shared contexts, there is a tendency for the explicit introduction of word meanings (via definition) to be associated with the written form.

Of course, definitional statements may occur in oral languages as well, particularly where formal knowledge is being shared, as in schools or learned assemblies. But in ordinary oral discourse, the speaker can appeal to the shared extralinguistic context or to the known presuppositional base of the hearer. In written texts, such appeals are impossible.

Furthermore, the prevailing view among philosophers of language is that definitions are reflective statements about words(Putnam, 1975) rather than statements about things or concepts, as earlier philosophers maintained (Robinson, 1950). This is not to suggest that things and concepts have no bearing on the structure of definitions. Such a statement would imply that no relation exists between the structure of the world, the structure of thought, and the structure of meaning in the language, which is not the case. The metalinguistic view of definition reflects rather a differentiation of reflective statements about word meaning from the inchoate word meanings that underlie use in ordinary discourse. Definitions are explicit expressions of the word meanings that remain tacit in ordinary discourse. The explicitness of definition allows reflection upon the structure of word meanings, much as texts in general allow reflection upon forms of discourse. They are also formal expressions of the conventions governing word use in literate cultures.

THE DEVELOPMENT OF DEFINITION

Children's first words are usually acquired implicitly (Bierwisch & Kiefer, 1969) in ordinary discourse contexts, and not through explicit definition. There still exists much disagreement about the relative influences of dialogue, cognitive processes, ontological factors, and language itself in the child's construction of word meaning (Anglin, 1986; Bloom, Lifter, & Broughton, 1985; Carey, 1983; Dore, 1985; Keil, 1983; Nelson, 1985), and even about the linguistic status of early word meanings (Atkinson, 1985). But it is generally things and events in the world that provide occasions for discourse events like labeling, requesting, and commenting, events in which the child is exposed to language. Through repeated episodes of this sort, the child constructs word meanings, however that may be accomplished. When explicit introduction of word meaning does occur, it is more likely to be in the form of ostensive definition (e.g., *That's a doggie!*) rather than in the form of a word definition (e.g., *A doggie is an animal with four legs*). Even so, words themselves have been observed to provide the occasion for requests for explicit expressions of meaning, even in very young children. J. Anglin (personal communication) observed that when his daughter was 2.8, she invented the word *wook,* and after using it several times, asked *What does dat (that) mean?* A. Gopnik (personal communication) also noted that when her son was 3.3, he used expressions such as *What means old-fashioned?* and *What means by and by?* Robinson (1980) however found that metalinguistic questions, such as statements involving the verbs *mean* and *understand,* were rare in the early acquisition contexts she observed.

The sheer volume of words that are learned by young children belies explicit introduction as a primary vehicle of early lexical acquisition. The rate at which words are acquired by children, derived from estimates of vocabulary size at given ages, has ranged from 1 to 3/day (Ballard, 1934; Terman, 1916) up to 21 words (or 14.5 root words)/day (Templin, 1957; cited in Miller, 1977). Miller (1977) has suggested that even this high estimate may underestimate the actual rate, and recent evidence indicates that a high rate persists even during the child's early school years (Nagy, Herman, & Anderson, 1985).

The child's early attempts to define words are more like descriptions of things and events in the world (Papandropoulou & Sinclair, 1974). When young (preliterate) children are asked *What is an X?* or *What does X mean?* (where X is a word), they usually respond with expressions like: *cat: you pet it* or *flower: it smells nice* (Al-Issa, 1969; Anglin, 1978; Krauss, 1952; Litowitz, 1977; Nelson, 1978; Norlin, 1980; Feifel & Lorge, 1950; Watson, 1985; Wolman & Barker, 1965). These early definitions emphasize the functional characteristics of the referent, rather than the meaning of the word (Anglin, 1978; Nelson, 1978). Children's definition attempts are also incomplete expressions of meaning, and are often not criterial to the meaning of the word. *Dog* may be defined by the expression *It's black,* for example. However, data on children's understanding of the concept dog suggest that these expressions do not fully reflect the child's representation of meaning. After defining a dog as black, the child may successfully categorize a white poodle as a dog and a black horse as not a dog (Anglin, 1978). Also, children may demonstrate knowledge of superordinate category terms in comprehension tasks (Watson, 1985) and object-sorting tasks (MacNamara, 1982) and not include this criterial information in their definitions. Anglin (1978) suggests that this reflects a lack of coordination between the intension (meaning) of the term and its extension (its set of referents).

We would suggest that these early "definitions," (or incomplete descriptions of the functions and properties of referents) are essentially unsuccessful attempts to render the inchoate meanings of oral discourse into expressible forms. They may reflect aspects of word meaning that subserve use on particular utterance occasions. For example, the featural marker *black* may suffice to distinguish a dog from other things in the world on particular occasions of use. It could also serve as a comment when dog is a topic in discourse. The inadequacy of black as a definition of *dog* derives from its inability to specify the meaning of *dog* across diverse speakers and occasions of use. Thus, early definitions could be characterized as reflecting an oral discourse bias, rather than a literate bias.

It may also be that the preliterate child does not interpret the definitional question as a request for a full, explicit expression of word meaning. Anglin (1978) noted that children 3 years old and younger had difficulty understanding the question. We also found that in conversations with 6 year olds, the question *What is an elephant?* was met with laughter and disbelief: how could an adult not know what an elephant was?

At least three requirements must be met in order for the child to produce an expression that resembles a word definition: (1) a sense of word as a meaningful constitutent of language that has some constant identity and meaning across speakers and occasions of use, (2) an understanding of the conventional meaning of the definitional question, and (3) a recognition that a conventional response is required by the definitional question. We discuss each of these in turn.

The Sense of Word

The ontogenetic development of children's sense of word as a constituent of language has been linked to literacy, not unlike the historical emergence outlined above. Before the age of 5, children generally do not differentiate between words and the characteristics of their referents (Papandropoulou & Sinclair, 1974; Vygotsky, 1962). When asked whether *strawberry* is a word, they may say yes, *because it grows in the garden, train* is reported to be a long word, and *tidy* a difficult word *because he has to tidy up all the toys* (Papandropoulou, 1978, p. 58). It is not until 6 or 7 years of age that children begin to base their responses on properties of the word itself. Papandropoulou (1978) speculates that the "permanent and objective" qualities of written language, and the segmentation of the word in the written form, may lead to words acquiring "a substantial identity of their own" (p. 61). This was supported by the observation that, when she asked children what a word was, she found them more likely to refer to the graphic properties of words than to their phonic substance. In our laboratory, we asked eight children at each of three ages (5, 6, and 8 years) what a word is. We found that reference to the properties of the written form occurred in 50% of the 5 year olds' responses, and that this increased to 100% by 8 years of age. Lundberg

(1978) also suggested that, like members of preliterate cultures, preliterate children have no sense that language consists of lexical constituents called *words*.

If preliterate children have not developed a sense of word, it is unlikely they would have a sense of word meaning that could remain constant across speakers and occasions of use, and even less likely that they could produce a definitional expression that would reflect this. The incompleteness and inconsistency of children's definitions supports this notion. This may be simply one aspect of a general sense that linguistic expressions have no identity distinct from their use on particular utterance occasions. Their own defining expressions do not seem to be held constant by children across their judgments and expressions of meaning. They do not "preserve" the linguistic form of their own definitions when making semantic decisions about words they have previously defined. After correctly defining *food* as *something you eat*, for example, they may not identify a lollypop or bread as food (Anglin, 1978). Nor do they adjust their definition to accommodate the conflicting exemplar. This is in contrast to literate adults, who hold their definition in mind when categorizing referents, change thier definitions to accommodate unanticipated exemplars, and change their categorization of exemplars to conform to their definitions. Thus, when asked if a penguin is a bird, for example, adults will modify their definition of *bird* to exclude the criterion of flight, or when asked if a person is an animal, they will hold the definition constant and include person as an animal (Anglin, 1978).

It seems that children either can't preserve the linguistic form of their own expression, or else they don't recognize the need to. Limitations on working memory might explain why definitions are not held in focal awareness as children solve categorization problems. But it does not explain why the semantic knowledge that bread is food (for example) may be easily demonstrated on linguistic comprehension tasks (Watson, 1985) or categorization tasks (Anglin, 1978) with preliterate children, and yet the expression *food* almost never occurs in their definitions of *bread*. It seems more likely that children do not recognize that words and their meanings are constant across occasions, and that word definition entails the explicit expression of these constant aspects of word meaning.

The Conventions of the Definition Question

It is not only the sense of word that is required to understand the task of definition; but also the intended meaning of the definitional question. According to Grice (1975), one of the maxims of ordinary conversation is sincerity: you ask a question because you want to know the answer. In ordinary discourse, the question *What is X?* has an intentional structure something like the following:

> I don't know what X is.
> I think that you know what X is.
> I would like you to tell me what X is, because *I would like to know what X is.*

When children ask *What means old-fashioned?*, as in the example above, this is roughly what they intend by the question. When a psychologist, or a teacher, or a parent in some contexts (such as bookreading, Snow, 1983) asks a child *What is X?* the intentional structure of the question is completely different. It is more like the following:

> I *know* what X is.
> I don't know whether you know what X is.
> I also don't know whether you can tell me what X is.
> I would like you to tell me what X is, because *I would like to know if **you** know what X is and if you can say what X is.*

It is not so much that the "knowing" adult is violating Grice's sincerity maxim, but rather than the question is different from the one the child has asked, and the child must come to understand the adult question. There are acquisition contexts in which this question is common, most notably parent–child bookreading (Snow, 1983) and classrooms (Heath, 1983; Mehan, 1979; Wells, 1981). Typically, the parents) (or teachers) elicit a label with the question *What's that?*, not because they don't know, but because they want to know if the child can supply the label. After the child successfully labels an object, teachers typically ask for a definition. The following examples are from show-and-tell sessions in two different kindergartens:

Episode 1

Teacher:	*What (do you have there), Joshua?*
Child:	*It's a C.B.*
Teacher:	*What's a C.B.?*
Child:	*Policemen use it to call the station.*
Child 2:	*It's a walkie talkie.*

Episode 2

Teacher:	*What's that?*
Child:	*It's an enchanted egg.*
Teacher:	*What does **enchanted** mean?*
Child:	*It means there's something inside it.*

Labeling and definition formats familiarize the child with this type of question, which requires a display of their knowledge (Mehan, 1979; Wells, 1981).

Conventional Definitional Responses

It is well known that around the time most children start school (5 to 6 years of age) the structure of their definitions begins to change. Superordinate categories begin to replace early functional descriptions, and definitions become more elaborated, complete, closer to conventional dictionary definitions (Al-Issa, 1969; Feifel & Lorge, 1950; Wolman & Barker, 1965). Anglin (1978), for example, compared the incidence of superordinate terms in preschool children's definitions with that in adults' definitions and found a dramatic difference. Approximately 90% of the definitions he collected from adults contained superordinate category terms, while only 18% of the definitions of children 5 years old and younger contained any reference to superordinate categories. As noted above, it is not that children do not possess the knowledge that, for example, dog is an animal. Children as young as 3 are capable of grouping diverse exemplars under the superordinate category term *animal* (MacNamara, 1982). What is it, then, that triggers this "functional-to-superordinate" shift in the structure of definitions? It parallels the well-known syntagmatic–paradigmatic shift (Nelson, 1977). On tasks such as word associations, young children (2–5 years of age) tend to give syntagmatic responses, such as *dog: bark,* that reflect the sentence frames in which the words are likely to occur. During the early school years (6–7 years) children begin to give paradigmatic responses (*dog: cat* or *dog: animal*), and by about 10 years of age, paradigmatic responses predominate. The onset of the shift is generally held to be around the time children start school, although it is not constant across all form classes and semantic categories (Nelson, 1977). Yet it may be significant that in the classroom definition routines that we observed, there is clear bias toward superordinate category terms.

Consider the following example from our transcripts of discourse in a junior kindergarten class:

Teacher: *What is a lullaby?*
Child 1: *It helps you to go to sleep at night.* (a)
Teacher: *But what **is** it?*
Child 2: *It's a song.* (b)
Teacher: *That's right.*

Why does the teacher accept (b), calling it *right,* and implicitly reject response (a) by repeating her questions? Most obviously, response (b) places the term within a superordinate category or genus, like a dictionary definition. Response (a) could be characterized as describing a function of the referent of the word, or alternately as reflecting a typical use of the word in ordinary discourse. The response that is acceptable is the superordinate term. Interestingly, the teacher places an intonational emphasis on the copula *is*, which emphasizes the particular form of the question (*tell me what it **is**, not what it does*). This seems to emphasize that in order to produce the right response, the child must keep in mind the linguistic form of the question. And, it so happens, preserving the copula *is* constrains the type of response the child gives (see Watson, 1985, for a fuller discussion). Response (a) does not answer the question, but rather uses a whole new construction: *it **helps** you (to go to sleep at night)*. In contrast, response (b) preserves the linguistic form of the question: *It **is** a song*. The same verb is used, the child simply pronominalizes the subject and supplies a complement that is both accurate and succinct. If the child cannot supply an adequate or conventional definition, one will be provided for him.

Another example from the kindergarten:

Teacher: *What's cancer?*
Child 1: *A little bug that eats your leg away.* (a)
Child 2: *My brother's going to get cancer because he smokes.* (b)
Teacher: *Cancer is really a terrible disease.*

The children's expressions reflect a naive hypothesis and an occasion meaning, respectively. The teacher's *really* implies that neither of the children's definitions is adequate. Her bias is toward the superordinate category definition "disease." Of course, the teacher is also giving the child new information—perhaps neither child knew the word *disease*, nor that it applied to cancer. However, the teacher does not choose to specify the symptoms of cancer, methods for its cure, the significance of contracting it for the victim, or other information that would probably be of more interest to the children than a simple verbal label. She rather chooses to model her expression, however unconsciously she may do so, on the archival, definitional form of word meaning. This episode illustrates a bias in school discourse that is consistent with what ultimately comes to be expressed in children's definitions: superordinate category expressions.

We have argued that a sense of *word* qua word, and an understanding of the discourse conventions governing both questions and responses in definition routines, may figure in the ontogenetic development of definition. The development of definition has been linked to literacy (Snow, 1986; Luria, 1976), although it is difficult to disentangle literacy effects per se from the effects of formal schooling, both literacy and schooling being text oriented (Scribner & Cole, 1981).

The study below explores the relation between the emergence of children's conventional definition responses and their attention to, and preservation of, features and forms of conventional definitional discourse.

A STUDY OF DEFINITIONS

Eight common nouns, familiar to most preschool children (Rinsland, 1945) such as *cat, flower, bread,* were used to elicit definitions from children. The sample comprised children from six school classrooms—two classes from each of three grade levels—in two middle-class schools in Toronto, Canada. The children's ages were: 5,0 (preliterate kindergarten children), 7,0 (first grade) and 10,0 (fourth grade). Between 30 and 40 children at each age level participated in the study.

Each child was interviewed individually. First, we simply asked the child the definitional question *What is (an) X?*; next, we encouraged the children to *Tell more about X,* using the standard, nonspecific probes for eliciting more information used in the WISC-R testing procedure (Wechsler, 1974). Subsequent to these standard procedures, we used a simple manipulation of intonation to focus the child's attention on the linguistic form of the definitional question: we repeated the question *is,* as did the teacher we described above in the lullaby example.

Finally, children were given a comprehension task to establish receptive language knowledge of the superordinate category terms for the words in question. The task consisted of target questions such as *Is a cat an animal?* balanced by foil questions of the type *Is a cat a plant?* The unit of analysis for scoring was the response pairs representing correct acceptance of the target question (hits) and correct rejection of the foil. (False alarm rates were close to zero.)

Results

Figure 11.1 clearly illustrates that in the comprehension task, even the 5-year-old children knew most of the superordinate category terms for the words they were asked to define. Figure 11.1 also shows the mean number of superordinates spontaneously produced in the children's definitions, again out of a maximum possible of 8. It is clear from Figure 11.1 that knowledge of the superordinate terms is not sufficient for its spontaneous inclusion in the child's definition.

This raises the question: Why is this known information not included?

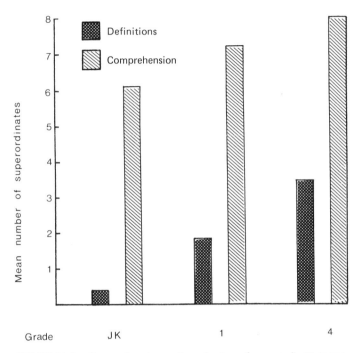

FIGURE 11.1.   Comprehension and production of superordinate terms.

The appearance of superordinates requires at least two things: first, the preservation of the linguistic form of the question predicate *is a*, and second, the use of a noun or noun phrase as a complement. This is congruent with the standard definitional form identified by Bierwisch and Kiefer (1969) that we discussed above. When a child gives a functional definition, as was illustrated with our lullaby example, they often disregard the response structure implied by the question. Instead of saying *a cat is a pet* (NP1 *is* NP2) they are more likely to say *you pet a cat* or *a cat purrs*. Also, the use of the copula *is* in a definitional sentence is not an ordinary use of the verb, as in sentences of type A (above): *John is in the kitchen.* Does marking the form of the question by adding intonational emphasis on the copula *is*, as the teacher did, help children to recognize its special form?

Figure 11.2 illustrates the cumulative means of the incidence of superordinate terms across the three eliciting expressions: *What is X?*, *Tell me more about X* and *What is X?* (again, maximum = 8). When the standard probe *Tell me more about X* is added to the initial definitional question *What is X?*, no significant increments are observed in the mean number

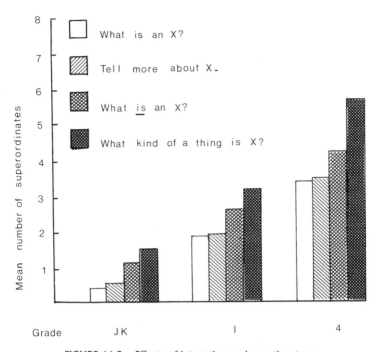

FIGURE 11.2.   Effects of intonation and question type.

of superordinate terms. In contrast, when intonational emphasis is placed on the copula *is* in the definitional question, the increment in superordinate terms elicited is significantly larger than that obtained with the nonspecific probe *Tell more about* X (univariate Dunnett contrasts): $F (1, 101) = 53.58$, $p < 0.0001$. Thus, when the linguistic form of the question is emphasized by stressing the copula, known superordinate terms are more likely to appear in the child's definition. It may be that emphasizing the copula leads to a greater preservation of the linguistic form of the question, which in turn leads to a response consistent with the X *is* _____ structure implied by the question.

Both the initial definition question and the emphasized question sometimes elicited responses of the structure X *is* **something that** . . . or X *is a* **thing that** . . . . These expressions fulfill the syntactic convention (NP1 *is* NP2) but do not fulfill the semantic convention of including a true superordinate term. They mark the fact that a noun phrase is required to complete the response X *is* _____, and could be referred to as **nominal complement markers.** This type of expression was higher in frequency than true superordinate expressions in the youngest group

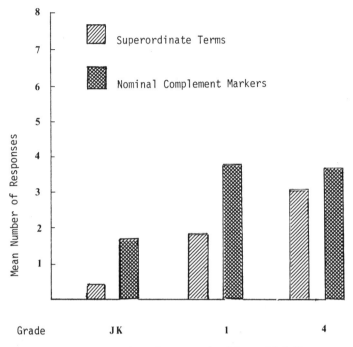

FIGURE 11.3.   Marking the conventional form of definition.

(5,0) (Figure 11.3). But it did not continue to increase in a monotonic manner, as the superordinate terms did. It began to decrease in the oldest (10,0) group, while high superordinate usage continued to increase in this group.

The use of superordinates and nominal complement markers was negatively correlated: age 5,0, $r = -.08$; age 7,0, $r = -.4$; age 10,0, $r = -.5$. Also, nominal complement markers continued to account for a high proportion of nonsuperordinate responses, even in the oldest group. It seemed, then, that marking the syntactic convention (NP2) of the definition by the use of nominal complement markers in place of true superordinate terms was an alternate strategy used by the children. It may also be a transitional phase in the emergence of true superordinate expressions, according to a suggestion made by Litowitz (1977).

To summarize, the overall pattern of data suggests first, that children know more superordinate terms than they spontaneously produce in their definitions; second, that attention to the linguistic form of the question (elicited by intonational emphasis) yields a higher proportion of superordinate responses than the standard definitional question and standard probe alone; and third, that responses which do not include superordinate terms are very likely to mark the conventional linguistic form of the definition by use of nominal complement markers (NP2).

CONCLUSION

The idea that definition is a contrived exercise, with a significance confined to scholarly domains, is evident in the following passage. It suggests the bizarre overemphasis upon formal definition found in Victorian schooling:

> "Bitzer," said Thomas Gradgrind, "your definition of a horse."
> "Quadruped. Gramnivorous. Forty teeth. namely twenty-four grinders. four eye teeth, and twelve incisive [sic]. Sheds coat in spring; in marshy countries sheds hoofs too. Hoofs hard, but requiring to be shod with iron. Age known by marks in mouth."
> Thus (and much more) Bitzer.
> "Now, girl number twenty," said Mr. Gradgrind, "you know what a horse is."
> Charles Dickens, *Hard Times*

What makes the episode striking and humorous is the assumption that girl number twenty did not know what a horse was (in fact, she was a circus rider) unless she could define it in formal lexical terms.

We have argued that, far from being a trivial classroom artifact, definition reflects one aspect of the general consequences of the uses of text. It illustrates the role of text in refiguring the relation between language and thought. This role can be summarized by listing four effects definitions have on words and their meanings: they render them **opaque, autonomous, generalizable,** and **conceptual.**

To treat words as opaque is to treat them metalinguistically, i.e., as linguistic elements with semantic structures rather than as simply indicating a particular referent in ordinary oral discourse. This metalinguistic turn reflects the general bias in literate and schooled discourse that language is "conscious" or opaque, whether at the phonological, lexical, or propositional level; that words and sentences have sense and structure independent of individual utterance occasions; and that some things can be inferred from language per se: If John "knows" X, then X must be true, or else John could not have "known" it, and so on. A large number of schooled tasks, and many classic problems in developmental psychology, such as Piaget's conservation tasks, depend upon just such careful attention to the structure of linguistic expressions (Donaldson, 1978; Donaldson, Grieve, & Pratt, 1983).

Second, definitions contribute to the autonomy of language by decreasing the speaker's reliance upon particular physical and social contexts in the construction and interpretation of meaning in discourse. When words are defined in terms of other words, they may be used to construct other word meanings stipulatively. This is a common use of definition in science and mathematics. The creation of word definition is critical in the stipulation of hypothetical meaning structure, and in the development of theory. This is one of the ways in which language becomes an explicit tool for thought, as well as being a means for the expression of thought.

The third effect is related to the second: definitions permit generalizability. Even if contexts of use change, the formalization of word meanings in the form of definitions creates the potential for fixing the meaning of a given term across diverse contexts and occasions of use, thereby permitting mutual understanding in a range of possible worlds.

Finally, and most importantly, definitions permit the explication and development of concepts. Of course, concepts are implicit in one's ordinary knowledge of the world and in one's ordinary speaking practices. One must have some concept of the truth of a belief, for example, to use the word *know* correctly. But the metalinguistic treatment of the word *know* in terms of a definition, the attempt to explicate the conditions entailed by its use and the structure of its nominalized form *knowledge,* and more important still, the reflection upon the nature of knowing, upon the construction and acquisition of knowledge, and so on, represent the most fundamental part of theoretical enquiry. This theoretical, conceptual procedure is, in a sense, a by-product of the metalinguistic treatment of words. And it is this theoretical orientation that makes definitions so important to formal education, and indeed, most literate uses of language.

In ordinary oral discourse, the intended meaning of interlocutors is primary, and words are the implicit means for sharing those intended meanings. Consequently, word meanings remain largely implicit in oral language and depend in any case on both the particular intention of the speaker and the occasion on which the utterance occurs. With the use of texts, whether in reading or writing, the sense of language as consisting of linguistic elements, that have some spatio-temporal identity begins to emerge. The sense that word meanings must of necessity have some consistency across diverse occasions of use begins with this process. Writing systems make the words of the language explicit, they render their meanings and structures available to analysis and reflection. This precipitates the formalization and explication of word meaning in the definitional form.

Children's induction into the practices of a literate culture, which for some children begins with parent–child interactions long before they actually learn to read independently, effects this process developmentally. Schools are one cultural institution which systematically encourage the transformation of the implicit meanings of ordinary oral discourse to the explicit definitions typical of literate language use. It is not surprising that with the acquisition of literacy in the context of formal schooling, children's definitions gradually become closer approximations of the archival definitional form prevalent in our literate culture.

ACKNOWLEDGMENTS

The work presented here was carried out with the assistance of the Social Sciences and Research Council of Canada Doctoral Research Fellowship #452-81-0553 held by the first author. Some portions of the empirical results were reported earlier in *The Journal of Child Language*.

REFERENCES

Al-Issa, I. (1969). The development of word definitions in children. *Journal of Genetic Psychology, 114,* 25–28.

Anglin, J. (1978). From reference to meaning. *Child Development, 49,* 969–976.

Anglin, J. M. (1986). Semantic and conceptual knowledge underlying the child's words. In S. A. Kuczaj & M. D. Barrett (Eds.), *The development of word meaning* (pp. 83–97). New York: Springer-Verlag.

Atkinson, M. (1985). How linguistic is the one-word stage? In M. Barrett (Ed.), *Children's single-word speech* (pp. 289–312). New York: Wiley.

Ballard, P. B. (1934). *Thought and language.* London: University of London Press.

Barrett, M. D. (1985). *Children's single-word speech.* New York: Wiley.

Bates, E. (1976). *Language and context: The acquisition of pragmatics.* New York: Academic Press.

Bierwisch, M., & Kiefer, F. (1969). Remarks on definitions in natural languages. In F. Kiefer (Ed.), *Studies in syntax and semantics.* Dordrecht, The Netherlands: Reidel.

Bloom, L., Lifter, K., & Broughton, J. (1985). The convergence of early cognition and language in the second year of life: Problems in conceptualization and measurement. In M. Barrett (Ed.), *Children's single-word speech* (pp. 149–180). New York: Wiley.

Bowerman, M. (1978). Systematizing semantic knowledge: Changes over time in the child's organization of word meaning. *Child Development, 49,* 977–987.

Bruner, J. S. (1983). *Child's talk: Learning to use words.* New York: Norton.

Carey, S. (1983). Constraints on the meanings of natural kind terms. In B. Seiler & W. Wannenmacher (Eds.), *Concept development and the development of word meaning* (pp. 126–143). New York: Springer-Verlag.

Chomsky, C. S. (1969). *The acquisition of syntax in children from 5 to 10.* Cambridge, MA: MIT Press.

Donaldson, M. (1978). *Children's minds.* Glasgow: William Collins.

Donaldson, M., Grieve, R., & Pratt, C. *Early childhood development and education.* New York: Guilford.

Dore, J. (1985). Holophrases revisited: Their 'logical' development from dialog. In M. Barrett (Ed.), *Children's single-word speech* (pp. 289–312). New York: Wiley.

Feifel, H., & Lorge, I. (1950). Qualitative differences in the vocabulary responses of children. *Journal of Educational Psychology, Vol. 41*, 1–18.

Garfinkel, H. (1964). Studies of the routine grounds of everyday activities. *Social Problems, 2* (3). Reprinted in D. Sudnow (Ed.), *Studies in social interaction.* New York: Free Press, 1972.

Goody, J. (1977). *The domestication of the savage mind.* London: Cambridge University Press.

Greenfield, P., & Smith, J. H. (1976). *The structure of communicating in early language.* New York: Academic Press.

Grice, H. P. (1975). Logic and conversation. In P. Cole & J. Morgan (Eds.), *Syntax and semantics* (Vol. 3). London: Academic Press.

Havelock, E. (1978). *The Greek concept of justice: From its shadow in Homer to its substance in Plato.* Cambridge, MA: Harvard University Press.

Havelock, E. (1963). *Preface to Plato.* Cambridge, MA: Harvard University Press.

Heath, S. (1983). *Ways with words.* London: Cambridge University Press.

Johnson, S. (1755). *A dictionary of the English language* (2 vols.). London: Strahan.

Karmiloff-Smith, A. (1979). Language development after five. In P. Fletcher & M. Garman (Eds.), *Language acquisition* (pp. 307–323). London: Cambridge University Press.

Keil, F. C. (1983). Semantic inferences and the acquisition of word meaning. In B. Seiler & W. Wannenmacher (Eds.), *Cognitive development and the development of word meaning* (pp. 103–124). New York: Springer-Verlag.

Kneale, W., & Kneale, M. (1962). *The development of logic.* Oxford: Clarendon Press.

Krauss, R. (1952). *A hole is to dig.* New York: Harper.

Kripke, S. (1972). Naming and necessity. In D. Davidson & G. Harman (Eds.), *The semantics of natural language.* Dordrecht, The Netherlands: Reidel.

Litowitz, B. (1977). Learning to make definitions. *Journal of Child Language, 4*, 289–304.

Lord, A. B. (1960). *The singer of tales* (Harvard Studies in Comparative Literature, 24). Cambridge, MA: Harvard University Press.

Lundberg, I. (1978). Aspects of linguistic awareness related to reading. In A. Sinclair, R. J. Jarvella, & W. J. M. Levelt (Eds.), *The child's conception of language.* Berlin: Springer-Verlag.

Luria, A. R. (1976). *Cognitive development: Its cultural and social foundations.* Cambridge, MA: Harvard University Press.

Lyons, J. (1977). *Semantics.* London: Cambridge University Press.

MacNamara, J. (1982). *Names for things.* Cambridge, MA: MIT Press.

Maratsos, M. P. (1974). Children who get worse at understanding the passive: A replication of Bever. *Journal of Psycholinguistic Research, 3*, 65–74.

McLuhan, M. (1962). *The Gutenberg galaxy.* Toronto: University of Toronto Press.

Mehan, H. (1979). "What time is it Denise?" Asking known information questions in classroom discourse. *Theory Into Practice, 28*(4), 285–294.

Miller, G. A. (1977). *Spontaneous apprentices.* New York: Seabury Press.

Nagy, W., Herman, P., & Anderson, R. (1985). Learning words from context. *Reading Research Quarterly, 202*, 233–253.

Nelson, K. (1977). The syntagmatic–paradigmatic shift revisited: A review of research and theory. *Psychological Bulletin, 84*, 93–116.

Nelson, K. (1978). Semantic development and the development of semantic memory. In K. E. Nelson (Ed.), *Children's language* (Vol. 1). New York: Gardner Press.

Nelson, K. (1985). *Making sense: The acquisition of shared meaning.* Orlando: Academic Press.

Norlin, P. F. (1980). The development of relational arcs in the lexical semantic memory structures of young children. *Journal of Child Language, 8,* 385–402.

Ochs, E., & Schieffelin, B. (1979). *Developmental pragmatics.* New York: Academic Press.

Olson, D. R. (1977). From utterance to text: The bias of language in speech and writing. *Harvard Educational Review, 47*(3), 257–281.

Olson, D. R. (1986). The cognitive consequences of literacy. *Canadian Psychology/Psychologie Canadienne, 27*(2).

Olson, D. R. (in preparation). *The world on paper.*

Papandropoulou, I. (1978). An experimental study of children's ideas about language. In A. Sinclair, R. J. Jarvella, & W. T. M. Levelt (Eds.), *The child's conception of language.* Berlin: Springer-Verlag.

Papandropoulou, I., & Sinclair, H. (1974). What is a word: Experimental study of children's ideas on grammar. *Human Development, 17,* 241–258.

Putnam, H. (1975). *Mind, language and reality: Philosophical papers* (Vol. 2). London: Cambridge University Press.

Rinsland, H. D. (1945). *A basic vocabulary of elementary school children.* New York: Macmillan.

Robinson, E. J. (1980). Mother–child interactions and the child's understanding about communication. *International Journal of Psycholinguistics, 7-1/2 17-18,* 85–101.

Robinson, E. J., Goelman, H., & Olson, D. R. (1983). Children's understanding of the relationship between expressions (what was said) and intentions (what was meant). *British Journal of Developmental Psychology, 1,* 75–86.

Robinson, R. (1950). *Definition.* Oxford: Clarendon Press.

Scribner, S., & Cole, M. (1981). *The psychology of literacy.* Cambridge, MA: Harvard University Press.

Sharpe, D., Cole, M., & Lave, J. (1979). Education and cognitive development: The evidence from experimental research. *Monographs of the SRCD, 44* (Serial No. 178) 1–2.

Snow, C. (1983). Literacy and language: Relationships during the pre-school years. *Harvard Educational Review, 53*(2), 165–189.

Snow, C. (1986). Paper presented to the Boston Child Language Conference.

Starnes, D. T., & Noyes, E. (1946). *The English dictionary from Cawdrey to Johnson.* Chapel Hill: University of North Carolina Press.

Stock, B. (1983). *The implications of literacy.* Princeton: Princeton University Press.

Sweet, H. (1900). *A primer of spoken English.* (3rd ed., revised). Oxford: Clarendon Press. (c. 1890).

Templin, M. C. (1957). *Certain language skills in children: Their development and interrelationships.* Minneapolis: University of Minnesota Press.

Terman, L. M. (1916). *The measurement of intelligence.* Boston: Houghton-Mifflin.

Vachek, J. (1976). *Selected writings in English and general linguistics.* The Hague: Mouton.

Vygotsky, L. (1962). *Thought and language.* (E. Hanfmann and E. Vakar, Trans.). Cambridge MA: MIT Press.

Watson, R. (1985). Toward a theory of definition. *Journal of Child Language, 12,* 181–197.

Wechsler, D. (1974). The Wechsler intelligence scale for children (revised.) New York: The Psychological Corporation.

Wells, G. (1981). *Learning through interaction.* Cambridge: Cambridge University Press.

Wittgenstein, L. (1953). *Philosophical investigations.* Oxford: Blackwell and New York: Macmillan.

Wolman, R. N., & Barker, E. N. (1965). A developmental study of word definitions. *The Journal of Genetic Psychology, 107,* 159–166.

Chapter 12

Language, Speech, and Print: Some Asymmetries in the Acquisition of Literacy*

Charles A. Perfetti

INTRODUCTION

One starting point for considering the relationship between the comprehension of spoken and written language is to acknowledge that there are both important commonalities and significant differences between the two. Discussions have sometimes dwelled on either the commonalities or the differences to the exclusion of the other. These discussions sometimes include extreme viewpoints that amount to slogans. One extreme is represented by the claim that "Writing is speech on paper," or "Print is speech writ down," or "Reading is listening plus decoding." Let's call this the commonality view. The opposite extreme is represented by the claim that spoken and written language are independent and have little in common except that they both are symbol systems mapping language forms and meanings. Let us call this the distinctiveness view.

These matters are, of course, quite important for the teaching of reading. If the commonality view is more nearly correct, then one might imagine that teachers of reading should teach children how to convert print to speech and everything else would take care of itself. Or, at least,

* This chapter is based on a talk given as part of a symposium at the 26th International Reading Conference in New Orleans.

children's reading level would reach their listening level. The distinctiveness point of view implies that teaching a child how to convert print to speech will not only fall well short of teaching the child how to read but will actually be misleading concerning the nature of reading. By this view, the child must learn the special characteristic demands of reading, or reading comprehension will not reach a level approaching speech comprehension.

Neither of these extreme views ought to be taken seriously. Reading print is more than understanding speech writ down. And writing is less than an independent symbol system contrived to serve special purposes. Once the extreme positions are recognized as mere slogans, the theoretical and practical relationships among language, speech, and print become interesting. In particular, there are four general points I wish to make: (1) The similarity between speech and print is essentially asymmetrical in some important ways. (2) This asymmetry in the similarity between speech and print changes as a child's reading ability improves. (3) For the child who has succeeded at decoding, the commonalities between speech and print are more important than their differences. (4) For the older child and adult who have acquired vast experience at reading, speech processes become more like reading in some conditions. In what follows I elaborate each of these four points.

THE ASYMMETRY RELATION BETWEEN SPEECH AND PRINT

The source of the asymmetry between speech and print is this: For the child learning to read, print is more similar to speech than speech is to print. This may seem a perverse logic. After all, if A is similar to B, then B is similar to A. However, psychological similarity does not necessarily follow this particular paradigm of symmetrical logic. Tversky (1977) has shown that the perceived similarity between two things depends on their relative psychological salience. My claim is that, for children and probably for adults of average literacy, print is more similar to speech because speech is psychologically primary. Inversely, speech is less similar to print because print is psychologically secondary, at least for children and adults of average literacy.

The general point that psychological similarity can be asymmetrical is best illustrated for cases other than reading, cases similar to those examined by Tversky (1977). Suppose a person is asked to rate the similarity of two countries on a scale of 1 to 7 as follows: *How similar is East Germany to the Soviet Union?* Judgments will vary with individuals, but most will judge similarity to be between 4 and 7, with an average of, say,

6. Now let's reverse the terms: *How similar is the Soviet Union to East Germany?* The average rating in this case is lower. Americans, on the average, do not think of the Soviet Union as similar to East Germany to the extent that they think of East Germany as similar to the Soviet Union.

That this is not a peculiarity associated with Eastern European and Soviet political relations can be demonstrated by considering a different example. *How similar is a space shuttle to an airplane? How similar is an airplane to a space shuttle?* Most people will judge more similarity between a space shuttle and an airplane than between an airplane and a space shuttle.

For an example closer to the issue at hand, consider learning two languages, English and German. *How similar is English to German? How similar is German to English?* For a native speaker of English with only an acquaintance of German, the judgment has an asymmetry. English is less similar to German than vice versa. However, for a native speaker of German with little acquaintance with English, the asymmetry will exist in the opposite direction: English is more similar to German than vice versa.

What does this all have to do with speech and print? The examples above follow Tversky's (1977) theory of similarity, and print and speech do also. In particular, for children learning to read, print is more similar to speech than speech is to print. For experts in reading, the similarity between print and speech is more nearly equal. For some people, hyperliterates, speech actually may become more similar to print than vice versa.

The principle in all these cases—countries, airplanes, and language modalities—is that the less salient or less familiar is more similar to the more salient or more familiar than vice versa. East Germany is more similar to the Soviet Union for someone more familiar with the Soviet Union. However, for an East German expert, the asymmetry does not exist or, indeed, it could exist in the other direction. Likewise, for most people, a space shuttle is more similar to an airplane than vice versa only if an airplane is more familiar. And reading is more similar to speech than vice versa only if speech is more familiar. For a child beginning school, there is no doubt about the familiarity difference. Reading, not speech, is unfamiliar.

While the examples so far have been for judgments of similarity, processing similarity may also follow this asymmetry principle. Processing in a less-familiar domain is more like processing in a more-familiar domain than vice versa. This suggestion, while it goes beyond what we have real evidence for, makes sense in terms of what we know about learning and transfer of skills. We perform a newer or less well-learned task by using older or more well-learned skills, not vice versa. For speech and print, the key to this suggestion is the experience the child has had with the two language forms.

This is illustrated in Figure 12.1, which shows four hypothetical observation points throughout a person's acquisition of literacy. the unique properties of speech and of print are represented by the size of the S (speech) square and the P (print) square. Their intersection (S ∩ P) represents their shared psychological attributes. Asymmetries in similarity will be present when the sizes of S and P are unequal. This can be seen informally by comparing the size of intersection (S and P's shared attributes) to S and to P separately. Where P is small and S is large, the ratio of this intersection is larger to P than to S. (See Tversky, 1977, for a formal treatment of such similarity relations based on set relations.) Thus P is more similar to S than S is to P. The relative sizes of S and P change with the relative amount of print experience and speech experience.

Thus the four observation points reveal changing similarity relations between speech and print. At point 1, children have considerable experience with speech and negligible experience with print, because they are just learning to read. The similarity asymmetry between speech and print is large. By observation point 2, they have been at reading for 3 or 4 years, and the similarity gap between reading and listening has been reduced. The two share more attributes and reading is still more like listening than vice versa. Observation point 3 represents a still later point after more reading experience. This may not be a typical child but a typical college student. The overlap between reading and listening is still larger. Furthermore listening is nearly as much like reading as reading is like listening. The final observation point (4) represents what I call "hyperliteracy." Print experience has exceeded speech experience and speech is more like print than print is like speech.

The core of the argument is that any two interrelated systems are unequal in their mutual interdependence. One system is psychologically primary and the other is psychologically secondary. The system that is secondary uses components of the system that is primary. In second language learning, for example, the second language is acquired in terms of the first language. Further, as skill in the second language develops, it may be used in a way that is dependent upon first language knowledge and habits. As the second language gains it becomes more independent. Finally, if it achieves a very high fluency, it may exert some influence on the primary language. Notice that I am suggesting the relationship between psychologically primary and psychologically

1. BEGINNING READING

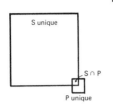

- ➤ Speech has many unique properties;
- ➤ Speech-print overlap (S∩P) is small
- ➤ Print is more similar to speech than speech is to print

2. INTERMEDIATE READING

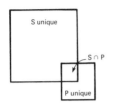

- ➤ Print has more properties than at 1, both unique and shared with speech
- ➤ Print has become more similar to speech and speech has become more similar to print
- ➤ Print is more similar to speech than speech is to print; however asymmetry much less than at 1

3. ADULT SKILLED READING

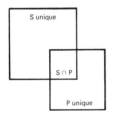

- ➤ Print experience has further increased both print's unique properties and those shared with speech.
- ➤ Speech has relatively fewer unique properties than before,
- ➤ Speech is nearly as similar to print as print is to speech.

4. HYPERLITERACY

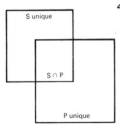

- ➤ Print experience has exceeded speech experience
- ➤ Speech experiences have become more like print
- ➤ Speech is slightly more similar to print than print is to speech; reversal of asymmetry

FIGURE 12.1. The similarity between speech and print over four hypothetical observation points.

secondary is one of actual processing, not simply of perceived similarity. Perceived similarity, e.g., the perceived similarity between English and German and German and English, is a result of the knowledge one has about the two languages, and this influences processes as well as perceived similarity. Thus, initially, the second language is, in some sense, processed more like the first language than vice versa. If we substitute *speech* for first language and *reading* for second language, we have the gist of the present proposal.

Given this general picture, I turn now to some of the ways print and speech differ, how this matters for reading, and how it changes with the child's development of reading skill.

HOW EARLY READING IS DIFFERENT FROM SPEECH

There are many apparent differences between speech and reading. Consider a brief list of their most obvious differences. (1) Speech has prosody to help signal meaning, but print does not.(2) Print relieves memory demands by allowing reinspection of the text. Speech, by contrast, makes high memory demands because of its impermanence. (3) Print imposes decoding demands. (4) Print conventions mark word boundaries unequivocally with spaces, even in nonalphabetic orthographies. Speech does not always mark word boundaries with silence. This is a consequence of the spatial layout of print versus the temporal layout of speech. (5) Speech requires, and is part of, social contact. By contrast, reading is an individual activity most often done in private. (6) The choice of speech content is seldom arbitrary, because of its social context. However, print content often is arbitrary, at least from the perspective of the child reader. It is fixed and unchangeable, arising from a sometimes mysterious source.

This list can be extended to accommodate finer distinctions. In fact, it can be extended to include many more contrasts than the six I have mentioned. For example, there are differences in the syntactic structures characteristic of print and speech, including the greater print use of subordinate clauses (Harrell, 1957; O'Donnell, 1974) and nominalizations (Chafe, 1982), among other features. However, such differences may be derivative of more fundamental differences. It is possible to develop a small number of principled design features of print that distinguish it from speech, parallel to Hockett's (1960) design features for language. For example, the six differences I have listed, and others as well, may derive from differences in a small number of fundamental features, perhaps just two: *I.* A contrast on physical dimensions, the spatial–visual presentation of print and the temporal–auditory presentation of speech. Such differences as (1), (2), (3), and (4) derive from this feature. *II.* A contrast on social-function dimensions, the asocial, individual, one-way commumication of print and the socialized interactive communication of speech. At a deeper level, this latter contrast may be derivative of the transience of the speech signal versus the relative permanence of print and thus a consequence of the physical properties of print and speech. In any case, semantic, syntactic, and stylistic differences between print and speech are probably traceable to this fundamental functional contrast.

We can consider the implications of these differences for differences in ease of language processing. If we keep score, we are likely to decide that most differences favor speech, with two exceptions: Reading makes memory less obvious because the words are there for reinspection, and reading makes words easier to identify because they are consistently marked by spaces. Other differences seem to favor speech through its advantageous communication context and, for the early reader, the decoding demands of print. In fact, these advantages for speech make the memory and word-boundary advantage of reading necessary. Memory and word identification are seldom a problem for speech because of the heavy contribution of context.

Thus, there are two differences between speech and print that especially favor speech processing and constitute an obstacle for reading. These two differences, coding and context, are especially significant because (1) they are critical in processing and (2) they reduce and perhaps disappear with increased familiarity with print.

The Coding Factor

There has been so much said about decoding that the only point required here is to emphasize its importance. The fact that print is constructed as a code on speech is a critical element of reading in an alphabetic system. There is no value in pretending that decoding is an obstacle to the child's enjoyment of reading created by phonics teachers or scribes or psychologists. Unless someone helps the child discover relations between print symbols and speech sounds, the child risks not discovering something very important to becoming an independent, skilled reader. Young children who have difficulty in reading almost invariably have imperfect knowledge of the symbol–speech code.

The Contextual Factor

Reading is decontextualized whereas speech is heavily contextualized. There are a number of things entailed by this contextual difference, but the most important have to do with the contribution of message context to interpretation. The uses of language of a child entering school are almost entirely restricted to speech events that take place in very rich contexts. When a child's mother says *Close the refrigerator*, there is an open refrigerator to see and there is a human speech agent whose general appearance supports the speech act she has just made. In other contexts, there are comparable contextual supports in the message environment. Speech interactions with a child's peers occur in rich, purposeful, play contexts. Even speech heard on television tends to be embedded in rich social and narrative contexts. In general, the child hears about the here and now and can often see what's being referred to in the speech as well as why someone is saying what they are saying. Even when confronting speech that refers to things remote in time or space, the child has contextual cues to support the speech and often has a speaker who is willing to rephrase something should it misfire.

Print is different. The message is in the printed sentences, more or less unsupported by context. Children's books contain pictures, of course, but those hardly serve the role of social context. Indeed, whether they even help children read is dependent on exactly how they relate to the printed message (Schallert, 1980). At best they serve a weakly supportive role to the primary communication burden borne by the print.

To put it another way, in reading, the printed sentences contains intrinsic meaning. This meaning is formalizable as propositions, i.e., formal abstractions of meaning. For speech, important meanings lie outside the propositions. The comprehension of formal propositions is often neither necessary nor sufficient for successful communication by speech.

Olson (1977) has made the argument that linguistic meaning, as defined by propositions contained in sentences, is a unique attribute of literacy. Furthermore, there may be specific cognitive consequences of literacy as a result of intrinsic meaning. Linguistic meaning, in a sense, does not exist in preliterate speech. For a culture, it exists only when an evolution toward written symbols confronts people with decontextualized symbolic content, permanently available for analysis and reflection (Scribner & Cole, 1981). For a child, it exists only when pages that contain meaning only in the properties of the printed sentences are confronted.

It is interesting, incidentally, that, by this line of reasoning, formal semantic and syntactic analyses are made possible only through print, an especially ironic perspective on a linguistic science which has traditionally assumed the primacy of speech. The reason is that semantic and syntactic analyses depend critically upon observations of multiple levels, at least two. At one level, the referring value of a sentence must be recognized. At another level, the arrangement of symbols must be brought into awareness. Dramatic counterexamples to the usual disassociation of reference and form come from self-referring sentences:

This sentence contains five words.
Although the preceding sentence is true, this one is false.

The first sentence above seems unremarkable, but the two sentences together illustrate the paradox of self-reference. Such paradoxes are well known to students of introductory logic and readers of Hofstadter (1979). I suggest that such sentences are enabled by literate language and perhaps are not possible without print. Oral language in context provides less opportunity for operating on a language at more than one level, and without this opportunity, self-referring sentences are less remarkable.

There is a speech analogue to a self-referring sentence, namely, a self-referring utterance. For example, *Am I talking too loud?* screamed at the top of one's voice is a self-referring utterance. However, note that, in contrast to a self-referring sentence, the scope of the self reference is the utterance token; i.e., it is self-referring to that particular utterance at that particular time. This context specificity is the essence of contextualized language. By contrast, the scope of sentence self-reference is the utterance type, i.e., the decontextualized sentence. Thus decontextualization is the key to sentence self-reference and it is the decontextualized property of print that makes this sort of self-reference possible.

Finally, it is useful to connect this decontextualization argument with observations about the child's linguistic competence at the age of six. Research on what the child knows about syntax prior to the school years is not consistent with the earlier view of a fully competent linguistic being. The idea that the 4-year-old child had developed all the basics of syntax and had only to be filled in on certain idiosyncratic details seems valid only within important limits. Instead, it may be more accurate to characterize the young child's knowledge of syntax as very context dependent. For example, a young child may appear to understand the sentence *The meat was eaten by the dog.* However, this "understanding" may be strictly based on pragmatic knowledge about eating and not on syntax (e.g., Bever, 1970; de Villiers & de Villiers, 1973). Thus the child will often fail to understand a sentence such as *The car was hit by the truck.* While the form of the *car–truck* sentence is the same as the *meat–dog* sentence, pragmatic knowledge is not helpful because the child knows either a car or a truck could have done the hitting. The point is that the child, while appearing to have control over a linguistic form, may in fact be very dependent on context. Similarly, while preschool children understand the difference between *before* and *after* in context, it's not clear that they can do so when only the linguistic forms govern the interpretation of temporal order (French & Brown, 1977). Ordinarily contextual cues to temporal order are sufficient. When they are not, the child has difficulty.

It's not that preschool children's linguistic knowledge is not considerable. Rather, it's that much of what they know about linguistic forms is rather tenative. They can demonstrate competence in one situation but not another. This is quite consistent with the picture of children who have had the luxury of almost totally contextualized speech encounters. Their reading experiences will confront them with decontextualized messages and provide the opportunity to master linguistic forms that are only partially mastered before then. This linguistic knowledge can extend to speech processing. This is one of the ways speech comes eventually to be more like print. But at the beginning, the dependence on form for meaning is a distinctive feature of reading.

HOW LATER READING BECOMES MORE LIKE SPEECH

A later observation of the relationship between speech and print shows a different picture. As reading is acquired, it becomes more speechlike. In terms of the two factors of coding and context, this is mainly due to the mastery of coding. As the child comes to first acquire the general requirement of decoding and then the more refined efficiency of it, reading becomes increasingly like listening. The two phases to decoding mastery are important—first accuracy and then efficiency, roughly speaking. There is, of course, consistent evidence linking decoding accuracy and decoding speed to reading comprehension skill. The accuracy link is elementary: Comprehension depends on accurate word recognition. The efficiency argument (e.g., Perfetti & Lesgold, 1979; Perfetti, 1985) also seems reasonable: Processes of comprehension are easy to the extent that processes of word recognition do not occupy limited-capacity processing mechanisms. Fast and automatic is better than slow and effortful.

The link this has with the present argument is that accuracy at decoding will be the first print component that can prevent reading from becoming like listening. The next component will be the effort of decoding. As these component skills improve, reading becomes more like listening. Equivalently, a child's reading level can reach his or her listening level (Sticht, 1979).

On this point, that reading becomes more like listening as decoding is mastered, there are supportive data. For example, Sticht's (1979) data on the relationship between listening skills and reading skills support the assumption that the two are closely related and the expectation that their relationship ought to become closer as the child becomes better at reading. Curtis (1980) has provided further evidence consistent with this expectation. Curtis compared second, third, and fifth graders of high and low skill on a number of tasks. To simplify, the results of interest in this context were that listening comprehension accounted for more unique variance in the reading comprehension of fifth graders than it did in that of second and third graders. For the younger subjects, a general factor that included both decoding and listening comprehension was most important. Similarly, less skilled subjects showed a general factor that included decoding and listening more than did skilled subjects of the same age. Thus, the general pattern is that as children get older and more skilled in reading, their reading comprehension looks more like their listening comprehension. However, decoding is not much of a unique factor unless they do not become good at reading.

The results of studies from my research group have been consistent with the picture that poor readers, as measured by a comprehension test, are also poor at listening comprehension. For example, a study by Berger (Berger & Perfetti, 1977) found that among IQ-matched fifth graders, low-skill and high-skill readers differed as much in recall and recognition of simple stories when the stories were spoken as when they were read. Similarly, we have found that memory for words spoken in a story, when measured seconds after hearing them, is just as poor for low-skill readers as when the text is read (Perfetti & Lesgold, 1979). These conclusions seem to hold especially well for older children, say fourth and fifth grade and beyond. Although we have no comparable evidence for younger readers, we would expect that memory during reading is less similar to memory during listening to the extent that decoding is a factor. Even for very young children, it is becoming increasingly likely that we must see their reading problems as intimately related to problems in speech processing (e.g., Byrne & Shea, 1979; Liberman & Shankweiler, 1979). Such children may have decoding problems that are partly dependent on failures of speech processing, including lack of explicit knowledge about speech and failures to encode speech sounds.

The evidence summarized so far illustrates that as the coding factor is reduced, the dependence of reading and listening on their common processes becomes more apparent. What about decontextualization, the second major factor distinguishing reading from listening? One empirical implication of the decontextualization argument is that the decontextualization factor should produce specific differences between reading and oral language comprehension. In fact, Hildyard and Olson (1982) seem to have found exactly the kind of difference that should occur. They found that among third- and fifth-grade children, recall of oral stories contained more implicit contextually plausible material than did recall of written stories. The latter contained relatively more explicit text material. It's as if listening produced more attention to the likely context of the story events and reading produced more attention to the exact story events explicit in the text. By the asymmetry argument, such differences should diminish with increased print experience.

HOW LATER SPEECH CAN BECOME MORE LIKE PRINT

Speech should become more like reading as the ability to process decontextualized speech develops. That is, reading requires decontextualized processing, and the generalization of this ability to speech, at least in some conditions, should be a key development. However, we are at a loss for evidence concerning changes in the contextual factor. One possibility is that the child in the elementary years begins to notice a lot of things about language as a result of successful encounters with print. (If the child's encounters with print are unsuccessful, such increased language awareness may not occur.) Part of this is noticing things about word boundaries and word constituents. For example, knowledge of speech segments seems to be promoted by learning to read (Ehri, 1981; Liberman, Shankweiler, Liberman, Fowler, & Fischer, 1977; Perfetti, Beck, Bell, & Hughes, in press). More to the point, through reading the child may really come to appreciate the truly expressive power of language and may learn that sentences contain meaning without reference to anything else. Certainly by the time the child learns to solve abstract problems of language, including algebra as well as natural language syntax, he has learned to deal with intrinsic meaning. But we have little research that would help fill in this picture.

One implication of this argument is that eventually speech will become more like print in its ability to express intrinsic meaning. Literate adults, and especially hyperliterate ones, become able to handle decontextualized messages in either speech or print. The very fact that we can listen to a talk that was written down illustrates this. Despite some differences between a scholarly talk and a scholarly paper—mostly related to deictic reference—the language in a talk is not necessarily less abstract and the meaning is not particularly contextualized. Intrinsic decontextualized meanings, while never as easy to process as extrinsic contextualized meanings, are not handicapped by a speech mode relative to a print mode for a hyperliterate. Thus, a hyperliterate adult is one for whom speech has become more like reading than reading is like speech. He or she is no longer more experienced in speech than in print; processing of speech may be more similar to processing of print than vice versa.

This, of course, is not the person we are worried about in the teaching of reading. For the child, the first two observation points are the important ones. Observation point 1 affords the view that the beginning reader confronts a task that has several differences from customary tasks, and at least two of these are especially important. That reading requires decoding is the first one, and it partly masks the second difference, that reading is decontextualized. At observation point 2, e.g., a third-grade child, if decoding has been mastered, is very dependent on listening abilities. Pushed beyond these abilities, the child will be better at speech as well as print, and will use print to learn more about linguistic forms and how to extract messages from them no matter how unfamiliar the context. For the child, reading is more like speech than speech is like reading, the situation may begin to be reversed.

SUMMARY

I have assumed that speech processes and print processes have both shared and distinctive features. I have offered the conjecture that there are asymmetries in their shared and distinctive features that change with the acquisition of literacy, focusing especially on decoding and decontextualization as two critical features. At first, print is more like speech than speech is like print. As decoding recedes as a print feature, the decontextualization feature of print can be gradually attached to language in general. This is part of language development that thus depends on literacy. Speech and print gradually become more similar and speech processes may become as much like print processes as vice versa. At the extreme, the asymmetry is reversed and hyperliteracy is observed.

ACKNOWLEDGMENTS

Preparation of this chapter was supported in part by the Center for the Study of Learning of the Learning Research and Development Center and in part by the Office of Educational Research and Improvement.

REFERENCES

Berger, N. S., & Perfetti, C. A. (1977). Reading skill and memory for spoken and written discourse. *Journal of Reading Behavior, 9*, 7–16.

Bever, T. G. (1970). The cognitive basis for linguistic structures. In J. R. Hayes (Ed.), *Cognition and the development of language.* New York: Wiley.

Byrne, B., & Shea, P. (1979). Semantic and phonetic memory codes in beginning readers. *Memory & Cognition, 7*, 333–338.

Chafe, W. L. (1982). Integration and involvement in speaking, writing, and oral literature. In D. Tannen (Ed.), *Spoken and written language: Exploring orality and literacy.* Norwood, NJ: Ablex.

Curtis, M. E. (1980). Development of components of reading skill. *Journal of Educational Psychology, 72*, 656–669.

de Villiers, J. G., & de Villiers, P. A. (1973). Development of the use of word order in comprehension. *Journal of Psycholinguistic Research, 2*, 331–341.

Ehri, L. C. (1981). Reading and spelling in beginners: The development of orthographic images as word symbols in lexical memory. In U. Frith (Ed.), *Cognitive Processes in spelling.* New York: Academic Press.

French, L. A., & Brown, A. L. (1977). Comprehension of before and after in logical and arbitrary sequences. *Child Language, 4*, 247–256.

Harrell, L. E., Jr. (1957). A comparison of oral and written language in school-age children. *Monographs of the Society for Research in Child Development, 22*(3, Serial No. 66).

Hildyard, A., & Olson, D. R. (1982). On the comprehension and memory of oral vs. written discourse. In D. Tannen (Ed.), *Spoken and written language: Exploring orality and literacy.* Norwood, NJ: Ablex.

Hockett, C. F. (1960). The origin of speech. *Scientific American, 203*, 88–96.

Hofstadter, D. (1979). *Gödel, Escher, Bach: An eternal golden braid.* New York: Basic Books.

Liberman, I. Y., & Shankweiler, D. (1979). Speech, the alphabet, and teaching to read. In L. B. Resnick & P. Weaver (Eds.), *Theory and practice of early reading* (Vol. 2). Hillsdale, NJ: Erlbaum.

Liberman, I. Y., Shankweiler, D., Liberman, A. M., Fowler, C., & Fischer, F. W. (1977). Phonetic segmentation and recoding in the beginning reader. In A. S. Reber & D. L. Scarborough (Eds.), *Towards a psychology of reading. The proceedings of the CUNY Conference.* New York: Wiley.

O'Donnell, R. C. (1974). Syntactic differences between speech and writing. *American Speech, 49*, 102–110.

Olson, D. R. (1977). From utterance to text: The bias of language in speech and writing. *Harvard Educational Review, 47*, 257–281.

Perfetti, C. A. (1985). *Reading Ability.* New York: Oxford Press.

Perfetti, C. A., Beck, I., Bell, L., & Hughes, C. (in press). Phonemic knowledge and learning to read are reciprocal: A longitudinal study of first grade children. In K. Stanovich (Ed), *Children's reading and the development of phonological awareness.* Special issue of *Merrill-Palmer Quarterly.*

Perfetti, C. A., & Lesgold, A. M. (1979). Coding and comprehension in skilled reading and implications for reading instruction. In L. Resnick & P. Weaver (Eds.), *Theory and practice of early reading* (Vol. 1). Hillsdale, NJ: Erlbaum.

Schallert, D. L. (1980). The role of illustrations in reading comprehension. In R. J. Spiro, B. C. Bruce, & W. F. Brewer (Eds.), *Theoretical issues in reading comprehension.* Hillsdale, NJ: Erlbaum.

Scribner, S., & Cole, M. (1981). *The psychology of literacy*. Cambridge, MA: Harvard University Press.

Sticht, T. G. (1979). Applications of the Audread model to reading evaluation and instruction. In L. B. Resnick & P. Weaver (Eds.), *Theory and practice in early reading* (Vol. 1). Hillsdale, NJ: Erlbaum.

Tversky, A. (1977). Features of similarity. *Psychological Review, 84,* 327–352.

Chapter 13

A Comparison of the Two Theories about Development in Written Language: Implications for Pedagogy and Research

Sandra Stotsky

INTRODUCTION

There seems to be no systematic comparison of theories about the nature of development in written language. In order to discover the essential differences among these theories, I have examined all available theoretical writings on the relationship of written to oral language and have concluded that there appear to be two basic theories about the relationship of written to oral language and the relationship between reading and writing. Because these theories imply fundamentally different research paradigms and instructional practices, especially at higher levels of literacy development, it is important to understand them clearly. It is also important to know whether there is evidence to support either one. This chapter first discusses the assumptions and claims made by each theory, then outlines the model of development in written language that can be derived from each one, and indicates the pedagogical implications of each. It then indicates what empirical evidence has been found to support each theory and concludes by suggesting what kinds of research might help to assess the claims of both theories.

Copyright © 1987 by Academic Press, Inc.

The critical differences between these two theories hinge on the resolution of three issues: (1) how written language is related to oral language; (2) how the reader derives meaning from written texts; and (3) from where the writer derives meaning in order to produce written texts. Figure 13.1 suggests where these critical differences occur in the interrelationship of the four language processes of listening, speaking, reading, and writing. The circles in this figure and in the subsequent ones as well represent these processes. The lines with arrows leading to MEANING indicate the processes that may contribute to growth in comprehending meaning; the boxes at the beginning of these lines indicate the possible sources of influence on these processes. The lines with arrows leading away from MEANING indicate the processes that may contribute to growth in expressing meaning; the boxes at the end of these lines indicate the results of these processes.

THE FIRST THEORY

In the first theory, which has several variations, oral language experience structures meaning in reading and writing at all levels of literacy development; reading and writing cannot independently influence each other. Further, written language is not considered qualitatively different from oral language. Greenberg writes, "The linguist views writing . . . as a derivative system whose symbols stand for units of the spoken language" (in Osgood & Sebeok, 1969, p. 9). Smith (1975) writes, "Spoken and written language . . . are alternative surface structure forms of a common underlying language (p. 350).[1] Goodman (1970/1982) writes that written language "must be seen as a different but parallel form to oral language" (p. 101). Moffett (1983) defines literacy as a "second layer of symbols, written words for spoken words" (p. 7). The critical assumption underlying this general theory is that the substance and structure of written language do not differ from the substance and structure of oral language.

The variations in the theory concern the mechanisms for gaining access to meaning in print and differ in their pedagogical implications only at the level of beginning reading and writing instruction. One variation views written language as a derivative of, or sequential to, oral language, while the other views written language as an alternate but parallel form of oral language. Figures 13.2 and 13.3, showing these variations, have been constructed (as have Figures 13.4 and 13.5) to match statements in the texts of the theorists discussed, using the basic model presented in Figure 13.1, for the purpose of comparison. Figure 13.2

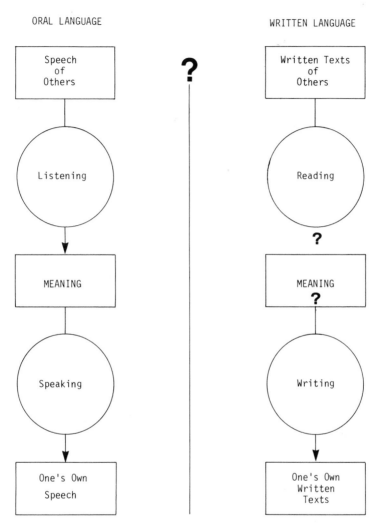

FIGURE 13.1.   Location of the critical differences between the two basic theories about the development of meaning in written language.

shows the first variation and represents Moffett's (1983) ideas. In his view, readers always decode when comprehending written language, and reading is always the matching of print with speech. Even the experienced reader never quite goes from print to meaning directly: "When people read, they are decoding print into speech at the same time they are decoding speech into thought" (Moffett, 1983, p. 143).[2]

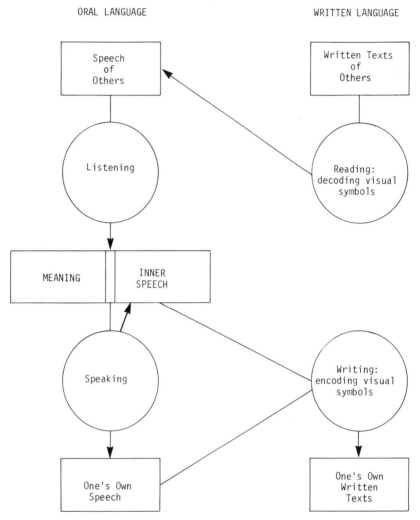

ORAL LANGUAGE   WRITTEN LANGUAGE

FIGURE 13.2. Sources of influence on the development of meaning in written language, after Moffett (1983).

Figure 13.3 is Goodman's and Smith's version, although there is a slight difference between them. In Goodman's (1970/1982) version, as in Moffett's version, beginning readers also need to decode (or recode) written language into speech; the dashed line indicates this process. But eventually, in Goodman's version, with increasing reading experience, beginning readers go directly from print to meaning. However, they

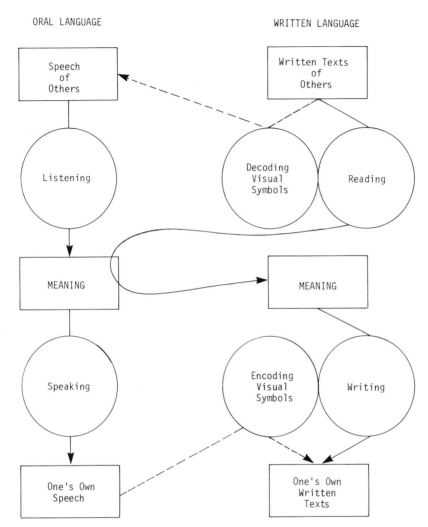

FIGURE 13.3.   Sources of influence on the development of meaning in written language, after Goodman (1970/1982) and Smith (1971, 1982).

continue to read by predicting and confirming meaning in print on the basis of previous meanings developed from their experiences with oral language. Smith (1971), on the other hand, argues against any decoding stage; the reader always goes directly from print to meaning. According to Smith, the beginning reader predicts meaning from the very beginning by sampling from whatever are determined to be the distinctive features of "visual configurations." The teacher simply provides "information" to the beginning reader, indicating whether or not the reader's predictions are correct (pp. 228–229). As in Goodman's version, these predictions are based on semantic/syntactic structures developed from experience with oral language. Hence, the loop through meaning derived from oral language experience in Figure 13.3.[3]

The critical feature in this theory is that the reader does not seem to be able to understand anything in the reading material that is of greater semantic/syntactic complexity than can be understood aurally. The reader reads by decoding from print to speech or by predicting meaning on the basis of prior language knowledge. The written texts the reader understands may be less complex than or as complex as what can be understood aurally, but they apparently cannot be more complex. What the reader understands aurally sets a ceiling on, or gates, what can be understood in written texts. As Moffett asserts, the developing reader cannot read with understanding anything that cannot be understood if heard in oral reading (p. 145). Thus, in this model of written-language development, oral-language knowledge always serves as the basis for deriving meaning from written texts. The reader's level of comprehension of written language seems to be dependent on level of comprehension of oral language at all levels of development. The development of written language does not seem to be independent of the development of oral language at any point.

Now let us examine writing development according to this general theory. In Moffett's version, writing is always the transcription of inner or outer speech (pp. 4–6); it derives at first from outer speech and, then, later, from inner speech, which is developed primarily from oral language activities and is the internalization of outer speech (p. 177). Because, in Moffett's theory, inner speech is derived primarily from outer speech, writing is therefore related to reading through the primary modes of speaking and listening at all levels of development. This means that the reader cannot produce semantic/syntactic forms and structures in writing that are more complex than those produced in spoken language. What has been read cannot independently influence what is being written, nor can what is being written reciprocally influence inner speech, or, ultimately, meaning itself.

In Goodman's and Smith's models, the language structures and forms the developing writer composes with and writes also cannot be of greater complexity than those the writer can understand aurally and produce orally.[4] Why? Because the level of complexity in the oral language internalized up to that point determines the level of complexity in the language patterns and resources understood in reading material and drawn upon for writing. Written language that is of greater complexity than one's level of comprehension of oral language cannot influence one's writing because oral language knowledge always determines what can be understood and, hence, absorbed from written texts. Thus, in this theory, in order to produce written texts the writer essentially derives meaning only from oral language.[5]

Pedagogical Implications of the First Theory

What are the pedagogical implications of this theory? Goodman (1970/ 1982) and Moffett (1983) have spelled them out quite clearly. If formal written language is not qualitatively different from oral language, and if the comprehension of written language depends on the level of comprehension of oral language, then, as Moffett asserts, the problems of comprehension and composition are essentially the same for the reader and writer as for the listener and speaker (p. 176). Accordingly, there is no need to spend much time on reading and writing since reading and writing pose no problems at any developmental level that cannot be dealt with pedagogically through oral practice (p. 6). Even "less developed learners" can learn through oral practice the "bulk of what they need to know in order to read and write" (p. 556) in any area of discourse. Thus, in Moffett's curriculum, we find a consistent emphasis on social interaction and the development of an oral language base as the focus of classroom activity.

Goodman's theory appears to be quite similar to Moffett's. Goodman (1970/1982) writes,

> Concepts and ideas can be introduced through demonstration, experimentation, concrete illustration. Vocabulary can be developed orally in relation to these experiences. Then, and only then, is the child ready for the task of reading about the same concepts in the text. He reads them not so much to gain new concepts as to reinforce them. (p. 113)

It should be noted that Goodman does state that by the time a student is in high school, "he may . . . be able . . . to initiate study at times through a textbook" (pp. 113–114). It is not clear whether or not he believes, as Moffett does, that reading problems at higher levels can be addressed primarily through oral language activities alone.

To conclude, in this theory of written-language development, growth occurs in reading and writing through growth in listening and speaking. Comprehension or composition of written language is always grounded in the comprehension or composition of oral language. When the comprehension and composition of oral language is postulated to derive from concrete experiences with the natural world, we have a curriculum shaped by the assumptions of a cognitive developmental model. When the comprehension and composition of oral language is postulated to derive from innate linguistic structures or a language acquisition device, we have a curriculum shaped by the assumptions of a psycholinguistic model. However, whether the curriculum is influenced by a cognitive developmental model or by a psycholinguistic model, the focus of instruction in reading and writing will be on the enrichment of natural language by means of a variety of oral language activities in conjunction with practical experiences.

THE SECOND THEORY

The second theory about the relationship of written to oral language and the relationship between reading and writing is suggested by the work of Vygotsky (1962, 1978), Bruner, Olver, and Greenfield (1966), Luria (1969), and Simon (1970), among others. In this theory, not only may written language influence meaning in oral language, but reading and writing may also influence each other directly. The basic assumption of this theory is that oral and written language differ in both their origins and in their purposes and, accordingly, are qualitatively different in nature. Vygotsky (1978) writes, "writing . . . is a new and complex form of speech" (p. 118). Luria (1969) writes, "written speech [differs] from oral speech in its origins and in its structural and functional features" (p. 141).[6] Simon (1970) writes that written language does not arise as a "twin" to spoken language; it may share some common elements but requires other resources for its full development, using different means to achieve different goals (p. 323).[7] Bruner *et al.* (1966) suggest the following differences between written and oral language:

> All the semantic and syntactic features that have been discussed in relation to concept formation—a rich and hierarchically organized vocabulary, as well as the syntactic embedding of labels—become necessary when one must communicate out of the context of immediate reference. It is precisely in this respect that written language differs from the spoken. (p. 310)

We might call this theory an epistemological theory of written language development because it seeks to explain how we come to know—and, hence, be able to use—the language of formal schooling.[8] According to this theory, writing, although initially dependent upon spoken language while students learn to decode and encode written language, becomes increasingly independent of spoken language and more influenced by written language itself. Although the language developing writers read is usually far richer and more complex than the language

ORAL LANGUAGE   WRITTEN LANGUAGE

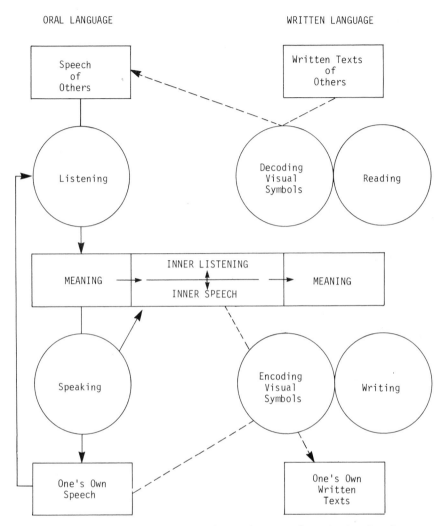

FIGURE 13.4.   Sources of influence on the development of meaning in written language at the onset of literacy learning, after Vygotsky (1962, 1978), Bruner *et al.* (1966), Luria (1969), and Simon (1970).

they can write, the theory suggests that students' writing may gradually become like the language they read with continuous experience and instruction in reading and writing this language.

Figure 13.4 presents a preliminary version of this theory in order to show what happens in beginning reading and writing. Again, the direction of the arrows indicates whether the process may contribute to the development of meaning or to an expression of meaning—or, in this theory, to both. As Figure 13.4 indicates, language learners first derive meaning from the spoken language of others; moreover, their own speech may also contribute to the development of meaning. They learn to read primarily by decoding and fusing written symbols into sounds that have meanings recognized from experience in listening to the speech of others (Luria, 1966, pp. 411–413). Thus, as beginning readers, they derive meaning from written texts on the basis of meaning gained from experience with spoken language. The written texts they read with understanding may be less rich and complex than, or as rich and complex as, what they can understand aurally. What they understand aurally sets a ceiling on, or gates, what they can understand in written texts.[9]

During this period, as Figure 13.4 also indicates, inner speech and inner listening continue to develop. Inner speech is the internalization of outer speech but has a "predicative, idiomatic structure" (Vygotsky, 1962, p. 149); inner listening refers to our ability to "hear" inner speech and would seem to be presupposed by the existence of inner speech (Sokolov, 1969, p. 568). In the preschool years, inner listening may simply be the internalization of external listening.

Eventually, with enough reading experience, the beginning reader no longer has to translate written symbols into sounds in order to understand the meaning they signify but can understand the meaning they signify directly. The reader now goes directly from print to meaning. Vygotsky (1978) writes,

> As second-order symbols, written symbols function as designations for verbal ones. Understanding of written language is first effected through spoken language, but gradually this path is curtailed and spoken language disappears as the intermediate link. To judge from all the available evidence, written language becomes direct symbolism that is perceived in the same way as spoken language. (p. 116)

The direct influence of reading upon meaning (and thought) is shown in Figure 13.5, a more fully developed model. It is possible that the development of inner listening facilitates the understanding of written language as "direct symbolism."

At the point when written language can be understood as direct symbolism, something very significant can occur in the reading process. Up to this point, the reader has understood written language on the basis of his or her understanding of spoken language. Now, however, the reader can go beyond the limits of spoken language experiences. Level of listening comprehension no longer sets limits on level of reading comprehension. The reader can now learn to read written language that is richer and more complex than his or her spoken language.

How can developing readers come to understand written forms and

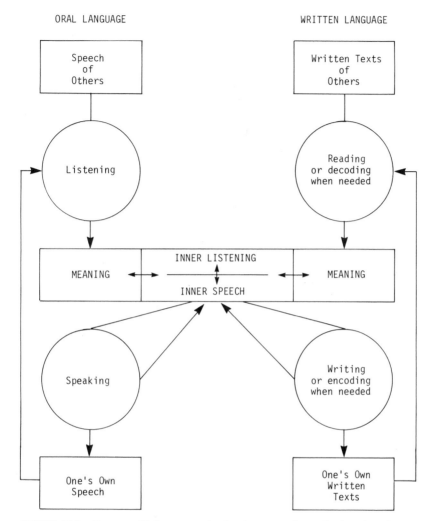

FIGURE 13.5.   Sources of influence on the development of meaning in written language at higher levels of literacy learning, after Vygotsky (1962, 1978), Bruner *et al.* (1966), Luria(1969), and Simon (1970).

patterns of language that differ from those they have heard? In general, in almost exactly the same way they have learned to understand greater complexity in oral language—through continuous exposure. Just as language learners come to understand greater complexity in oral language through frequent exposure to more complex oral language, so, too, do they learn to understand more complex written language through continuous exposure to more complex written language. New meanings are gradually incorporated through frequent experiences reading them; in other words, developing readers use the same processes for absorbing the lexical richness and density of written language that they use for absorbing or internalizing more complex oral language.

How more precisely do developing readers go beyond the limits of the level of their comprehension of spoken language? This is not spelled out by Vygotsky or Luria. One may hypothesize that the development of the readers' ability to understand as "direct symbolism" written forms of language that are familiar to them may gradually enable them to understand as direct symbolism some written forms of language that are somewhat unfamiliar. These newly acquired semantic/syntactic forms and structures then provide the context for developing readers to understand other written forms of language that are also unfamiliar. In this way, written forms of language that differ from forms in the reader's spoken language system function as new resources that serve to accelerate growth in understanding written language beyond the level of listening comprehension. It is in this way that literacy nourishes itself. Eventually, mature readers can absorb language visually that is far richer and denser than spoken language. (Indeed, it is difficult to listen to language that is as dense and as rich as the mature language we can read.)

Now let us turn to the development of writing. As Figure 13.4 indicates, beginning writers may encode spoken language directly or they may encode from inner speech, which in the preschool years is a transformed form of external speech. In either case, the only independent source from which beginning writers derive meaning is spoken language. Written language that is of greater richness and complexity than the oral language they can comprehend cannot influence their writing because their experience with spoken language determines what they can understand and, hence, absorb from written texts. So long as what beginning writers read must be translated into meaningful sounds for comprehension to occur, their writing cannot be richer or more complex than the language they have heard. The language of beginning writing will therefore be very much like speech written down.

How is the language of the beginning writer transformed into the language of more mature writing? Here one may hypothesize that the development of the ability to understand written language directly, together with frequent reading experiences at progressively more difficult levels, enables developing writers to internalize written forms of language that differ in quality and density from the language they experience aurally, and, eventually, to use or reproduce them in their writing. With sufficient experience and instruction in reading and writing, mature writers can produce language that is far richer than the language they speak. (Indeed, we cannot easily produce language orally that is as dense and as rich as the language we can write.) Note that by positing a source of influence on meaning that is not gated by the writer's level of listening comprehension, the model in Figure 13.5 accounts for the writer's ability to use or produce language that is richer and denser than spoken language.

As suggested by Luria (1969), inner speech develops even more after the onset of literacy training. Thus, Figure 13.5 also shows the direct influence of writing upon inner speech. Luria writes,

> Because it delays the direct appearance of speech connections, inhibits them, and increases requirements for the preliminary, internal preparation for the speech act, written speech produces a rich development of inner speech which could not take place in the earliest phases of development. (p. 143)

Because meaning and thought are related but not identical (Sokolov, 1969; Bruner *et al.*, 1966, pp. 43–44), the direct influence of writing upon inner speech and inner listening means that meaning and thought are also enhanced by writing.

Finally, Figure 13.5 shows that what one has written becomes in its own right a text to be read and "listened to" directly. Critical reading of one's own writing may become at least as great a stimulus for mental activity and intellectual development as the reading of others' texts. Ong (1983) asserts that written words make possible "psychological operations so complex as to defy total description" (p. 8).

It is important to note that in this model speech itself is affected by written language development. However, it is possible that the longer established habits of speech, the speed with which it must be produced, and its lack of permanence probably keep speech less complex than writing at all levels of development. The relative slowness of writing and the objectified nature of written language enable the writer to produce or work out forms of written language that the nature of spoken language precludes.

Pedagogical Implications of the Second Theory

What are the pedagogical implications of this model? If the significant characteristics of mature written language are not present in spoken language and are therefore not a part of the language learner's natural language environment at home or at school, then the density and richness of mature written language cannot be absorbed through oral language experience and practice. Teachers will need to provide students with regular exposure to increasing levels of textual density to help them absorb the lexical richness and density of written language (see Stotsky, 1983a, for a more detailed discussion of this issue). In other words, the focus of instruction in reading will be on the development of academic language by means of a carefully planned curriculum that requires students to undertake progressively more challenging reading assignments of an expository informational nature.[10] Teachers will also have to provide students with regular practice in writing about what they are learning about the world around them and about their own ideas concerning what they have learned in order to help them use this language and develop mastery of its resources.[11]

In general, this theory of written language development suggests that the bulk of what developing readers and writers need to learn will be learned through their own individual efforts and experiences in reading and writing academic language. Note that this model does not suggest that students should not engage in oral language activities; such activities are valuable for their own sake and for the contribution they do make to written language development. What the model does imply is that oral language experiences are not a substitute for reading and writing experiences.

SUMMARY OF THE TWO THEORIES

Both of the theories about the relationship of written to oral language and the relationship between reading and writing agree that oral language experience structures meaning in beginning reading and writing (normally, Grades 1 to 3). However, while the first theory claims that oral language retains its primacy at higher levels of literacy development, the second suggests that the relationship may be more than reversed at higher levels of literacy development; not only may written language influence meaning in oral language, but reading and writing may also influence each other directly. The first theory suggests only a unidirectional relationship: oral language influences written language but not the reverse. The second theory suggests a reciprocal relationship, even a multidirectional one, among the four language processes: oral language may influence written language, written language may influence oral language, and reading and writing may each enhance the other directly in different but equally profound ways. The first theory suggests that growth in reading and writing is always a function of growth in oral language; the second theory suggests that growth in reading and writing becomes less a function of growth in oral language and more a function of exposure to written language itself. In addition, each theory makes a different assumption about the nature of oral and written language: the first theory assumes that oral and written language are identical in nature; the second theory assumes they are qualitatively different in nature.

Research Evidence for the Two Theories

Research evidence may be found in support of both theories. However, the evidence so far for the first theory is at best inconsistent. Sticht *et al.* (1974), after an intensive review of the literature, noted that 10 of the 12 studies measuring the effects of listening instruction or activity on reading comprehension and finding improvement in listening skills also found improvement in reading skills. However, Belanger (1978), in his review of the literature, reported two other studies (Binzer, 1974; Lewis, 1976) that found no effects on reading comprehension after significant improvement in listening comprehension. Belanger also noted that three other studies (*Improving Reading*, 1972; Campbell, 1973; Drumm, 1976) that sought to improve reading through oral language activities also found inconsistent or nonsignificant effects. Groff (1979) reviewed studies that attempted to use oral language activities to facilitate growth in writing and concluded that "research that is available indicates that such activities do not well serve this function" (p. 36). Belanger also concluded from his review of the literature that investigators attempting to enhance writing skills by teaching oral skills have failed to demonstrate consistent improvement, if any, in writing skills (p. 35). Although a study by Meyers (1979) and an earlier one by Gatlin (1974) found significant differences in compositions written after a talk–write method was used, five other studies using this method have found inconsistent or nonsignificant results (Tovatt & Miller, 1967; Radcliffe, 1969; Zanotti, 1970; Moore, 1971; Davis, 1975).

On the other hand, there appears to be stronger and more consistent evidence in support of the second theory. Stotsky (1983b) Synthesized the results of all the experimental and correlational studies that could be found on reading/writing relationships to determine what seems to be known about these relationships and to suggest directions for further research. The experimental studies were classified into two categories: these studies examining the influence of writing on reading and those studies examining the influence of reading on writing. Most of the correlational studies were classified into one of three major categories: those correlating measures of reading achievement with measures of writing ability; those correlating measures of reading experience with measures of writing ability; and those correlating measures of reading ability with measures of syntactic complexity in student's compositions. Stotsky found direct support for the second theory in three groups of studies. First, almost all experimental studies that used writing activities or exercises specifically to improve reading comprehension or retention of information in instructional material found significant gains; depending on the length and type of study, the gains varied from better recall of specific material read to improved scores on standardized reading tests or achievement tests in academic subjects. It is worth noting that most of these studies used reading material that was expository or informational in nature. Second, experimental studies that sought to improve writing by providing reading experiences in place of grammar study or additional writing practice found that these experiences were as beneficial as, or more beneficial than, grammar study or extra writing practice; studies that used literary models also found significant gains in writing. Third, studies that correlated measures of writing ability with measures of reading experience, based on questionnaires, also found a relationship between reading and writing.

Only two groups of studies found no significant influence of reading or writing upon the other: experimental studies that taught writing or used writing exercises primarily to improve writing and measured effects on reading did not tend to find significant effects on reading; experimental studies that sought to improve free writing through reading instruction were almost all ineffective.

Although the studies correlating measures of reading achievement with measures of writing ability or syntactic maturity in writing did find significant relationships, the results of these studies in themselves do not provide direct evidence for either theory because no cause-and-effect relationship can be clearly inferred. A correlation in these studies does not indicate whether reading or writing has influenced the other independent of oral language development or whether both are simply a reflection of oral language development.

There are, however, other types of correlational studies whose results clearly suggest the influence of reading on writing. A small number of studies of samples of speech and writing at two or more grade levels all found that most students' writing becomes syntactically more complex than their speech by the middle grades, regardless of the type of discourse examined (Lull, 1929; Harrell, 1957; O'Donnell, Griffin, & Norris, 1967; Loban, 1976; Golub & Fredrick, 1971). Within each study, similar measures were used for each mode. Similarly designed, Bushnell's study (1930) found that the oral English of only 2 of 100 students in Grade 10 was rated of higher quality in both thought and sentence structure than was their written English in response to the same topic.

Further evidence that children's writing gradually becomes increasingly different from their oral language comes from a 5-year longitudinal study by Simon (1970) of 120 French schoolchildren from Grades 1 to 5. After studying yearly samples of their writing and speech, which were elicited by the same picture-story stimulus, Simon concluded that written language differs qualitatively from oral language from the very first year of schooling, notably with respect to greater precision in lexical choices and greater correctness in certain syntactic constructions, e.g., the rapid disappearance of the pleonastic subject in written language (pp. 220–250). To explain all these findings, one must infer that writing is being influenced by sources other than speech.

Further, almost every study on writing development using T-unit measures for analysis reported a plateau in increases in the dependent clause ratio for the average student by Grade 8 (e.g., Hunt, 1970; Rubin & Piché, 1979). Blount, Johnson, and Fredrick (1969) also reported that by Grade 8 clause length is a more powerful influence on T-unit length than the subordination ratio, i.e., increases in T-unit length are beginning to occur by means of additions within the clause rather than by means of increases in the number of subordinate clauses per T-unit. Because this phenomenon occurs at about the same time that writing demonstrates greater overall complexity than speaking, it seems reasonable to conclude that this phenomenon indicates a movement toward the structures of mature written prose and away from the structures of oral language. Thus, this phenomenon might also suggest that writing is being influenced by sources other than speech. Moreover, if high overall writing ability is associated with high reading ability, if high reading ability is associated with the use of more mature syntactic structures in written texts, and if the use of more mature syntactic structures in written texts indicates a movement away from the structures of oral language, then the results of the studies correlating measures of reading achievement with measures of writing ability or syntactic maturity in writing may be interpreted as providing indirect evidence for the second theory. Clearly, a viable theory of written language development must account for all these findings.

SUMMARY AND SUGGESTIONS FOR FURTHER RESEARCH

Overall, there seems to be little evidence to support the first theory; clearly, much stronger and more adequate evidence is needed to maintain its viability. On the other hand, there seems to be substantial support for the second theory. However, there can be some reluctance in concluding that clear or strong enough evidence has been provided to support this theory. While the second theory claims that most growth in reading and writing results from experience and instruction in reading and writing, it does not rule out the possibility that some growth in reading and writing may be attributable to growth in oral language. Further, the second theory also suggests that growth in reading and writing may also lead to growth in listening and speaking. It may therefore be difficult to disambiguate the effects of either theory over any prolonged period of time since normal classrooms usually provide many opportunities for students to speak, listen, read, and write; growth in both oral and written language will occur regardless of the research design and the focus of instruction.

Nevertheless, there are at least three possible areas for research if we wish to determine more conclusively whether or not reading has a separate and special influence on writing independent of the continuing influence of oral language on both: research with English as a Second Language (ESL) students with varying degrees of proficiency in reading, research with deaf children who have learned to read reasonably well, and case studies of developing writers. If speech is more important than reading, then ESL students with reading levels that are similar to native English-speaking students should produce writing of lower quality. If speech is not as important as reading level, then the writing of the ESL students should be of similar quality to the writing of the native English-speaking student, given similar reading levels. However, the reading level itself may make a difference. The writing of the ESL student with a reading level below Grade 6 or so may be more influenced by language differences than the writing of the ESL student with a reading level above Grades 6 to 8. At higher levels of reading ability, oral language differences may exert much less influence. Thus, reading level, not oral language proficiency, may be the more critical variable. The nature of the writing task itself is another significant variable that must be taken into consideration in such research.

A similar line of investigation could be pursued with deaf students. Although the average deaf child apparently rarely goes beyond a fourth-grade reading level (Ewoldt, 1981), there are some who do. Given similar ages, degree of deafness, and degree of facility with sign language, would deaf children with higher reading scores produce higher quality writing than those with lower reading scores?

Case studies of developing writers that clearly show the presence of specific language structures in a student's writing before their appearance in the student's spoken language are another promising area for research on this question. Data from such research could help us to assess the relative influence of reading and speech on writing and would have considerable theoretical and pedagogical significance.

Research also needs to be directed toward the assumptions about the nature of oral and written language. Do oral and written language have the same underlying structures or do oral and written language have different underlying structures? A number of scholars and researchers have suggested differences between the process of speaking and the process of writing, but few have examined the formal differences in what is being processed. (However, see Stotsky, 1986, for one research approach.) It may in fact be far more fruitful for researchers to reconceptualize the difference between spoken and written language as one between natural and academic language, or between literary and academic language, even though all these dichotomies may sometimes be synonymous with each other. There are many differences between expository informational prose and narrative literary prose (Stotsky, 1984b), and the distinctions between them should be noted. We have barely begun to probe the nature of academic language, the language for developing and communicating knowledge, and an essay by Stotsky (1985b) suggests how widely and deeply we must extend our research. The scholarship that exists appears primarily in the classics (see, e.g., Snell, 1960; Havelock, 1980) or in rhetoric, and, as Kinneavy (1980) points out, there is "no systematic coverage of [the style of reference discourse] either historically, critically, descriptively, or comparatively" (p. 166). A more complete understanding of the differences between natural and academic language, or between literary and academic language, might lead to entirely new ways to investigate the process of comprehending or composing each one. Although Ingarden (1973) sees no formal differences between literary language and academic language, he discusses at length how the understanding of a literary work of art differs from the understanding of a "scientific" work (pp. 146–167).

Finally, if it is the case that we learn to comprehend academic language not only by reading it but also by writing it, then we need far more research to explain more precisely how the final connections in the language learning process are made, i.e., the lines in Figure 13.5 going from Writing to Inner Speech and from One's Own Written Texts to Reading. Such studies as the one on paraphrasing by Glover, Plake, Roberts, Zimmer, & Palmere (1981) and the one on notetaking by Peper & Mayer (1978) are examples of the kind of research on writing about reading that may have fruitful implications for pedagogy. We especially need studies that examine the effects of formal, idea-centered essay writing on language learning and intellectual development.

The essential problem in reading research is to explain how we learn something new during or after the act of reading. A theory that sees reading as an act of predicting and confirming meaning on the basis of prior knowledge is incapable of explaining how new knowledge is acquired and assimilated, i.e., how semantic structures are changed. Both the reading and writing of expository texts should be seen as the active working out of meaning, either one's own or someone else's. They are not the prediction and confirmation of meaning nor its transcription. Because mental effort is required to understand another's ideas and to integrate them with one's own ideas, the value of various kinds of writing activities for the comprehension of expository texts may lie in their power to elicit and structure the reader's active attention to meaning during or after the act of reading. However, it is possible that formal, idea-centered essay writing in particular may be even more valuable than the personal essay or more informal kinds of writing activities, such as paraphrasing or note-taking, because it requires the writer to focus on abstract concepts, not the self, as the subjects of predicates and to work out logical relationships among these abstract ideas in extended stretches of expository discourse. Discovering how writing helps us to acquire and integrate knowledge will help us to explain more powerfully than do current theories of language comprehension how the comprehension of written language is achieved.

NOTES

[1] Smith (1982) still maintains that there is one underlying structure for oral and written language, even though he repeatedly asserts that oral and written language are not identical. He clearly indicates in his text that what he means by this statement is that the processes and uses of speaking and writing differ.

[2] On the basis of Moffett's theory, it is difficult to explain the widespread and well-known phenomenon of being able to comprehend directly a text written in a foreign language (i.e., without having translated it mentally into one's native language), given enough reading experience with that language. No translation into speech is possible if the foreign language has not been acquired as a spoken language.

[3] The major differences among these theorists for pedagogy in beginning reading seems to be in the role each attaches to instruction in decoding. Goodman (1970/1982) suggests that children learn decoding better without direct instruction; Moffett (1983) suggests that direct instruction is probably helpful, if not necessary (p. 422). Smith (1971, 1982), on the other hand, sees no role for decoding instruction at all.

[4] In recent articles, both Goodman & Goodman (1983) and Smith (1981) have suggested that reading influences writing. Both of them as educators are of course free to write anything they believe. However, both of them as theorists have outlined in earlier writings a theory of the reading process that does not allow for the separate and special influence of reading on writing independent of the influence of oral language on both. Moreover, neither has ever, to my knowledge, explicitly revised his theory in any way to account for such an influence. My essay deals with both Goodman and Smith as theorists and points

out the relationships among the four language processes that can be logically inferred from their theoretical statements. My essay also points out the pedagogical practices that can be validly derived (or that they themselves have derived) from their theories. It is not the purpose of my essay to deal with the inconsistencies between their theories and their recent statements.

From the perspective of Goodman's model of the reading process, it is not at all clear how good readers learn to spell. However, because good readers do learn, inductively at least, to decode written language in his model, it is possible that they may learn, inductively as well, to encode written language.

But it is even less clear how good readers ever learn to spell in Smith's model. In his latest work (1982), he claims that writers spell by remembering "thousands of spellings" (p. 152) and/or by remembering "whole groups of letters, often entire words, which [the brain] produces as integrated movement sequences" (p. 153). Given his belief that good readers do not read by decoding letters into sounds or by seeing individual letters, it is wholly unclear how thousands of spellings or integrated movement sequences are learned. His theory also leaves us with no way to account for the dialect speaker who reads and writes inflectional endings that conform to the conventions of written language but are not in his speech patterns (see, e.g., Groff's 1979 review of some of this literature). Nor can it explain the results of programs that are successful in teaching adult dialect speakers to eliminate syntactic errors in their writing (Epes, Kirkpatrick, & Southwell, 1980). Finally, Smith's theory suggests that only poor readers are apt to read letter-by-letter. This might imply that fluent readers are poor spellers and that poor readers are good spellers. Yet, studies on the relationship between spelling and reading ability (see, e.g., the review by Sherwin, 1969) have consistently found that good readers tend to be good spellers and that poor readers tend to be poor spellers. The evidence from these studies also raises serious questions about the validity of Smith's theory about the reading process.

[5] The model of language development proposed by Sticht et al. (1974) is also compatible with this theory. They too deny the possibility of qualitative differences between written and oral language. Their review of the literature suggests that after decoding ability is fully acquired, reading ability becomes comparable to "auding" ability by Grade 7 or 8, but their model rules out the possibility that reading performance can ever exceed auding performance except in terms of amount of information obtained (p. 83). However, from his research in designing equivalent tests of reading and listening, Durrell (1970) found that reading comprehension equaled listening comprehension by Grade 6, thereafter exceeding it, and that reading vocabulary equaled listening vocabulary by Grade 8, thereafter exceeding it. Apparently, after Grades 6 to 8, students could understand written language better by reading it than by listening to it.

Schema theory also seems to be compatible with this theory. Adams and Collins (1977, p. 4) write,

> A fundamental assumption of schema-theoretic approaches to language comprehension is that spoken or written text does not in itself carry meaning. Rather, a text only provides direction for the listener or reader as to how he should retrieve or construct the intended meaning from his own, previously acquired knowledge.

Apparently, in schema theory, the reader never grapples with new ideas in order to work out their meaning, since the ideas he reads have no meaning independent of the meaning he imposes on them from prior language knowledge. This theory seems to suggest that readers cannot read to assimilate something new, only to recognize what they already know. This theory raises profound difficulty for composition teachers who are attempting to teach their students to write "explicit" and "autonomous" texts. By assumption, such texts cannot exist. On the basis of this theory, the essays a writer writes have no meaning independent of the meaning construed by a particular reader. This notion would seem to create havoc with a writer's relationship to his own texts, especially his motivation to revise them and his ability to judge the effects of his own revisions.

⁶ Although the word *speech* is used in the English translations of Vygotsky's and Luria's statements, it seems to make better sense to understand the word as *language*, since neither Vygotsky nor Luria considers writing as "speech written down."

⁷ The original passage is as follows: *La langue écrite naît chez l'enfant; parturition douloureuse. Et elle ne naît pas soeur jumelle de la langue parlée, mais nouvelle Eve, elle lui emprunte ses éléments et non pas ses aliments car elle se nourrit à d'autres sources, ne vise pas les mêmes buts et dispose d'autres moyens techniques.*

⁸ According to Snell (1960), philosophical and scientific discourse was created by the ancient Greeks to develop knowledge and lives in all languages today "by virtue of taking over, translating and elaborating upon the original Greek" (p. 50).

⁹ Although language learners who are regularly exposed to literate conversation and the oral reading of literature or nonliterary formal prose will be able to understand richer and more complex language as beginning readers than those without this exposure, their oral language experience will still determine meaning in beginning reading and writing.

¹⁰ Achieving this goal will necessitate the redesign of most current reading instructional series K–8. The majority of reading selections in most series is narrative or fictional in nature.

¹¹ One of the critical deficiencies in most schools with respect to the development of writing ability is the lack of instruction and practice in informational writing. Broadly speaking, informational writing is writing that organizes and presents ideas and facts and usually has a logical, not a chronological, structure. Most writing in the content areas assigned for students to demonstrate their understanding of a particular body of knowledge and too often consists of individual words to fill in blanks or short answers to essay-type questions. Rarely is informational writing taught through draft stages, with a stress on imaginative or creative thinking, as well as on a clear presentation of the information. Current instructional approaches to informational writing badly need to be modified (see Stotsky, 1984a, 1985a, and 1987 for a wide variety of suggestions for teachers).

REFERENCES

Adams, M., & Collins, A. (1977). *A schema-theoretic view of reading.* Urbana, IL: Center for the Study of Reading.

Belanger, J. (1978). *Reading skill as an influence on writing skill.* Unpublished doctoral dissertation, University of Alberta, Edmonton. (ERIC Document Reproduction Service No. ED 163 409)

Binzer, P. (1974). The effect of direct instruction in comprehension through listening on reading comprehension. (Doctoral dissertation, State University of New York at Albany, 1974). *Dissertation Abstracts International, 34,* 538A.

Blount, N., Johnson, S. L., & Fredrick, W. C. (1969). *A comparison of the writing of eighth and twelfth grade students* (Tech. Rep. No. 78). Madison: University of Wisconsin, Wisconsin Research and Development Center for Cognitive Learning.

Bruner, J., Olver, R., & Greenfield, P. (1966). *Studies in cognitive growth.* New York: Wiley.

Bushnell, P. P. (1930). *An analytical contrast of oral with written English* (Contributions to Education, No. 451). New York: Columbia University, Teachers College, Bureau of Publications.

Campbell, J. (1973). The effect of oral language on reading achievement. (Doctoral dissertation, Lehigh University, 1973). *Dissertation Abstracts International, 34,* 5575A.

Davis, J. (1975). The language laboratory as a medium and model in a talk–write composition course. *NALLD Journal, 9,* 16–19.

Drum, I. (1976). The effects of instruction in oral language-experience activities, synonym generation, and kernel sentence expansion on language development and reading achievement. (Doctoral dissertation, Temple University, 1976). *Dissertation Abstracts International, 37,* 2033A.

Durrell, D. (1970). *Durrell Listening–Reading Series Advanced Level: Form DE Manual for Listening and Reading Tests.* New York: Harcourt.

Epes, M., Kirkpatrick, C., & Southwell, M. (1980). *An evaluation of the Comp-Lab project: Final report. A project of the Exxon Education Foundation, 1978–79* (Mimeo). New York: York College.

Ewoldt, C. (1981). A psycholinguistic description of selected deaf children reading in Sign language. *Reading Research Quarterly, 17,* 58–89.

Gatlin, E. (1974). The extent of the relationship between the maturity of oral and written extemporaneous compositions in the language of community college freshmen. (Doctoral dissertation, University of South Carolina, 1974). *Dissertation Abstracts International, 35,* 6534A.

Glover, J., Plake, B., Roberts, B., Zimmer, J., & Palmere, M. (1981). Distinctiveness of encoding: The effects of paraphrasing and drawing inferences on memory from prose. *Journal of Educational Psychology, 73,* 736–744.

Golub, L., & Fredrick, W. C. (1971). *Linguistic structures in the discourse of fourth and sixth graders* (Tech. Rep. No. 166). Madison: University of Wisconsin, Wisconsin Research and Development Center for Cognitive Learning.

Goodman, K. (1982). Behind the eye: What happens in reading. With Olive Niles. In F. V. Gollasch (Ed.), *Language and literacy: The selected writings of Kenneth S. Goodman* (Vol. 2). London: Routledge & Kegan Paul. [Originally published in K. S. Goodman & O. S. Niles (Eds.), *Reading process and program.* Urbana, IL: National Council of Teachers of English, Commission on the English Curriculum, 1970]

Goodman, K., & Goodman, Y. (1983). Reading and writing relationships: Pragmatic functions. *Language Arts, 60,* 590–599.

Groff, P. (1979). The effects of talking on writing. *English in Education, 13,* 33–37.

Harrell, L. E., Jr. (1957). A comparison of the development of oral and written language in school-age children. *Monographs of the Society for Research in Child Development, 22* (3).

Havelock, E. (1980). The coming of literate communication to Western culture. *Journal of Communication, 30,* 90–98.

Hunt, K. (1970). Syntactic maturity in schoolchildren and adults. *Monographs of the Society for Research in Child Development,* Ser. no. 134, Vol. 35, No. 1, February. Chicago, IL: Univ. of Chicago Press.

Improving reading through an oral language program. (1972). Bulletin No. 39. Brisbane, Australia: Queensland Department of Education. (ERIC Document Reproduction Service No. ED 113 701)

Ingarden, R. (1973). *The cognition of the literary work of art.* Evanston, IL: Northwestern University Press.

Kinneavy, J. (1980). *A theory of discourse.* New York: Norton.

Lewis, S. (1976). Effects of listening instruction on the reading comprehension of black inner city children at levels one, two, and three. (Doctoral dissertation, St. Louis University, 1976). *Dissertation Abstracts International, 37,* 1962A.

Loban, W. (1976). *Language development: Kindergarten through grade twelve.* Research Report No. 18. Urbana, IL: National Council of Teachers of English.

Lull, H. G. (1929). The speaking and writing abilities of intermediate-grade pupils. *Journal of Educational Research, 20,* 73–77.

Luria, A. (1966). *Higher cortical functions in man.* New York: Basic Books.

Luria, A. (1969). Speech development and the formation of mental processes. In M. Cole & I. Maltzman (Eds.), *A handbook of contemporary Soviet psychology.* New York: Basic Books.

Meyers, D. (1979). The influence of using speaking as a pre-writing activity on community college freshmen's performance in writing. (ERIC Document Reproduction Service No. ED 203 316)

Moffett, J., & Wagner, B. (1983). *Student-centered language arts and reading: K–13* (3rd ed.). Boston: Houghton.

Moore, P. (1971). A descriptive analysis of R. Zoellner's talk–write theory: A behavioral pedagogy for composition. (Doctoral dissertation, State University of New York at Buffalo, 1971). *Dissertation Abstracts International, 32,* 2534A.

O'Donnell, R., Griffin, W. J., & Norris, R. C. (1967). *Syntax of kindergarten and elementary school children: A transformational analysis* (Research Rep. No. 8). Urbana, IL: National Council of Teachers of English.

Ong, W. (1983). Beyond objectivity: The reader–writer transaction as an altered state of consciousness. In P. Stock (Ed.), *FForum: Essays on theory and practice in the teaching of writing.* Montclair, NJ: Boynton/Cook.

Osgood, C., & Sebeok, T. (1969). *Psycholinguistics.* Bloomington, IN: Indiana University Press.

Peper, R., & Mayer, R. (1978). Note taking as a generative activity. *Journal of Educational Psychology, 70,* 514–522.

Radcliffe, T. (1969). *The results of an empirical study using talk–write composition* (Mimeo). Unpublished pilot study, University of Montana, Missoula.

Rubin, D., & Piché, G. L. (1979). Development in syntactic and strategic aspects of audience adaptation skills in written persuasive communication. *Research in the Teaching of English, 13,* 293–316.

Sherwin, S. (1969). *Four problems in teaching English: A critique of research.* Scranton, PA: International Textbook.

Simon, J. (1970). *Evolution génétique de la phrase écrite chez l'écolier.* Unpublished doctoral dissertation, University of Paris.

Smith, F. (1971). *Understanding reading.* New York: Holt.

Smith, F. (1975). The relations between spoken and written language. In E. H. Lenneberg & E. Lenneberg (Eds.), *Foundations of language development: A multidisciplinary approach* (Vol. 2). New York: Academic Press.

Smith, F. (1981). Myths of writing. *Language Arts, 58,* 792–98.

Smith, F. (1982). *Writing and the writer.* New York: Holt.

Snell, B. (1960). Forging a language for science in ancient Greece. *Classical Journal, 56,* 56–60.

Sokolov, A. (1981). Studies of the speech mechanisms of thinking. In M. Cole & I. Maltzman (Eds.), *A handbook of contemporary Soviety psychology.* New York: Basic Books.

Sticht, T., Lawrence, J., Beck, J., Hauke, R., Kleiman, G., & James, J. (1974). *Auding and reading: A developmental model.* Alexandria, VA: Human Resource Research Organization.

Stotsky, S. (1983a). Types of lexical cohesion in expository writing: Implications for developing the vocabulary of academic discourse. *College Composition and Communication, 34,* 430–446.

Stotsky, S. (1983b). Research on reading/writing relationships: A synthesis and suggested directions. *Language Arts, 60* (5). [Reprinted in J. Jensen (Ed.), *Composing and comprehending,* Urbana, IL: NCRE-ERIC, 1984.]

Stotsky, S. (1984a). Imagination, writing, and the integration of knowledge in the middle grades. *Journal of Teaching Writing, 3,* 157–190.

Stotsky, S. (1984b). A proposal for improving high school student's ability to read and write expository prose. *Journal of Reading, 28* (1), 4–7.

Stotsky, S. (1985a). Helping beginning writers develop writing plans: A process for teaching informational writing in the middle school. *The Leaflet, 84,* 2–17.

Stotsky, S. (1985b). From egocentric to ideocentric discourse: The development of academic language. In J. Niles & R. Lalik (Eds.), *Issues in Literacy: A Research Perspective,* Thirty-fourth Yearbook of the National Reading Conference.

Stotsky, S. (1986). On learning to write about ideas. *College Composition and Communication, 37,* 276–293.

Stotsky, S. (1987). Civic writing in the classroom. Co-sponsored by the Social Studies Development Center, ERIC/ChEES, and ERIC/RCS. Published by the Social Studies Development Center, Indiana University.

Tovatt, A., & Miller, E. (1967). *Oral–aural visual stimuli approach to teaching written composition to 9th grade students* (Report No. BR-5-0398). Muncie, IN: Ball State University, Burris Laboratory School. (ERIC Document Reproduction Service No. ED 015 204)

Vygotsky, L. (1962). *Thought and language.* Cambridge, MA: MIT Press.

Vygotsky, L. (1978). *Mind in society: The development of higher psychological processes.* Cambridge, MA: Harvard University Press.

Zanotti, R. (1970). A study of the use of the tape recorder as an aid to written composition at the sixth-grade level. (Doctoral dissertation, State University of New York at Buffalo, 1970). *Dissertation Abstracts International, 31,* 1520A.

Index